Money & Banking

FINANCIAL INSTITUTIONS AND ECONOMIC POLICY

2nd Edition

Money & Banking

FINANCIAL INSTITUTIONS AND ECONOMIC POLICY

2nd Edition

Marilu Hurt McCarty

Associate Professor of Economics
Georgia Institute of Technology

Assistant Dean
College of Management

Longman Financial Services Publishing
a division of Longman Financial Services Institute, Inc.

© 1988 by Longman Group USA Inc.
Published by Longman Financial Services Publishing, Inc.,
a division of Longman Financial Services Institute, Inc.

Printed in the United States of America.

88 89 90   10 9 8 7 6 5 4 3 2 1

Executive Editor: Richard Hagle
Project Editor: Carole Bilina
Cover and Interior Design: Edwin Harris
Manager, Composition Services: Gayle Sperando
Copy Editor: Jean Berry
Proofreader: Loretta Faber
Indexer: Sharon Johnson
Typesetting: Impressions

3 2280 00699 2200

Library of Congress Cataloging-in-Publication Data

McCarty, Marilu Hurt.
  Money & banking.

    Includes bibliographies and index.
    1. Money. 2. Banks and banking. I. Title.
II. Title: Money and banking.
HG221.M43 1988   332.1   87-29662
ISBN 0-88462-731-4

Contents

v

Preface

A serious problem in teaching any course in economics is convincing students of its relevance. This is less true of a course in money and banking, because the significance of money to their own health and happiness is lost on few students. Still, many textbooks in the field fail to take advantage of students' natural interest in money and forfeit the opportunity to make economic thinking an integral part of everyday living.

Typically, a textbook in money and banking includes sections focusing on (1) the origins and development of financial institutions, (2) monetary theory and (3) the course and consequences of government economic policy. Many good students absorb information within each of these categories without integrating their thoughts into a coherent understanding of the relationships among them. To the instructor the essential unity of the topics is so self-evident as to require little clarification. The student, on the contrary, may need frequent repetition of course objectives to reinforce the relevance of each new topic for understanding the total structure.

This text constructs a *framework* for considering economic ideas and a set of *criteria* by which they can be evaluated. The framework is built around three fundamental questions that underlie the study of money: What is money? How much money should there be? And, once determined, how does the supply of money affect our own well-being? In a general way, these questions reflect the three levels of economic study: description, analysis and policy. Learning to think in these stages should help students understand the monetary aspects of economics and attack other economic topics more systematically.

The criteria by which students are encouraged to evaluate economic ideas involve efficiency, equity and externalities: how financial institutions and monetary policy contribute to efficiency in the allocation of resources, the equity considerations that modify the behavior of our financial institutions and the externalities that flow from particular financial decisions. The context for evaluating economic decisions places particular emphasis on maximizing the nation's total wealth, an approach the author believes is superior to a "cookbook" approach focusing solely on mechanistic applications of technical processes.

Thus, a continuous thread ties together the sections of this text, connecting new information to the fundamental questions raised initially and evaluating new ideas in terms of the fundamental criteria. Frequently, the context for discussion is a political one: how differing consequences for various citizen groups give rise to opposing policy positions. Exposure to the economic basis for political conflict should help students look for the political origins of other policy proposals.

Each chapter includes important pedagogical tools: learning objectives at the beginning and a summary of important ideas at the end, a glossary of terms, a reading list of descriptive and interpretive articles and books, and selected questions for discussion and research. Additionally, all chapters include sections entitled Money and Banking in Practice—short articles describing significant current issues—that invite students to debate the opposing positions. Topics added to this edition include such critical issues as the crisis of the thrifts, Third World inflation, home ownership and the FHA, institutional investment, the Gold Bugs, the nationalization of Continental Illinois, home equity loans, interstate banking, electronic funds transfer, international monetary reform and Federal Reserve Chairman Alan Greenspan. The writing style is clear and uncluttered, giving particular attention to topics and procedures for engaging readers' interest and attention.

Part I addresses the question, What is money? It describes money's changing forms domestically as well as the international integration of money supplies. Terms and concepts are introduced clearly and explained in an interesting and relevant context. Public and private nonbank financial intermediaries are described fully, along with an up-to-date description of recent developments in financial markets. Then a discussion of risk and return on investment portfolios introduces the concept of specialization among financial intermediaries, followed by a discussion of how newly developing sources and use of funds have brought on the breakdown of specialization.

Finally, Part I includes a chapter on international trade and the significance of international currencies for spending in an open economy.

Part II considers the question, How much money should there be? It shows how the money supply decision has been accomplished over time and the consequences of unregulated growth. Particular emphasis is placed on the significance of bank size and structure for money growth and economic stability. The evolution of banking regulation is described in detail, along with the mechanism for supplying reserves. Other public agencies for regulating agricultural and housing credit are described, together with their implications for efficiency and equity in the allocation of financial resources. The chapter on international transactions addresses international capital flows as important factors that increase or decrease the nation's money supply.

Part III explores the question, How does money affect our economic goals? It constitutes the theoretical core of the text. Monetary theory is presented clearly and in detail, all the while relating theoretical concepts to actual behavior and historical observations. Discussion of the Keynesian model is thorough, and the IS-LM synthesis is accomplished in an easily readable style. The influence of government is described, analyzed and evaluated in the context of the problems of unemployment and inflation. Emphasis is placed on such significant concepts as selection of a target for policy, aggregate supply, nominal versus real interest rates and lags in the effectiveness of policy. The dilemma between internal and external balance is explored, along with automatic and policy-induced forces for stability. The progress and implications of international cooperation and institutions are examined in detail.

To write a text that includes such a range of institutional and theoretical topics requires intellectual contacts over a wide range of professional specializations. I have been fortunate in my associations with many members of the Atlanta academic and financial community whose ideas and influence I greatly appreciate. I would like to thank especially my friends at the Atlanta Federal Reserve Bank for their helpful suggestions.

I would also like to thank the many colleagues who provided reviews and advice on all or parts of the first and this new, second edition of the text: Douglas Agbetsiafa, Indiana University at South Bend; Ronald J. Balvers, University of Notre Dame; James Barth, George Washington University; Christopher Baum, Boston College; John W. Bay, University of Maine, Portland-Gorham; Jeffery A. Born, University of Kentucky; Robert B. Carson, State University of New York at Oneonta; Jack E. Gelfand, State University of New York at Albany; William C. Hunter, Emory University and Federal Reserve Bank of Atlanta; Robert F. Herbert, Auburn University; Walter Johnson, University of Missouri; Richard Kinonen, University of Arizona; Robert McGee, Florida State University; Alden Shiers, California Polytechnical State University; Elinor H. Solomon, George Washington University; Marjorie T. Stanley, Texas Christian University; Larry Steinhauser, Albion College;

Samuel C. Webb, Wichita State University; Loretta S. Wilson, Radford University and Dwayne Wrightsman, University of New Hampshire.

Errors and omissions are, of course, my own.

Marilu H. McCarty

Money & Banking

FINANCIAL INSTITUTIONS AND ECONOMIC POLICY

2nd Edition

PART I

What Is Money?

What is money? How should money be defined? How does money work for us? Experts agree on one definition of money: Money is anything that performs the functions of money. Beyond this simple definition, there is little agreement. The reason is that money takes many new forms in our modern, complex economy. Defining and measuring money is no longer so simple as counting bills and weighing coins—or even balancing checkbooks!

New forms of money have been a response to the changing needs of our economy. We have found new ways that money can work for us—new ways to stimulate production and exchange, new ways to allocate resources toward future production, and new ways to store wealth. Like most change, changes in money require new ways of managing money. Policymakers must understand how money works in all its new forms and decide on policies for helping money serve us better.

The chapters in Part I explore these questions, beginning with the oldest forms of money and describing how new forms developed. We will describe how early banks sprang up to store money and how, later, other kinds of financial intermediaries were established to transfer money from savers to spenders. We will see that an efficient financial system helped provide the funds for investing in new capital resources, promoting economic growth and raising living standards. Finally, we will discuss how new ways to borrow and lend continue to fuel our nation's prosperity and raise new questions about maintaining stable economic growth.

C H A P T E R

1

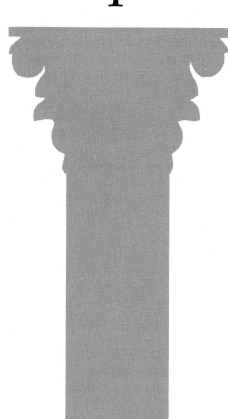

LEARNING OBJECTIVES

- ■ To understand how money evolved with the evolution of economic systems and how new money forms are continuing to evolve today
- ■ To see how money works to promote efficiency in production
- ■ To see the effect of changing money forms on the equity of our economic system and on the production of positive and negative externalities
- ■ To understand the relationship between money and real wealth, particularly with respect to government's role in regulating the money supply

The Many Forms of Money

"The use of money is all the advantage there is in having money."

Benjamin Franklin

A computer consultant working after-hours in a bank in Los Angeles presses a few keys, and within seconds his own bank account in New York acquires a deposit of almost a million dollars. By the time the Los Angeles bank discovers the theft, the money has been used to buy diamonds, which are hidden away in a safety deposit box in Switzerland. (Lest we leave the impression that such actions go unpunished, we should quickly add that the computer bandit was apprehended and brought to justice.)

We said "money," but how can a series of electronic impulses be money? By what mysterious process can the airways spanning North America carry money—whether for legal or illegal purposes?

Certainly there have been changes in what we call money since Columbus received a million gold pieces from Spain's Queen Isabella to finance his historic adventure. It isn't necessary to go back that far, however, to note substantial changes in what we think of as money. Most of today's college students can remember when the exchange of green bills constituted a much greater portion of spending than is true today. Now we are accustomed to conducting many transactions without using them at all. Someday our engraved portraits of a solemn George Washington may be collectors' items like Columbus's Spanish coins of five centuries ago.

What is money anyway? Who decides what should serve as money? What does money do for us? Why is defining and measuring money important for our well-being?

Money as an Intermediator

Money is important because it is an *intermediator*. An intermediator "stands between" participants in a transaction and does some of the work that occurs between them. It allows work to occur even when the parties have no direct, face-to-face contact. The principal work of money as an intermediator is to facilitate exchange.

Economists are interested in intermediators because they help achieve *efficiency* in the allocation of resources. Allocation is efficient if resources are used to produce the largest possible quantities of goods and services with a given level of expenditure. Intermediators smooth the flow of resources out of inefficient kinds of production and into efficient kinds. With more efficient uses of resources, a society can enjoy more and better products and, hence, a higher standard of living.

Throughout history, people have learned to use money more and more efficiently. We are still learning today. We are learning other things about money: how the use of intermediators can promote *equity* in the distribution of goods and services and how intermediators can yield *externalities* over and above the gains in efficiency.

Equity refers to fairness in the way a society shares the benefits and costs of production—*benefits* in terms of the distribution of the goods and services our economy produces and *costs* in terms of the resources required to produce them. Different people have different opinions as to what pattern of distribution is fair. Differences of opinion lead to differences in support for various forms of intermediation. Most of us tend to support systems that result in greater benefits for ourselves and fewer costs. Needless to say, we cannot all achieve that result!

Externalities are benefits and costs that occur outside the primary function of intermediators. External benefits are called *positive externalities*, and external costs are called *negative externalities*. A positive externality from the use of money to support a research scientist might be greater international competitiveness for the nation's high-tech industries. A negative externality from the use of money to purchase vacation homes might be a shortage of funds locally for restoring urban neighborhoods.

These themes will underlie our study of money and intermediation: the efficiency in resource allocation that comes from an efficient system of intermediation, the equity associated with various kinds of intermediation, and the externalities that can make our nation stronger and better. In some instances we will note that a sacrifice of efficiency has been the price we pay for a gain in equity. Or that a sacrifice in equity has yielded positive externalities. These themes represent the most fundamental trade-offs in economics and pose the most fundamental choices.

A World Without Money

Primitive societies do not need money. Furthermore, the absence of money keeps them primitive. This is because primitive societies, though austere by today's standards, are generally self-sufficient. They subsist only on the meager production that is carried on within the community itself. When a primitive tribe can satisfy all its own perceived needs for food, clothing, tools and shelter, there may be no need for exchange and no need for money.

Eventually, there may be some specialization among certain groups within a primitive society. Persons with particular physical attributes or mental abilities begin to perform appropriate jobs, and they develop skills for doing them better. Primitive engineers build the roads and bridges; strong, athletic youths capture the game; and careful artisans do work requiring meticulous detail. Many of our names are a result of our family's specialization as carpenter, fisher, miller, tailor or goldsmith in some primitive community.

With some degree of specialization within the tribe, exchange can take place through *barter*. Barter is the exchange of goods and services for goods and services of another type. When there are old, established patterns of production and consumption within a small, closely knit community, barter is fairly simple. Engineers, hunters and artisans can freely share the products of their work.

Things are not so simple when the society expands. Specialists develop new kinds of production that create opportunities for even finer specialization. A broader market covering greater distances makes increased production worthwhile. Old kinds of production and consumption constantly break down and are rebuilt in entirely new ways. Barter is not as convenient as before. To depend on face-to-face exchange of what one person has for what another person wants would become so complicated that all exchange— and all production—would slow to a halt. What is needed is a symbol to represent the value of goods in exchange and to entitle the holder to receive goods of equal value. In a word: money.

The availability of money encourages producers to increase their special output of particular goods. Thus, production becomes more efficient. Then the receipt of money enables consumers to spend for a wider variety of the things they need. When money replaces barter for making trades, both production and consumption can grow.

Early Money

Almost as many different symbols have been used as money as there have been societies using them. The most familiar in our history books are animal bones and giraffe tails, gunpowder and salt, and stones and strings of shells. In colonial America tobacco was used in exchange—for more years than gold was standard money. Some of these primitive forms of money are still used. In fact, in some islands of the South Pacific stone disks measuring four feet across still function as money.

What do all these symbols have in common? Certain characteristics are common to all money in some degree (although some forms of money exemplify certain characteristics more than others). For a material to serve as money it must be relatively rare; it should be easily carried and stored without spoiling; and it should be divisible into smaller pieces for making small payments. The commodity that best exemplifies these characteristics is precious metal. Gold and silver are rare relative to their demand for ornamental or industrial uses. Their rarity makes them highly valuable per unit of weight, so that they are easily carried. Both are fairly durable, subject to very little deterioration over long time and much use. They are easily fashioned into small shapes and easily stamped with identifying marks. Furthermore, badly worn metal coins can be melted down and made into fresh new ones.

The first use of precious metals as money was probably in southern Asia about 10,000 years ago. Nuggets circulated as money around the Persian Gulf and in trading settlements along the China coast. Exchange using precious metals was difficult at first because the metal had to be *assayed* each time it changed hands. Assayers would weigh and test a nugget for purity to determine its value. Eventually assayers began to stamp their special mark and the certified weight on each nugget so that it would not have to be weighed and tested over and over again. This worked rather well except for the common practice of chipping or shaving small pieces from the edges of several nuggets and combining them to produce another one. To reduce the value of money is called *debasing* the currency. Authorities tried to prevent debasement by flattening nuggets, making them round, and serrating the edges. Coins of this kind began to be used 9,000 years ago in eastern Mediterranean countries. By the time of Christ mints were producing coins in trading cities along the Mediterranean coast.

The arrival of money into medieval Europe helped destroy the old feudal society and made way for the development of a commercial and, finally, an industrial economy. The old system of feudalism had been based on strong ties of dependency between land-owning nobles and serfs, or slaves who worked the land. Barter worked well in such a closely knit society, where serfs turned over their surplus crops to the noble who, in turn, provided his serfs protection against marauding tribes. Money changed all this. Serfs could sell their grain and wine to traveling merchants and use the money to buy their freedom from the noble. Then the freed serfs moved to newly developing towns to become merchants themselves or, eventually, small manufacturers. The availability of money encouraged many nobles to sell their land and free their serfs and use the money to buy the silks and spices traders were bringing from the Orient.

A Bimetallic Money System

In the beginning, the United States used two precious metals for making coins: gold and silver. Two metals were needed because there was not enough of either one to satisfy the nation's need for money. A money system using two metals is called a *bimetallic system*. Bimetallic systems generally do not last long because of what is known as *Gresham's Law*. Gresham's Law describes the effect of a difference between the mint value and the market value of the two metals.

To understand Gresham's Law, it is helpful to look at the values of two metals over the 1800s. In the early 1800s, the mint values of gold and silver were set so that 24.75 grains of gold or 371.25 grains of silver were each worth one dollar. This was a *mint ratio* of 15 to 1; that is, gold was 15 times as valuable as silver at the mint. In the market at the same time, buyers of gold and silver for making ornaments and utensils were willing to pay 16 times as much for gold as for silver, making the *market ratio* 16 to 1. Naturally, sellers of gold tended to take it to where they could get the best price: in this case, to the market where gold would be used for purposes other than money. Even gold coins would be melted down and sold in the market. Only the less highly valued silver would be taken to the mint, so that eventually the nation would be using only silver for money.

Later in the 1800s, the mint values of the two metals were reversed to value gold more highly. This time the value of gold was set higher at the mint than in the market, and the nation came to use only gold for money. Sir Thomas Gresham is said to have noticed the problem with bimetallic money systems back in the sixteenth century and proclaimed the law that bears his name: "Cheap money drives dear money out of circulation." The principle arises from the fact that people will use the cheaper commodity for money and save the more highly valued commodity for other purposes.

Commodity Money and Representative Commodity Money

Money that is useful in itself apart from its value as money is called *commodity money*. Gold, silver and tobacco are all examples of commodity money. When large quantities of gold or silver became difficult (or risky) to carry around, owners would deposit their coins, or *specie*, with goldsmiths or banks. In return they would receive *representative commodity money*, certificates issued to stand in place of a particular quantity of coins or specie. At first, certificates were issued only piece-for-piece with the precious metal, so that the paper money was fully backed by the commodity. When the certificates were exchanged in trade, they entitled the new owner to reclaim the gold or silver. We say that such certificates were "redeemable in specie." Gold certificates were commonly issued during the Middle Ages in Europe and even earlier in China. In the United States, silver certificates were issued from the late nineteenth century until the early 1960s. A few remain outstanding today, generally in the hands of collectors.

A monetary system based on a rare commodity has the advantage that money itself remains rare. A scarcity of money relative to the quantity of goods for sale helps retain its value and keeps prices low. There is an offsetting disadvantage, however. When money is too rare, it serves less well to encourage sufficient production and to facilitate consumption. The result may be slower growth in economic activity and lower living standards for the community.

Credit Money

Modern monetary systems are not based on a useful commodity like gold or silver, but on credit. *Credit money* (or fiat money) has no value apart from its value in exchange. It is accepted by sellers because they know it will be accepted by other sellers with whom they trade. Credit money is a claim for assets of whatever kind desired by the holder, but it cannot be used to reclaim a certain quantity of gold or silver coins. Whereas credit money can be used to buy anything, including gold, at the market price, it is not necessarily redeemable in specie.

Banks began issuing credit money only about 500 years ago. Along with gold certificates, a bank would issue notes, adorned with the bank's own identifying design. Bank notes were paid out as loans to trusted borrowers who used the money to finance trading expeditions or productive enterprises of one kind or another. The expectation was that the borrower would be successful in the venture, earning enough gold and other paper money to repay the loan with interest. During periods of increasing prosperity, the expectation often proved to be correct. Successful borrowers would return bank notes (and gold) to the banks, which could then destroy them. This was to ensure that the total volume of commodity and credit money would never grow faster than the quantity of goods available for sale.

Sometimes things did not work as expected. In particular, during periods of depression loans might not be repaid, and the bank's notes remained in private hands. When business got bad, holders of gold certificates rushed to convert their representative commodity money to commodity money, so that gold flowed out of banks into safekeeping in homes and businesses. With the loss of its gold, a bank also lost its credibility as a depository, and many banks went out of business. Their notes continued to circulate, however, often at values substantially less than *par*, the face value of the note. Merchants learned to discount the value of bank notes according to the reputation of the issuing bank and the ease with which its certificates could be redeemed in specie.

Credit money was also issued by governments. Governments often needed money to finance wars or major public projects. When raising taxes was not practical, governments printed paper money to pay their bills. The American colonies began issuing paper money in 1690. During the Revolution they issued so much Continental money that its value fell to practically zero. This loss in value gave rise to the old saying, "It's not worth a continental." Both the North and the South issued credit money to finance the Civil War. The South had less money to begin with, so it issued substantial amounts of Confederate money—whose eventual loss of value is extolled in story and song. By the end of the war, Confederate money had lost almost all of its purchasing power. The North's Greenback remained only slightly more valuable. After the war, the U.S. Treasury collected Greenbacks in taxes and then, instead of spending them, destroyed them. The result was to reduce the volume of credit money in circulation and bring on a general decrease in economic activity. About $300 million in Greenbacks remain outstanding today, again mostly in the hands of collectors.

Some credit money was issued by private business firms. Firms involved in international trade often arranged payment through *bills of exchange*. An importer would pay an exporter a signed bill promising to pay the value of a particular shipment 30 or 60 days in the future. The bill then became valuable to its holder and could be "spent" like money. It might be exchanged by several merchants before the final holder presented it to the importer for payment. Inevitably, some exporters wrote bills of exchange on fictitious shipments and used them for carrying out their own business transactions. Sometimes they paid off at maturity and sometimes they did not.

Gresham's Law applies also to the use of credit money versus commodity money. If commodity money is available, it will normally be hoarded and credit money used for exchange. The expectation is that the value of the commodity is not as likely to fall. (Hoarding a commodity may even cause its value to increase as it becomes scarcer.) This creates some problems for government and may lead to a decision not to issue any more commodity money. During the 1960s, Americans stashed away so many silver coins that there began to be shortages, and the price of silver rose sharply. Finally, the government acted to remove silver from new coins and release all silver for industrial and decorative purposes.

The most common form of credit money used today is checks written on the holder's checking account. U.S. banks began to offer checking accounts to borrowers in the mid-1800s. Checks have many of the necessary characteristics of money: they are easily carried and stored, and they can be written in large or small amounts. Whether they are rare or not depends on the ability and willingness of banks to offer them—a subject we will discuss later in detail.

Today in the United States about nine-tenths of the dollar value of all transactions is carried on by check. This makes checking accounts the largest single type of money in use. Most of our coin and currency is credit money, too, having no significant value apart from its value as money. Federal Reserve notes comprise most of our currency and fall in this category, as do the few remaining Greenbacks. A few silver certificates remain as representative commodity money. They are no longer redeemable in specie, however, and thus are no longer representative commodity money.

MONEY AND BANKING IN PRACTICE: COINS AND PAPER MONEY

U.S. coins are produced at mints located in San Francisco, Denver and Philadelphia. Coins are made from layers of metal pressed together to form a thin sheet. Coin-cutting machines work like cookie cutters to turn out 20 million coins a day at the Philadelphia mint alone. The weight of each coin is controlled precisely so that a bag of coins can be "counted" by weighing it. Producing coins costs less than the face value of coins produced. The result is a profit for government called *seigniorage*. Seigniorage earns government more than $250 million a year. See Figure 1–1 for the market value of today's coins.

U.S. paper currency is printed at the Bureau of Engraving and Printing in Washington. Every day 6 tons of secret-formula ink and 25 tons of special rag paper are transformed into $75 million in bills—about $30 billion a year. Every bill (regardless of its face value) costs about one-tenth of a cent to produce. Most of our paper money is Federal Reserve notes, issued to the nation's 12 Federal Reserve banks and then sold to local commercial banks when they need currency to pay their customers. Years ago, Federal Reserve banks were required to hold gold worth at least 40 percent of the value of their notes in circulation. In 1945, the amount was reduced to 25 percent, and in 1968 the requirement was removed entirely.

Most of our remaining paper money is U.S. Treasury currency, a carryover from years past when the Treasury printed money to pay its bills. Currently, new Treasury money is issued only to replace existing money.

FIGURE 1–1   Market Value of Metals: What Today's U.S. Coins Are Worth

---

Dollar: Minted from March 1971 to date. Content: 91.67% copper, 8.33% nickel. **Value:** 3.34 cents.

Half Dollar: Minted from January 1971 to date. Content: 91.67% copper, 8.33% nickel. **Value:** 1.67 cents.

Quarter: Minted from August 1965 to date. Content: 91.67% copper, 8.33% nickel. **Value:** 84/100 of 1 cent.

Dime: Minted from December 1965 to date. Content: 91.67% copper, 8.33% nickel. **Value:** 1/3 of 1 cent.

Nickel: Minted from late 19th century to date. Content: 75% copper, 25% nickel. **Value:** 1.03 cents.

Penny: Minted from late 19th century to date. Content: 95% copper, 5% zinc. **Value:** 36/100 of 1 cent.

Silver Coins: Dimes, quarters, half dollars and dollars of 90% silver and 10% copper have all but vanished from general circulation. Except for numismatic coins, silver dollars have not been minted since 1935, dimes and quarters since 1965, half dollars since 1966 and a half dollar of 40% silver, also virtually out of circulation, since 1970.

SOURCE: U.S. Department of the Treasury; USN and WR Economic Unit, based on metal prices on October 31, 1977.

The Four Functions of Money

Remember that money is an intermediator. Most money in itself is worthless; its value is derived from its use. Money is useful as a link between the world's producers and the world's consumers. It enables people to consume things they did not produce, and it encourages people to produce things they do not want to consume.

Its function as a link makes money a *medium of exchange*. It is a means of exchanging the things we have produced for the things we want to consume. The availability of money simplifies the process of production and exchange and makes it more efficient. The more developed our money system, the more we are encouraged to produce, and the greater our desire to consume exotic things. We are encouraged to specialize in the production of cotton cloth, kitchen tables and haircuts so that we can enjoy oranges, tape players and sports events. Through specialization, we each become more productive. Without money to link producers with consumers, we would be limited to the self-sufficient production of our own hands—or we would spend much of our energy bartering our production for the things we want.

If money is to be a medium of exchange, it must also be a *standard of value*. It must provide a common measure for evaluating all items in exchange. Under barter, evaluating goods is enormously complex. One female goat may be worth four clay bowls or two cutting tools. A cutting tool may be worth a jug of oil, which in turn is worth six animal pelts or two male goats. Just making all the necessary calculations for trade can become tiresome, using time that could be better spent in real production.

A uniform symbol of value measures all these items by a single language and simplifies trade. It ensures that producers of, say, clay bowls are rewarded fully for their contribution to world output. By contributing to world output, producers earn the right to an equal quantity of goods and services for their own consumption. Most of us believe that a society that distributes output roughly according to contributions to production is more equitable than one that does not.

If money is to serve as an equitable measure of production and consumption, it must not change in value. This is particularly true when production and consumption take place in two different time periods. Some producers of goods or services intend to store the value of their work today as a basis for consuming other goods at some time in the future. When their own production cannot be stored for later sale, they will sell it today and save a portion of their earnings. In this sense, money is used as a *store of value*. Most of us store a part of our earnings regularly to provide for our consumption needs at some future time.

The reverse is also true. Often we need or want to consume goods and services before we ourselves have contributed to production. We will be allowed to do this if we can demonstrate our willingness to produce goods of equal value in the future. In this sense, money serves as a *standard of deferred payments*, a measure of our debt to the economy that must be settled by future production.

Money serves these four functions as a means of encouraging specialization in production and to allow consumption to take place regularly and according to our individual preferences. It is a medium of exchange, a standard of value, a store of value, and a standard for deferred payments. In general, money serves as a link between producers and consumers, making production and consumption more efficient. Furthermore, money helps make sure that those who contribute goods and services to world production receive an equal value of goods and services in return. Thus, money helps

---

TABLE 1–1   Hyperinflation in History

U.S. Civil War

Inflation in the Confederate states averaged 10 percent a month for almost three years. At
  the end of the Civil War, prices were almost 75 times their prewar level.

World War I and Postwar Years

Between 1913 and 1923, wholesale prices in Germany increased by almost a trillion times.
  Russia's prices increased by 4 billion times, Poland's by 2.5 million times, and Hungary's
  by 23 thousand times.

World War II and Postwar Years

During World War II, Hungary's prices increased by a factor of (1.4×10^{30}); that is, 1.4 with
  the decimal point moved 30 places to the right. By 1946, prices were increasing by 20,000
  percent a month. Between 1945 and 1948, U.S. prices increased 33 percent, an average
  annual rate of 10 percent.

1950–1965

Latin American prices increased by 31 percent a year in Brazil, 25 percent a year in
  Argentina, and 33 percent a year in Chile from 1950 through 1965.

1972

The cost of living increased 64 percent in Argentina, 94 percent in Uruguay, and 163 percent
  in Chile in a single year, 1972.

1984

In Argentina prices rose 1,000 percent in 1984.

---

distribute goods and services in a way that most of us consider equitable.
For this reason, it is especially important that the value of money not change.
When the value of money changes dramatically and in unpredictable ways,
the distribution of output also changes in ways that we may consider unfair.

Money and Prices

To say that the value of money changes is to say that the general price level
changes. When many prices change by different amounts and in different
directions, this does not necessarily mean that the value of money has
changed. It may only mean that some goods have become more desirable
(and costly) and others have become less desirable (and cheap). Or it may
mean that technology has simplified production of some goods, making them
cheaper than others. When most prices change in the same direction in
similar proportions, however, the value of money itself is changing.

Most of us are familiar with rising prices. When prices rise, the value
of money falls. We are experiencing *inflation*. (The opposite of inflation is
deflation, a condition unfamiliar to most of us.) Inflation weakens money as
a standard of value, a store of value, and a standard for deferred payments.
It means that money stored in return for production in one year will buy

fewer goods and services in another year. This is especially hard for those of us who prudently save part of our incomes each payday so that we can consume goods in the future. It is more pleasant for others who consume more than their incomes now, promising to pay in the future. For them, the value of the money they pay back in the future will be less than the value of the goods they consumed today.

Severe inflation may even weaken money as a medium of exchange. Producers of goods and services may be afraid to accept money whose value is falling and may insist on payment in other goods. The ultimate result of rampant inflation may be a return to barter and all the problems barter brings. Even worse, rampant inflation may arbitrarily destroy the money savings of productive, law-abiding citizens, causing them to lose faith in their government and forcing them to seek new and possibly destructive ways to protect their interests. Thus, inflation may bring a loss of efficiency and equity to the economic system. (Might it also bring negative externalities?)

Periods of extreme monetary crisis are often the result of war and its aftermath. In periods of crisis, the lack of a stable money system has led to the use of strange commodities as a medium of exchange, standard of value, store of value, and standard for deferred payments. Some examples are cigarettes, coffee and even pianos!

Some of the major periods of inflation in world history are listed in Table 1–1.

MONEY AND BANKING IN PRACTICE: HYPERINFLATION IN THE THIRD WORLD

Most of the world's industrialized countries had inflation under control in 1986. After 13½ percent inflation in 1980, the United States had reduced the growth of its money supply, and European countries had slowed the growth of government spending to hold down prices.

Things were different in the less developed nations of Latin America and the Middle East—nations often referred to as belonging to the Third World. Inflation in Bolivia was running at 3,400 percent annual rate, in Argentina 851 percent, in Israel 407 percent, in Brazil 220 percent, and in Peru 130 percent. The average inflation in less developed nations was running at 59 percent a year. With prices rising so fast, some governments wiped out old currencies and replaced them with new ones with more zeros!

Hyperinflation makes carrying on business especially difficult. Merchants must change prices as often as twice a day. Consumers must stock up on essential goods to try to beat price hikes. Unless house payments are increased with inflation, a home buyer may wind up paying for a house what it costs to buy a loaf of bread.

Inflation is often a result of poverty. When a nation is poor and the people are starving, it is easier for government to print money than to collect taxes to pay its bills. Unless new money is used productively—to build factories, irrigation systems, transportation networks—there may be no more goods and services to share. The new money will be worth less and less in terms of real wealth.

No painless solution exists for Third World inflation. Mexico cut inflation from more than 100 percent in 1983 to 50 percent in 1985 by cutting money growth and reducing government spending. Israel later tried to do the same, but when Israel's Prime Minister cut wage increases, 1½ million workers went out on strike. Argentina and Brazil tackled inflation with wage-and-price freezes and cuts in government spending.

Efforts to stop inflation may destroy jobs. Instead of working for government, workers must find jobs producing goods for sale to other countries at competitive prices. Until prices stabilize, workers will have to accept a lower standard of living.

Question for Discussion

1. Is there a "vicious cycle" in Third World inflation?

Portfolios of Assets

Money held for use in the future becomes part of an individual's portfolio of assets. Assets can be classified according to their *liquidity*: the ease with which they can be converted to purchasing power without significant loss of value. We might define *portfolio* broadly to mean all assets held, from the most liquid (money) to the least liquid (real goods and property). Particular assets in an individual's portfolio range from one end of the liquidity spectrum to the other:

- Money, including currency and all checkable deposits savings and time deposits
- Paid-up life insurance policies with cash values
- U.S. government securities

- High-grade bonds of cities, states and corporations
- Lower ranking bonds and notes
- Corporate stocks, futures and options
- Real goods, including gold
- Real estate

The ranking in the portfolio depends on the ease of converting each asset to purchasing power *without significant loss of value*. Thus, government securities rank above securities issued by private enterprises; bonds rank above stocks; and marketable financial assets rank above real estate. The riskier the asset and the more difficult to liquidate, the lower it ranks in the liquidity spectrum.

Note that the financial assets in an individual portfolio are *claims*: claims for real goods and property a person accumulates with the expectation that he or she can exercise the claim at another time. Currency and checking accounts are claims that can be exercised immediately. Other financial assets represent claims that have been temporarily relinquished to banks, business firms, or governments. Holders expect to be rewarded for giving up their immediate claims by receiving regular payments of interest or dividends over the life of the agreement.

Liquidity, Risk and Interest Yield

Although money is immediately usable as purchasing power, it has a major disadvantage. Stored money yields no explicit interest. When there are other reasonably safe ways to store purchasing power, most individuals will prefer them. After their immediate spending needs are satisfied, however, individuals will select a balanced assortment of financial assets and real property. The choice of other assets depends on relative liquidity, risk of loss, and expected *interest yield*. Generally an asset that is relatively liquid and safe pays a relatively low interest yield. Government securities and savings accounts are examples. A less liquid and more risky asset must pay a relatively high yield to compensate for its illiquidity and risk. Corporate stocks are examples; the issuing firm may go out of business (like Studebaker) or it may be wildly successful (like Coca-Cola) and make its stockholders very wealthy. Corporate bonds are more liquid than stocks because if the firm goes out of business, bondholders must be paid before any payment can be made to stockholders. Careful portfolio management involves choosing a collection of assets with enough advantages in terms of liquidity, safety and high interest yield to offset the disadvantages of illiquidity, risk and low interest yield.

Some typical returns on portfolio assets are listed in Table 1–2.

Near Money

Some items in an asset portfolio are so much like money they are called *near money*. Savings and time deposits experience no loss in principal value. They can be converted to the full amount of purchasing power fairly easily,

TABLE 1–2 Returns on Portfolio Assets, January 1987

Savings Accounts in Commercial Banks	5.25%
Savings Accounts in Savings and Loans	5.50
2-Year Time Deposits in Commercial Banks	6.00
2-Year Time Deposits in Savings and Loans	6.50
8-Year Time Deposits in Commercial Banks	7.75
8-Year Time Deposits in Savings and Loans	8.00
3-Month Treasury Securities	6.00
1-Year Treasury Securities	6.00
3-Year Treasury Securities	7.00
20-Year Treasury Securities	7.60
State and Local Securities (tax exempt)	
High Grade	6.00
Medium Grade	7.00
Corporate Bonds	
High Grade	9.00
Medium Grade	10.00
Utility Bonds	9.00
Common Stocks (dividend/price ratio)	3.00

often by pressing a series of buttons on an automatic teller machine; at worst they require a quick trip to the bank. Including near money in a portfolio increases its liquidity and makes it possible to substitute interest-earning assets for idle money. With less of the community's money held idle, more is available for lending to government or private borrowers, and more can be used for purchasing real goods and property.

Money and Real Wealth

Most of us associate large holdings of money with real wealth, and generally this assumption is correct. But by now we know that money in itself is not wealth. Money represents wealth, but it is not actual wealth. In fact, money is a claim against wealth. It is a means of storing up one person's contribution to the world's wealth, entitling that person to consume an equivalent amount.

Much of the money of the past was wealth, in the sense that gold and silver coins could be melted down and shaped into useful ornaments or utensils. Today's money, however, is worthless in itself, valuable only because it confers claims to real wealth.

Other portfolio assets are also claims for real wealth, entitling their holder to receive in exchange either wealth or other, more liquid claims to wealth. Near moneys like savings and time deposits and short-term government securities provide almost immediate access to real wealth. Stocks, bonds, and insurance policies take somewhat longer to convert to wealth and involve some exchange costs paid to brokers. Of an individual portfolio, only real goods and property are themselves wealth.

In a primitive economic society, the quantity of real wealth and claims against wealth remained roughly in balance. Each year farmers and small craftsmen received money income equivalent to the value of the production they sent to market. Their total claims against the world's new wealth remained roughly equal to total production. When real wealth and claims against wealth are in balance, there is no problem about excessive claims for a limited supply of goods. Producers can consume only as much as they have added to world production, whether in the current year or in years past.

The problem of balance between wealth and claims against wealth becomes more difficult as an economy develops. A large, complex economic system occasionally creates more claims against wealth than actual wealth. (The reverse is also possible but not likely. Why? It is easier to produce claims to wealth than to produce wealth itself.) Today, farmers and small manufacturers may receive claims to wealth before production actually takes place. When this happens, liquid claims accumulate in financial portfolios even when there has been no equivalent increase in the world's stock of real wealth.

If money were the only type of claim, balancing newly produced wealth with new liquid claims would not be especially difficult. The Treasury or the banks could issue new money precisely in the amount of new production. Maintaining the balance between claims and real wealth becomes more difficult when there are so many different types of claims. When many private businesses and individuals issue claims against their *capacity to create wealth in the future*, total liquid claims may multiply faster than new goods and services available for sale. An individual portfolio contains many claims issued by these private issuers. If all of us tried at once to exchange all our claims for real wealth, there would not be enough to go around. Some claims would not be satisfied.

Money and Policy: Measuring Money

The job of balancing liquid claims with the world's production of new wealth is the responsibility of monetary policymakers. To carry out their responsibility, policymakers must first measure the quantity of claims and then adjust the quantity to meet the spending needs of the economy. They must make sure there are enough new claims to encourage efficient production of new goods and services and to enable consumers to spend regularly for the things they need. But they should not allow liquid claims to grow to the point that they cannot be exchanged at some time for real goods and services. This is a difficult task.

Before policymakers can deal successfully with this task, they must know how much money there is. Economists define money most narrowly to include only the most liquid claims: currency, travelers checks, and checkable deposits, all in the hands of the public. Some examples of checkable deposits are checking accounts in commercial banks, negotiable orders of withdrawal (or NOW accounts), automatic transfers from savings (or ATS accounts), and credit union share drafts. Because all these claims can be exchanged immediately for goods and services, they provide the closest relationship between buyers and sellers.

M1

In December 1986 the quantity of currency and checkable deposits was about $730 billion, of which $184 billion was currency, $6 billion was travelers checks, and $540 billion was checkable deposits. Notice that the total $184 billion includes only currency held by people and business firms; to include currency deposited in banks would be double counting, because currency would also be counted as deposits. Currency held by the U.S. Treasury is not counted as part of the money supply either; Treasury currency becomes money only after it is paid out to an individual or business firm.

During 1986, the money supply of $730 billion was spent to purchase $4,208 billion of newly produced goods and services. Throughout the coming years, additional goods and services will be produced, and new claims must be created.

The $730 billion of money in 1986 was only one way to count liquid claims; it was the value of currency, travelers checks, and checkable deposits only, the most liquid of all claims against real wealth. Economists designate this class of claims *M1*.

M2

Adjusting the quantity of money to the needs of the economy is the job of the nation's monetary policymakers. The job has grown more complicated with the recent growth of other types of claims. Near moneys are the best example. Remember that near moneys can be used to purchase wealth almost as quickly as currency and checking accounts. Savings and time deposits in all depository institutions can be transferred to checking accounts very easily. Even ownership shares in money market funds are readily convertible to currency; money market funds are a means by which small savers can join a pool of investors for purchasing short-term securities. Because short-term claims come due frequently, members of the pool may quickly convert their shares to currency.

FIGURE 1–2   Money Stock Components

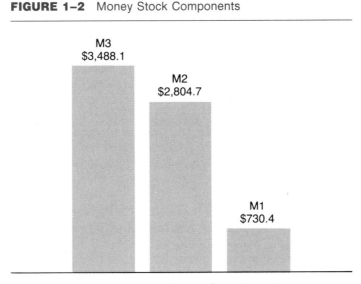

Ways to Measure Money: December 1986

M1 – Currency plus checkable deposits at commercial banks,
thrift institutions and credit unions
M2 – M1 plus savings and small time deposits at banks and
thrift institutions plus money market fund shares plus
overnight borrowings and Eurodollar loans
M3 – M2 plus large time deposits of banks and thrift
institutions
L – M3 plus bankers' acceptances, commercial paper, savings
bonds, short-term Treasury bills.

Including all these near moneys in the quantity of money gives a broader definition, which economists have labeled *M2*. The quantity of M2 in December 1986 was about $2,805 billion. M2 includes currency and travelers checks, all checking and savings accounts, and money market accounts. (Overnight repurchase agreements and Eurodollar deposits owned by U.S. residents also constitute a small part of M2.) When policymakers adjust the nation's supply of claims to its annual production of real wealth, they must consider the supply of this very liquid form of near money as well as the more narrow supply of currency, travelers checks and checkable deposits.

M3 and L

Another near money is large-denomination time deposits, including certificates of deposit and large deposits made by business firms. These are included in a third measure, *M3*, amounting to $3,488 billion in 1986. It is possible to define other measures of liquid claims, each new measure adding another less liquid type of financial claim. Economists have named the broadest measure of all *L*, for liquidity. This category includes bankers' acceptances, commercial paper, savings bonds, and short-term Treasury bills. We will have more to say about these liquid claims later. At this point, it is enough to say that measuring money is not a simple and straightforward process. Simply counting the dollars won't do. It is important to consider all the other less liquid ways to hold wealth.

Figure 1–2 summarizes some of the most commonly used money measures and shows their values.

Difficulties of Measurement

All new kinds of money represent claims against the nation's supply of goods and services. Thus they add to the complexity of the policymakers' job. Whereas once it was sufficient just to measure M1 (not a simple matter in itself), now policymakers must decide which of the other measures is the most appropriate guide to policy. Which M should be kept in balance with the nation's production of real goods and services? How much near money is too much? How much M represents too many claims against the nation's real wealth?

Increasingly, policymakers are looking to the broader definitions of M as better ways to measure the potential spending power in the hands of the nation's consumers and business firms. Whichever M is used, there are difficulties of measurement. M1 is easiest to measure. The quantity of paper money issued is known and the amount of currency stored in bank vaults and at the Treasury can be subtracted from the total. About two-thirds of the nation's checking accounts are held by commercial banks that report their deposits to the Federal Reserve. M2 and M3 require estimates of the other kinds of liquid claims.

MONEY AND BANKING IN PRACTICE: ELECTRONIC FUNDS TRANSFER

The growth of the U.S. economy and the development of our financial system have been phenomenal. Especially since World War II, the number of daily financial transactions has mushroomed. More and more our transactions are carried out by checks drawn on commercial banks, savings banks and credit unions. By the mid-1970s, some said that U.S. financial institutions were "drowning in a sea of paper."

Processing billions of checks annually has become so difficult that new technology is constantly being developed to speed up the process. A major improvement has been the use of "magnetic ink character recognition" and automatic sorting machines. Magnetic ink is used to print oddly shaped numbers on your checks. The numbers identify your bank, your account and the amount of the check. Machines can read the numbers and route checks easily to the appropriate banks. The result is to add your payment to the recipient's account and quickly deduct it from yours, with very little human labor required.

Continuing to carry on transactions through transfers of paper is likely to present even greater problems in the future. The latest technology for making financial transactions is electronic funds transfer (EFT). Most currently used EFTs involve automatic teller machines, plastic cards and code numbers. The user inserts a card, punches in a code number, then punches in the amount to be transferred to another account, also identified by a code. Many commercial banks and savings and loans provide automatic tellers for their customers to transfer funds from savings to checking, to withdraw cash, or to make loan payments.

Automatic tellers could be used in a more comprehensive payments system. Installed in retail stores, they could transfer payments automatically from a customer's account to the store's account. (The equipment is already widely used to verify customers' checks and could be adapted easily to transfer payments.)

They could also be accessed by push-button telephone, allowing the caller to pay a series of bills by pushing the code numbers of the local power company, water department and retail store. Electronic transfer of funds might mean a cashless and checkless society—all transactions carried on by electronic blips.

Financial institutions would welcome the change. Processing checks costs about 30 cents each. While electronic equipment is expensive, economies of scale would push the average cost of each transaction down. The public has been slow to accept the idea, however. Most of us like to have our checks as a written record and legal evidence of payments. There is also the issue of privacy; having our payments permanently on record in a computer is distasteful to some.

An even stronger public objection to EFT involves what the banks regard as an advantage: speed. We must confess that many checks are written before funds to cover them are actually in the accounts! Many of us depend on the *float* occasionally to tide us over a day or so before our paycheck arrives. Float refers to the excess payments over and above deposits actually in the banking system. When checks are slow to be deducted from the payer's account, float increases. To deduct payments instantaneously would eliminate float altogether.

Question for Discussion

1. What are the implications of electronic funds transfer for efforts to regulate the supply of money?

Some Conclusions and a Look Ahead

We have described how money has evolved from primitive times to the present, increasing the efficiency of economic systems the world over. The increasing use of money provides the basis for economic growth and development and helps ensure rising standards of living. Because money represents claims to real wealth, it is important to keep the supply of money in balance with the nation's production of goods and services. New types of claims make this more difficult and create problems with respect to equity and externalities.

Deciding on the correct measure of money is a job for monetary policymakers. In the next chapter we will discuss the use of gold as standard money. Under the gold standard the quantity of money was regulated by flows of gold. Thus, the money supply was determined apart from the acts of policymakers. We will see that this system brought some problems, too.

Glossary of Terms

assay. to evaluate a precious metal in terms of its purity and weight

barter. the exchange of goods for other goods without the use of money

bill of exchange. a promise to pay issued by an importer and used to pay the exporter

bimetallic money system. a money system that uses two precious metals

commodity money. money that is valuable in itself, apart from its value as money

credit money. money that has no value apart from its value as money; fiat money

debase. to reduce the value of money through chipping, overissue, etc.

deflation. general decreases in prices that reflect changes in the value of money; the opposite of inflation

efficiency. a condition in which productive resources are allocated in a way to achieve the greatest production with the smallest expenditure

equity.   fairness in the distribution of the benefits and costs of production; different people have different definitions of fairness

externalities.   benefits and costs that occur outside the primary activity of exchange in markets

Gresham's Law.   the principle that people will prefer to use as money the cheaper of two commodities and hoard the dearer commodity; thus "cheap money drives dear money out of circulation"

inflation.   general increases in prices that reflect changes in the value of money; the opposite of deflation

intermediator.   a person, institution or instrument that "stands between" participants in a transaction and does some of the work that occurs between them

L.   M3 plus nonbank public holdings of government securities, commercial paper and bankers' acceptances; net of money market fund holdings of these assets

liquidity.   the ease of converting an asset to purchasing power without significant loss of value

M1.   currency and checkable deposits in the hands of the public

M2.   M1 plus savings and small time deposits, repurchase agreements and money market deposit accounts

M3.   M2 plus large deposits, U.S.-owned Eurodollars and institutional money market mutual funds

market ratio.   the ratio between the values of two precious metals when sold in the market

medium of exchange.   the use of money for making purchases

mint ratio.   the ratio between the values of two precious metals when sold to the mint

near money.   assets that can be used as purchasing power almost as easily as money, including savings and time deposits

par.   the face value of money or securities

portfolio.   a collection of real and financial assets owned by an individual or business firm

representative commodity money.   certificates that stand for a certain quantity of commodity money

seigniorage.   the difference between the face value of money and the cost of producing it

specie.   coins made of precious metals, usually gold or silver

standard of deferred payment.   the use of money for paying in the future for goods and services obtained in the present

standard of value.   the use of money to compare the values of different goods or services

store of value.   the use of money to hold a claim for goods and services to be purchased in the future

wealth.   real goods and property

Summary of Important Ideas

1. As an intermediator, money contributes to the efficiency of the economic system. An efficient monetary system may also contribute to equity and add positive externalities.

2. Primitive societies did not need money, because they were largely self-sufficient. The growth of specialization made exchange and money necessary.

3. Nuggets and coins of precious metals were early forms of money, which contributed to broad economic and social change. Bimetallic money systems were difficult to maintain because of the operation of Gresham's Law.

4. Representative commodity money was the forerunner of bank notes, which could expand to meet the needs of trade. The value of early credit money depended on the reputation of the issuing bank or government. The most common credit money used today is checks drawn against their owners' checking accounts.

5. Money links consumers with producers and is thus a medium of exchange. It also serves as a standard of value, a store of value over time, and a standard for deferred payments. When money functions properly, it allows goods and services to be distributed according to each person's contribution to total production.

6. Changes in money's value are called inflation and deflation and often result from too much or too little credit money.

7. Persons hold money and other claims to wealth along with real wealth in their asset portfolios. Items in a portfolio are ranked according to their liquidity: the ease of converting to purchasing power without significant loss of value.

8. The use of many new claims to real wealth may present problems of liquidity and inflation and make it difficult to measure purchasing power. This complicates the task of monetary policymakers.

Questions for Discussion and Research

1. Describe the various procedures and instruments used in exchange: barter, commodity money, representative money, credit money.

2. Explain the reasons for bimetallic money systems and tell why they were often unsuccessful. What circumstances affected mint ratios and market ratios?

3. Illustrate the process by which the use of credit money might lead to boom-and-bust cycles for the economy. How is Gresham's Law significant in these cases? Does Gresham's Law still operate? Give examples.

4. How is Gresham's Law related to the four functions of money? Explain why satisfactorily performing any one of money's functions is necessary for the performance of the other three.

5. Define: portfolio, liquidity, real wealth, near money.

6. Explain why the correct supply of money is critical for healthy, stable economic growth. What are the likely consequences of too-slow or too-fast money growth?

7. Consult recent (Friday) issues of *The Wall Street Journal* for information about the nation's current supply of money, using the M1, M2 and M3 definitions. Compare current quantities with data on past values given in the text. Comment on the behavior of the values in the recent past.

Additional Reading

"Changes in the Use of Transaction Accounts and Cash from 1984 to 1986." *The Federal Reserve Bulletin*, March 1987, pp. 179–198.

C H A P T E R

2

- To understand the historical role of gold as money and the reasons gold was finally abandoned as a money standard
- To examine the relative advantages and disadvantages of gold as an investment or as part of a portfolio of assets
- To look briefly at the significance of silver in the nation's money supply

Gold as Standard Money

"You might as well base the monetary system on pork bellies."

Milton Friedman

Au. That's the chemical symbol for gold. Hardly an exciting name—it doesn't begin to convey the mysterious attraction that humans have felt for gold from antiquity to the present.

Certainly one of the most exciting events in the lives of American students is the day they receive their class rings. By taking part in this ritual we are continuing a tradition almost as old as civilization—adorning ourselves with gold. And not in an insignificant way either. Production of class rings is probably the largest single use for gold in the nation: about 15 tons every year!

Philosophers struggle to explain our fascination with gold. They point out its physical attributes: (1) malleability that enables artisans to create delightful works of beauty, (2) durability that preserves the beauty over thousands of years, (3) brilliance that excites the eye and (4) atomic structure that makes it an almost perfect conductor of electricity. To coldly recite the list of attributes is not sufficient, for such a list leaves out the most important reason for our historical love affair with gold: People want it. Gold is desirable because others desire it. People who own gold have command over the behavior of others. More than silver, platinum or precious gems, gold satisfies human hunger for the ultimate value, the standard by which all other values can be compared.

Such a prized commodity understandably became the basis for money. Money systems based on gold dominated the Western world during the period roughly corresponding to the Industrial Revolution.[1] It was only after

TABLE 2–1 Estimated Annual Gold Production

	Metric Tons	Value in Millions of Dollars*
South Africa	730	15,450
Soviet Union	380	8,042
Canada	55	1,164
United States	35	740
Ghana	25	529
New Guinea	20	423
Australia	18	381
Philippines	17	360
Rhodesia	15	317
Central and South America	53	1,122
Europe	11	233
Rest of World	30	635

*Computed at a price of $600 an ounce.

a series of international crises that the United States could—reluctantly—break the last ties that bound our money to gold. And even today there are many who yearn for the stability and security they believe gold guaranteed.

How completely does gold achieve these benefits for an economic system? What does gold actually do?

Producing and Using Gold

The largest producers of gold in the world today are the Soviet Union and the Union of South Africa. The Soviet Union does not reveal data on gold production, but South Africa produces almost 800 tons a year, probably two-thirds of world production. This amounts to about 4 tons, or 7 cubic feet, every working day. The United States produces roughly 35 tons a year, about one-fourth from Homestake Mine in South Dakota. See Table 2–1 for estimates of annual gold production around the world.

An ancient sea deposited microscopic particles of gold in banks of rock called reefs, reaching across 300 miles of the South African nation. Today, workers descend shafts as far as two miles into the earth where temperatures reach more than 100°. (Their average weekly wage is less than $50.) They insert explosives into the earth, and then they load the broken rock into buckets for lifting to the surface. There, the rocks are ground up and mixed with water and cyanide, which releases the gold. Filters separate out the rock, and zinc dust removes the cyanide. The resulting powder is heated along with certain chemicals that float away impurities and leave—finally—

FIGURE 2-1 Gold Holdings

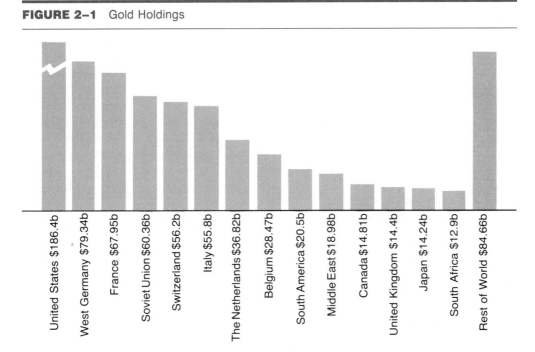

United States $186.4b
West Germany $79.34b
France $67.95b
Soviet Union $60.36b
Switzerland $56.2b
Italy $55.8b
The Netherlands $36.82b
Belgium $28.47b
South America $20.5b
Middle East $18.98b
Canada $14.81b
United Kingdom $14.4b
Japan $14.24b
South Africa $12.9b
Rest of World $84.66b

Value computed at an arbitrary price of $600 an ounce. Amounts stated in billions.

SOURCE: Adapted from *Newsweek*, December 16, 1974, p. 80.

a gleaming bit of gold. For each ounce of gold, 2½ tons of rock must be processed in this way.

For all the years that people have sought gold and struggled to produce it, their efforts have yielded only about 80,000 metric tons (1 metric ton equals 2,204.6 pounds). Only an estimated 41,000 tons remain underground. The world's total stock of mined gold would fill about 30 railroad boxcars or cover a football field to a depth of 2½ feet. The largest single stock of gold (12,600 metric tons) is in the Federal Reserve Bank of New York, which holds it for 80 other nations. The United States owns about 8,584 tons, much of which is stored at Fort Knox, Kentucky. See Figure 2–1 for estimates of national gold holdings.

Gold is rated according to its purity. Refined to 99.5 percent purity, it is rated 24 karat. Most jewelry in the United States is rated 14 karat. Goldsmiths test the purity of gold by rubbing it against a touchstone and applying nitric acid. If the color does not change, the substance is pure gold.

Ancient artisans fashioned gold into splendid works of art. The largest that has survived is Tutankhamen's coffin, made in Egypt 3,330 years ago and weighing 244 pounds. Smaller gold ornaments were made by the lost-wax method. First, jewelers made wax models, working carefully and painstakingly to produce precisely the desired design. Then they painted thin layers of plaster over the wax model again and again to make a solid mold. Heating the mold caused the wax to melt and drain out so that molten gold could be poured in. When the gold cooled, the plaster mold was broken and a gleaming treasure remained.

Coins were originally works of art, too, depicting victorious armies, religious themes or simply the face of a ruler. The first coins were probably made 2,500 years ago by King Croesus of Lydia, an island in the eastern Mediterranean Sea. A Roman coin of 215 A.D. was sold at auction in 1973 for nearly $65,000, the price more a reflection of its antiquity than its value as gold. In 1979, a gold doubloon minted in New York in 1787 brought $725,000.

Whether fashioned into coins or not, gold still serves as a store of wealth in many parts of the world. Brides in India adorn themselves with rings, bracelets, earrings, necklaces and even spots of gold dust on their cheeks. Gold provides security against life's adversities. For nations lacking social insurance and pension plans, gold may be the next best alternative.

Gold and the Economy

The Spanish explorers who followed Columbus to America were looking for spices, but when they saw natives wearing golden ornaments and helmets and carrying golden shields, all else was forgotten. Shiploads of treasure were taken back to Europe, where the magnificent cargo was melted down and fashioned into coins (or specie) for fueling a century of enormous prosperity. The prosperity was not confined to Spain. By an interesting principle first explained by David Hume, the flow of gold into Spain eventually spread growth and prosperity through much of the trading world.

The Specie-Flow Principle

David Hume explained the *specie-flow principle* this way. A flow of gold into a nation increases its money supply and stimulates spending. Merchants and manufacturers prosper, and employment and production increase. Living standards of workers increase, and prosperity spreads. If the supply of new money increases faster than the production of new goods for sale, prices rise; that is to say, the value of money falls.

Rising prosperity and prices in one nation cause an increase in its imports, as prosperous citizens spend their incomes for goods made abroad. Exports don't increase as fast and may even decrease, as domestic prices rise relative to prices abroad. The excess of imports over exports causes a drain of specie abroad, reducing the money supply in the first nation and increasing it in the second. As a result, price inflation tends to fall in the first and speed up in the second. This process continues until the new gold is spread around and business is growing in all trading nations.

Hume and other economists of the seventeenth and eighteenth centuries saw this result as ideal. It meant that flows of specie among trading nations would tend to equalize their prices and incomes. The promise of prosperity would stimulate the search for gold, and the availability of new money would stimulate production of goods and services. The money supply would tend to stabilize at levels that reflect the real productive capacities of trading nations.

The most attractive feature of the specie-flow principle was that it occurred automatically. Because it depended only on the independent acts of profit-seeking people, it required no policymakers at all. It confirmed the expectations of supporters of *laissez-faire*. This is the economic theory that free market decisions without government intervention produce ideal results in terms of efficiency in resource allocation, equity in distribution of goods and services, and positive externalities in the form of maximum personal freedom. The nineteenth century was the zenith of support for the theory of laissez-faire, and an important basis for that support was faith in the specie-flow principle.

Faith in the specie-flow principle was not exactly misplaced. When the ideal results failed to materialize, it was not entirely the fault of the process itself. More correctly, the problem was a failure to operate the system according to the rules. Under the rules of the system, the money supplies of all nations must be based on the *gold standard*.

Rates of Exchange

One of the rules of the gold standard was that nations must establish *exchange rates* between their currencies and gold. In the 1950s, for instance, the U.S. dollar was exchanged for 0.0286 ounce of gold and the British pound for 0.1 ounce. Fixing all currencies relative to gold establishes their values relative to one another; thus, the relative values of the pound and the dollar were:

$$\frac{1 \text{ pound}}{1 \text{ dollar}} = \frac{0.1 \text{ ounce}}{0.0286 \text{ ounce}}$$

so that:

$$\pounds 1 = \frac{0.1}{0.0286} \times \$1.00 = \$3.50 \,.$$

Fixed ratios between currencies and gold would ensure stability of exchange rates among currencies. An example may illustrate this point. Suppose a U.S. consumer orders a cashmere sweater from Britain for a price of £20. According to the existing exchange rate above, £1 equals $3.50, so the cost to the buyer would be: 20 × $3.50 = $70.00. Unless exchange rates were fixed, the price of pounds might rise to $4.00, for a cost of: 20 × $4.00 = $80.00.

Uncertainty about exchange rates tends to discourage international trade and reduce production and living standards worldwide. Fortunately, the gold standard would work to stabilize exchange rates. No U.S. consumer would pay $4.00 for British pounds if he or she could buy $70.00 worth of gold:

$$\$70.00 \times 0.0286 \text{ ounce} = 2.0 \text{ ounces}$$

and ship it to Britain where it could be sold for 2.0/0.1, or £20, which is just enough to buy the sweater. The result of the gold standard is to maintain exchange rates very close to the ratio established by the treasuries of the two nations. (Shipping gold adds a small charge to the cost of pounds, so the exchange rate might rise slightly before gold would be exported.)

Stable exchange rates help keep trade flowing among nations, but there is a disadvantage. When many U.S. consumers buy goods from abroad, the result may be to depress U.S. industry, reducing domestic production and employment. In this case it might be desirable to allow the price of pounds to rise. Then, the higher cost of buying British goods would discourage consumer purchases. Furthermore, the more valuable pound would enable British consumers to buy more U.S. goods and stimulate production in the United States. In our previous example, the price of dollars to British consumers might fall from:

$$\$3.50 = \pounds1 \text{ and } \$1.00 = 1/3.5 = \pounds0.29$$

to:

$$\$4.00 = \pounds1 \text{ and } \$1.00 = 1/4.0 = \pounds0.25 \ .$$

Unless exchange rates are allowed to fluctuate, trade flows will tend to continue in the same direction, stimulating production in one nation and retarding it in another.

Limits on the Money Supply

A second rule of the gold standard involved the supply of paper money. In order that paper currencies remain convertible into a fixed quantity of gold, a nation had to be careful not to issue too much currency. Gradually, however, throughout the Western world the need for currency for trade required creation of more paper money. In fact, a nation's money supply came to look like an inverted wedding cake. The bottom (smallest) layer represented the nation's stock of gold; the next (larger) layer represented bank notes and certificates redeemable in gold; the top (largest) layer represented checking accounts issued to borrowers on the basis of banks' holdings of currency and specie reserves. The size of the total cake was limited by the quantity of gold in the smallest layer.

By the rules of the gold standard, a nation would have to adjust its money supply to reflect its gold holdings. Should gold flow out of the nation to pay for imports, the entire wedding cake would have to shrink proportionally. Gold certificates and bank notes would be drawn out of the spending stream through taxes; checking accounts would be reduced as banks collected old loans and cut down on new lending. The reduction in the money supply would cause incomes and prices to fall; then gold would stop flowing out and might even begin to flow in. This is because other nations would be receiving more gold and experiencing an increase in the money supply. Their prosperity and inflation would cause their imports to increase and exports to fall.

Violating the Rules

Abiding by the rules of the gold standard brought on agonizing cycles of inflation and deflation, with alternating prosperity and depression in trading nations. Democratically elected public officials could not afford to inflict such pain on voters—so they ignored the rules. More specifically, they found ways to avoid reducing the money supply, thus aggravating a tendency toward inflation. With world currency supplies far in excess of gold stocks, there were frequent money panics. People would rush to convert their currency to gold and hide it away in private hoards. Inconvertible paper money would decline in value as merchants refused to accept it in trade (another example of Gresham's Law). In the Great Depression of the 1930s many nations were forced off the gold standard. All currencies became inconvertible except among Central Banks and since 1971 even for Central Banks.

Freeing money from its gold backing has had two results. It has allowed nations to expand their money supplies without fear of losing gold, and it has accelerated tendencies toward inflation. Holders of paper money have seen their value erode away. Some, called goldbugs, have recommended a return to the "discipline" of the gold standard. The French people are particularly aware of the dangers of holding inconvertible paper money. (Perhaps they have been burned too often by spendthrift governments.) French citizens are believed to hold large amounts of gold (some say 5,000 tons), and their government frequently urges a return to the gold standard for all nations.

The goldbugs are correct in their belief that a return to the gold standard would impose some discipline in the tendency of governments to overissue paper currency. The results might be unpleasant—periods of reduced production, high unemployment and slow growth—but there would be less danger of uncontrolled inflation. A quaint side effect, however, might result from a return to the gold standard. Because South Africa and the Soviet Union produce the bulk of the world's gold, they would have significant power to affect global politics through their enhanced economic power. It is not clear that this would be desirable.

Most economists agree with John M. Keynes, who called gold a "barbarous relic"—a memento from the past that should not interfere with money management in today's world. In this view, the money supply should be controlled in a way that promotes efficiency, equity and positive externalities for the society as a whole—not made to depend on the generosity of Mother Nature.

"Paper Gold"

Recent history has seen three great periods of gold production. Discoveries in California and Australia in the 1850s, in Alaska and the Yukon in the late 1800s, and in South Africa and the Soviet Union in this century all led to periods of great new production. Probably two-thirds of the earth's gold has already been extracted, and further production is likely to be slow and costly.

The slowing growth of gold production has created some problems. As the world's capacity to produce goods and services grows, the need for money grows also. Too little money means slower growth of spending and incomes, lower production and employment, and falling prices and reduced efficiency in resource allocation. These problems characterized the world economy of the 1930s and continued to affect trade after World War II.

After World War II, the United States agreed to supply the world with dollars as a means of dealing with the shortage of other currencies. The dollar was convertible to gold, and other currencies could be exchanged for dollars. Trading nations were said to be on a gold-dollar standard. The United States created billions of new dollars that it sent abroad in trade. Eventually, dollar holdings abroad came to exceed our capacity to redeem them in gold. The exchange value of the dollar declined, impairing our ability to import needed materials and aggravating domestic inflation.

To place on one nation the major burden of supplying the world's money was an unworkable solution to the problem of the scarcity of gold. An international solution had to be found. The solution involved an organization established after World War II: the International Monetary Fund (or IMF), whose purpose is to hold international accounts and make loans for trade. In 1970, IMF member nations agreed to allow the IMF to create a new form of money for use in international trade. The new money is called *Special Drawing Rights (SDRs)*, but it might well be called "paper gold." The

IMF adds SDRs to nations' accounts as if they had discovered new supplies of gold. In the future it is expected that new issues of SDRs will help regulate the supply of international money. IMF issues of SDRs would relieve any one nation of the burden of creating excess supplies of its own currency. We will have more to say about international financial institutions in Chapter 12.

MONEY AND BANKING IN PRACTICE: INVESTING IN GOLD

Money and precious ornaments are not the only uses for gold. Because gold is chemically stable, it is especially suitable for filling teeth and for making electrical circuitry in calculators, TV sets and computers. It can be rolled so thin that light will pass through but the sun's infrared rays are reflected away; this makes it suitable for lining the plastic visors of space helmets and for coating office windows. Industrial uses like these once constituted three-fourths of the demand for gold. The remaining one-fourth was bought for investment or speculative purposes. In recent years these proportions have just about reversed. See Figure 2–2 for an illustration of how gold is used.

Investors have seen the price of gold rise from a controlled $35 an ounce in 1968 to almost $870 in January 1980 and then fall below $300 in 1985 before rising again. (See Figure 2–3 for gold prices since 1970.) The downward trend of gold production (about 1,430 tons annually) and increasing world demand portend an eventual further rise in gold prices. World calamities, revolutions and shortages all stimulate demand for that most storable, most desirable of all commodities.

Some of the increasing demand for gold has been satisfied by sales from U.S. Treasury stocks. Treasury sales help hold the price of gold down—and the value of the dollar up— and draw in dollars from abroad. During 1978–1979, the United States sold 1.5 million ounces a month to the gold market from its holdings of 275 million ounces. The leading centers for the gold market are Zurich and London. Since 1919, the worldwide gold price has been set twice a day in London by five leading dealers. The price is based on buy and sell orders received during the day.

Most of the investors who became wealthy in the gold boom of the 1970s were not Americans. Until 1975, it was illegal for Americans to own monetary gold, and by then the price was already high. Since 1975, an investment in com-

FIGURE 2–2 How Gold Is Used

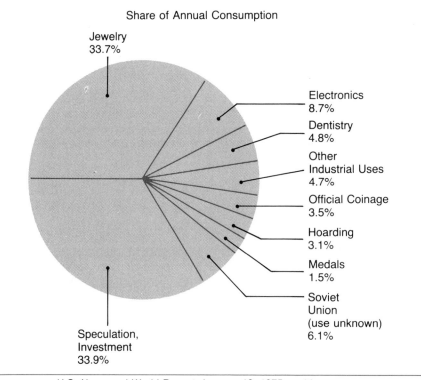

Share of Annual Consumption

Jewelry
33.7%

Electronics
8.7%

Dentistry
4.8%

Other
Industrial Uses
4.7%

Official Coinage
3.5%

Hoarding
3.1%

Medals
1.5%

Soviet
Union
(use unknown)
6.1%

Speculation,
Investment
33.9%

SOURCE: *U.S. News and World Report*, January 13, 1975, p. 11.

mon stocks would have yielded a greater return than an investment in gold. Gold pays no dividends, requires storage and insurance costs, and is generally bought from dealers at retail prices (with markup) and sold back at wholesale prices (without markup).

Investors can buy gold in numerous forms. The most popular in recent years has been gold coins, specifically the South African Krugerrand. The Krugerrand contains exactly one ounce and sells for the wholesale London gold price plus a 5 percent to 8 percent commission. The coins are easily stored, rec-

ognizable and readily sold. In the late 1970s Americans bought almost four million Krugerrands annually. (In 1986 the U.S. Treasury got into this profitable market by selling its own one-ounce and half-ounce gold medallions.)

Large investors often prefer to own gold bars, which can be bought in amounts from one to 100 ounces. The commission charge is generally lower than for coins, but the bars cannot be broken down for sale in smaller amounts as coins can.

Furthermore, it is generally necessary to have a gold bar assayed before

FIGURE 2–3 Gold Prices, 1970–1986

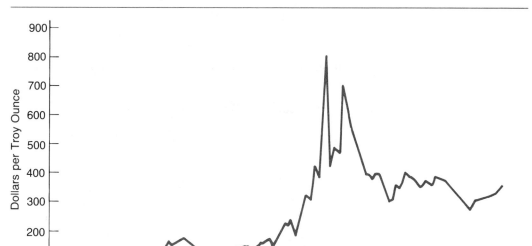

resale. The owners need not actually take possession of the gold bar, but they may pay a small storage fee to a bank depository.

The newest form of dealing in gold is *futures contracts*. Investors buy contracts entitling them to receive gold at some future date; the price is the expected future gold price plus commission. Other investors who expect the gold price to fall sell contracts promising to deliver the gold; if their expectations are correct, they will eventually buy cheaper gold to fulfill the contract. Often no gold changes hands at all. When the contract comes due, holders of futures contracts resell them to sellers. The resale price depends on the current price of gold. Thus, the original buyer makes a profit if the price has

risen higher than expected, and the original seller makes a profit if the price has fallen. Futures trading requires no storage, insurance or assaying costs, but it is risky.

Some investors prefer to hold stock in gold-mining companies. Like any other stocks, their dividend return and market value depend on the quantity and price of the firm's output; so they may be risky. Holding gold ornaments or jewelry is satisfying in many ways but is not very profitable as an investment. This is because so much of the purchase price represents labor rather than the intrinsic value of the metal. Melting down a gold ornament yields gold worth only a fraction of the price of the ornament.

Question for Discussion

1. How does investing in gold affect the efficiency, equity, and externalities of our economic system?

MONEY AND BANKING IN PRACTICE: THE PRICE OF GOLD

What determines the price of gold? Many investors would like to know the answer to that question.

To many investors gold is an asset that increases in value as the value of money falls. They see gold as a hedge against inflation. Indeed, investors' purchases of gold tend to rise with inflation, so that the price of gold also tends to rise. Between 1972 and 1986, U.S. prices rose by about 7 percent a year. Over the same period, the price of gold rose from less than $100 an ounce to $400, an annual increase of about 10 percent. Thus, investors in gold earned an average return over inflation of about 3 percent a year (10 percent less 7 percent).

Some economists argue that it is not inflation that causes gold's price to rise but the *real* return on other financial assets. The real return on a financial asset is the difference between the interest yield and the rate of inflation.

When the real return on other financial assets falls below the increase in the price of gold, investors buy gold, and its price rises. In contrast, when the real return on other financial assets rises above the increase in gold's price,

investors tend to buy other financial assets, and gold's price remains stable or falls.

To understand this point, it is helpful to look at gold's price over the recent decade. In the late 1970s the real return on financial assets was negative. (The reason was that inflation was higher than the interest rate.) Negative real returns on financial assets pushed gold prices up to reach a peak in 1980.

Then in the early 1980s gold's price fell sharply and has since remained about $400 an ounce. Over the same period, the real rate on U.S. Treasury securities has been about 6 percent. Thus, it has been more profitable for investors to purchase government securities than gold.

Will gold's price rise again in the future? There are two circumstances that could bring about an increase in gold's price. Inflation could rise above interest rates, so that real returns again become negative on financial assets. Or interest rates could fall so far as to make holding other financial assets unprofitable. In the 1980s, most investors seem to expect neither of these events to occur.

Question for Discussion

1. Consult current business publications for information about the real return on financial assets and the current price of gold. Evaluate your findings in terms of the theory proposed here.

A Note on Silver

Next to gold, silver is the most malleable and ductile of all minerals; that is, it can be formed into useful shapes, and it can be drawn into fine wires. Silver is also suitable for conducting heat and electricity, and it can be mixed chemically for use in photography, medicine and other industrial purposes. About one-third of silver mined goes for silverware, ornaments and jewelry. Of course, its rarity and fine qualities have made silver useful also as money.

Canada, Mexico and the western states supplied the United States with silver for coins throughout the period of bimetallism in the 1800s and during the early 1900s. In 1834, the value of the dollar was fixed at:

$$\$1.00 = 0.773 \text{ troy ounce of silver}$$
$$1 \text{ ounce of silver} = \$1.292.$$

The dollar's value in terms of gold was:

$$\$1.00 = 0.0484 \text{ ounce of gold}$$
$$1 \text{ ounce of gold} = \$20.67.$$

The ratio of their values at the mint was 16 to 1.

The price of silver to be used for industrial purposes was allowed to fluctuate according to supply and demand. During the 1800s, production of silver grew so fast relative to demand that the market price threatened to fall. Voters in western states pressured Congress for legislation to support the price of silver. To maintain the agreed-on price, the Treasury would have to buy all the excess supplies of silver offered in the market. Buying silver cost the Treasury nothing except the cost of printing silver certificates used for the purchase. The Treasury accumulated substantial amounts of silver, some of which was made into coins and some stored as backing for the silver certificates.

Eventually production of silver slowed relative to demand for its use in industry. As the market price of silver rose, the Treasury stopped buying and began to sell from its accumulated stocks. The result was to hold down the price, discouraging new production and threatening future shortages. To

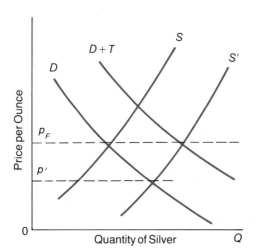

FIGURE 2–4a 1800s Silver Market

Increased supply threatens to push price down to p'. Treasury purchases increase demand to D + T and maintain a price floor at p_F.

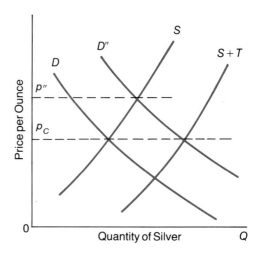

FIGURE 2–4b 1900s Silver Market

Demand grows faster than supply and threatens to push price up to p'. Treasury sales increase supply to S + T and maintain ceiling at p_C.

continue to sell silver at prices below the market price, however, would have exhausted the Treasury's entire supply. Then the price would have soared.

In 1961 the Treasury stopped selling silver and allowed the price to rise to the market level. At the same time, the Federal Reserve Banks were authorized to begin withdrawing silver certificates from circulation and to replace them with Federal Reserve notes. This freed all the Treasury's silver for use in coins. Unfortunately, U.S. citizens were beginning to realize that coins were worth more as metal than as money. In expectation of further price increases, they began hoarding coins. The Treasury had to forbid melting or exporting silver coins and to replace silver with copper and nickel in many new coins.

Figures 2–4a and 2–4b illustrate the effects of the government's silver policy. The fast growth of production during the 1800s is shown on Figure 2–4a as a shift to the right of the supply curve of silver. Market price falls from p_F to p'. Adding the Treasury's purchases of silver shifts the demand curve to the right. The result is a *price floor*: a fixed price below which price is not allowed to fall.

Figure 2–4b shows slower growth of silver production in the 1900s and increasing demand for silver to be used in industry. The market price rises.

Sales from Treasury stocks shift supply to the right and create a *price ceiling*: a fixed price above which price is not allowed to rise.

Interferences with market adjustments, such as these attempted by the Treasury, often have results different from those intended. Furthermore, they involve bureaucratic and storage costs for the government, and they distort the production and use of the metals themselves. All these considerations make the change from commodity and representative commodity money to credit money a much more efficient decision for the nation.

Our nation's money supply is no longer based on gold or silver. The needs of a modern economy dictate a more accommodating money supply. Even representative commodity money can no longer serve as a medium of exchange, standard of value, store of value, and standard of deferred payments. Credit money is needed—particularly the modern form of checking accounts created by banks.

MONEY AND BANKING IN PRACTICE: BACK TO GOLD?

Lewis E. Lehrman, Chairman of Citizens for America, believes that removing currency from its gold backing has produced anarchy in the world's monetary system. Without the discipline of gold, he says, nations can issue more currency, causing its value to fall and encouraging an increase in sales of goods and services abroad. Or they can reduce their outstanding currency to increase its value and allow domestic consumers to import foreign goods and services more cheaply. Either way, the strains on world trade can lead to national policies to restrict trade, which would damage productive relationships the world over.

Lehrman blames the lack of discipline in currency issue on political motives. Increasing the money supply is popular with many voters, who gain increased job opportunities and rising prices for their products. They frequently fail to see the long-term damage done by changes in the value of money.

A return to the gold standard would require that nations manage their money supply in accordance with their gold holdings. All the world's Central Banks now own 1.1 billion ounces of gold, which under Lehrman's plan would become the backing for national currencies. Current holdings of gold are roughly proportional to the nation's annual production and trade. The important question is what price is to be placed on gold. Setting the correct price would provide just enough money for full employment with low interest rates and stable wages and prices.

Lehrman says the correct price is determined at the average cost of producing additional gold. That price would place the price of gold correctly in proportion to production costs of all U.S. goods and services. It would also ensure about a 2 percent annual increase in production and, therefore, a 2 percent increase in the nation's money supply. (He estimated the correct price in 1987 at about $500 an ounce.)

Lehrman would not depend on the specie-flow mechanism to adjust nations' gold holdings. He points out that even under the gold standard, very little gold moved among nations. Instead, when one nation experienced an increase in gold and the money supply, the accompanying increase in prices reduced sales abroad and increased purchases. This left foreigners with more of the nation's currency, which they used to buy more of its products. Thus, instead of shipping gold abroad, the nation would ship goods and services.

Critics argue that staying with the gold standard may create unemployment unless the price of gold is increased frequently—to allow the nation to issue more currency. When the price of gold is increased, the nation's money will buy less, which imposes hardships on low- and middle-income families that lack investments tied to gold.

Questions for Discussion

1. Suppose Lehrman's proposal is followed and the United States returns to the gold standard. What would be the result of setting a gold price that is "too low"?

2. What groups are likely to favor Lehrman's proposal and what groups oppose? Explain your answer.

3. What far-reaching implications are there in a program to fix the nation's money supply relative to gold?

A Look Ahead

In the next chapter we will look closely at the origins and functions of banks. We will be especially interested in the process by which banks create credit money. Through money creation, banks can help achieve the appropriate rate of growth in the money supply. Or banks can complicate enormously the job of monetary policymakers to keep money growth in line with the nation's production of real goods and services.

Glossary of Terms

exchange rate. the price of one nation's currency in terms of another's for use in trade

futures contracts. contracts promising to deliver a certain asset on a certain day at a certain price

gold standard. a money system in which paper currency is evaluated according to a specific weight of gold; the Treasury buys and sells gold at the stated price

laissez-faire. the belief that economic activity is most efficient when government interferes least

price ceiling. a maximum price maintained by government sales of a commodity from stockpiles

price floor. a minimum price maintained by government purchases of a commodity for adding to stockpiles

SDRs. Special Drawing Rights issued by the International Monetary Fund for the purpose of increasing world liquidity

specie-flow principle. the principle that explains how flows of gold lead to proportional changes in incomes and prices

Summary of Important Ideas

1. Gold has certain characteristics that make it especially well suited to serve as money. Most gold produced today comes from the Soviet Union and the Union of South Africa.

2. David Hume described how the flow of gold into a nation would raise prices, stimulate production and income, and spread prosperity through increased trade. The result would be a tendency toward equality in prices and incomes among nations, with no need for government to regulate money flows. The gold standard also helped ensure stable exchange rates among currencies.

3. Adherence to the gold standard declined when democratic governments refused to inflict high levels of unemployment on their citizens. The supply of money was often allowed to grow too fast, so that it was no longer convertible to gold. Since 1971 no nation has redeemed its currency in gold.

4. The slow growth of gold production in recent decades has placed limits on world liquidity. For some years after World War II, the U.S. dollar served as a major source of liquidity for trade, but this presented some

problems. The International Monetary Fund (IMF) created a new form of world money called Special Drawing Rights (SDRs).

5. A decline of confidence in credit money has contributed to increased investment in gold. Investment can take the form of coins, bars, gold futures or stock in gold mines.

6. Silver is also useful as money and for other purposes. During the 1800s the price of silver was supported by Treasury purchases, paid for with newly issued silver certificates. In the 1900s, the Treasury sold silver to keep its price from rising. Finally in 1961, the Treasury ceased its silver dealings and began withdrawing silver certificates from circulation. The increasing scarcity of silver has made it necessary to use copper and nickel in today's new coins.

7. Today's coins and paper money are credit money, having no "backing" in gold or silver.

Questions for Discussion and Research

1. Write a good definition for "gold standard."

2. What circumstances prevented the specie-flow principle from operating the way David Hume expected? Could it work today?

3. Why were free market economists attracted to the use of gold as standard money? Why were kings less likely to be?

4. Explain the process by which the gold standard helped preserve stable exchange rates among currencies used in international trade. Why were gold flows necessary to achieve this stability?

5. Consult recent issues of *The Wall Street Journal* for information about currency values. Then estimate the mark-price of a vacation in Florida, the yen-price of a bushel of U.S grain, and the pound-price of a computer. Compare with corresponding prices a decade ago.

6. How has declining gold production affected global economic systems? What are the advantages and disadvantages of including gold in an individual portfolio of investments?

7. What economic and political circumstances are likely to accompany a rising gold price? A rising silver price? What are the consequences for the nation's output, income and prices?

8. Illustrate the effects of Treasury silver purchases and sales on silver prices. How do changing silver prices confirm Gresham's Law?

9. Look for information about recent gold prices and add them to Figure 2–3.

Additional Readings

Hein, John.   "In Gold They Trust." *Across the Board* 16 (April 1979): 46–56.

"Investing in Gold." *Business Week* (5 February 1979), 96–98.

McCulloch, J. Huston.   *Money and Inflation: A Monetarist Approach.* New York: Academic Press, 1975. Ch. 5.

Endnote

[1]Gold had been used as money for more than a century before the gold standard was established in Great Britain in 1821 and in the United States and other Western nations in 1870. The gold standard was abandoned in the 1930s.

C H A P T E R

3

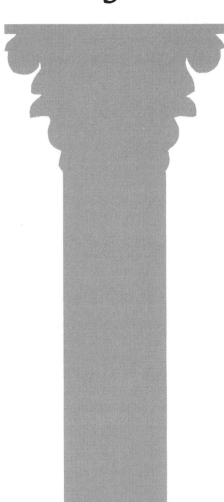

LEARNING OBJECTIVES

- To understand how banks developed and the basis for fractional reserve banking
- To examine the considerations that determine bank loans and investments
- To analyze the political concerns that affect the efficiency and equity of the U.S. banking system
- To study the internal structure of a bank as it performs the functions of a financial intermediary

Banks

*"Man to bank teller: I'll tell you what. You give me a thousand
dollars and I'll give you a toaster."*

The Wall Street Journal

If money is essential for developing an
efficient economic system, a banking system is almost as important. Banks
belong to a large group of institutions that are described as *financial intermediaries*. Financial intermediaries "stand between" savers and depositors,
on the one hand, and borrowers and spenders, on the other.

Nearly a thousand years ago, banks began accepting depositors' money,
making loans to merchants and manufacturers, and creating new kinds of
money to satisfy the growing needs of an expanding economy. Even today,
in the bustling cities of Southeast Asia, banking is carried on as it has been
for hundreds of years. Ordinary storefronts hide dark rooms where men sit
on straw mats among teakwood money boxes, counting out loans to borrowers. Typically, the men wear dhotis—a garment like a draped white
sheet—and they are members of India's ancient class of moneylenders. They
bring money from India and lend at high rates of interest in the cities of
Malaysia. These may not seem much like the banks we are used to, but
lately our own banks are not like those we are used to either. Today in the
United States much lending takes place by stamping a plastic card, often
for no interest charge at all. And many of a bank's customers carry on all
their banking business without ever entering the bank.

Like other financial intermediaries, banks have an important responsibility toward achieving efficiency in the allocation of resources. That responsibility has to do with the allocation of idle funds toward production
of new capital resources: buildings and equipment, specialized skills and

new technology, public works projects. Without financial intermediaries, investors in capital resources might have trouble acquiring the savings that make new investments possible. Without new investments, our nation could lose its potential for growth and its capacity to provide citizens with a rising standard of living.

In this chapter we will explore the origins and functions of banks. In subsequent chapters we will expand our discussion to describe the functions of other, nonbank financial intermediaries. Understanding how banks work will help us understand the similar functions of other financial intermediaries.

To begin, we will be concerned with how early banks helped people to work more efficiently: providing a safe place to store money assets, relieving income earners of the worry of loss or theft, and transferring funds quickly from buyer to seller and from seller to spender. Then we will focus on an important function of banks: creating new credit money in line with our nation's growing capacity to produce real wealth. It is through their ability to create money that banks encourage new production and permit new consumption to take place. It is through their money-creating ability, also, that banks are of interest to monetary policymakers.

How do banks create money? What determines their money-creating ability? How can creating new money improve or worsen our standards of living?

Early Banking

Banks typically developed where there was trade: at river ports along the China coast, at watering holes on the arid plains of Asia Minor, and in the Mediterranean ports of Italy, Greece and Spain. The word *bank* evolved from the Italian word *banco*, meaning bench and signifying the bench where the money changer sat. In Italian markets the banco was the place where merchants deposited their gold and silver specie for safekeeping until they selected what they wanted to buy. They would receive certificates to represent their claims for coins, and they would pay certificates to the sellers of goods. The sellers could redeem the certificates when they needed coins. Without bancos, conducting business would have been much more difficult.

The first bankers were careful not to issue more certificates than their actual holdings of gold and silver coins. But bankers soon came to realize how unlikely it would be for all certificates to be presented for redemption at once. As some merchants drew out coins, other merchants were bringing in new coins for deposit. In fact, many merchants were content to hold paper certificates indefinitely, passing them around among themselves over and over again in trade. As long as merchants were confident specie would be available if they needed it, banks would have to pay out very little gold and silver at all.

This fact led to what is known as *fractional reserve banking*: Banks would issue additional certificates for lending at interest to creditworthy borrowers; they would hold in reserve specie equal to only a fraction of their outstanding certificates. Although certificates would bear the promise "redeemable in specie," bankers hoped that few holders would insist on actually redeeming them.

Bank Balance Sheets

Fractional reserve banking can be illustrated through use of a bank's *balance sheet*. A balance sheet lists the value of everything a bank owns and everything a bank owes. Every business firm has a balance sheet with listings of the things the firm owns—such as buildings, property, equipment and money on one side—and the amounts the firm owes to individuals, banks, and other business firms on the other. Individuals have balance sheets, too, listing the values of personal property, real estate, cash and personal loans. On any balance sheet, properties owned are called *assets*; amounts owed are called *liabilities*.

Assets and Liabilities

Because a bank is a financial intermediary, its balance sheet is a little different from that of an ordinary business firm. The main items on a bank's balance sheet are not buildings and equipment but financial items. A bank's financial assets include cash, deposits in other banks, and loans made to the bank's customers. Loans are assets because they are promises to pay certain amounts, they are signed by the borrower, and they indicate the method and schedule of repayment. A bank's financial liabilities are primarily deposit accounts owed to the bank's customers and subject to immediate withdrawal; other liabilities include a bank's borrowings from other banks.

In days of old, before a bank began lending, its balance sheet might have looked like the one in Figure 3–1. On the left side are listed the bank's holdings of gold and silver coins. On the right side are listed the bank's obligations to its depositors. A depositor could transfer ownership of his or her deposits by endorsing certificates and passing them to another person, perhaps to a farmer or merchant who delivered a good or service. Transferring the ownership of deposits from a buyer to a seller had no effect at all on the total supply of money available for trade.

FIGURE 3–1

Assets		Liabilities	
Specie	100	Outstanding Certificates	100

With fractional reserve banking, a bank could lend a fraction of its specie holdings and keep the remaining fraction as a reserve against withdrawals. When a bank made a loan, its balance sheet changed as shown in Figure 3–2. Loans of 50 monetary units represent promises to pay signed by the borrowers. The remaining specie reserve of one-half of its deposits would be sufficient to meet normal withdrawals by bank depositors.

FIGURE 3–2

Assets		Liabilities	
Specie	50	Outstanding Certificates	100
Loans	50		

The important difference is that fractional reserve banking actually increases the quantity of money available for trade. Borrowers now have 50 units of specie to spend, and the bank's depositors have 100 units in certificates that they can also spend.

Making loans was an attractive source of income for banks. Interest earned on loans helped pay banks' operating costs and permitted banks to serve their depositors without charge. Bank lending was helpful to the community, too, because it transferred idle funds from the hands of depositor-savers to active use by borrower–spenders. Borrowers who used their loans for productive purposes helped increase economic activity, increasing incomes and advancing technology. In this way, banks contributed significantly to economic growth and development.

Making a loan did not necessarily mean the loss of a bank's specie. In fact, a loan was more likely to be in the form of bank notes, some of which were redeemable in specie. When a bank made a loan of bank notes, its balance sheet would change as shown in Figure 3–3. Outstanding bank notes of 50 monetary units represent the bank's obligations to pay in specie when notes are presented for redemption. Bankers hoped that all notes would not be presented for redemption at once. In fact, many of a bank's notes were never presented for redemption at all, circulating indefinitely as a new form of money as long as the holders were confident specie would be available for redemption if needed.

FIGURE 3–3

Assets		Liabilities	
Specie	100	Outstanding Certificates	100
Loans	50	Outstanding Bank Notes	50

Bank notes were credit money, worthless in themselves and useful only in exchange for goods and services. Creation of credit money was helpful to the community because it provided new forms of purchasing power as the economy developed. To limit a community's purchasing power to its limited supply of gold and silver would have placed unnecessary restrictions on its capacity for growth. There were problems with bank notes, however. Without any limit to their issue, the quantity might grow faster than the community's capacity to produce goods and services. Too much credit money would mean rising prices, rising loan demand and an upward spiral of money creation.

This kind of currency confusion eventually led to efforts to place some restrictions on issues of bank notes. Seeking to survive, banks discovered an alternative way to make loans. Instead of paying out specie or bank notes, they would simply create a new checking account. With a checking account, a borrower could make payments without using any currency at all. In this case, the bank's balance sheet would change as shown in Figure 3–4. The created money is the checking account created for the new borrower.

FIGURE 3–4

Assets		Liabilities	
Specie	100	Outstanding Certificates	100
Loans	50	Checking Accounts	50

Checking accounts are as important a source of new money as were the old bank notes. In the same way as currency, checking accounts provide additional purchasing power as the economy's productive capacity grows. Notice that issuing new deposit money always involves increasing a bank's liabilities. This is true of lending both through issuing bank notes and through new checking accounts. To offset each new liability, the bank receives an asset in the form of the borrower's promise to repay the loan with interest at maturity.

Capital Accounts

Our simplified bank balance sheet showed bank assets *owned* and liabilities *owed*. Early banks' primary assets were specie, and their primary liabilities came to be checking accounts. However banks, like other business firms, have other ways of acquiring cash for carrying on bank business. Banks sell shares of ownership, or stock, to savers and investors. A share of ownership entitles its holder to a voice in bank policy and to dividends paid from bank profits. Unlike checking accounts, ownership shares cannot be used directly for making purchases, but they can be sold to other investors fairly easily and the proceeds spent. Also their dividend income and a possible increase in value make some bank stocks attractive financial investments.

Sales of ownership shares are recorded in a bank's *capital account*. The issue of bank stock is shown in Figure 3–5. The sale of 100 units of bank stock for gold coins increases the bank's specie reserve by 100 monetary units. The outstanding stock does not represent actual amounts owed to stockholders; more correctly, it represents stockholders' shares in the ownership of the bank's assets.

FIGURE 3–5

Assets		Liabilities and Capital Account	
Specie	100	Checking Accounts	100
Loans	100	Bank Stock Outstanding	100
Total Assets	200	Total Liabilities and Capital Account	200

Issuing stock enables a bank to accumulate more funds for lending, collecting interest on its loans and paying dividends to stockholders from its profits. Some profits may be retained in the bank, increasing the bank's ability to make loans and increasing the value of bank assets. Stockholders generally approve of this practice because it generally means an increase in the resale value of their stock. The balance sheet in Figure 3–6 illustrates the effect of retained bank profits.

FIGURE 3–6

Assets		Liabilities	
Specie	100	Checking Accounts	100
Loans	110	Capital Account:	
		Outstanding Bank Stock	100
		Retained Profits	10
Total Assets	210	Total Liabilities and Capital Account	210

In our balance sheets we have shown gold and silver as a bank's principal liquid asset. Gold and silver were important assets for early banks. However, as governments began to issue paper currency, paper money replaced gold as the major liquid asset of banks. In 1934, the U.S. government made it illegal for banks to hold specie. Now, paper currency is a major financial asset for U.S. banks, along with banks' own deposit accounts in other banks. We will have more to say about these accounts later. For now, it is enough to note that cash and deposits in other banks (instead of specie) are a modern bank's principal liquid assets.

Bank Assets

A modern bank's principal earning assets are its loans. Banks make loans as a source of interest income for paying operating costs and dividends to stockholders. They seek creditworthy borrowers who can be depended on to repay with interest when the loan is due. Like private lenders, bankers want a portfolio with a high interest yield, low risk and an acceptable degree of liquidity. In Chapter 1 we saw that these three objectives cannot all be achieved at once. Higher interest yields are associated with loans of high risk, and vice versa. Higher interest yields may also accompany lower liquidity, because a borrower may be willing to pay a high rate of interest only if loan payments are spread out over a long period of time. Long-term loans are less liquid than loans that come due within a shorter time.

Because the three objectives of lending are not all possible to achieve, banks look for some combination of them all that may be somewhat less than ideal. Like individuals, they give up some interest yield for greater safety, and they give up some liquidity for a higher interest yield. The result is a balanced portfolio of financial assets including some safe, liquid, low-yielding loans and some risky, illiquid, high-yielding loans.

In practice, a typical bank's asset portfolio is divided into two types of lending: loans and investments. Loans are generally "face-to-face" lending to a bank's own customers. Investments are "secondhand" lending: the purchase of promises to pay from someone else who may have done the initial lending. Here, the bank and the ultimate borrower seldom meet face-to-face. The major borrower in this category is government.

Today in the United States bank asset portfolios average about 65 percent in loans and 20 percent in investments. The asset side of a bank's balance sheet also includes currency and *reserve accounts* in other banks.

Currency and Reserve Accounts in Other Banks

Bank currency and reserve accounts are only about 8 percent of total assets. They are liquid and safe, but they earn no interest income. Banks are required to hold some fraction of their deposits in currency or reserve

accounts in other banks. We will have more to say about reserve requirements later.

Loans

Loans to Other Banks.   Interbank loans are generally very short-term (often
overnight) at a low interest rate. The interest rate on interbank loans is called
the *federal funds rate* and was about 7 percent in 1987.

Commercial and Industrial Loans.   The largest single category of bank
lending is commercial and industrial loans. Most of these loans are short-
term (about three months), although large ones may run three or four years.
The rate for each borrower may be based on the bank's *prime rate*: the
publicly announced rate large money-center banks charge their most creditworthy corporate borrowers. Other less creditworthy borrowers may pay
from one-half to three percentage points above the prime rate. (Remember
the trade-off between risk and return.) In 1987, the prime rate on short-
term business loans was about 9 percent.

Agricultural Loans.   Loans to farmers are generally small loans for purchasing livestock and farm equipment and for paying farm operating expenses. The term on agricultural loans is about ten months, and the interest
charge is generally somewhat higher than that on industrial loans.

Real Estate Loans.   Real estate loans are a growing category of bank loans.
Construction and land development loans range from three months to two
years. Mortgage loans are less liquid, maturing in up to 30 years, but they
are *amortized*; that is, a portion of the amount borrowed is repaid regularly.
Mortgage interest rates rose to 17 percent in 1980 but fell to around 10
percent in the middle of the decade.

Consumer Installment Loans.   The second largest type of bank lending
consists of consumer installment loans. They are loans to bank customers
for the purchase of automobiles, mobile homes, and appliances and for
making home improvements. Revolving credit from the use of bank credit
cards is a growing type of installment lending; consumers buy on credit and
make regular payments of some fraction of the total owed. Interest charges
may be as high as 18 percent annually.

Loans to Brokers and Dealers.   Loans to brokers and dealers are a relatively
specialized type of lending. Securities dealers borrow short-term to finance
their inventories of corporate and government securities. The security is the

collateral for the loan. Such loans are generally *call loans*; that is, the bank can call them in for payment at any time.

Investments

U.S. Treasury Securities. Treasury *bills* mature in less than a year and earned around 6 percent in 1987. Interest rates are relatively low on Treasury bills because bills are liquid and safe. Treasury *notes* and *bonds* run for up to 30 years and earned between 7 percent and 8 percent in 1987 to compensate for their lower liquidity and greater risk. The risk is not because the U.S. government may default on its obligations, but because the market value of a long-term security may change with changes in interest rates. If a long-term security paying a low interest rate is sold before maturity, it may have to compete with new securities paying higher rates. In this case, the seller would have to accept a price lower than the purchase price.

State and Local Government Securities. Interest on most state and local government securities is not subject to federal income tax. This makes them an attractive investment for a profitable bank, even though interest earned in 1987 was only about 7 percent (depending on the soundness of the borrowing government). For a bank that pays income tax of 33 percent on profits, interest income of 7 percent is equivalent to about 10 percent on a taxable security.

Corporate Bonds. Corporate bonds are the smallest category of bank investments, in part because of legal restrictions on holdings of corporate securities. In 1987 high-grade corporate bonds were earning between 8 percent and 9 percent. The other major form of corporate borrowing used by bank and nonbank corporations is commercial paper: short-term obligations sold by corporations to other firms having temporary cash surpluses.

Bank Liabilities

A principal liability of banks is deposit accounts. About a third of the deposit accounts in U.S. banks are checking accounts. Until 1981, banks were not allowed to pay interest for this source of funds, but they provided bank services to depositors at little or no charge. For example, they provided check clearing, regular statements of account balances, and safekeeping for depositors' funds.

The other two-thirds of deposit accounts in U.S. banks are savings or time deposits. These accounts earn interest that varies according to their liquidity. Typically, the longer the depositor is willing to leave funds on deposit, the higher the interest rate paid. Regular savings accounts can generally be withdrawn at any time; because they are fairly liquid they earn less interest (about 5 percent in most bank savings or passbook accounts in 1987). *Time deposits* are amounts deposited for a particular period of time—for example, three or six months, seven or ten years. The depositor may receive a *certificate of deposit (CD)* to represent a type of time-deposit claim against the bank. Long-term CDs paid interest up to 7 percent in 1987.

Checking, savings and time deposits constitute a bank's liabilities to its customers. Banks may also borrow from other banks, paying interest according to current rates on interbank lending, about 7 percent in 1987. Banks may borrow from the Federal Reserve Bank, a process we will describe in more detail later. And banks may borrow from foreigners who hold dollars from their sales of goods and services to U.S. consumers.

FIGURE 3–7

Assets	Liabilities
Cash and Reserve Accounts in Other Banks	Deposit Accounts:
Loans:	Checking Accounts
Loans to Other Banks	Savings Accounts
Commercial and Industrial Loans	Time Deposits
Agricultural Loans	
Real Estate Loans	Borrowing from Other Banks
Consumer installment Loans	
Loans to Brokers and Dealers	Borrowing from Foreigners
Investments:	
U.S. Treasury Securities	
State and Local Government Securities	
Corporate Bonds	

Naturally, a bank tries to acquire funds with the lowest possible obligation in terms of interest costs to be paid. This permits relending with a favorable spread between the costs of the bank's borrowing and the earnings received for its lending. It enables the bank to offer borrowers more favorable interest terms than offered by competitors and thus ensures the bank's position in the market.

Banks must also consider the liquidity of their own borrowing; that is, the time within which their own obligations must be satisfied. If their obligations come due quickly, banks should only make loans that will be repaid often. For example, a high fraction of checking and savings accounts would limit a bank to short-term loans like commercial or call loans. On the other hand, if the maturity dates of its own obligations are a definite time rather far in the future, the bank's own lending may be for longer terms also. A high fraction of long-term CDs permits a bank to purchase more government bonds or make more loans for mortgages and real estate development. In every case, the bank would compare the cost of acquiring funds with the expected interest income on the loan.

The important categories of bank assets and liabilities are summarized in Figure 3–7. Bank assets are listed on the left as on a balance sheet. Bank liabilities are listed on the right.

Obtaining and Managing Bank Reserves

Sound banking management, as well as federal and state law, requires banks to maintain reserve accounts equal to some fraction of bank deposits. If a bank owns excess reserves over and above required reserves, the fractional reserve system permits the bank to make loans and investments. Lending only excess reserves enables a bank to create new deposits and increase the nation's money supply. This makes the level of excess reserves especially important, not only to the profit-seeking bank itself but also to the economy as a whole. Excess reserves permit lending for interest income, and the level of lending determines the growth (or decline) of the nation's money supply. The nation's economic activity and the stability of the banking system depend on achieving and maintaining the proper level of reserves.

Concern over the proper level of reserves and banks' use of excess reserves is the reason for much of government regulation of banks. In Chapters 10 and 11 we will see how the Federal Reserve System influences bank reserves as a means of influencing money growth. Whereas banks may prefer unlimited freedom to expand bank credit, the Federal Reserve seeks to moderate money growth. Particularly during periods of inflation, the Federal Reserve may act to restrain bank lending, holding down bank reserves and eliminating excess reserves.

Faced with zero excess reserves, a bank may be forced to turn down opportunities for lending at high interest rates. A bank has two ways to acquire new reserves. In banking circles, they are called *asset management* and *liability management*.

Asset Management

Asset management involves exchanging some of the bank's assets for currency or reserves. A bank might sell some of its current holdings of government securities, for instance, and use the proceeds for new lending.

It might also sell some of its own loans—commercial paper, corporate bonds, consumer credit—to individuals or other business firms. Note that asset management results in a simple shift of total commercial bank reserves from one bank to another. This is because the buyer of one bank's asset must pay by reducing another bank's deposits and reserves. Unless an asset is sold to an individual or business outside the U.S. banking system, there is no net increase in total bank reserves. What one bank gains, another loses.

There is another problem with asset management. During prosperous times when excess reserves are scarce, many banks will attempt to sell assets. The increased supply of old loans and investments will hit financial markets at a time when there are likely to be few buyers. The result may be a fall in the price of securities and a fall in the value of the bank's portfolio. Only if the bank expects new lending to be substantially more profitable than old lending is this a wise move.

Liability Management

In the 1970s, banks were faced with the problems associated with asset management. Demand for loans was increasing, but reserves were scarce. Interest rates reached historic peaks in the mid-1970s, and bank reserves hardly grew at all. Competition among banks for the limited supply of excess reserves made asset management impractical. The result was a general shift to what bankers call liability management.

Liability management involves increasing a bank's liabilities, thus adding to reserves and increasing lending ability. One form of liability management was to encourage new deposits (and their associated new reserves), especially deposits having low (or zero) reserve requirements, thus freeing up the maximum quantity of excess reserves. Large certificates of deposit with long maturities are preferred for this purpose. Like asset management, this form of liability management may result only in a shift of reserves from one bank to another without increasing total reserves. Still, by offering various inducements—luggage, silver trays, food processors, personalized checks and so on—many banks hoped to increase their deposit liabilities.

Some liabilities were acquired from other sources. Foreign holders of dollars were offered opportunities to earn interest on dollars deposited in U.S. banks or their branches abroad. Foreign dollar holdings are called *Eurodollars* because they tend to accumulate in European banks or in the hands of European exporters. During the 1970s Eurodollars accumulated in European banks as a result of the high price of petroleum. Until the late 1980s the dollar's high exchange rate and high U.S. interest rates encouraged holders to deposit their Eurodollars in U.S. banks. All these dollars became an important source of new deposit liabilities.

When faced with a scarcity of reserves, a bank may also increase its borrowings from other banks. The federal funds market for interbank borrowing provides the means for actively using all available reserves.

The Difference

An important difference between asset management and liability management as a means of acquiring reserves creates a potential problem for some banks. Asset management changes only the composition but not the value of a bank's portfolio. It involves a shift from one earning asset to reserves and then from reserves to another earning asset. The expectation is that the bank's revised portfolio will produce a better combination of liquidity, safety and interest yield than the original portfolio. Asset management alone leaves the totals on the bank's balance sheet unchanged.

Liability management may be different. New deposits and deposits with lower reserve requirements mean an increase in a bank's reserves and an increase in excess reserves. The result is an expansion in the bank's portfolio and, perhaps, a corresponding increase in the money supply. The danger in practicing liability management arises from the possibility that the bank's new deposits might be quickly withdrawn, leaving it without enough reserves to meet its reserve requirements. There are some limitations on withdrawals of time deposits; still, many deposits are subject to quick withdrawal in response to favorable opportunities elsewhere. This is particularly true of Eurodollar deposits, whose owners respond quickly to differences in interest earnings anywhere in the world.

When deposits are withdrawn, a commercial bank may experience an abrupt decrease in reserves, so that it is forced to reduce its lending. A bank that has accepted short-term deposits and made long-term loans may be unable to collect its loans fast enough to satisfy reserve requirements. To sell its loans to other institutions might mean such a loss in value that bank profits disappear. Several of the nation's large banks faced this problem in the 1970s and 1980s.

Increasing Capital Accounts

Until now, we have neglected a method of acquiring reserves that avoids the problems associated with asset and liability management; that is, increasing the bank's capital. The sale of capital stock yields funds that remain an asset to the bank, increasing balance sheet totals and increasing the bank's ability to make loans. A large capital account relative to liabilities also preserves bank earnings, because dividends need not always be paid but interest charges must always be paid. Perhaps this advantage was used too often by some banks, so that their stocks have become so unattractive to investors that they are unable to sell new issues at reasonable prices. To reduce stock price low enough to make a sale would add so little to total assets as to reduce the book value of all shares. (Book value is the value of total assets less total liabilities divided by shares of stock outstanding.) Furthermore, bank earnings would have to be distributed among more stockholders, diluting the dividend payment to each one.

Bank Solvency

A bank's liabilities and capital accounts are the sources of funds for acquiring interest-earning financial assets. Loans and investments earn income for satisfying the bank's liabilities to depositors and paying dividends to stockholders. Bank profits depend on a balanced portfolio of lending to creditworthy borrowers. A careful lending policy is essential for bank *solvency*. Solvency refers to the value of a bank's assets relative to its liabilities. It is important that the value of assets be at least as great as the value of liabilities; otherwise, the claims of depositors cannot be repaid and the bank is said to be *insolvent*.

How might the value of assets fall below the value of liabilities? The answer involves the lending policy of the bank. Lending to creditworthy borrowers is generally safe—loans are repaid on time, promises to pay are cancelled out, and cash replaces loans on the bank's balance sheet. Lending to less creditworthy borrowers is more risky—payments are not made, borrowers default on their obligations, and the value of their promises to pay falls to zero. Long-term lending is especially risky, because interest rates paid to next year's depositors may rise above rates received from last year's borrowers. When a risky lending policy reduces the value of a bank's assets, the bank may be unable to pay its depositors.

Insolvency and bank failures have been characteristic of the U.S. banking system in the past. However, since the 1930s, far fewer incidents of insolvency and bank failure have occurred. The Federal Deposit Insurance Corporation (FDIC) has protected most depositors' accounts. Too, bank boards of directors have been found to be legally liable for risky lending practices (which has tended to make directors more cautious about lending). Most banks face restraints on the types and amounts of lending they can do.

MONEY AND BANKING IN PRACTICE: REGULATING BANK CAPITAL ACCOUNTS

There are two ways to look at banks' capital accounts. Monetary policymakers look upon capital accounts as a way to limit bank lending. Capital accounts serve as a kind of cushion between a bank's assets and liabilities. Because bad loans reduce the cushion between assets and liabilities, policymakers expect larger capital requirements to make banks more cautious in extending loans. In contrast, bankers look upon capital accounts as a costly source of funds for lending. Satisfying bank stockholders requires banks to keep stock prices high which, in turn, requires payment of dividends. Paying dividends reduces the profits a bank retains from lending, particularly when compared with loans based on banks' interest-free deposits.

Monetary policymakers in the United States and Britain are considering a change in requirements regarding bank capital accounts. The change would require larger holdings of capital in financial institutions that make riskier loans. Specifically, lending to private borrowers would have higher capital requirements than would purchases of government securities (federal, state or local). On the other hand, all loans to private borrowers would have the same capital requirements, regardless of the borrowers' creditworthiness.

Some economists worry that the result of the proposed capital requirements would be to encourage banks to shift their asset portfolios more toward government securities, where the spread between what a bank earns on investments and what it costs to acquire funds is greatest. With respect to loans to private borrowers, banks would be encouraged to make more risky loans at higher interest rates, where the

spread between interest yield and the cost of funds is greatest. In the meantime, the more creditworthy borrowers would seek loans from other nonbank financial institutions, whose lower costs of funds would permit lower interest charges on loans. The result of all these tendencies would be to weaken the asset portfolios of many banks.

Policymakers' concerns about the size of bank capital accounts may be unfounded. An average bank already maintains more than 6 percent of total loans and investments in its capital accounts, selling stock and retaining profits to achieve this objective. In addition, banks hold about 1 percent of total loans and investments in an allowance to cover loan losses. Furthermore, less than 0.5 percent of bank loans go bad, even in today's relatively insecure credit environment. All this means that most banks already have sufficient capital to support their lending activity; only a few have too little capital to protect against a series of defaults and a major run on deposits. Requiring all banks to increase their capital accounts will not help (and may hurt) the ones with bad loans.

Requiring sound banks to increase their capital accounts may create other problems. Selling more stock will require higher dividends, which may drive still more creditworthy borrowers away from banks as a source of funds and leave banks with still more risky borrowers.

Questions for Discussion

1. Less than one-eighth of the nation's banks account for almost one-half the bad loans. How would a requirement to increase its capital account affect one of these banks?

2. What would be the likely result of uniform capital requirements for all government securities, including federal, state and local, on bank purchases of these securities? What would be the likely result in terms of allocation of the nation's resources?

3. How would the proposed change in capital requirements affect the efficiency of the nation's financial sector?

MONEY AND BANKING IN PRACTICE: INSOLVENCY OR ILLIQUIDITY?

A bank can get into trouble even though the value of its assets exceeds the value of its liabilities. A problem can arise if there is a mismatch between the maturities of the bank's assets and liabilities. In 1980 the Federal Deposit Insurance Corporation (FDIC) was called upon to rescue First Pennsylvania Bank from collapse resulting from the bank's liability management policies of the previous several years.

First Pennsylvania is the nation's oldest bank, having been established in 1782, and the 23rd largest. During the late 1970s, the bank's managers viewed the abnormally high long-term interest rates as an opportunity to increase earnings on the bank's portfolio. The bank purchased $900 million in long-term government securities cheaply, expecting to enjoy the interest income and capital gains for years to come. The bonds paid interest of 7 percent, close to the all-time high. The bank paid for the bonds by issuing short-term liabilities at moderate rates: large corporate certificates of deposit and Eurodollar borrowings paying 6 percent or less.

First Pennsylvania did not expect the credit crunch that sent short-term rates sky-high at the end of 1979 and reduced their hoped-for profits to crushing losses. At an average interest rate of 9 percent, earnings on the bank's portfolio were millions of dollars short of interest costs on short-term liabilities, whose costs rose to 18 percent. Selling the long-term bonds when rates were high would have involved capital losses of such magnitude that the bank was forced to hold on. Nevertheless, the bank's low earnings were reported in the financial press, destroying depositor confidence and causing substantial short-term deposit withdrawals. Throughout 1979, First Pennsylvania was unable to sell its CDs and was forced to borrow repeatedly from the Federal Reserve Bank. Still, losses in the first quarter of 1980 were $6.4 million.

Bank regulators analyzed the bank's accounts and decided that the bank was fundamentally sound and would recover from its liquidity crunch in time. The FDIC and 22 other banks (led by Citicorp, Chase Manhattan, Morgan Guarantee and Philadelphia National) agreed to lend $500 million and to extend lines of credit up to $1 billion. The rescue package was the largest ever put together by the FDIC. The loans will enable the bank to pay its depositors, but current stockholders will have to forego dividends until the loans are paid. Moreover, issuing new First Penn stock to lenders will so increase the number of shares outstanding that bank earnings per share will drop sharply. After the bank recovers, however (a likely prospect, given the involvement of the FDIC), its stock will become valuable again.

To allow First Penn to fail would have required the sale of its long-term securities at substantial losses. Stockholders would have lost heavily, and other financial institutions would have suffered, too. So the intervention of the FDIC was in the interests of the financial community at large. The participation of banks in the rescue had other implications as well; ownership of bank debt and preferred stock is only a short step away from interstate banking—an objective long sought by some of the nation's largest banks.

Questions for Discussion

1. Explain First Penn's problem in terms of solvency and liquidity.

2. What are the arguments *against* bank rescues?

3. How do other banks gain from the rescue of First Penn? How do bank customers gain?

Banking in the United States

The structure of U.S. banking was a major source of controversy surrounding the formation of our government. The Founding Fathers were divided in their views on the appropriate role of government in the financial system. One reason had to do with banks' lending policies. Careful lending policies would ensure a bank's solvency and protect depositors and stockholders against loss. But careful lending policies might also deny loans to potentially profitable businesses.

Representatives of wealthy merchants generally favored careful bank lending policies. After all, they were the savers who would stand to lose the most if risky loans were not repaid and banks failed. Farmers and small manufacturers were the spenders who needed funds for expanding and carrying on new business. What others saw as risks, they saw as opportunities to contribute to the growth of the nation's productive capacity.

Debate over the proper level of government intervention in the financial system has continued throughout our history. In general, we have resisted placing substantial control over the nation's financial resources in the hands of the federal government. We have allowed states to set their own laws regulating banks within their borders. Because states generally want to encourage local business, their laws tend to be more lenient than federal laws would be. Today the United States has a *dual banking system*, consisting of state banks chartered by state banking authorities and national banks chartered by the U.S. Comptroller of the Currency. National banks are supervised by the Federal Reserve System, the subject of Chapters 10 and 11. State banks are supervised by the Federal Reserve, the Federal Deposit Insurance Corporation (FDIC) and state banking authorities.

In all, there are about 14,000 banks in the country, 4,700 of which are national banks. Most U.S. banks are *unit banks*; that is, they operate only one bank. This is in contrast with banking in some states and in many other countries where *branch banking* is more highly developed. Our states have the power to forbid branch banking, and some continue to do so. Where branches are permitted, banks are often restricted as to the number and location of branches. Bank *holding companies* are permitted to operate under certain restrictions. Holding companies hold stock in operating companies and manage them for a profit.

A typical U.S. bank in 1987 would have had a balance sheet like the one in Figure 3–8.

FIGURE 3–8

Assets		Liabilities and Capital Account	
Currency and Coin	2%	Deposit Accounts:	
Reserve Accounts in		Checking	22%
Federal Reserve Banks	6	Time and Savings	50
Loans	66		
Investments	18	Capital Accounts	6
Other	8	Other	22
Total Assets	100%	Total Liabilities and	
		Capital	100%

Look first at the source of bank funds: liabilities and capital accounts. Deposits are by far the largest source of bank funds, with time and savings accounts much larger than checking accounts. Paid-in capital of stockholders and retained profits amount to about 6 percent of total assets. In case of insolvency, holders of bank stock are more likely to lose the value of their contribution to bank funds than are depositors. The larger the amount of paid-in capital and retained profits, the larger is the gap between assets and liabilities and the safer is depositors' money.

Now look at the asset side for the uses banks make of depositors' and stockholders' funds. Only a small fraction of bank funds is held as idle currency or in reserve accounts in Federal Reserve Banks. Banks are required to keep some idle funds, and reserve accounts at the Federal Reserve are useful for making payments. However, because they earn no interest, banks minimize the use of their funds this way. Loans make up the major portion of a bank's income-earning portfolio. A variety of loans provides a bank with a combination of interest yield, safety and liquidity appropriate to the bank's objectives. Investments are also attractive assets because of their liquidity: They are easily sold if a bank needs funds for making more profitable loans.

The simple balance sheet in Figure 3–8 illustrates the most important function of commercial banks: their function as financial intermediaries. Financial intermediaries make possible the transfer of idle funds to persons, business firms and governments who will use the funds productively. Commercial banks are not our only financial intermediaries, although they are our most important ones. Savings and loan associations, mutual savings banks, credit unions and even insurance companies also "stand between" groups of savers and spenders. There is one important difference between banks and these other financial intermediaries. Because of fractional reserve banking, commercial banks can create deposits and make loans and investments greater than their initial cash deposits. Most other financial intermediaries cannot do this and thus have no part in actually increasing the nation's stock of money. Their power to increase the nation's money supply makes commercial banks an important instrument for economic growth and stability. Poor management in our banking system can lead to inflation or recession, international payments crises, or stagnating economic growth. Managing banks' ability to affect the nation's supply of money is a major concern of monetary policymakers.

MONEY AND BANKING IN PRACTICE: BANKING ETHICS

Commercial banks have enormous responsibility for the financial security and prosperity of their customers, responsibility they should exercise with care. In the absence of clear ethical standards, there is the potential for abuse of the public trust. In recent years, banking authorities have intensified their supervision of bank practices, and bankers have had to face up to the issue of banking ethics.

Some activities are and always have been strictly prohibited. Misleading regulatory agencies, filing false financial statements, and use of bank funds for personal benefit are examples. Preferential loans to insiders and overdrafts by bank directors have been prohibited since October 1978. Other activities are less clearly contrary to banks' primary responsibility to the community. One issue concerns the extent to which an individual bank should risk depositors' funds for the sake of the community's economic development. Stated differently, what guidelines should govern a bank's lending policies?

These questions surrounded the trial of President Carter's first Director of the Office of Management and Budget. Bert Lance was indicted for offenses allegedly committed while he headed a small-town bank in Georgia. Lance and his codefendants were accused of acquiring personal loans on the basis of the bank's assets. One alleged procedure was to deposit bank funds in another large bank in a distant city. (The second bank would be called a *correspondent bank*.) The deposit would be used for clearing customers' checks in the other city, but it would provide the receiving bank with a welcome source of funds for relending at a profit. Supposedly, the receiving bank would be sufficiently grateful so that it would provide personal loans to the executives of the smaller bank. In Lance's case the loans were used to buy other bank stock, extending his control over other banks. The practice is not clearly illegal, but it raises the question whether the correspondent bank would have made the loan in the absence of the smaller bank's deposit. Because Lance was well-known to the lending bank, there was never any doubt about his creditworthiness.

Most banks extend overdraft privileges to certain valued customers. The quantity of the customer's business may justify permitting overdrafts at little or no charge. But an overdraft is essentially a loan, for which there has been no loan agreement, including collateral and schedule for repayment. The issue involves the extent to which a bank should take such risks for the sake of a customer whose business practices may or may not be vital to the local economy.

Some economists argue that certain risks are necessary and desirable for stimulating economic development. In fact, Congressman Wright Patman once suggested that "there ought to be more bank failures." It isn't necessary to go that far to acknowledge that the line between exercising a bank's responsibility to depositors and promoting community development is not clearly drawn.

MONEY AND BANKING IN PRACTICE: NATIONALIZING A BANK

How safe *should* banks be? How far *should* the government go toward protecting banks from failure? Should all bank liabilities be guaranteed? How might the fate of one bank affect others?

All these questions revolved around the U.S. government's decision to, in effect, nationalize the Continental Bank of Illinois. By purchasing a block of Continental's stock, an agency of the federal government actually assumed a role in managing the bank and sharing its future profits (or losses).

Continental was once the eighth largest bank holding company in the United States. It got into trouble by making bad loans—bad loans amounting to $5 billion! Some of the loans were purchased from Penn Square Bank in Oklahoma, which had loaned billions of dollars to firms in the oil industry. Other loans were made directly to Latin American governments, whose exports of oil were requiring major investments in transportation and processing facilities. When oil prices plunged in the early 1980s, many of these borrowers were unable to make their regular loan payments, and the value of their loans fell. Not only did Continental's earnings fall, but the company was in danger of becoming insolvent.

As depositors and stockholders got wind of Continental's problems, they began to withdraw deposits and sell their stock. Continental lost $10 billion in deposits and a total of $25 billion in assets. The rush to withdraw deposits accelerated, and the Federal Deposit Insurance Corporation entered the bank to protect its depositors.

The FDIC is pledged to guarantee deposits up to $100,000, but in order to shore up depositor confidence in Continental, it offered to guarantee all deposits, as well as all bank borrowings and preferred stock. But still the run on deposits continued. The FDIC looked for another bank to purchase Continental, but there were so many bad loans that other banks stayed away. In the meantime, the FDIC put up $4.5 billion, and other agencies of the government put up additional billions. Other U.S. banks contributed $5.5 billion to a "safety net" to enable the bank to pay its depositors without liquidating all its assets at a loss.

In the end, the FDIC purchased $3 billion in bad loans for $2 billion and required the bank to absorb the difference by deducting the loss from profits. The FDIC purchased $1 billion in preferred stock that is convertible to common stock, giving the FDIC power to make bank policy. Unless the FDIC can collect on most of the bad loans, the bank's original stockholders will be wiped out.

Questions remain about the way the Continental rescue was handled and about how such rescues should be handled in the future. One question involves deposit guarantees. In the past, large deposits in small banks have not been guaranteed. This meant that large depositors divided their deposits among a number of large, powerful banks, and it damaged the competitiveness of small banks. Concentrating deposits in large, money-center banks may not be a good thing. Their problems make headlines that make depositors nervous. There may be a greater tendency to move deposits around when news is bad.

Another question involves the treatment of bad loans. If the FDIC pressures borrowers to pay, some may give up and default. When a major borrower defaults on one loan, holders of similar loans may become nervous, too. If they also pressure their borrowers to pay or if they refuse additional loans, the result may be a series of defaults that damages the entire banking system.

Questions for Discussion

1. What is the significance of large holdings of Latin American loans in U.S. banks? How should a bank react to problems of collecting Latin American loans?

2. Someone once said that if you owe a bank a little, the bank owns you, but if you owe a bank a lot, you own the bank. Explain.

3. What are the implications of the Continental rescue for the practice of banking in the United States? What are the implications for the U.S. taxpayer?

Glossary of Terms

amortize. to pay off a portion of the amount borrowed with each regular interest payment

asset management. acquiring additional reserves by selling some of a bank's assets

assets. real and financial properties owned

balance sheet. a financial statement listing bank assets, liabilities and capital accounts

bills. securities with maturity of less than a year

bonds. securities with maturity of one or more years; compare with bills and notes

branch banks. banks that operate more than one closely linked banking office

call loans. loans that are due when "called" by the lender

capital accounts. accounts listing the value of stockholder shares plus accumulated profits

CDs. certificates issued for certain time deposits

dual banking system. a system in which banks are chartered by states and by a national authority

Eurodollars. dollars or dollar deposits owned by foreigners

federal funds rate. the interest rate paid on borrowings among banks

financial intermediaries. institutions that stand between savers and borrowers

fractional reserve banking. an arrangement by which banks hold only a fraction of depositors' funds in reserve; fractional reserve banking permits banks to lend from holdings in excess of this fraction

holding companies. firms that own stock in other companies and manage them for a profit

insolvent. holding assets that are of less value than liabilities

liabilities.   amounts owed to lenders

liability management.   acquiring reserves by receiving new bank liabilities

notes.   securities with maturity of one or more years; compare with bills and bonds

prime rate.   the interest rate charged a bank's most creditworthy corporate customers

reserve accounts.   a portion of a bank's deposits, generally held on deposit in another bank

solvency.   a condition in which assets are greater than liabilities

unit banks.   banks that operate only one banking institution

---

Summary of Important Ideas

1. Banks developed to facilitate trade, hold gold deposits and issue certificates. Eventually, fractional reserve banking came about, and banks made loans by issuing additional certificates or bank notes to borrowers.

2. Bank assets came to include loans as well as specie. Too many outstanding bank notes often led to rising prices and brought on government attempts to limit money growth. Then banks began issuing checking accounts to borrowers. The sale of capital stock to stockholders was a means of acquiring additional funds for lending.

3. Bank loans include lending to other banks, commercial and industrial loans, agricultural loans, real estate loans, consumer installment loans and broker loans. Bank investments are purchases of promises to pay from someone else who did the initial lending. Investments include U.S. Treasury securities, state and local government securities, and corporate bonds.

4. Checking, savings and time deposits are the main bank liabilities. Banks may also borrow from other commercial banks, the Federal Reserve Bank, and foreigners. As holders of the community's savings and as lenders to individuals, businesses and governments, banks are important financial intermediaries.

5. If the value of a bank's assets falls below the value of its liabilities, the bank is said to be insolvent. Careful lending policies help guard against insolvency.

6. In the United States banks are chartered by the states or by the federal government. Nationally chartered banks are supervised also by the Federal Reserve Bank.

7. Banks can acquire additional reserves for lending by selling a part of their asset portfolios, by encouraging the inflow of new deposit liabilities,

or by borrowing. In general, these sources merely shift reserves from one bank to another. The sale of additional capital stock may increase total bank reserves, however.

8. Although their actions strongly affect the nation's economic health, commercial banks exist primarily to serve their customers and earn a profit. Profit depends on after-tax income relative to total assets or to capital. Another measure of bank health is the ratio of capital to total assets.

Questions for Discussion and Research

1. Request a copy of your bank's balance sheet. Compute the relationships between: liabilities and total assets, capital accounts and total liabilities plus capital, demand deposits and total liabilities, loans and total assets, investments and total assets, total cash plus reserve accounts and total deposits. Compare your ratios with ratios for the typical bank in Figure 3–8 and comment on the results.

2. What are the advantages and disadvantages of a bank's issuing more capital stock? How are stock issues related to bank solvency?

3. What considerations influence the composition of a bank's portfolio? Discuss the advantages and disadvantages of various portfolio assets. Show how a bank would compute the return on its portfolio.

4. Define: dual banking system, unit banks, asset management, liability management and Eurodollars.

5. Discuss the advantages and disadvantages of a strong profit-seeking drive among commercial banks.

6. What are the economic implications of business failures in a free market economy? How might the failure of financial institutions differ from other failures? To what extent should the public be protected from bank failures? Discuss.

7. What is the meaning of the statement that deposit insurance has become a substitute for bank capital?

Additional Readings

David, Richard G.   "The Recent Performance of the Commercial Banking Industry." *The Federal Reserve Bank of New York Quarterly Review*, Summer 1986, pp. 1–11.

Duckworth, S.M. "Problems in Liability Management." *Federal Reserve Bank of Boston Research Report* 56, October 1974.

Fiedler, Edgar R. "Bank Runs and Errors." *Across the Board,* June 1985, 10–15.

Mayer, Martin. *The Bankers.* New York: Weybright and Talley, 1974.

Nadler, Paul S. *Commercial Banking in the Economy.* 3d ed. New York: Random House, 1979.

Piper, Thomas R. "The Economics of Bank Acquisitions by Registered Bank Holding Companies." *Federal Reserve Bank of Boston Research Report* 48, March 1971.

Rhoades, Stephan A. "The Competitive Effects of Interstate Banking." *Federal Reserve Bulletin* 66 (January 1980): 1–7.

Appendix. Managing a Commercial Bank

Commercial banks are privately owned, profit-seeking institutions; yet their actions strongly affect the efficiency of the nation's economy. They hold deposits and make payments, smoothing the process of exchange and promoting the advantages of specialization. They create new purchasing power that permits new investment spending and encourages economic growth. Without a well-developed system of commercial banks, our living standards would not have improved so dramatically over the years.

Promoting economic efficiency is not their primary objective, of course. Banks' contribution to economic efficiency is an incidental result (sometimes) of the pursuit of their main objective: earning a return for depositors and stockholders. A commercial bank's profitability depends on its ability to use funds to purchase loans and investments whose return is greater than the cost of the funds. Like any other business, banks are judged according to the difference between income earned and costs paid.

Bank profits can be measured in three ways.

1. The most important measure of profitability is the ratio of bank income after taxes to its total assets. For any business firm, return on assets is a measure of efficiency. For a bank, return on assets shows how efficiently a bank is using its total funds.
2. A second measure of profitability is return on capital stock. Capital accounts represent the ownership shares of a bank's stockholders. An adequate return on capital relative to returns on other corporate stocks ensures that new stock issues can be sold at high stock prices.
3. Some economists use a third measure: the ratio of capital accounts to total assets. This is a useful measure because it shows the bank's net worth relative to its total size. A high value for this ratio means that liquidating assets and satisfying all liabilities would leave a

substantial amount for distribution to stockholders. Capital accounts typically comprise from 6 percent to 10 percent of total assets.

Hypothetical bank balance sheets for two consecutive years are shown in Tables 3A–1 and 3A–2. Bank revenues and costs for the two years are shown in Table 3A–3.

TABLE 3A–1   Balance Sheet for Hypothetical Bank, December 1986
(in millions of dollars)

Cash and Reserve Accounts	576.25	Demand Deposits	756.70
Investments	227.47	Time Deposits	601.01
Loans	960.68	Borrowings	447.79
Other Assets	153.30	Capital Accounts	112.20
Total Assets	1917.70	Total Liabilities and Capital	1917.70

TABLE 3A–2   Balance Sheet for Hypothetical Bank, December 1987
(in millions of dollars)

Cash and Reserve Accounts	799.16	Demand Deposits	939.11
Investments	224.70	Time Deposits	719.06
Loans	1053.78	Borrowings	463.85
Other Assets	162.56	Capital Accounts	118.18
Total Assets	2240.20	Total Liabilities and Capital	2240.20

TABLE 3A–3   Revenues and Costs for Hypothetical Bank
(in millions of dollars)

	1986	*1987*
Revenues from Operation	136.16	162.86
Costs (interest on deposits, overhead, salaries, taxes, and so forth)	−122.74	−146.95
Net Income	13.42	15.91

It is helpful to compute ratios for the two years and evaluate the bank's performance.

1.   Return on assets is:

$$13.42/1917.7 = 0.70\%$$

and

$$15.91/2240.2 = 0.71\%.$$

TABLE 3A–4 U.S. Commercial Banks, 1986 (in millions of dollars)

A. Report of Income for All Insured Banks		
Total Operating Income		$269,292
Interest on Loans	$168,429	
Interest on Investments	42,219	
Other	58,644	
Operating Expenses		$250,399
Interest Paid		$140,467
Employee Expense		42,258
Occupancy Expense		14,551
Other		53,123
Income before Taxes and Securities Gains or Losses		$ 18,893
Income Taxes	$ 5,261	
Net Income before Securities Gains or Losses	13,632	
Securities Gains	3,773	
Net Income (including extraordinary items)	17,674	
Cash Dividends Paid	9,135	
B. Profit Rates for Insured Commercial Banks		
Return on Total Assets		
All Banks	0.64%	
Banks with Assets of Less Than $100 Million	0.53	
Banks with Assets of $100 Million to $1 Billion	0.71	
Money Center Banks with Assets of More Than $1 Billion	0.46	
Return on Capital Stock		
All Banks	10.23%	
Banks with Assets of Less Than $100 Million	6.24	
Banks with Assets of $100 Million to $1 Billion	9.87	
Banks with Assets of More Than $1 Billion	9.50	

SOURCE: Federal Reserve Bulletin, July 1987.

For each $100 of the bank's assets, earnings are about 70 cents. The largest banks in the country earn only about 80 cents, placing this bank among the most efficient in the use of its assets.

2. Return on capital stock is:

$$13.42/112.27 = 11.95\%$$

and

$$15.91/118.18 = 13/46\%.$$

Every $100 of stockholder investment is earning $12 to $14 annually, with some apparent improvement in the second year shown. J.P. Morgan and Co. earned about $18 per $100 of stockholder investment in 1986, placing this bank in the mid-range of return on capital stock. Earnings are not distributed entirely to stockholders, of course. Dividends paid may amount to only about half of earnings, with the remainder placed in surplus accounts and providing additional funds for new lending. If the new lending is profitable, stockholders may reap larger dividends in the future.

3. The capital-asset ratio is:

$$112.27/1917.7 = 5.85\%$$

and

$$118.18/2240.2 = 5.28\%.$$

This bank's capital accounts appear healthy relative to those of other banks. However, there is some room for expanding assets through new lending without endangering stockholders' cushion of capital. A high value for bank assets increases the book value of outstanding shares and increases stockholder wealth. Book value per share equals total assets less total liabilities, divided by the number of shares outstanding.

Financial information on the nation's commercial banks in 1986 is presented in Table 3A–4.

MONEY AND BANKING IN PRACTICE: THE AFTERMATH OF BANK FAILURES

The number of U.S. banks that failed in 1986 was 145. They were victims of excessive lending to oil producers, farmers and Latin American countries. The 99 percent of U.S. banks that remain have tried to clean up their loan portfolios, deducting bad loans from annual earnings and making substantial additions to their capital accounts. With lower inflation worldwide, interest rates are lower also, making it easier for borrowers to keep up their loan payments.

Question for Discussion

1. Interpret this information in terms of a typical bank's balance sheet.

C H A P T E R

4

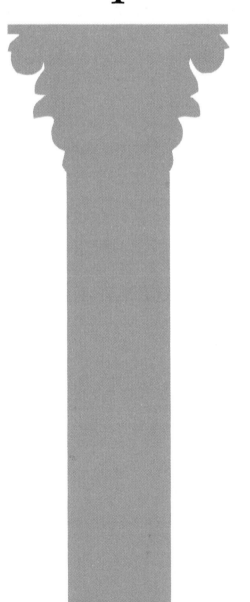

LEARNING OBJECTIVES

■ To understand how financial markets transfer claims from lenders to borrowers

■ To understand the instruments used in money and capital markets

■ To analyze the forces that influence market interest rates

■ To evaluate financial information in terms of current economic conditions

Financial Markets

"Don't gamble! Take all your savings and buy some good stock and hold it 'til it goes up, then sell it. If it don't go up, don't buy it."

Will Rogers

We have seen that money is an intermediator between producers and consumers. Money is not real wealth, but it may be exchanged for real wealth. The use of money increases the efficiency of production and permits higher levels of consumption. With money, greater division of labor is possible, workers learn specialized skills, and a modern exchange economy develops. Improving the efficiency with which money performs these functions is the goal of monetary theory and policy.

Simple exchange of goods and services is a major function of money. But, perhaps more important, money is needed for storing and transferring claims to real wealth. Money claims to wealth are collected and exchanged in markets similar to markets for goods. Suppliers of money are individual savers, business firms with extra cash, commercial banks, and governments with temporary excess of tax revenues over spending needs. Demanders are the individuals, businesses or governments whose spending needs exceed their own money holdings. As in other kinds of markets, price is determined by the relationship between supply and demand. The price of holding money is the interest rate. If the supply of money exceeds the public's demand for money to hold at the current price, the interest rate tends to fall. If demand exceeds supply, the interest rate will rise.

Money claims, and the markets where they are traded, are generally distinguished according to the time period for which the money is exchanged. Claims exchanged for less than a year are traded in *money markets*. Claims exchanged for more than a year are traded in *capital markets*.

In this chapter we will discuss the use of money as a means of transferring claims to wealth. We will describe various types of financial instruments traded in financial markets. We will examine the behavior of interest rates and the role of interest rates in allocating money among alternative kinds of financial instruments.

Money and Capital Markets

Development of financial markets is an important milestone in the growth of an economy. It means that the funds of savers can be channeled more efficiently to borrowers. Financial markets help allocate idle money toward productive use.

Individuals, business firms and governments participate in financial markets according to their own money holdings and their spending needs. Participants can be classified as surplus units (holders of idle money for lending) or deficit units (those who need money for spending). Surplus units normally use their idle money to purchase debt instruments issued by deficit units. Thus, surplus units are suppliers of financial capital, and deficit units are demanders. Alternatively, surplus units are demanders of debt instruments, and deficit units are suppliers.

The initial savers and borrowers carry on their financial transactions in the *primary markets*. They buy and sell new issues of *debt instruments*. Debt instruments are contracts in which the borrower states intentions with respect to the conditions of the loan: the proposed schedule of interest payments, the time to maturity, and the redemption value at maturity. Once debt instruments are sold, they become financial assets to their holders. They earn interest and are redeemable at maturity. The existence of *secondary markets* makes them also liquid. Secondary markets are markets for the resale of previously issued securities. Lenders might refuse to buy long-term securities if there were no way to collect on them before maturity.

Face Value, Price and Interest Yield

Many short-term debt instruments are issued in denominations of $100, $1,000 or $10,000. This amount is called the *face value* and is the amount returned to the holder at maturity, generally three months, six months or a year. The actual selling price depends on interest rates prevailing in financial markets at the time of sale. When securities are first issued, they may be sold at *discount*; the discount below face value reflects the interest to be paid at maturity.

A simple illustration may be helpful. Suppose you purchase a three-month security with a face value (*FV*) of $100 and a current price (*p*) of $98.

You are promised a payment of FV ($100) at maturity for an interest yield of:

Interest Yield $= FV/p - 1 = 100/98 - 1 = 1.0204 - 1 = 2.04\%$

for three months, or an annual rate of 8.16 percent. If the same security had been offered for sale at a price (p) of $97, your interest yield would be:

Interest Yield $= FV/p - 1 = 100/97 - 1 = 1.0309 - 1 = 3.09\%$

for three months, or 12.37 percent annually. The lower price would imply a higher interest yield.

If a security changes hands before maturity, the buyer pays a price that reflects market interest rates at the time of the exchange. Thus, in the example above the security initially purchased for $98 may be worth only $97 in the secondary market if market interest rates have risen from 8.16 percent to 12.37 percent before the maturity date. (This simple explanation ignores the time to maturity at resale.)

"Coupon" Rates of Interest

Long-term debt instruments are issued in varied denominations. The face value is payable at maturity, which may be as long as 30 years. Many long-term securities pay a *coupon rate* of interest at regular intervals over its life. A $1,000 bond with a semiannual coupon rate of 8 percent, for instance, pays $40 twice a year for a total annual payment of $80. The holder receives payments throughout the life of the security and the face value at maturity. Again, the original selling price depends on prevailing interest rates at the time of issue. If current interest rates are precisely 8 percent, the security sells for its face value. If current rates are less than 8 percent, the contract becomes more valuable and its selling price will increase to include a premium above face value. If current rates are higher than 8 percent, the selling price will drop below face value. The lower price ensures that the $80 coupon payments provide the buyer with an interest yield comparable to current interest rates.

The same relationship between price and interest rates prevails if a long-term security is sold before maturity. Its selling price in secondary markets is higher or lower depending on prevailing interest rates at the time of resale. If the security has a long time remaining before maturity, it is particularly sensitive to interest rates. This is because many coupon payments are yet to be received, and payment of the entire face value is far in the future. Holders of long-term securities may experience substantial losses if they sell when prevailing interest rates are higher than at the time of issue. As the date of maturity nears, however, the price of a security is less sensitive to prevailing rates. Because few coupon payments are expected and the entire face value is due soon, the security sells for a price closer to its face value.

Money Market Instruments

Short-term debt instruments trade in the money markets. Sellers are business firms, financial intermediaries and governments with temporary cash needs: for purchasing inventory, for carrying on other financial transactions or, in the case of governments, for meeting normal cash needs in advance of expected tax revenues. Households also borrow short-term to finance large purchases or emergency expenses. Buyers of short-term debt instruments are primarily business firms, financial intermediaries and Federal Reserve banks. Surplus funds of these institutions are frequently used to purchase interest-earning assets with short maturities. Households may also purchase short-term securities.

Commercial Paper

An important type of short-term debt instrument is *commercial paper*, of which more than $300 billion was outstanding in 1987. Commercial paper includes the unsecured promissory notes of corporations; that is, their promises to pay, unsecured by any specific collateral. Most commercial paper is sold directly by the issuing corporation to the lender, frequently another corporation. Some is sold by dealers. Because corporations want to protect their credit ratings, they rarely fail to pay on time, so commercial paper is considered quite safe. Commercial paper is attractive to borrowers because the low administrative costs keep interest charges below charges on bank loans. Corporations can borrow large sums without registering with the Securities and Exchange Commission (required for other forms of debt issue).

As short-term paper becomes due, firms may "roll over" the debt by issuing new paper for money to pay off the old. Bank holding companies are major issuers of commercial paper, lending the proceeds of their borrowing to their own subsidiaries.

Bankers' Acceptances

Another form of short-term borrowing, generally associated with international trade, is *bankers' acceptances*. A U.S. importer, for example, may order a shipment of Italian shoes. To ensure payment when the order arrives, the importer will submit a promise to pay to the local bank. When the bank accepts the debt instrument, it assures the Italian exporter that payment will be made on a specific date. The acceptance is sent to the exporter, much as a check would be. It differs from a check in that the promise to pay is for a future date.

The acceptance may remain in the hands of the exporter until maturity, when it is presented to the bank for payment. More likely, the exporter will sell the paper at a discount before maturity, and payment will be made to the final holder. Major holders are banks and other financial intermediaries, who purchase acceptances at a discount that reflects current interest rates. More than $65 billion in acceptances were outstanding in 1987.

Large-Scale Time Deposits

Certain time deposits of commercial banks are also considered money market instruments. Certificates of deposit are funds deposited for a stated time period, with interest paid according to current market rates. Corporations and some individuals purchase CDs for $100,000 or more. These CDs are negotiable; that is, they can be exchanged in secondary markets before maturity. Negotiable certificates of deposit are an important source of funds for banks and an important earning asset for corporations.

Federal Funds

Banks have another source of short-term funds for meeting temporary financial needs. Recall that loans among banks are called federal funds. Their maturity is frequently only one day, and interest charges reflect current demand and supply conditions in the interbank market. The ability to make interbank loans helps ensure that bank funds are not left idle but are put to use for profitable purposes.

U.S. Treasury Bills

The largest quantity of short-term debt instruments is issued by the U.S. Treasury. Short-term debt instruments enable the Treasury to obtain funds for regular expenses and for refunding maturing debt. (To refund is to pay off one debt with the proceeds of another.) Short-term Treasury debt is marketable; that is, it can be exchanged before maturity and is therefore quite liquid. About $6 billion of U.S. Treasury bills are transferred every day by securities dealers in New York City. Treasury bills are issued with maturities of three months, six months or one year and are sold at discount to commercial banks, other financial and nonfinancial institutions, and state and local governments. The discount reflects current interest rates on short-term loans; in 1987 Treasury bills earned less than 6 percent, compared with almost 10 percent in 1984. They are attractive investments because of their low risk. Because Treasury bills have minimum denominations of $10,000, they are not available to many private individuals. State and local governments also issue small amounts of short-term debt.

Capital Market Instruments

Securities with maturities greater than a year trade in the capital markets. Sellers are business firms or governments needing funds for large capital expenditures. Individuals also enter capital markets for funds to purchase a home. Buyers of capital market instruments are banks, other financial intermediaries and individuals. Other buyers include agencies established by the federal government for the sole purpose of buying and selling capital market instruments.

Corporate Bonds

Each year private corporations issue about $100 billion in *corporate bonds* with maturities greater than one year. Manufacturing firms, real estate and financial firms, and public utilities account for the greatest portion of long-term borrowing. Corporate bonds are sold at prices that, when compared with coupon interest payments and face value, reflect current interest rates. Furthermore, corporate bonds are rated according to the corporation's past performance in the credit markets.

Corporate Stocks

Corporations also obtain long-term financing through the issue of corporate stocks. Stocks are classified as *common* or *preferred*. Owners of common stock are generally allowed to vote to select a board of directors who decide corporate policy and hire managers. Common stock pays dividends that vary with company profits. It is never redeemed unless the company sells all its assets, pays all its liabilities, and divides the proceeds remaining among stockholders. Preferred stockholders may not be allowed to vote on company policy, but they are guaranteed a specific regular dividend. As long as profits are sufficient, preferred dividends must be paid according to the agreement in the stock certificate. Remaining profits after taxes may or may not be paid to common stockholders.

Stock prices depend on public expectations of the future earnings of the issuing firm. This makes their value fluctuate rather widely with fluctuations in economic activity. One measure of stock prices is Standard and Poor's Index of 500 industrial, transportation, utility and financial stocks. Against a base of 10 in 1941 to 1943, the S&P Index reached 265 in 1987.

Corporate stocks and bonds are issued through investment banks, which sell them to individuals and financial intermediaries, or they may be sold directly to a large buyer. The secondary market for stocks and bonds includes the New York Stock Exchange, the American Stock Exchange and the over-the-counter markets throughout the country. About 150 million shares are traded daily.

MONEY AND BANKING IN PRACTICE: INSTITUTIONS IN THE STOCK MARKET

Small investors used to constitute the main holders of corporate stocks. That changed in 1985. In 1985, for the first time, most of the stocks exchanged on the New York Stock Exchange were exchanged by *institutional investors.*

Institutional investors are large pension funds, insurance companies, mutual funds, banks and brokerage firms that hold many individual savings and invest wherever earnings are expected to be greatest. They typically trade stocks in blocks of 10,000 shares at a time. The largest ten institutions alone control more than half a trillion dollars in assets.

Once institutions began to trade on the stock exchange, individual investors began to disappear. The sale of a large block of stock could push its price down so far as to wipe out small investors. Many small investors lack the current information necessary for acting quickly to take advantage of changing market conditions. By joining a fund of some sort, small investors can achieve some of the gains of a rising market and avoid the worst losses.

Institutional investors follow a variety of strategies for making money in stocks. Some firms analyze market statistics to try to predict changes in investor psychology. Others combine fundamental economic information with intuition about market trends. A few even consider offbeat indicators like women's hemlines, football games and cover pictures on business news magazines.

Question for Discussion

1. Some investors consider a time of extreme optimism the time to get out of stocks. Why?

Mortgages

Individual needs for long-term capital are generally satisfied by home mortgages. Business firms obtain mortgages to finance apartment buildings and business property. The borrower agrees to a schedule of payments over the life of the *mortgage.* Payments are amortized; that is, they include a payment toward the principal of the loan along with the interest due. Early in the life of a mortgage the interest payment is generally greater than the principal payment. This is because of the substantial debt remaining. The low principal payment means that the homeowner's ownership share increases very slowly. Home mortgages typically represent three-fourths of the purchase price and run from 25 to 30 years. Total mortgage loans outstanding amounted to more than $2.5 trillion in 1987.

Newly issued mortgages are bought by commercial banks, other financial intermediaries and mortgage companies. Existing mortgages are frequently resold among financial intermediaries or government agencies. In 1938, the federal government established the Federal National Mortgage Association (FNMA) to buy mortgages in secondary markets during periods when the demand for funds is great. FNMA is now a privately owned company that acquires funds for purchasing mortgages by issuing its own securities to the public or borrowing from the Treasury. The Government National Mortgage Company and the Federal Home Loan Mortgage Company now perform the same function. (These federally sponsored agencies are familiarly known as Fannie Mae, Ginnie Mae, and Freddie Mac. We will have more to say about their function later.)

Exchanging mortgages in secondary markets helps ease interest rate pressures in capital markets. If the demand for mortgages is great relative to supply, interest charges tend to rise; then an institution can sell a part of its mortgage holdings and acquire liquidity for making new ones. Later, if demand for mortgages falls relative to supply, an institution can use its excess cash to buy back previously issued mortgages. In general, the important consideration should be whether making a new mortgage is profitable enough to offset a possible loss in the resale price of an existing mortgage. In 1987 new mortgages were made for between 10 percent and 11 percent, and existing mortgages sold in secondary markets for somewhat lower interest yields. (The quoted rate understates the effective rate because of the points that must be paid up front to the lender. Points amounted to 3 percent to 4 percent of the purchase price in 1987.)

Revenue Bonds

Governments are major participants in capital markets. State and local governments issue more than $100 billion in long-term securities every year. Many are classified as *revenue bonds*: bonds issued to finance a particular project, the revenue from which is used to pay interest and face value to bondholders. Others are classified as *general obligation bonds*: bonds secured only by the taxing power of the issuing government. In recent years, the power to issue bonds has been extended to special districts or authorities. A district may include more than one city or county that may need long-term funds for a district-wide capital project; some examples are mass transit, water resource development and industrial development. Such districts are increasingly taking over the job of financing major public investments.

U.S. Treasury Bonds

The U.S. Treasury is an important borrower in capital markets. Some Treasury debt instruments are nonmarketable. Savings bonds, for instance, are sold to individuals and cannot be resold in secondary markets. Series EE bonds are sold in small denominations; a bond selling for $25 can be redeemed in five years for an interest rate of 6 percent. Others are sold with face values up to $10,000. Because Series EE bonds cannot be resold, their value cannot fluctuate; however, holders can redeem them before maturity for a small loss of yield. Series H bonds are income bonds; they differ from Series EE bonds because they pay interest currently rather than in a lump sum at maturity.

Nonmarketable Treasury bonds are held primarily by individual savers. Because there is no risk of default, they are a valuable addition to an individual's asset portfolio. Unfortunately, interest yields are low and sometimes fail to keep pace with inflation. Other nonmarketable bonds are held by state and local governments, foreign central banks, and government agencies and trust funds.

Most Treasury debt instruments are marketable. Bonds are issued in $1,000 denominations and mature in from 5 to 30 years. Bonds are auctioned and sold to the highest bidder. The price determines the interest yield, just as is true in the market for corporate bonds. Regrettably for the Treasury, Congress has limited the quantity of bond sales for interest yields greater than 4¼ percent. This makes new issues difficult, because investors can buy higher yielding securities elsewhere.

Treasury notes mature in up to ten years and have no interest ceiling. More than $800 billion in notes was outstanding in 1987, with recent issues earning around 7 percent. They were held by banks, other financial intermediaries, and state and local governments.

MONEY AND BANKING IN PRACTICE: RATING SECURITIES FOR RISK

What determines the interest rate corporations must pay their bondholders? We have discussed the relationship between interest yield and liquidity: the ability to convert holdings quickly to cash. Short-term securities are highly

TABLE 4–1   Rating Systems of Standard & Poor's Corporation and Moody's Investors Service, Inc.

S&P's	Rating	Moody's	Rating
Highest quality	AAA	Best quality	Aaa
High quality (only slightly more risky than AAA)	AA	High quality (somewhat higher long-term risk)	Aa
Good grade (safe but with one weakness, such as quality of management)	A	Upper medium grade	A
		Strongest upper medium	A1
Medium grade (more than one weakness or one serious weakness)	BBB	Medium grade (speculative)	Baa
Lowest investment quality grade	BBB		

liquid, and long-term securities that can be exchanged in secondary markets are liquid also. The more liquid a security, the lower the necessary interest yield to bondholders.

Interest yield depends also on a security's risk. Very safe securities require a lower yield than risky securities. U.S. Treasury securities are the best example of safe securities. The more risky a security, the higher the interest yield must be. Risk depends on the reliability of the issuing body in meeting its scheduled interest and principal payments. A corporation with a clear record of payments is considered quite safe and can borrow at relatively low interest rates.

Two nationally known investor services rate securities in terms of safety or risk. Moody's Investors Service, Inc., a subsidiary of Dun & Bradstreet, Inc., has been in the business since 1918. Standard & Poor's Corporation, a subsidiary of McGraw-Hill Corporation, has been rating securities since 1949.

Basically, the job of the rating services is to judge the ability of the borrower to repay its debts with interest when due. Then the business firm or government is given a rating to describe its relative risk. The ratings systems of the two firms are summarized in Table 4–1.

A potential borrower in the capital markets is understandably concerned about maintaining high ratings. A drop from AAA to AA may mean a half percentage point increase in the interest rate it must pay to borrow. That may not seem like much, but when the bond issue amounts to as much as $100 million over, say, 20 years, the additional borrowing cost may be almost $5 million. This is an amount worth worrying about!

Rating services look at several features of a firm or a government's financial condition to determine its rating: existing debt, current income and expenditures, and the quality of management. In 1978, Chrysler Corporation lost $205 million, giving Moody's and S&P reason to drop ratings on new issues. The result was higher borrowing costs and greater difficulty in financing purchases needed for meeting new environmental and safety regulations. Finally, Chrysler appealed to the federal government for funds, and Congress agreed to guarantee up to $1.5 billion in loans. The state of Connecticut saw its ratings drop in 1979. Interestingly,

New York City retained its rating up to the time it defaulted on $12 billion in short-term notes. Even the rating services make mistakes.

Questions for Discussion

1. What are the advantages and disadvantages of rating services?

2. Are there cases where "expectations can make it so"?

MONEY AND BANKING IN PRACTICE: STOCKS, BONDS AND COMMODITIES

For owners of corporate stock the 1950s were fabulous, the 1960s sensational, and the 1970s downright sickening. Two major recessions, an oil embargo and a ten-fold increase in oil prices, apparently uncontrollable inflation and wage-price controls, the largest corporate bankruptcy in history, and the resignation of a President in disgrace—all these events combined to destroy investors' confidence in economic prospects for the future and to hammer stock values to the lower depths. The Dow Jones average of industrial stock prices closed out the 1970s only a few points higher than when the decade began.

Over the 1970s private investors drew $7 billion out of stock-owning investment companies, major financial institutions scaled back their stock purchases, and private pension funds reduced their holdings of stock. Investors were painfully aware that the 5 percent average return per year on stocks—including dividends paid and price appreciation—was not enough to offset their loss of purchasing power through infla-

tion running at 7 percent a year. Many turned to purchases of precious metals, works of art, antiques and commodities. Others turned to purchases of bonds, giving the bond market a significant boost over the period.

Bonds became especially attractive to investors because of their high yields. The large volume of corporate and government borrowing during the 1970s reduced the price of bonds and raised their yields to record levels. Total volume outstanding was about $1.5 trillion at the end of the decade, about half issued by the U.S. Treasury and federal agencies, about a third by corporations, and a fifth by state and local governments. When the 1970s ended, high-grade utility bonds were paying yields of more than 11 percent.

The enormous volume of new issues and increased competition for investors' savings began to take hold as the 1980s began. Fixed-income securities became less attractive in an environment characterized by fears of inflation. Portfolios experienced heavy capital losses on bonds issued when interest rates were lower. Low stock prices began to attract investors back into the stock market, and stock prices began to rise. From 900 at the beginning of the 1980s, the Dow Jones Industrial Average rose to 2400 in 1987.

Another difference between the 1970s and 1980s has been the difference in investor interest in commodities. Worldwide food shortages, accelerated industrial demand and threats of international crises in the 1970s increased the demand for commodities. Stocks of resource-oriented firms—like oil, gold, silver, forest products and other industrial commodities—rose more sharply than other stocks. The 1980s began with two recessions, which reduced demand for commodities and brought their prices down. Likewise, the stocks of resource-oriented firms plummeted.

Volatility in stock prices has increased the demand for futures contracts: contracts promising to deliver a certain asset on a certain day at a certain price. Futures contracts are essential to many industrial users of industrial commodities, but in recent years they have become important investments for speculators as well. Speculators gain on purchases of futures contracts when the price of the commodity rises above the price specified in the contract. Speculators gain on sales of futures contracts when the price of the commodity falls below that specified in the contract. More than a hundred million futures contracts trade each year.

Questions for Discussion

1. What factors other than those mentioned contribute to a rise in commodities prices?

2. What factors contribute to a fall in prices of stocks and bonds?

3. Consult recent issues of *The Wall Street Journal* for information regarding the current behavior of stocks, bonds and commodities.

MONEY AND BANKING IN PRACTICE: SELLING MORTGAGES IN SECONDARY MARKETS

Markets are the means by which wanted goods and services are made available to those who want them. Financial markets make securities available to those with money to buy them. More fundamentally, financial markets are the means by which a nation allocates its capital resources to one kind of activity or another.

As our wants for capital resources have increased, the number and variety of financial markets have increased, too. Participants in financial markets have devised more and more ways to bring the funds of buyers together with the needs of sellers, so that our financial sector can operate more efficiently. Because competition is vigorous among been perfectly smooth or without conflict.

The largest single type of capital market instrument issued each year in the United States is a home mortgage: almost half a trillion dollars worth in 1986. The Tax Reform Act of 1986 gave special tax advantages to a new kind of security designed to raise money for making still more mortgages. The new securities are called REMICs, for Real Estate Mortgage Investment Conduits, and they are sold by major thrift institutions and certain brokerage firms. By issuing REMICs, a financial institution acquires funds for purchasing mortgages in secondary markets and then uses the yield to pay a return on the security.

Mortgage-backed securities are relatively new financial instruments. Although they financed only about one-tenth of new mortgages as recently as eight years ago, today they account for more than two-thirds of new mortgage money. Many mortgage-backed securities are issued by Fannie Mae, Freddie Mac, or Ginnie Mae. To increase the flow of mortgage money, in 1987 the U.S. Secretary of Housing and Urban Development Samuel Pierce proposed to allow Fannie Mae to issue the new REMICs and enjoy the tax advantages allowed these securities.

Private thrifts and brokerage firms opposed the granting of such authority to Fannie Mae, which they still regarded as a government lending program even though it went public in 1968. Some minority real estate brokers, thrifts and builders supported the idea, however. They accuse private thrifts of discrimination regarding mortgage lending in inner cities populated by minorities, and they expect to get better service from Fannie Mae. The thrifts contend that they are already suffering from competition with Fannie Mae, which they say is already too big to be economically efficient. In contrast, the thrifts generally hold onto their mortgages for the entire term of the contract and maintain a continuing commitment to their borrowers.

Questions for Discussion

1. Some economists worry that, when financial institutions "securitize" debts, they lose the close contact with borrowers that helps ensure debts will be paid on time. Describe the particular advantages and disadvantages associated with securitizing home mortgages.

2. Name the efficiency and equity characteristics of securitized home mortgages.

The Term Structure of Interest Rates

Interest yields on borrowed funds differ according to the time to maturity of the loan. Interest yields on loans of successively greater term are shown

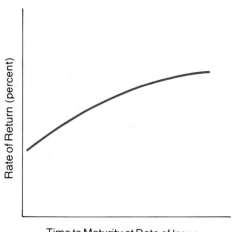

FIGURE 4–1a Typical Yield Curve with Upward Slope

Rate of Return (percent)

Time to Maturity at Date of Issue

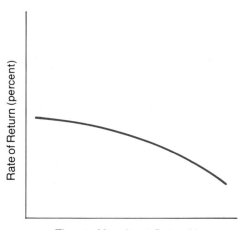

FIGURE 4–1b Yield Curve with Downward Slope

Rate of Return (percent)

Time to Maturity at Date of Issue

graphically as a *yield curve*, where yields are shown relative to time to maturity of the loan. Typically interest yields on long-term loans are higher than rates on short-term loans. When this is true, the yield curve slopes upward. Occasionally interest yields on short-term loans are higher, and the yield curve slopes downward. Examples of yield curves are shown in Figures 4–1a and 4–1b.

There are several explanations for the shape of the yield curve and several interpretations of its shape.

The Liquidity Preference Theory of Interest Rates

Our normal preference is to hold money in its liquid form, rather than near money or other money substitutes. Because we are reluctant to part with our money, we require a reward for doing so. Generally, lenders require a larger reward the longer they are to be without liquidity. Similarly, borrowers may be expected to prefer loans of longer duration. Long-term loans give borrowers liquidity over several years during which capital projects may be brought into production. Borrowers' preference for long-term loans causes greater demand and raises their interest yields.

This explanation is often sufficient for explaining an upward sloping yield curve. Lenders may be willing to buy bonds maturing in one year for an interest yield of 7 percent, but for bonds maturing in 20 years they insist on 10 percent. Borrowers must pay 10 percent to acquire liquidity over the

20 years. Throughout the range of maturities, the required interest yield is directly related to time to maturity.

The liquidity preference theory of interest rates is more difficult to apply when the yield curve slopes downward. When this happens, it appears that lenders want a lower interest yield for giving up liquidity for a longer period of time. They lend for one year at, say, 12 percent but require only 10 percent for longer loans. A possible explanation involves the presence of inflation, which makes all rates abnormally high. Borrowers seek short-term loans to avoid locking in high rates over the long term. Lenders avoid making long-term loans, fearing a loss of purchasing power through inflation. The result is to increase demand for short-term loans, driving rates up, and to reduce activity in long-term markets, keeping rates from rising as high as they might otherwise. Short-term loans also require greater administrative costs, because short-term loans are turned over more frequently. To compensate for these higher costs and for the current rate of inflation, interest charges must be higher.

The Risk-Premium Theory of Interest Rates

The usual pattern of short-term and long-term interest rates has another explanation. Long-term loans are believed to be more risky than short-term loans. The higher risk means that a risk premium must be built into the interest charged on long-term loans.

Risk is divided into two types: default risk and market risk. *Default risk* is greater over a long term because it becomes more likely that borrowers will be unable to pay. Unexpected developments in product markets or in the markets for materials, energy or labor may reduce a borrower's profits. The borrower may be unable to pay interest on schedule or the face value of the loan at maturity. For these reasons, holders of long-term securities may find the value of their assets declining. To allow for the possibility of default on some long-term securities, all must carry a premium for risk.

Market risk is the risk of loss in value when a security is resold in secondary markets. Market risk is greater over the long term because of the greater likelihood that interest rates on new securities might rise. When new securities are issued at higher interest rates, existing securities become less valuable. If holders of existing securities resell them before maturity, the new holder will receive all remaining interest payments and the face value at maturity. The selling price must be competitive with newly issued securities. If the existing security is paying 9 percent but new issues are paying 10 percent, the selling price must fall until earnings to the new owner are 10 percent of the selling price.

The Expectations Theory of Interest Rates

The liquidity-preference theory and the risk-premium theory focus on prevailing attitudes toward risk and reward. They assume that people seek to avoid risk and that they prefer a high level of liquidity. Another explanation of the yield curve focuses on the plans and expectations of borrowers and lenders. It assumes that expectations will drive long-term interest rates into a particular relationship with short-term rates.

The expectations theory states that long-term interest rates are a geometric average of expected short-term rates. The reasoning goes like this. Suppose a lender has cash for lending over a three-year period. The lender can buy a three-year bond or three successive one-year bonds. If the decision is made to purchase three one-year bonds, the value of the loan at the end of three years is

$$TV = \text{Loan } (1 + r_1)(1 + r_2)(1 + r_3)$$

where

$$TV = \text{terminal value,}$$
$$\text{Loan} = \text{amount of the original loan, and}$$
$$r_1, r_2, \text{ and } r_3 = \text{short-term interest rates}$$
prevailing in each of the next three years.

The interest earned for three years is determined by

$$\frac{TV}{\text{Loan}} = (1 + r_1)(1 + r_2)(1 + r_3)$$

and the annual interest yield is

$$r_a = \sqrt[3]{(1 + r_1)(1 + r_2)(1 + r_3)} - 1.$$

An illustration may be helpful. With short-term rates of

$$r_1 = 5\%,$$
$$r_2 = 8\%, \text{ and}$$
$$r_3 = 10\%,$$

a $100 loan will be worth:

$$TV = 100(1.05) = \$105 \text{ after one year}$$
$$105(1.08) = \$113.40 \text{ after two years}$$
$$113.40(1.10) = \$124.74 \text{ after three years.}$$

Its average annual yield is

$$r_a = \sqrt[3]{(1.05)(1.08)(1.10)} - 1 = 1.0765 - 1 = 7.65\%.$$

Computing a geometric average differs from an arithmetic average because the quantities are not added but multiplied. Therefore, the average is the root of the product of the quantities. The value of the root is the number of quantities multiplied. Three successive one-year securities would earn

$$(1 + r_a)^3 - 1 = (1.0765)^3 - 1 = 1.2475 - 1 = 24.75\%$$

or an average of

$$r_a = \sqrt[3]{1.2475} - 1 = .0765.$$

The lender in our example could purchase three successive one-year securities for an annual interest yield of 7.65 percent. Or if a three-year security is earning 7.65 percent, the lender could purchase a single three-year security.

Borrowers are making the same sort of calculations to decide on the term of borrowing: three successive one-year loans or a single three-year loan. While lenders seek the highest annual interest yield, borrowers seek the lowest. Competition among borrowers and lenders pushes the three-year interest rate to the geometric average of expected one-year rates. In our example the current one-year rate is 5 percent and the three-year rate is 7.65 percent. Because one-year rates are expected to increase over the period, the yield curve slopes upward.

Suppose we now reverse our circumstances and assume current and expected short-term rates are

$$r_1 = 10\%,$$
$$r_2 = 8\%, \text{ and}$$
$$r_3 = 5\%.$$

The process of computing the geometric average is the same as before and

$$r_a = 7.65\%.$$

But this time

$$r_1 > r_a.$$

Because one-year rates are expected to fall, the yield curve slopes downward.

The Contributions of Hedgers and Speculators

When borrowers (or lenders) enter the financial markets for loans equal in length to the time funds are actually needed (or are available for lending), we say they are hedging. *Hedgers* are financial investors whose transactions correspond in length to their own particular needs. Other financial investors enter markets in order to profit from the borrowing and lending process itself. They are called *speculators,* and their gains or losses depend on their ability to borrow funds at one rate of interest and relend at another (higher) rate. The behavior of speculators is significant also for bringing the yield curve in line with expected future short-term rates.

It works this way. Speculators hope to profit by borrowing funds at low interest rates and relending at high rates. They may borrow long (for several years) and relend short (in successive short-term loans), or they may take the opposite position, borrowing three successive times to make one long-term loan. The choice depends on the actual long-term rate relative to the expected future behavior of short-term rates; that is, the actual long-term rate relative to the geometric average of expected short-term rates.

Suppose the actual long-term rate is less than the geometric average ($r_a = 7.65\%$) calculated in the example above. With a long-term rate of, say, 7.25 percent, speculators could borrow for three years. Then, if their expectations are correct, they can relend at 5 percent, 8 percent and 10 percent for a net gain of

$$(1.05)(1.08)(1.10) - (1.0725)^3 = 1.2474 - 1.2336 = .0138 = 1.38\%$$

over three years. The percentage gain seems small, but for a large loan the absolute interest earnings may be substantial. If many speculators have similar expectations about future short-term rates, they will do the same. In this case, many speculators would attempt to borrow long whenever long-term rates are less than 7.65 percent. Their demand for long-term loans will help push the long-term rate up to the level consistent with expected short-term rates.

The reverse strategy will work to keep the long-term rate from rising above the geometric average of expected short-term rates. If the long-term rate should rise too high, say to 8 percent, speculators will attempt to borrow short in order to relend long. Then, if short-term rates behave as expected, speculators will gain:

$$(1.08)^3 - (1.05)(1.08)(1.10) = (1.2597 - 1.2474) = .0123 = 1.23\%$$

over the period. This time their willingness to lend long helps push the long-term rate down.

The Segmented Markets Explanation of Interest Rates

A final explanation of the term structure of interest rates assumes no relationship between lending for various time periods. In this view, borrowers and lenders each have preferences with respect to liquidity and risk and individual expectations about future short-term rates. The wide range of attitudes and plans in the market means there is no consistent relationship between long- and short-term interest rates. In fact, long- and short-term securities trade in separate markets in which supply and demand depend upon many individual decisions. The result is a unique set of prices and interest rates in different markets.

Some borrowers require short-term loans for financing inventories or providing working capital. Some corporate lenders have idle funds only temporarily. Because neither wants a long-term financial arrangement, both enter the short-term market only. If inventory financing needs are exceptionally high and corporate liquidity exceptionally low, the demand for short-term funds will exceed supply at existing interest rates. Short-term rates will tend to rise, rationing out the scarce funds to the most urgent needs and encouraging more lenders to enter the short-term market.

Other borrowers and lenders prefer long-term financial arrangements. Borrowers have major construction projects that require long-term financing before they become profitable. Lenders want to ensure a stable level of earnings far into the future. These borrowers and lenders enter long-term markets, and the supply of long-term funds relative to demand determines price, or interest rate. An economy with few construction projects would not have much demand for long-term loans. If at the same time many lenders are attempting to lock in high long-term yields, the supply of long-term funds would be great. The small demand relative to supply would cause the long-term rate to fall.

The segmented markets explanation of the yield curve allows for two possible behavior patterns among borrowers and lenders. One possibility is that borrowers and lenders will attempt to match maturities; that is, they will choose loans that match the maturity of their cash needs (or of their available cash). In effect they are hedgers, acquiring cash or loans that correspond to their own particular needs. If borrowers and lenders match maturities, then it is appropriate for them to enter a particular market only.

A second possibility is that borrowers and lenders seek a diversified collection of debt or earning assets, balanced with respect to time to maturity of loans. Borrowers prefer a variety of loans coming due regularly through time rather than in one large payment. Lenders prefer loans that are paid back regularly, adding frequently to liquidity and avoiding the danger of major default. Such behavior is consistent with the segmented markets theory of interest rates, in that borrowers and lenders enter several markets simultaneously to satisfy diverse financial needs.

MONEY AND BANKING IN PRACTICE: KEEPING UP WITH THE YIELD CURVE

Investors use information about the yield curve to make investment decisions. Policymakers consider the shape of the yield curve when deciding policy—both at the level of the individual firm and at the national level. The relationship be-

FIGURE 4–2a Yield Curves for 1978 and 1979

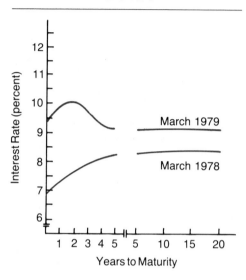

Years to Maturity

FIGURE 4–2b Yield Curves for Mid-1980s

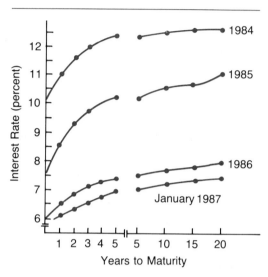

Years to Maturity

tween short-term and long-term interest rates reflects the combined judgment of many borrowers and lenders, each using all available information to plan his or her market activity.

A typical yield curve slopes upward, like the one for 1978 shown in Figure 4–2a. In 1978 many participants in financial markets expected interest rates to rise in the future. Some were borrowing long term to avoid higher rates in the future; others were lending short so that their funds would be readily available later for lending at more profitable rates. The result was higher long-term and lower short-term rates.

Inflation picked up at the end of the 1970s, so that nominal interest rates rose and the yield curve shifted up. Long-term rates rose so high that many borrowers abandoned the long-term market entirely; then increased short-term borrowing raised short-term rates,

so that the yield curve changed from upward-sloping to relatively flat. When short-term rates finally rose above long-term rates in 1979, the yield curve changed again to slope downward, as shown in Figure 4–2a. Investors and policymakers interpreted the downward-sloping yield curve in 1979 as a signal of a coming recession, and in fact the economy moved into recession in 1980.

A downward-sloping yield curve suggests excessively fast economic growth, with rising inflation and disorder in financial markets. Such conditions frequently culminate in recession, with defaults and business failures and a collapse of interest rates. All these developments occurred in the "double-dip" recessions of 1980 and 1981–1982.

Recovery from recession was strong but accompanied by a marked slowdown in inflation and a drop in interest rates. Short-term rates fell farther than long-term rates, however, suggesting that market participants expected inflation to return and hesitated to make long-term loans except at relatively high rates. Throughout the early 1980s, the yield curve continued to shift downward, as expectations of inflation gradually abated. See Figure 4–2b.

Policymakers were pleased with the shape of the yield curve in 1987. Its downward slope signaled moderate economic growth, without the excesses that generally precede recession.

Question for Discussion

1. Discuss the climate in financial markets when the yield curve slopes upward. Look for information regarding current interest rates and construct a current yield curve. Comment on your results.

A Look Ahead

This chapter has focused on transfers of wealth claims from savers to spenders. In the next chapter we will look at a particular use of savings: the use of savings to construct and exchange capital goods like buildings and equipment, business inventories, and homes. Capital goods require large expenditures, but they yield services over a long period of time. Because spending occurs at once but earnings return slowly over time, it is often necessary to borrow for making capital expenditures. Money needed for purposes of capital construction is called *financial capital*.

Glossary of Terms

bankers' acceptances.   agreements by banks to pay private debts incurred in international trade

capital markets.   markets for lending funds for more than a year

commercial paper.   unsecured short-term debt instruments of corporations

common and preferred stock.   shares of ownership issued by corporations

corporate bonds.   long-term debt instruments issued by corporations

coupon rate.   interest paid regularly on the face value of a long-term debt instrument

debt instrument.   an agreement stating the amount borrowed and the terms for repayment

default risk. the risk that a borrower will not pay interest and principal as agreed in the debt instrument

discount. a reduction in the selling price of a debt instrument that reflects the interest paid the lender

face value. the amount marked on the face of a debt instrument to be paid at maturity

financial capital. savings made available for borrowers to use in constructing new capital resources

general obligation bonds. bonds issued by governments, interest and principal to be paid from the government's general revenue

hedgers. market participants whose purchases and sales reflect their own needs for funds or for interest-earning assets

liquidity preference. the preference for holding liquid assets rather than illiquid assets

market risk. the risk that the resale value of a security will fall as a result of a rise in interest rates

money markets. markets for lending funds for less than a year

mortgage. long-term lending, usually for the purpose of buying a home or commercial property

primary markets. markets where the initial borrowing and lending is done

revenue bonds. bonds issued by governments to build a particular project, the revenue from which will be used to pay interest and principal

secondary markets. markets for trading previously issued debt instruments

speculators. market participants who purchase and sell financial assets with the aim of profiting from differences in their prices

yield curve. a graph showing the term structure of interest rates

---

Summary of Important Ideas

1. In addition to facilitating transfer of real goods and services, money is important for financial construction of new capital resources. Financial capital is traded in money and capital markets through exchange of debt instruments.

2. Demand for debt instruments depends on their interest yield, risk and time to maturity. Demand and supply determine price, which in turn reflects the interest rate.

3. Many debt instruments are traded in secondary markets, but trading before maturity involves a risk of loss. This is because the resale price reflects current interest rates.

4. Money market instruments are short-term debt and include commercial paper, bankers' acceptances, large certificates of deposit, federal funds and short-term government securities.

5. Capital market instruments are long-term debt and include corporate bonds, common and preferred corporate stocks, home and business mortgages, revenue and general obligation bonds of state and local governments, and U.S. Treasury bonds.

6. The interest yield on debt instruments of various maturities is shown on a yield curve. The yield curve frequently slopes upward because lenders require a higher yield the longer they are asked to sacrifice liquidity and because market and default risk are greater for long-term debt instruments.

7. Another explanation of the yield curve states that the long-term rate is a geometric average of expected short-term rates. This result is ensured by the borrowing and lending activity of hedgers and speculators.

8. A final explanation of the yield curve states that investors acquire short- and long-term debt for different portfolio reasons: to meet individual financing needs, to match maturities of assets and liabilities, or to diversify their financial holdings.

9. Shifts in the shape of the yield curve may indicate changes in credit conditions and foreshadow financial crises.

Questions for Discussion and Research

1. Compute the interest paid on a $100 three-month security sold at discount for $96.

2. What circumstances influence the interest rate paid on new debt instruments? What circumstances influence the yield to maturity on a long-term security purchased after the date of issue but before maturity?

3. Consult recent issues of *The Wall Street Journal* for a list of prices and corresponding yields on outstanding U.S. Treasury securities. Comment on the relationships among securities of various maturities.

4. Outline the characteristics of securities traded in the money and capital markets in terms of liquidity, risk and yield.

5. Distinguish between default risk and market risk. What factors increase both kinds of risk?

6. Use the expectations theory of interest rates to compute the three-year interest rate, given that current rates are 12 percent and expected to decline 1 percent a year. Demonstrate the process by which speculators and hedgers would push the rate to this level.

7. What are the implications of the segmented markets explanation of the yield curve for financial institutions? For the U.S. Treasury?

8. In recent years, practically all new issues of U.S. government securities have been sold by auction. What are the advantages and disadvantages of this form of marketing?

Additional Readings

Foweraker, Joe. "What's Good for Citicorp . . . ." *Challenge* (January/February 1987): 47–50.

Malkiel, Burton G. *A Random Walk down Wall Street.* rev. ed. New York: Norton, 1975.

"Oh, That Market." *Business Week*, February 2, 1987, cover story.

Stigum, Marcia. *The Money Market: Myth, Reality, and Practice.* Homewood, Ill.: Dow Jones-Irwin, 1978.

C H A P T E R

5

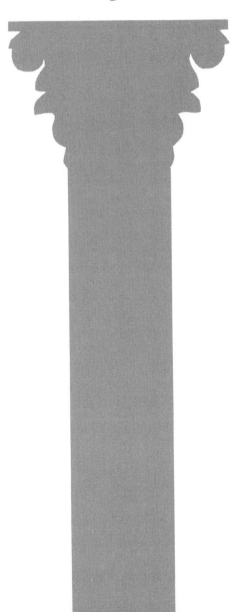

LEARNING OBJECTIVES

- To understand the relationship between saving (the supply of financial capital) and investment (the demand for financial capital) and how saving and investment contribute to a nation's economic growth
- To learn present-value techniques for evaluating investments and choosing among alternative investments
- To measure the risk of an investment and learn how diversification reduces risk

Saving and Investment

"The capital of all the individuals of a nation is increased in the same manner as that of a single individual, by their continually accumulating and adding to it whatever they save out of their income."

Adam Smith

There are two fundamental sources of economic growth. The labor supply may grow with the population and with an increase in the population's participation in the labor force. Highly motivated workers may develop more specialized skills and organize their work more efficiently so as to produce more units of output per hour of labor. Increasing the quantity and quality of labor resources brings growth in total production, but the growth of per capita production from this source is limited. Growth that depends primarily on an increasing labor force cannot yield increasing standards of living.

The second source of growth is less subject to such limits. Construction of *capital* resources enlarges the capacities of workers so that production can grow substantially faster than population. The result is rising per capita living standards. The growth of the U.S. economy has been largely a result of increases in the quantity and quality of capital resources.

To build capital requires sacrifice. Resources must be used in what has been called "roundabout" production. Instead of producing goods and services for immediate use, workers build machines that will become productive only at some future time. If the time is far distant, the postponement of current consumption can be painful. Some nations are unable to forego current consumption for long enough to carry out capital formation, and they remain underdeveloped as a result. Their production continues to be limited by the quantity and quality of labor resources alone.

The process of current sacrifice for the sake of future production is called *saving and investment*. To save is to forego consumption so that resources can be released from production of consumer goods and services. To invest is to use resources for production of capital goods. Capital goods are expected to produce goods or services over some period in the future. They include buildings and equipment, component parts and raw materials, finished goods, and residential housing. As the labor force grows, more capital goods are needed to equip the growing numbers of workers. To add capital just equal to the growth of labor is called *capital widening*. In contrast, *capital deepening* is increasing the quantity and quality of capital available for each worker. Capital deepening is largely responsible for the growth of the U.S. economy.

Growth through capital construction depends on two necessary conditions: first, that some sacrifice of current consumption is possible without intolerable hardship and, second, that idle resources (if any) will indeed be channeled into the production of capital goods. Essentially, savings must be made available for investment. To collect savings and offer them to investors is the job of financial intermediaries. An efficient, innovative system of financial intermediaries has contributed significantly to U.S. economic growth.

The Demand for Investment Funds

Investment requires first a willingness to sacrifice current consumption for the sake of increased production in the future. To sacrifice today for an uncertain future requires careful thought. Investors want some assurance that the value of future production will fully offset today's sacrifice.

Savers require similar assurance. Savers who deposit a portion of income in a financial intermediary have foregone the use of the money for current consumption. They expect to be compensated for the sacrifice, the compensation to be measured by the interest received. With an annual interest rate of $r = 5$ percent, for instance, a deposit of $100 will earn a return of 5% ($100) = $5 after one year. Thus, in return for the sacrifice of consumption for a year, the saver will receive a total of:

$$\text{Current deposit } (1 + r) = \text{Future Compensation}$$

$$\$100 \ (1.05) = \$105.00.$$

If the deposit and interest are left to accumulate interest for a second year, the saver will receive a total of:

$$\text{Current deposit } (1 + r)(1 + r) = \text{Future Compensation}$$

$$\$100 \ (1.05) \ (1.05) = \$110.25.$$

In general, future compensation can be determined by the equation $C(1 + r)^t = F$, where the exponent t is the number of years the deposit is left to accumulate interest, C is the amount of the current deposit, and F is the future compensation. The rate of return r represents both the increased production expected from new investment and the interest paid the saver for the use of savings.

Compounding, Discounting and Present Value

To apply interest on interest (as above) is called *compounding*. In the preceding example, interest was paid or compounded annually. If interest is paid semiannually at half the annual rate, the equation is changed somewhat. This is because interest is earned on interest more frequently. When interest is paid twice a year, future compensation is:

$$C [1 + (r/2)]^{2t} = F,$$

or after one year:

$$100 (1.025)^2 = \$105.06,$$

and after two years:

$$100 (1.025)^4 = \$110.38.$$

The larger exponent reflects more frequent compounding, and the higher total compensation is the result of adding interest on interest more frequently. The formula for quarterly compounding is:

$$C [1 + (r/4)]^{4t} = F,$$

for monthly compounding:

$$C [1 + (r/12)]^{12t} = F,$$

and so forth. Computing compensation for more frequent compounding becomes more tedious, but there are tables available that list the values.

The equation for compensation can be rearranged to show the current deposit required if the saver wants to receive a certain compensation at a certain future date:

$$C = F/(1+r)^t$$

when interest is compounded annually.

A saver who would like to receive \$100 for each of the next five years would have to make a current deposit of:

$$C = \frac{100}{(1.05)^1} + \frac{100}{(1.05)^2} + \frac{100}{(1.05)^3} + \frac{100}{(1.05)^4} + \frac{100}{(1.05)^5}$$

$$= 95.24 + 90.70 + 86.38 + 82.27 + 78.35 = \$432.94.$$

A saver who wants to receive \$500 in a single payment five years in the future would have to deposit:

$$C = 500/(1.05)^5 = 500/1.28 = \$391.76.$$

The above equations can be generalized as:

$$C = \sum_{t=1}^{n} \frac{F_t}{(1 + r)^t}$$

where

$$C = \text{amount deposited in current period,}$$
$$F = \text{amount to be received at the end of future period } t, \text{ and}$$
$$r = \text{interest rate paid annually.}$$

The expression

$$\sum_{t=1}^{n} \frac{F_t}{(1 + r)^t}$$

is called the *present value* of a future payment or series of payments. To multiply a future quantity by

$$\frac{1}{(1 + r)^t}$$

is called *discounting*. (Note that discounting is the inverse of compounding.) The effect of discounting is to reduce the present value of future payments by larger amounts according to the level of interest rates (r) and the length of time before the payment is to be received (t). For a bank deposit where r and t are known, the values of C and F must be such that the current outlay is equal to the present value of the future compensation.

Net Present Value

The relationship between a current outlay (C) and future compensation (F) is important in the investment decisions of a business firm. Firms purchase equipment in the present that they expect will yield revenues in the future. Often the interest rate (r) that could be earned on competing uses of the firm's funds is known, and future revenues can be estimated on the basis of past experience operating similar equipment. Or firms may set a required *rate of return* based on their cost of borrowing. Then the firm's managers compare the current outlay (C) with the present value of future revenues

$$\sum_{t=1}^{n} \frac{F_t}{(1 + r)^t}$$

to decide whether the proposed investment should be made.

To illustrate, suppose a business firm is considering purchasing a five-year lease on mining equipment. The initial outlay would be $100,000, and using the equipment is expected to increase cash inflows after taxes by the following amounts over the next five years: $25,000, $35,000, $30,000, $20,000 and $15,000. The firm is considering other investments that would yield 8 percent after taxes and would be no more risky than this proposal. Therefore, the value ($r = .08$) is the required rate of return on investments that will be used to discount the future stream of revenues as follows:

Present Value of Future Revenues

$$= \frac{25}{1.08} + \frac{35}{1.08^2} + \frac{30}{1.08^3} + \frac{20}{1.08^4} + \frac{15}{1.08^5}$$

$$= 23.15 + 30.01 + 23.81 + 14.70 + 10.21$$

$$= \$101.88 \text{ thousand.}$$

Comparing the present value of cash inflows with the current outlay yields the following:

$$\$101.88 > \$100$$

and

$$\sum_{t=1}^{n} \frac{F_t}{(1 + r)^t} > C$$

Because the present value of future revenues exceeds the current outlay, the investment should be made.

The difference between the present value of future compensation and the current outlay is called *net present value (NPV)*:

$$NPV = -C + \sum_{t=1}^{n} \frac{F_t}{(1 + r)^t} = \$1.88 \text{ thousand.}$$

Positive net present value indicates the investment should be made. In general, negative net present value indicates the investment should not be made.

The Marginal Efficiency of Investment

It is frequently necessary to compare investment proposals and choose among them. The relationship

$$C = \sum_{t=1}^{n} \frac{F_t}{(1 + r)^t}$$

is helpful also in this case. The initial outlay will be known for each investment, and future revenues (after out-of-pocket costs and taxes) can be estimated. Then it is useful to compute the value r that brings the present value of future revenues into equality with the initial outlay. The result is the expected rate of return on the investment project; the rate of return on investments is a useful basis for comparison and selection among them.

To illustrate, suppose two investment proposals have the following initial outlays and future revenues (figures are in thousands of dollars):

Investment	Initial Outlay (C)	Cash Inflows			
		F_1	F_2	F_3	F_4
X	100	36	45	38	0
Y	50	13	25	10	15

The equations are:

$$100 = \frac{36}{(1 + r)} + \frac{45}{(1 + r)^2} + \frac{38}{(1 + r)^3} + \frac{0}{(1 + r)^4}$$

$$50 = \frac{13}{(1 + r)} + \frac{25}{(1 + r)^2} + \frac{10}{(1 + r)^3} + \frac{15}{(1 + r)^4}$$

Solving the equations for r yields

$$r_X = .09 \text{ and } r_Y = .10.$$

(Solving for r requires trial and error, substituting various values until the equation balances. The process may be simplified through use of a computer program.)

Normally a firm will be considering a number of possible investments and can compute the rate of return for each one. Then projects can be arranged in descending order according to their expected rates of return and plotted on a graph that relates the expected rate of return to the initial outlay. Figure 5–1 illustrates the rates of return on a combination of hypothetical investments W, X, Y and Z. The cumulative total of investment expenditures is shown on the horizontal axis, and the rate of return (r) for each proposal is shown on the vertical axis.

The curve in Figure 5–1 is called the firm's *marginal efficiency of investment (MEI)*. It shows the expected rate of return associated with proposed investment outlays. Many firms use the MEI curve for making investment decisions. The MEI curve is important whether or not the firm expects to borrow funds for making the initial outlay. Even if the firm has internal funds for investing, it is important that the funds be used most efficiently to generate the highest possible return.

On Figure 5–1 a dashed line has been drawn at the current interest rate ($i = .09$). For a firm that expects to borrow funds for investment, the current interest rate represents the firm's borrowing costs. With an interest rate of 9 percent, only projects earning a rate of return greater than 9 percent would be considered. For a firm that has internal funds for investment, the current interest rate represents the firm's opportunity to lend its own funds out at interest. With an interest rate of 9 percent, the firm will lend its funds to other firms rather than invest in projects that earn a lower return.

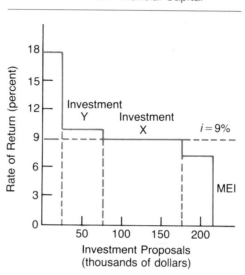

FIGURE 5–1 A Firm's Demand Curve
for Financial Capital

Demand for and Supply of Financial Capital

A single business firm's MEI curve is that firm's demand curve for financial capital. The vertical axis measures the expected rate of return on investments, and the horizontal axis measures the outlays for investments that would yield various rates of return. Adding the individual MEI curves for all business firms produces a total demand curve for financial capital in the economy as a whole. The demand curve in Figure 5–2 is determined by adding all the investment outlays along the horizontal axis and plotting them against rates of return on the vertical axis. The horizontal axis in Figure 5–1 is in thousands of dollars; the horizontal axis in Figure 5–2 is in billions.

The demand for financial capital in Figure 5–2 is a typical demand curve. It shows the quantities of financial capital that would yield various rates of return and, thus, the interest rates business firms would be willing to pay to borrow for investment. The downward slope of the demand curve indicates that larger quantities will be demanded when the price of financial capital (the interest rate) is lower. The steepness of the curve reflects the responsiveness of business firms to changes in the cost of borrowing. As in the markets for goods and other resources, the equilibrium price is determined by supply and demand.

A hypothetical supply curve of financial capital is drawn on Figure 5–3. The supply of financial capital depends on the willingness of savers to

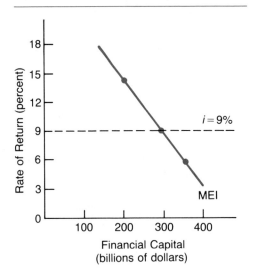

FIGURE 5–2 Total Demand Curve for Financial Capital

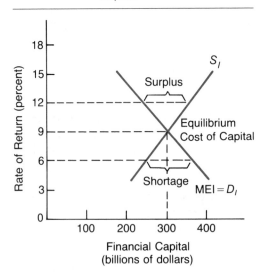

FIGURE 5–3 The Market for Financial Capital

FIGURE 5–4a Shift in Demand for Financial Capital

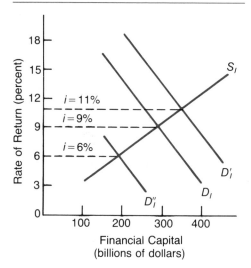

An increase in demand causes an increase in *i*; a decrease causes a decrease in *i*.

FIGURE 5–4b Shift in Supply of Financial Capital

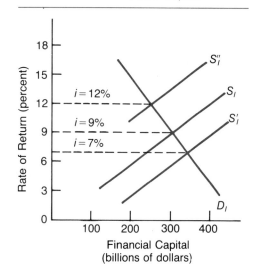

An increase in supply causes a decrease in *i*.

provide funds to borrowers and on the ability of the banking system to create new funds. Normally we might expect the supply of funds from both sources to be greater the higher is the expected return on investments and the higher the interest rate paid to savers. This makes the supply of financial capital an upward sloping curve. The slope of the supply curve reflects the responsiveness of savers and banks to changes in the interest rate on loans and, thus, the rate of return on investments.

The intersection of demand and supply identifies equilibrium in the market for financial capital. At equilibrium the interest cost of borrowing is such that the quantity of funds demanded is just equal to the quantity supplied. A higher interest rate would create a surplus of financial capital, which would tend to push the interest rate down. A lower interest rate would create a shortage, which would cause the interest rate to rise. Only at equilibrium is the demand for financial capital precisely equal to supply.

Figure 5–4 shows the effects of shifts in demand and supply. Note the effect on the interest rate when demand or supply changes. We have not shown the effect of a simultaneous shift in both curves. How would you estimate the interest rate effect of such a shift?

The interest rate effect of a single shift in both curves would depend on the relative magnitude of the shifts. The effect can be demonstrated by

FIGURE 5–5 The Market for Securities

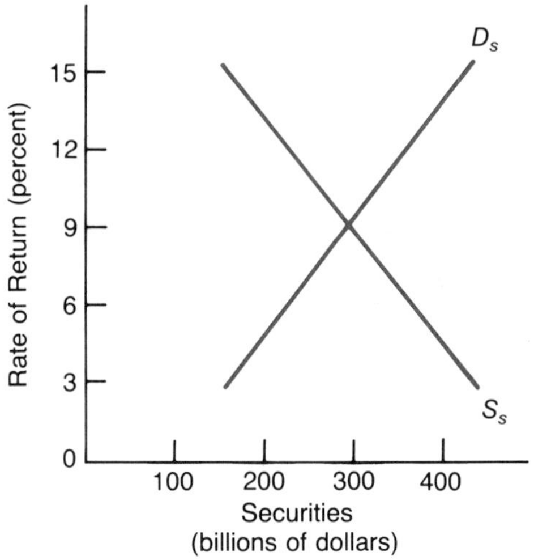

drawing a simple graph and observing the result of changes in the curves. For example, if the demand for financial capital should increase much more than supply, the interest rate will rise significantly. If the supply of financial capital should decrease much more than demand, the interest rate will rise.

Demand for and Supply of Securities

There is another way to regard the market for financial capital. Those who demand funds for investment can be thought of as suppliers of securities. When business firms borrow funds they are, in effect, supplying new securities. The quantity of securities supplied may be expected to be greater, as the interest rate is lower (the selling price higher). Thus, the supply curve for securities slopes downward. An increase in the supply of securities (a shift of the S_s curve of Figure 5–5) has the same effect as an increase in the demand for financial capital (a shift of the D_I curve of Figure 5–4): an increase in the interest rate and a decrease in price.

Similarly, suppliers of financial capital can be thought of as demanders of securities. By buying new securities, suppliers of funds are making funds available to borrowers. The demand curve for securities slopes upward because the higher the interest rate (the lower the price), the greater is the

FIGURE 5–6a Shift in Supply of Securities

FIGURE 5–6b Shift in Demand for Securities

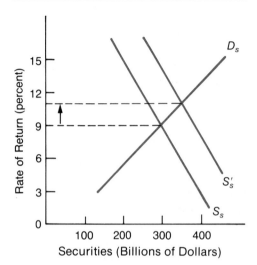

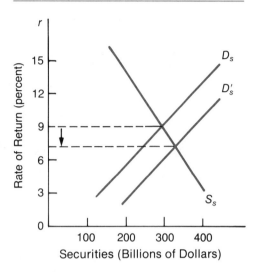

Securities (Billions of Dollars)

Securities (Billions of Dollars)

An increase in supply raises interest rates and reduces security prices.

An increase in demand reduces interest rates and increases security prices.

quantity of securities that will be bought. An increase in the demand for securities has the same effect as an increase in the supply of financial capital: a decrease in the interest rate and an increase in price. In Figure 5–5 the curves of Figure 5–3 have been renamed from supply and demand for financial capital to supply and demand for *securities*. Note the effect of an increase in the supply of securities (Figure 5–6a) and an increase in the demand for securities (Figure 5–6b). In each case, the resulting change in the interest rate implies an opposite change in the price of securities.

The Importance of Saving and Investment

The relationship between a business firm's marginal efficiency of investment and the supply of financial capital is important because it determines the quantity of new capital investment. Regular increases in capital resources are the nation's major source of economic growth. First, business firms must expect that additions to capital will earn revenues sufficient to justify their initial outlay; that is, the rate of return on investment must be at least as great as the cost of borrowing. And second, financial markets must operate efficiently so that savers are encouraged to provide their savings for investment.

One goal of economic policy is to ensure that these two conditions will be met so that new investment expenditures will continue to enhance the nation's productivity. Growth of capital resources should proceed in line with increases in labor resources and with advances in technology. Increases in productive capacity will help reduce inflationary pressures and promote rising living standards.

Achieving the goal of regular growth of capital resources is often difficult, in part because of frequent shifts in demand and supply curves for financial capital. The marginal efficiency of investment depends on business expectations of consumer spending, production costs, taxes, foreign competition and so forth.

Favorable changes in business expectations mean a rightward shift in the demand for financial capital and a tendency for interest rates to rise. (See Figure 5–4a.) The actual increase in investment depends on the responsiveness of savers and banks to higher interest rates. More pessimistic changes in business expectations lead to the opposite results: a downward shift in demand for financial capital and a tendency for interest rates and investment to fall.

Shifts in the supply of financial capital result from changes in savings and changes in the ability and willingness of banks to create money. When consumers increase their purchases of goods and services, the quantity of personal saving for lending falls. When banks reduce their lending, the same result follows. The market supply curve shifts to the left, and the interest rate tends to rise. (See Figure 5–4b.)

At the higher interest rate, fewer investment projects will earn a rate of return sufficient to justify the current outlay. The actual decrease in borrowing for investment depends on the responsiveness of business firms to changes in the interest rate. If a certain quantity of investment must be undertaken regardless of the interest rate, the resulting decrease in investment may be small.

An increase in the supply of savings and bank lending tends to push the interest rate down and increase investment spending. Again, the actual increase in investment depends on the responsiveness of business firms to the cost of borrowing. If many new proposals appear profitable at the lower rate, the actual increase in investment may be substantial.

The responsiveness of business firms to changes in the interest rate is reflected in the slope of the MEI curve for the economy as a whole. We will have more to say about the determinants of investment demand and the effects of investment expenditures in Chapters 14 and 15.

MONEY AND BANKING IN PRACTICE:
SAVING IN THE UNITED STATES

Of all the world's industrial nations, the United States has the lowest saving rate. In 1986 U.S. families saved $116 billion of take-home pay of $2,974 billion, for a saving rate of less than 4 percent. Throughout the past decade, the saving rate has declined fairly consistently from more than 9 percent in the mid-1970s. Unless U.S. families can be persuaded to forego current consumption, investment in future productivity may fall, and economic growth will slow.

How can the decrease in saving be explained? One explanation for lower saving involves fears of inflation; consumers spend heavily for goods for which prices are expected to be higher in the future. By this explanation, purchases of durable goods like autos, furniture and appliances tend to rise as a proportion of consumers' take-home pay. A related explanation involves the effect inflation has on the real value of workers' incomes: As their real purchasing power falls, workers have to spend a larger fraction of their take-home pay just to maintain the same standard of living. In either case, increasing the saving rate requires policies to hold down inflation and the expected rate of future inflation.

Another explanation for the low level of saving has been more important in the 1980s. It involves U.S. government policies that discourage saving. In the United States, interest earnings from savings are subject to income tax, almost to the same extent as income from work. Other industrial nations exempt larger amounts of interest income from taxation. Canada allows $1,000 of interest income to escape taxation, and the saving rate is 10.4 percent. Japan's rate is close to 25 percent, and Germany's about 15 percent.

Until 1987, another feature of U.S. tax laws discouraged saving and encouraged spending. This was a provision that interest *paid* on consumer or business borrowing could be deducted from personal income before computing federal tax owed. The result was to discourage saving for large purchases and encourage borrowing. Investments purchased with savings continue to suffer under current U.S. tax laws. Gains on the sale of an investment that has increased in value are subject to the *capital gains tax*. The capital gains tax applies even if the gain reflects only price inflation during the time the investment was held. Until 1987, capital gains tax rates were less than half the saver's income tax rate. The tax law that took effect in 1987 includes a capital gains tax rate that is equal to the saver's income tax rate. A high capital gains tax often means that the net resale value of investment property is less than its initial cost (when both are corrected for inflation).

Some economists recommend a completely new approach to taxation in the United States. Instead of taxing income, as we do, they recommend taxing spending, as many other nations do. Under this proposal, a family's tax bill would depend on the difference between earnings for the year and the amount saved. A nationwide sales tax of this kind, it is said, would encourage increased saving to avoid the tax.

Some small movement away from income taxation began in the 1970s. Under prevailing tax laws, many workers are allowed to set aside part of their income in a tax-free retirement account. Until the fund is actually drawn out for spending, it is not subject to tax. The tax law that went into effect in 1987 reduced the allowed contributions to tax-free retirement accounts.

Questions for Discussion

1. What sorts of information frequently bear on congressional decisions to change tax laws? What sorts of information *should* be used?

2. What opposing arguments might be made in the debate over U.S. tax policy?

MONEY AND BANKING IN PRACTICE: THE RISING LEVEL OF HOUSEHOLD DEBT

Not only are U.S. consumers small savers, they are big borrowers. The borrowings of many U.S. households must be subtracted from the savings of others to arrive at the supply of saving available for lending to investors. By 1987, household debt in the United States had reached the highest level ever as a percent of disposable personal income: 83 percent. As recently as 1975 household debt was only 58 percent of disposable income. Household debt includes home mortgage debt, consumer installment debt and other consumer credit.

Economists cite two reasons for concern about the high level of debt. Heavily indebted consumers may be forced to reduce their future expenditures, thus bringing on a decrease in economic activity. And heavily indebted

consumers may default on loans, thus reducing the assets of financial institutions. Other economists are less concerned about the high level of debt, reasoning that while the debt level has risen sharply, the debt-service level has not risen as fast. Debt service refers to regular payments on debt, including interest and principal. Debt service on home mortgages and consumer installment loans was only 17½ percent of disposable personal income in 1986, compared with about 15 percent at its low point in 1976.

One reason for the large increase in consumer debt has been the deregulation of financial institutions in the United States. Today, banks and other financial institutions can pay interest on checkable deposits, and many compete freely for deposits. Then they offer a wide range of consumer loans at higher and higher interest rates. Another reason is the age level of the population. Today's young baby-boomer families are spending heavily for homes, furnishings, vehicles and education. Many such families have two wage earners, however, and have good earning potential for paying off debt.

The nation's high debt ratio can come down in either of three ways. The most pleasant way would be through healthy economic growth, which reduces the burden of debt service. A more productive population can enjoy a more lavish lifestyle and satisfy its debt obligations at the same time. A less pleasant way to reduce the debt ratio would be through higher inflation, which increases the nominal level of income while leaving existing debt obligations fixed. But inflation weakens money as a standard of value, a store of value, and a standard for deferred payments and arbitrarily redistributes the wealth of the population. The least pleasant way

of all would be through a severe recession, which brings loan defaults and bank failures. This is the result economic policymakers would like to avoid.

The fundamental concern regarding household debt should be whether debt increases or decreases the nation's productive capacity: that is, whether debt encourages investments that increase the nation's capital resources. Only if this is true does the nation accomplish the goal stated by Adam Smith at the beginning of this chapter.

Much of business borrowing does, in fact, increase the nation's productive capacity. This may or may not be true of consumer borrowing. Borrowing to construct a home clearly increases the nation's capacity to produce housing services. Borrowing to buy a personal automobile or a pleasure boat may not. Only if the purchase of an auto or boat leads the manufacturer to invest in new capital resources, can the original consumer borrowing be said to increase the nation's productive capacity.

Questions for Discussion

1. What is the effect of longer loan maturities on the debt-to-income ratio? On the ratio of debt service to income?

2. As more of the limited supply of saving is used to finance consumer borrowing,

what is the likely result in terms of interest rates? Suppose consumer borrowing has the effect of increasing production and employment. Would your answer be any different?

Making Allowance for Risk

We have suggested that supply and demand for financial capital determine interest rates and the quantity of new investment. Our discussion has focused on a single market with a unique interest rate. In fact, there are many markets for financial capital and various interest rates appropriate to conditions in each market. (For simplicity in this text, we will use "the interest rate" and "interest rates" interchangeably to refer to the entire spectrum of rates that tend to move up and down together.) Savers may supply funds in any one market or, what is more likely, in a number of different markets.

Financial markets may be classified according to their risk and liquidity. Borrowers whose prospective earnings are more risky are distinguished from borrowers with more stable earnings. Because savers generally prefer safe, liquid investments, the supply of savings in such markets is greater and interest rates lower than in markets used by more risky borrowers. A reluctance to finance risky, illiquid investments keeps supply smaller in those markets and interest rates higher. Most savers and financial intermediaries participate in both types of markets, earning high interest yields on risky, illiquid investments and low interest yields on safe, short-term investments.

Mathematical Supplement: Calculating Risk

Risk is a difficult concept to define and measure. One way to measure risk is to measure the tendency of a security to pay a return that differs from investors' expectations. Suppose an investor studies the previous behavior of a particular security and records these returns:

Year	Return	Year	Return
1	8%	6	8%
2	5	7	7
3	4	8	9
4	9	9	10
5	10	10	10

On the basis of historical data the *expected return* for this security is the average of its past returns:

$$\text{Expected Return} = r = \sum_{t=1}^{n} \frac{r_t}{n} = \frac{80\%}{10} = 8\%$$

where

$$r_t = \text{return in year } t \text{ and}$$
$$n = \text{number of years.}$$

More simply, the expected return is a weighted average of returns when returns are weighted by the fraction of the total time each occurred:

$$r = \sum_{i=1}^{n} r_i p_i$$

where

$$r_i = \text{individual returns and}$$
$$p_i = \text{fraction of the time the return } r_i \text{ occurred.}$$

In our example:

$$r = 4\%(.1) + 5\%(.1) + 7\%(.1) + 8\%(.2) + 9\%(.2) + 10\%(.3) = 8\%.$$

(Note that the sum of the decimal fractions p_i must equal 1.00.)

Although the investor may expect a return of 8 percent, historical experience with this security suggests that the return may be as low as 4 percent or as high as 10 percent. By this measure, the *risk* of a security is computed as a weighted average of the difference between actual returns and the expected return. A simple weighted average would sum to zero, because positive and negative deviations from the expected return would be exactly equal. Therefore, we must square the deviations and take the square root of the final result. The risk statistic is called the *standard deviation* and its formula is:

$$S = \sqrt{\Sigma \ (r_i - r)^2 p_i}$$

where

$$r_i = \text{individual returns,}$$
$$r = \text{expected return, and}$$
$$p_i = \text{fraction of the time the return } r_i \text{ occurred.}$$

The risk of our hypothetical security is:

$$S = [(4\% - 8\%)^2(.1) \ + (5\% - 8\%)^2(.1) + (7\% - 8\%)^2(.1)$$
$$+ (8\% - 8\%)^2(.2) + (9\% - 8\%)^2(.2) + (10\% - 8\%)^2(.3)]^{1/2} = (4)^{1/2} = 2\%.$$

A standard deviation of 2 percent means that the actual return on the security will be within a range 2 percent above or below the expected return at least two-thirds of the time.

The low risk on this security results from the rather narrow fluctuations of the returns. A zero or negative return in some past year would increase its risk substantially.

Selecting an Investment Portfolio

Savers and financial intermediaries select portfolios of financial assets that reflect their own preferences for interest yield, risk and liquidity. The process of selection requires trade-offs between interest yield, on the one hand, and risk and illiquidity, on the other. The securities available in the various financial markets can be ranked according to these characteristics and plotted in risk/return space. In Figure 5–7 points A, B, C and D identify the return

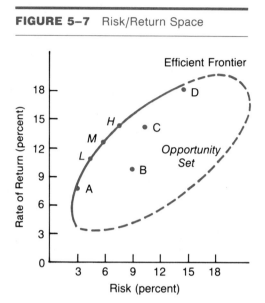

FIGURE 5–7 Risk/Return Space

and risk of securities A, B, C and D. Return is measured on the vertical axis, and risk is measured on the horizontal axis. (Because illiquidity is closely associated with risk, we combine these characteristics.) Security A is expected to yield a return of 8 percent and its risk is only 2 percent; that is, its return may vary by plus or minus 2 percentage points about two-thirds of the time. Security D is expected to yield about 18 percent and has a risk of 15 percent; two-thirds of the time its return will be at least 3 percent and no greater than 33 percent. The higher expected interest yield for this security is necessary to compensate savers for the higher risk. Points identifying all securities available in the market comprise the saver's *opportunity set*. Note that the points are arranged in an upward direction, reflecting the positive relationship between risk and return.

The Efficient Frontier

Most savers would want to hold A, B, C and D in a combination that satisfies their own preferences for interest yield and risk. Some possible combinations are listed in Table 5–1.

Combining securities in various proportions produces portfolios for which the expected return is a weighted average of the returns on the individual securities. Weights are the fractions of each security in the portfolio. Thus, the expected return on a portfolio is:

$$r_p = \Sigma r_s p_s$$

where

TABLE 5–1 Some Possible Combinations of Securities in Figure 5–7

Low Risk/ *Low Return* *Portfolio (L)*	*Medium Risk/* *Medium Return* *Portfolio (M)*	*High Risk/* *High Return* *Portfolio (H)*
$400 of A	$250 of A	$100 of A
$300 of B	$250 of B	$200 of B
$200 of C	$250 of C	$300 of C
$100 of D	$250 of D	$400 of D
$1,000	$1,000	$1,000

r_s = expected return of each security and
p_s = fraction of that security in the portfolio.

The low risk/low return portfolio in Table 5–1 has a return of

$$r_L = 8\%(.4) + 10\%(.3) + 15\%(.2) + 18\%(.1) = 11\%$$

and the high risk/high return portfolio:

$$r_H = 8\%(.1) + 10\%(.2) + 15\%(.3) + 18\%(.4) = 14.5\%.$$

(What is the return on the medium risk/medium return portfolio?)

When securities are combined in a portfolio, the risk of the portfolio is generally less than a weighted average of the risks of the individual securities. This is because all securities do not vary in the same amounts and in the same direction during changes in business activity in general. When different securities behave differently, a downward movement of one may be at least partially offset by an upward movement of another. The absence of perfect correlation among securities has the effect of reducing risk. To reduce risk through holdings of several securities is called *diversification*.

In Figure 5–7 points *L, H* and *M* identify the low risk/low return, high risk/high return, and medium risk/medium return portfolios in Table 5–1. Note that *L, H* and *M* lie to the northwest of A, B, C and D, indicating a reduction of risk through diversification. Savers select among *L, H, M* and many other possible portfolios containing A, B, C and D in various proportions. All possible combinations of the available securities occupy a space along the upper left portion of the opportunity set. A curve can be drawn showing all portfolios with highest return and lowest risk. For any level of risk, a portfolio on the curve yields the highest possible return. Alternatively, for any return a portfolio on the curve involves the lowest risk. Because portfolios on the curve yield the highest return relative to risk at every level of risk, the curve is called the *efficient frontier*.

FIGURE 5-8   Indifference Curves for
Consumer Goods

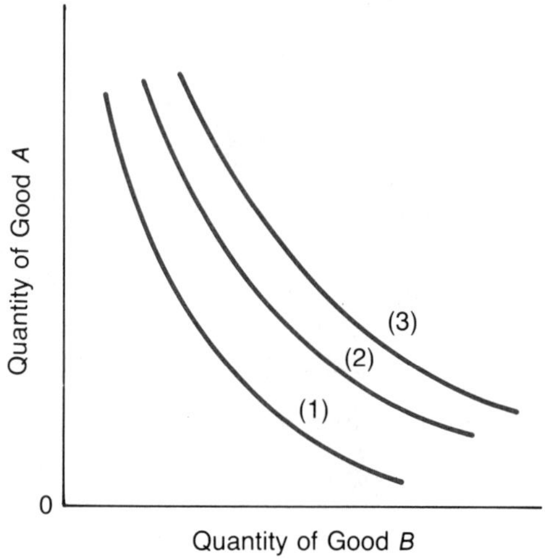

Quantity of Good A

(1)   (2)   (3)

Quantity of Good B

The Risk/Return Preferences of Savers

Selection of a specific portfolio depends on a saver's preferences with respect to risk and return. Preferences are often shown as *indifference curves* in which higher levels of satisfaction are associated with larger amounts of two items measured on the horizontal and vertical axes. To illustrate, indifference curves for two consumer goods are shown in Figure 5-8. A particular level of consumer satisfaction is associated with indifference curve (1); larger quantities of both goods increase consumer satisfaction and involve a movement to indifference curves (2) and (3). Movements along a single indifference curve reflect a consumer's trade-off between goods: the quantity of one good a consumer will give up to receive an additional quantity of the other, all the while continuing to experience the same level of satisfaction.

Indifference curves that illustrate risk/return preferences have a different shape from indifference curves describing consumer preferences for goods. The difference is that increasing the quantities of the item measured on the horizontal axis *reduces* the consumer's satisfaction. To experience higher levels of risk would place savers on lower indifference curves. In Figure 5-9 higher levels of satisfaction are associated with indifference curves drawn closer to the vertical axis and farther from the horizontal axis. Movements along a single indifference curve reflect the individual saver's preferences with respect to risk and return. Savers who consistently require safe in-

FIGURE 5–9 Indifference Curves for Securities

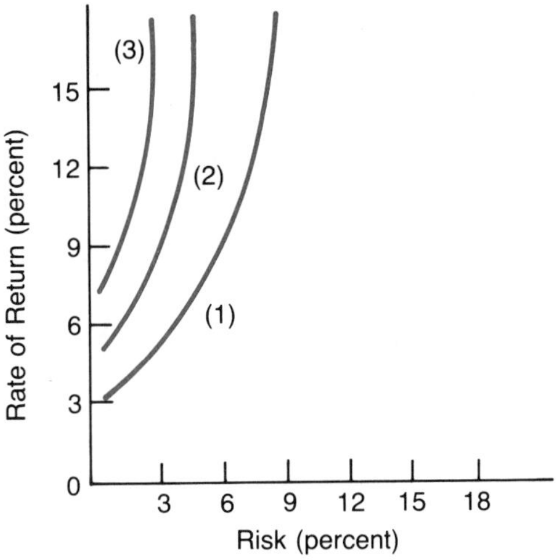

vestments have steeper indifference curves than savers who are more willing to accept some risk.

Figure 5–10 combines the opportunity set of available securities, the efficient frontier including all efficient portfolios, and indifference curves for two savers with different risk/return preferences. Saver I is highly averse to risk and chooses portfolio L; this portfolio provides the highest risk/return ratio available to meet saver I's investment objectives. At the other extreme, portfolio H provides the highest risk/return ratio within saver II's objectives. Savers in all markets evaluate the risk/return characteristics of all portfolios and select the particular portfolio that satisfies their individual preferences for risk and return.

A Risk-Free Security

Our discussion thus far has included only securities with some measurable risk. Some securities, however, are acknowledged to have no default risk: U.S. Treasury bills. Moreover, because they are short-term, market risk is negligible, too. To include riskless securities in a portfolio reduces total risk. Because riskless securities do not require compensation for risk, their return is low also. Therefore to include riskless securities in a portfolio reduces its return. Portfolios including risk-free securities appear in Figure 5–11 on the straight line drawn from the risk-free rate ($i = 6\%$) to touch the efficient frontier. With a risk-free security the efficient frontier is trans-

FIGURE 5–10 Securities Available in the Market, along with Indifference Curves for Savers I and II

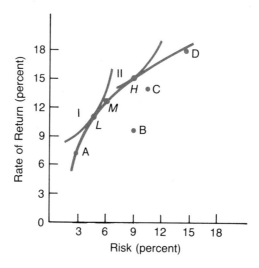

FIGURE 5–11 Portfolio Selection with Risk-Free Security

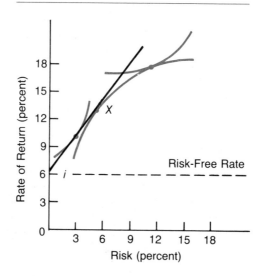

formed so that a portion is the straight line *iX* and the remainder is the curved line beyond *X*.

As before, savers are free to select portfolios that satisfy their own preferences. A strongly risk-averse saver selects a portfolio far down the straight-line portion of the new efficient frontier; the greater the proportion of risk-free securities in the portfolio, the lower its return and risk. A more aggressive investor selects a portfolio high on the straight-line portion or on the curved portion of the efficient frontier. This investor expects higher return on a higher risk portfolio.

Asset Portfolios of Financial Intermediaries

Some savers purchase securities through brokers and accumulate portfolios of financial assets that satisfy their individual preferences for return and risk. More often, savers deposit funds regularly in a bank or thrift institution, or they make regular payments to other nonbank financial intermediaries: insurance companies, pension funds or investment companies. In either case, they become part owners of the financial assets accumulated by the financial intermediary. In the next chapter, we will see that financial intermediaries, too, demonstrate different preferences for return and risk. Credit unions, for instance, make low-risk investments for relatively low return, and life insurance companies make more risky investments for higher return. Portfolio selection for these intermediaries follows a pattern similar to the pattern described here.

The final result of portfolio selection is a flow of funds into financial markets according to the particular goals of savers. Goals and intentions may change, shifting the distribution of funds in various ways and altering the pattern of interest rates for various types of securities. Demand for financial capital changes also, as borrowers change their expectations of return on particular investment projects. Efficient financial markets adjust smoothly to such changes, with the result that financial resources are allocated among sectors according to the collective attitudes and goals of the nation.

Summing Up

Understanding portfolio selection is important for understanding monetary theory and policy. The reason is that decisions regarding investment portfolios affect the demand for and the supply of money. The public's willingness to hold their wealth in the form of securities permits the existing supply of money to work harder; that is, to circulate faster and provide more spending power and higher incomes to productive resources. The purchase of securities facilitates investment in capital resources, which are the principal means of economic growth and rising per capita living standards.

In this chapter we have described the forces that govern behavior in private financial markets. In the following chapters we will examine financial intermediaries and instruments in detail. Private individuals and institutions are led by their own interests to seek funds for investment or to supply funds to borrowers. Decisions based on private interests may at times conflict with the goals of efficiency, equity and the production of positive externalities. Wide fluctuations in spending or investment, accompanied by fluctuations in interest rates and severe unemployment or inflation, are examples. Unemployment indicates inefficiency in the use of scarce resources, and inflation distorts the distribution of goods and services in ways that may be inequitable. Both unemployment and inflation create negative externalities that reduce living standards for the nation as a whole.

When individual decisions regarding saving and investment conflict with the goals of efficiency, equity and the production of positive externalities, the powers of government may be called upon to resolve the conflict. In Part II, we will examine the institutions and procedures for government's intervention in financial markets.

Glossary of Terms

capital deepening. producing enough new capital resources to increase the amount available for each worker

capital gains tax. a tax on the gain from resale of an asset

capital widening. producing enough new capital resources to supply a growing labor force with a constant quantity of capital

compounding. applying interest on interest earned on a long-term asset

discounting. reducing the value of a future revenue according to the interest rate and the distance in the future it is to be received

diversification. selection of a variety of securities whose behavior is likely to differ with cycles in economic activity

efficient frontier. the curve showing the portfolios with the highest return relative to risk

expected return. the weighted average of past returns on an asset

indifference curves. curves representing individual preferences with respect to risk and return

marginal efficiency of investment. rates of return on investment projects arranged in descending order to form a firm's demand curve for financial capital

opportunity set. an arrangement of points representing the risk and expected return of available investments

present value. the value of a future stream of revenues, discounted according to the interest rate and the distance in the future the revenues are to be received

rate of return. the discount rate that makes the present value of an asset equal to the initial outlay

risk. the average of squared deviations of past returns from the expected return on an asset

saving and investment. refraining from consumption and using resources to produce capital goods

standard deviation. a statistic that measures the risk of an investment

Summary of Important Ideas

1. Increasing per capita production and income depends on improvements in the quantity and quality of capital resources. Buildings and equipment, materials and component parts, and housing are necessary for increasing worker productivity. Capital investment requires the sacrifice of current consumption and is especially painful for very poor countries.

2. Business firms compare the current outlay for a new capital good with the present value of its expected future earnings, discounted according to the interest rate and the time before earnings are to be received. A positive net present value indicates the investment should be made.

3. When a number of investment projects are under consideration, a rate of return should be computed for each. The firm's marginal efficiency of investment curve ranks the return from all investment proposals and is the firm's demand curve for financial capital. It is also the supply curve for new securities, a downward sloping curve because lower interest rates mean higher security prices and a larger quantity supplied.

4. The supply of financial capital is also the demand for new securities. Equilibrium between supply and demand determines the interest rate and the quantity of new capital resources.

5. Bringing savers together with borrowers smoothly and efficiently is the job of financial intermediaries.

6. Savers allocate funds for lending according to expected return and risk. Expected return is a weighted average of past returns, and risk is measured according to past deviations from expected return. Savers select

portfolios according to individual preferences for return and safety; the process is similar to selection of a combination of consumer goods. Adding risk-free U.S. Treasury bills to a portfolio reduces return as well as risk.

7. Savers frequently purchase portfolios through financial intermediaries whose preferences for risk and return differ according to the character of the institution. Changing preferences of savers and changing expected return on investment projects cause shifts in the nation's allocation of financial capital and in the direction of new capital construction.

Questions for Discussion and Research

1. Define roundabout production, saving, investment.

2. Consult the latest *Economic Report of the President* for data on annual investment. Compare the nation's growth in capital with labor force growth and comment on the relationship. Is the nation experiencing capital widening or capital deepening? Explain.

3. Compute the final value of a $100 deposit left to accumulate interest for five years at 10 percent. Assume interest is compounded semiannually.

4. How much would an investor be willing to pay for a security that earns $5 a year for ten years and then is redeemed for $80? Assume the investor has other investment opportunities that would earn 9 percent.

5. Use a mathematical example to show the relationship between: compounding and discounting, present value and net present value, expected return and risk.

6. What factors affect the position and shape of a firm's marginal efficiency of investment curve? What factors might cause a rightward or leftward shift in the curve? Show how a firm's MEI curve is at the same time its demand curve for financial capital and its supply curve of securities.

7. Illustrate graphically the opportunity set of financial portfolios available to savers. Show how savers with different risk/return preferences would be expected to select different portfolios.

8. Compute the expected return of a portfolio composed of the following securities:

Security	Total Investment	Expected Return
A	$50,000	10%
B	30,000	8
C	10,000	12
Treasury bills	10,000	6

What conclusions might be drawn about the risk of such a portfolio? Explain.

Additional Readings

Brown, Lynn E., and Richard F. Syron.   "The Municipal Market since the New York City Crisis." *New England Economic Review* (July/August 1979): 11–26.

Campbell, Claudia R., and Jean M. Lovati.   "Inflation and Personal Saving: An Update." *Federal Reserve Bank of St. Louis Review* 61 (August 1979): 3–9.

Fiedler, Edgar R.   "Capital." *Across the Board* 14 (September 1977): 40–46.

Modigliani, Franco.   "Saving and Growth." *Challenge* (May/June 1987): 24–29.

Tatom, John A., and James E. Turley.   "Inflation and Taxes: Disincentives for Capital Formation." *Federal Reserve Bank of St. Louis Review* 60 (January 1978): 2–8.

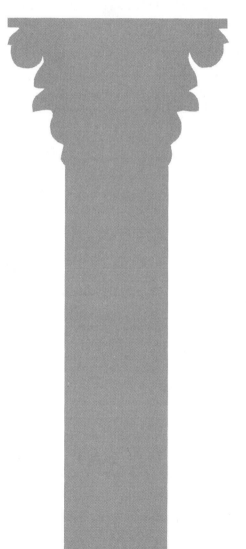

C H A P T E R

6

LEARNING OBJECTIVES

- To understand the functions of nonbank financial intermediaries and the economic and legal circumstances that led to specialization among them
- To distinguish among financial intermediaries on the basis of their assets and liabilities
- To understand the role and objectives of government-sponsored financial intermediaries and some of the disadvantages of government intervention in financial markets

Nonbank Financial Intermediaries

"Put not your trust in money, but put your money in trust."

Oliver Wendell Holmes

Americans are creative people, especially where money is concerned. New ways to borrow and lend money are constantly being "invented" by participants in America's financial markets. The goal of profit is an important incentive to this type of creativity. When artificial restraints prevent certain activity, determined borrowers and lenders develop ways to get around the restraints. The result is often a whole new set of financial instruments and intermediaries, each responding to particular market circumstances and each earning a return in accordance with supply and demand in a particular market.

Until the mid-1970s most financial intermediaries in the United States specialized in particular types of borrowing and lending. Commercial banks specialized in holding short-term deposits and making commercial loans; savings and loan associations specialized in holding savings accounts and making home mortgages; insurance companies specialized in collecting premiums and providing insurance coverage; finance companies specialized in consumer loans; and credit unions made short-term loans to employees of a particular firm.

In part, specialization in financial intermediaries was a result of legal barriers to competition among them. Some legal barriers were established by state-chartering agencies, many with the intent to protect the public. Restrictions against commercial bank mergers and branching, for example, were intended to protect the public against the growth of excessive market power. It was felt that small, independent financial intermediaries would be more competitive and more eager to serve the public at low cost. Restrictions on the types of loans and investments owned were intended to preserve savers' assets against misuse. It was felt that absolute freedom to make all kinds of loans might encourage risky lending on preferred terms to favored customers. These kinds of restrictions at the state level tended to maintain a system of small- to medium-sized financial intermediaries, each specializing in performing a particular function set forth in its state charter.

Federal regulations also encouraged specialization. Federal tax laws provided special tax advantages to certain types of investments. Although commercial banks are taxed like other corporations at the corporate income tax rate, other financial intermediaries are allowed deductions that reduce their tax bills. Some are allowed to distribute all income from investments to their shareholders without paying taxes. Then shareholders must pay taxes based on their own personal income tax rates. (Note that profits of commercial banks may be taxed twice: once as corporate income and again if they are paid out as personal income to depositors and shareholders.) Other federal legislation regulates financial intermediaries with respect to disclosure of information to shareholders and other business practices.

Laws passed in the 1930s were the basis for much federal regulation of commercial banks. The Great Depression drove many banks out of business. The worst casualties were the small banks, in part because they were unable to survive the vigorous competition that had preceded the collapse. To guard against ruinous competition in the future, Congress passed a series of laws limiting the activities of banks. The Glass–Steagall Act of 1932 and the Banking Acts of 1933 and 1935 were the most important. A major provision of the Banking Acts was the restriction on interest paid by commercial banks. Commercial banks were forbidden to pay any interest at all on checking accounts and by Regulation Q were limited in the amount of interest payable on savings and time deposits. Savings and loan associations were allowed to pay one-quarter percent higher interest on their savings deposits than commercial banks. Restrictions on interest rates were intended to discourage financial intermediaries from competing vigorously, and perhaps unwisely, for funds and using funds to purchase risky investments.

Restrictions also had the effect of encouraging the development of new kinds of financial intermediaries. Because new, nonbank financial intermediaries accepted no deposits, they were not bound by the restrictions placed on banks and savings and loan associations. They were free to solicit new sources of funds and enjoyed wider opportunities in their uses of funds. Whenever the community's financial needs could not be served efficiently by traditional financial intermediaries, new financial intermediaries grew up to serve them. Each new institution developed a speciality on which to concentrate its resources for investment.

Specialization kept financial intermediaries small, but specialization may also have created expertise. Specialization also affected profitability. A characteristic of specialized institutions is that they are subject to the behavior of supply and demand in relatively limited markets. Profits may rise or fall sharply with particular market conditions. A small specialized financial intermediary is more subject to risky market circumstances than one that operates in many markets. As the risks of specialization grew and became more apparent, many financial intermediaries looked for ways to diversify their operations.

Balance Sheets Again

Another look at balance sheets of financial intermediaries will be helpful. Like other business firms, financial intermediaries list the value of their assets, liabilities and capital accounts on a balance sheet, as shown in Figure 6–1.

FIGURE 6–1

BALANCE SHEET	
Assets	Liabilities and Capital Accounts

Unlike other business firms, financial intermediaries own few *real* assets. Their assets are financial assets: loans and investments that are expected to produce income. In fact, the sides of a financial intermediary's balance sheet might be relabeled as shown in Figure 6–2.

FIGURE 6–2

BALANCE SHEET	
Uses of Funds	Sources of Funds

The principal sources of funds are liabilities owed to depositors or borrowed from other creditors. Other sources are capital accounts: ownership shares sold to individuals or businesses, retained profits, and special accounts. All these sources are used to purchase financial assets.

A financial intermediary selects a portfolio of assets that provides acceptable levels of yield, safety and liquidity. Adequate yield is essential for paying interest income to depositors and dividends to shareholders. Safety against default risk and market risk helps ensure the institution's solvency.

Liquidity is necessary for paying claims against the institution as they come due. No portfolio can provide maximum levels of yield, safety and liquidity, because a high level of one of these advantages is generally associated with a low level of another. This means that some financial intermediaries seek a particular combination of the three in their portfolio, and others seek another. The objective in each case is to purchase a portfolio with the combination of yield, safety and liquidity appropriate to the needs of the particular institution.

The type of portfolio actually selected depends primarily on the sources of funds for each type of institution. Because financial intermediaries differ in sources of funds, their requirements for yield, safety and liquidity differ also. As you read about the structure and functions of various financial intermediaries, keep in mind the opportunities and the limitations imposed on each by the character of its liabilities and capital accounts.

Savings and Loan Associations

Our most familiar nonbank financial intermediaries are savings and loan associations (S&Ls). In the beginning they were called building societies, and they held small deposits from middle-income working people for lending to homebuilders. In England, building societies began as far back as the eighteenth century. The first U.S. building society met in a Philadelphia tavern in 1931 and made a $375 mortgage loan to Comly Rich. Rich was a lamplighter, and his home still stands in Philadelphia.

The small savings of many depositors have always been the S&Ls' major source of funds: 70 percent of total liabilities and capital accounts in 1987. We think of our savings as constituting deposits, but for most S&Ls they are properly known as shares. As part owners of the association, savers receive dividends on their shares, rather than interest. Moreover, shareholders may vote to select directors who hire managers and direct policy. S&Ls known as mutual savings associations offer traditional deposits as well as shares of ownership.

Many types of accounts are available to savers in S&Ls and mutuals. Regular passbook accounts are the most familiar, paying interest formerly limited by government regulation at 5½ percent. Savings can generally be withdrawn on demand, although the association retains the right to ask 30 days' notice before withdrawal. Various club accounts are also popular, calling for regular deposits and accumulating to a Christmas or vacation fund.

Time deposits differ from savings deposits in that a specific date is set for maturity. An example is 90-day accounts, which require 90 days' notice before withdrawal but earn higher interest than regular passbook accounts. Another is savings certificates, which are issued with various maturities and pay higher interest for longer maturities. Holders of savings certificates may redeem them before maturity, but only with a substantial loss of interest income. Certificates of deposit greater than $100,000 pay interest at market rates, unrestricted by government ceilings.

Advantages and Disadvantages

The variety of claims against S&Ls provides some advantages and some disadvantages. Because many ownership shares have maturities at definite times in the future, these funds can be used for long-term lending. The relative stability of S&L sources of funds permits lending for the important purpose that began with the English building societies: lending for building new homes and purchasing existing homes.

Four-fifths of the assets of S&Ls are residential mortgages or mortgages for business properties. In fact, S&Ls provide almost half the nation's mortgages for one- to four-family nonfarm dwellings. Most mortgages are *conventional* loans, but some are insured by the Federal Home Administration (FHA) or guaranteed by the Veterans' Administration. In addition to direct mortgage lending, S&Ls also purchase mortgages originally issued by mortgage companies or other financial intermediaries. To retain liquidity, S&Ls also purchase short-term U.S. Treasury bills and notes, state and local securities, acceptances, and the securities of federal agencies.

Interest charges on new mortgage loans rise and fall according to supply and demand in the current market. Although an S&L's loan portfolio has been accumulated over past periods when interest rates may have varied widely, its annual earnings remain fairly stable. This is because current lending (whether at abnormally high rates or low) will not change the composition of the total portfolio very much. Stability of earnings makes an S&L a safe, secure financial intermediary, but it has a disadvantage also. The disadvantage arises from the fact that interest paid to sources of funds may not be stable.

When government ceilings on interest were lifted in 1986, S&Ls were allowed to compete for funds with other financial intermediaries. If the bulk of an S&L's depositors insist on higher rates of interest, interest paid on savings may rise substantially relative to interest earned on the S&L's mortgage portfolio. Even worse, when market rates rise, savers might be expected to withdraw their funds from low-yielding passbook accounts and purchase higher yielding investments directly.

The Problem of Disintermediation

Withdrawing funds from a financial intermediary for the purpose of direct purchase of investments is called *disintermediation*; to disintermediate is to eliminate the middleman or intermediary. Thus, rising market interest rates present S&Ls with two problems: rising costs on certain sources of funds and a drain of other important sources from the institution. Profits will suffer, and new lending may have to be cut back sharply.

A reduction of new lending is especially painful for the housing industry. Because homebuilders depend strongly on S&Ls for funds, rising interest rates and disintermediation may bring new homebuilding to a virtual standstill. Housing construction is not the only industry affected either. A decline in homebuilding reduces expenditures for appliances, carpets, furniture, heating and plumbing equipment, landscaping materials—the list could go on and on. When housing is cut back, production and employment in many related industries suffer also, contributing to a general decrease in economic activity and possibly causing a recession.

The problem of disintermediation became so serious in 1978 that S&Ls (and banks) were given permission to issue *money market certificates* (MMCs) in denominations of $10,000 with interest rates tied to rates on U.S. Treasury bills. Some S&Ls took advantage of this opportunity to attract funds, but others were reluctant to pay the higher interest charges. The result was a slowdown in the rate of housing construction and a decrease in S&L profits for the year.

Like commercial banks, S&Ls may be chartered by the federal or state governments. Federally chartered institutions are subject to supervision and examination by the Federal Home Loan Bank Board (FHLBB) in Washington. State-chartered institutions may be supervised and examined by state agencies or by the FHLBB if there is no state examining body. Federally chartered institutions are required to purchase deposit insurance from the Federal Savings and Loan Insurance Corporation (FSLIC). Deposits are insured up to $100,000. Most state-chartered institutions are also insured by the FSLIC, although a few states have their own insurance programs. (The number of states with state insurance programs is decreasing.)

MONEY AND BANKING IN PRACTICE: CRISIS IN THE THRIFTS

The nation's thrift industry is in trouble. With assets valued lower than their liabilities, many thrifts have negative net worth: They are insolvent.

Insolvent thrifts may not be able to satisfy their obligations to their depositors. The Federal Savings and Loan Insurance Corporation (FSLIC) was established in 1934 to insure depositors of thrift institutions, but by 1987 so many thrifts had failed that the FSLIC lacked sufficient funds to continue deposit insurance. Congress was trying to decide whether to provide funds from tax revenues or to authorize additional borrowing.

Some of the problems of the thrifts were a result of deposit insurance itself. Insurance tends to lead to two kinds of behavior: moral hazard and adverse selection. Moral hazard refers to the increased willingness to take risks when insurance is expected to offset any losses. Adverse selection refers to the tendency of risk-prone individuals or groups to enter fields protected by insurance. Both these tendencies have increased the potential obligations of the FSLIC without increasing its capacity to satisfy the obligations.

Other problems have been a result of deregulation in financial markets. Interest-rate ceilings held down the cost of funds for thrifts and enabled them to earn a profitable spread on their mortgage loans. When rising market interest rates brought on disintermediation, thrifts were allowed to offer money market accounts at market interest rates. Higher rates on deposits reduced profits and led to deregulation of thrifts' investments. By 1982 thrifts were increasing their lending in commercial real estate, consumer loans, commercial paper and debt securities. When many of these more risky loans went bad, insolvent thrifts faced liquidation by the FSLIC.

Closing a thrift is costly: in terms of funds paid to insured depositors and in terms of financial assistance paid to another institution that is allowed to merge with the failed institution. To ensure the FSLIC sufficient funds for carrying out its mission, some economists recommend increasing the insurance premium of more risk-prone institutions. Others recommend stricter regulation of thrifts' lending powers. Still others recommend removal of regulations to allow thrifts to compete freely in financial markets.

In one sense, the problems of the thrifts have resulted from their contribution to the nation's housing stock. As specialized institutions making home mortgages, the thrifts made possible home ownership for many U.S. families. Their problems today are a result of low-cost mortgages issued decades ago. For the future, the nation's policies with respect to home ownership may have to be carried out in ways other than through the thrift industry.

Questions for Discussion

1. Can you cite other examples of moral hazard and adverse selection?

2. Discuss the various alternatives for financing the FSLIC.

3. Discuss the merits of a policy to subsidize the nation's housing industry through low-cost mortgages. How might this result be accomplished without endangering the health of the thrift industry?

Mutual Savings Banks

Mutual savings banks are similar to savings and loan associations except for the wider range of sources and uses of funds they enjoy. All mutual savings banks are chartered by states, mostly in the northeastern part of the United States and the states of Washington, Oregon and Alaska. Some state-chartering agencies permit mutual savings banks to offer interest-earning checking accounts as well as savings and time deposits. In 1980 this privilege was extended to savings and loan associations and banks. Third-party payments like these are called negotiable orders of withdrawal—or *NOW accounts*. They have the advantage for the holder of earning interest up to the date a payment is made. A disadvantage for the financial intermediary is that the source of funds is more costly and less dependable than other deposit accounts.

State-chartering agencies permit mutual savings banks to purchase U.S. government securities, certain municipal bonds, high quality corporate bonds and certain corporate stock. Mortgage loans are their major investment, however, making them second only to S&Ls and commercial banks in this form of lending.

Both savings and loan associations and mutual savings banks have enjoyed healthy growth in recent decades. Post–World War II population growth has increased both the demand for housing and the supply of savings. Lately, growth has slowed somewhat and competition has become more intense. Mergers have increased the average size of these institutions, and branches have penetrated new markets. In general, profitability has been good, varying only with cycles in the level of business activity.

Life Insurance Companies

Most of us believe strongly in what Benjamin Franklin said 200 years ago about the inevitability of death and taxes. So we try to plan for them. One way we do this is by purchasing life insurance to provide benefits to our dependents after we die.

Life insurance companies hire actuaries to predict the level of death benefits that will have to be paid during any period of time. Actuaries are specialists in human statistics. By studying historical death rates for particular population groups, they are able to recommend the necessary accumulation of funds to satisfy the firm's insurance obligations.

The business of providing life insurance has not changed much since the Corporation for Relief of Poor and Distressed Presbyterian Ministers and of the Poor and Distressed Widows and Children of Presbyterian Ministers was established in the 1750s. Policyholders still pay premiums based on actuarial estimates of the risk of imminent death. Premiums are invested in interest-earning assets for the benefit of insured policy owners and stockholders. In 1987, accumulated premiums and investment income of life insurance companies amounted to almost $1 trillion.

Because sources of funds are stable and long-term and because claims can be predicted fairly accurately, investments may be long-term also. Mortgages constitute almost a third of life insurance company investments; large mortgages are often made for business properties, office complexes, entertainment facilities or other income-earning properties. An even greater share of life insurance company funds goes for purchase of corporate bonds. Bonds are more popular than stocks because of their fixed income, but preferred stock and some common stock are also owned. Other securities and loans to policyholders complete the portfolio.

Life insurance companies are licensed by the states and must comply with state regulations with respect to premium rates, investments and liquid reserves against claims.

Property and Casualty Insurance Companies

Some property and casualty insurance companies specialize in particular types of policies, and others provide many kinds of insurance coverage: from wind and fire insurance to burglary and health insurance. Like life insurance companies, their sources of funds are premiums paid by policyholders.

Property and casualty insurance companies differ from life insurance companies in an important respect. Because they deal with smaller claims and smaller premiums than a life insurance company, they have less to invest in large, long-term mortgages. Furthermore, their claims are generally less predictable than death claims. For both these reasons, property and casualty companies invest primarily in more liquid, short-term securities. State and local bonds are most popular and together with U.S. government bonds and corporate bonds constitute about half the asset portfolio. Common stock of utilities, banks and insurance companies; some preferred stock; and a few mortgages complete the portfolio.

Property and casualty insurance companies are also regulated by the states.

Finance Companies

We have seen that savings and loan associations, mutual savings banks, and life insurance companies invest primarily in mortgages and government or corporate securities. The character of their liabilities enables them to make large, long-term investments. An important source of small, short-term loans for consumers is finance companies. Consumer finance companies make direct loans to consumers. Sales and commercial finance companies lend to retailers who, in turn, lend to consumers. An example of a sales finance company is General Motors Acceptance Corporation. GMAC is owned by General Motors, and its purpose is to provide consumer auto loans through GM dealers.

Finance companies acquire funds through bank loans or through sale of commercial paper. Almost half their loans are personal loans, and another third are auto loans. Because loans are small and short-term, they are costly to administer. Loans are often risky, too. For both these reasons, interest charges tend to be higher than commercial bank rates. Interest charges are generally computed on the original amount of the loan. Thus, a one-year $1,000 loan at 12 percent requires an interest charge of $120. But the borrower has use of the full $1,000 only briefly—just until making the first loan payment. Although the unpaid balance declines through the year, interest is charged on the full amount borrowed. The result is a true interest charge almost twice the quoted rate.

Finance companies are subject to state regulation, which varies among states. The Consumer Credit Protection Act (Truth-in-Lending Act) requires that borrowers be given information about loan agreements and regulates collection practices. In 1987, domestic finance companies had assets of $350 billion, more than double their assets of 1980.

Credit Unions

A rapidly growing type of financial intermediary in the United States today is the credit union. Credit unions were originally established to take factory workers out of the clutches of loan sharks. Their members have a common bond—usually a job, union, church or club. (Mill Creek Credit Union in Portland, Oregon, allows only convicts and ex-convicts to join!) Credit union members purchase shares similar to savings deposits, and they may borrow from the credit union. Interest income on loans is used to pay dividends to members. Dividends are generally higher than the interest paid on regular passbook savings at commercial banks or savings and loan associations.

Credit unions are chartered by the federal or state governments and operated by members, many of whom serve without pay. Deposits are generally small but frequent, making short-term lending a major form of investment. Recently, however, some credit unions have begun making real estate loans. Because their expenses are low and their lending relatively safe, interest charges can be rather low also. They are exempt from taxes on investment income and are generally profitable to their shareholders.

State banking agencies supervise state-chartered credit unions. Federally chartered credit unions are supervised by the National Credit Union Administration. Most are insured by federal or state agencies.

Some credit unions offer members accounts similar to conventional checking accounts. Their members are allowed to write *share drafts* similar to checks, making credit unions a new source of competition for commercial banks. In 1987, the nation's credit unions held total assets of $150 billion.

Investment Companies

An important financial intermediary in today's economy is the investment company. Investment companies exist only to hold securities. They pool the savings of individuals whose own funds are too limited to purchase a diversified portfolio.

Investment companies are called *open-end* if the number of outstanding shares changes with supply and demand: Savers can purchase additional shares from the company at any time and resell shares to the company at current market value. Investment companies are called *closed-end* if there is a constant number of shares outstanding at any time: Savers can purchase shares only from current owners. Typically, an investment company is operated by a management company, and shares are bought and sold by independent dealers. The selling price often includes a *load*, or commission, to the underwriter or dealer, although some investment companies sell *no-load* shares.

Investment portfolios vary among companies. Some investment companies purchase only common stocks, some a balanced portfolio of stocks and bonds, and others a specialized type of securities: growth stocks, income stocks, commercial paper, Treasury bills or municipal securities. The Securities Act of 1933 regulates such matters as information provided to stockholders and other management practices. Other more recent legislation aims to protect investors from fraud. As long as the investment company pays out to shareholders 90 percent of investment income and short-term capital gains, it pays no taxes. Shareholders are taxed on earnings when they receive them, along with their personal income tax.

Profits depend on performance of the investment company's portfolio. The return on assets tends to fluctuate with the business cycle. In recent years, some funds have turned to a new technique for ensuring that the return on their portfolio does not deviate sharply from the return on the market as a whole. They have begun to *index* their asset holdings; that is, they have purchased a combination of securities that precisely duplicates the combination of securities used for computing a popular market index. Standard and Poor's Index of 500 stocks, for example, might be the basis for an indexed portfolio. With indexing, a 5 percent return on the market index guarantees a 5 percent return on the investment company's portfolio as well.

When open-end investment companies redeem more shares than they sell, they experience a decrease in total assets. This was a problem of the mid-1970s when assets fell from $60 million in 1972 to $40 million in 1975. At one point in 1980 assets fell again to $47 billion. By 1987, assets of all investment companies were more than $400 billion.

Pension Funds

In times past, U.S. workers were expected to provide individually for their retirement years. Some workers found this difficult, because their current earnings were often barely enough to pay their current living expenses. This was not a really serious problem then, for life spans were short, and aged parents could live with adult sons and daughters. These conditions changed dramatically in the past half century with improved health care, movement of young families about the country, and pressure toward early retirement from a growing pool of talented young workers on the way up. An improved system of retirement benefits was needed.

Some firms and state and local governments have set up individual retirement programs, supported by employee and employer contributions. Frequently, funds are placed in the hands of a bank or trustee to be invested, with investment income to be added to the fund. Other programs provide for purchase of insurance policies at group rates, with contributions invested along with other premiums collected by the life insurance company.

Individually managed *pension* funds have greater freedom in the types of investments selected. Typically more than half a pension fund's portfolio is invested in common and preferred stock. Another fourth is in corporate bonds. These pension funds are exempt from federal taxation if they meet certain standards. The *Employee Retirement Income Security Act (ERISA)* of 1976 was designed to protect employees from misuse of retirement funds. The law also established eligibility requirements, benefit vesting according to age or years of service, adequate funding to meet the plan's obligations, insurance against termination of the plan, and standards for sound and ethical asset management. An acceptable pension program is becoming an important part of contract arrangements in many labor negotiations.

The pension plans that we have described are said to be *funded*: funds are collected and invested, with earnings used to pay benefits to participants. Other pension funds are *unfunded*: funds are collected from today's workers and paid out immediately to beneficiaries. The largest unfunded pension program is the Social Security system. To collect and invest enough funds to provide benefits for all Social Security recipients would absorb a large part of the wealth of the nation. Therefore, funds are collected from currently employed workers and paid directly to retired workers. Some idle funds are invested in U.S. government securities, however.

MONEY AND BANKING IN PRACTICE: PENSIONS

For many U.S. workers their most important financial asset is their pension fund. Workers and employers make regular payments to a fund to be invested by a professional manager. Contributions and earnings accumulate for paying benefits to workers at retirement.

For years, private pension funds were governed somewhat loosely by the "prudent man" rule. This rule of law says that any person entrusted with another person's money must manage that money as prudently as if it were his or her own. Otherwise, he or she might be subject to a lawsuit. In 1974, for example, a New York bank trustee was found to be "imprudent" because a few securities in the total pension fund portfolio he managed were found to be losers. The Employee Retirement Income Security Act of 1976 (ERISA) stated more precisely the acceptable uses of pension funds for protecting the interests of covered workers.

In the United States today, fewer than half of private sector employees are covered by pension plans. Most large companies provide plans that, along with Social Security benefits, guarantee workers about two-thirds of their pay after retirement. Automatic cost-of-living escalators are rare in these plans, however. Many small companies have no plans at all or provide only minimum benefits. Low- and middle-income workers may set aside up to $2,000 a year in an Individual Retirement Account (IRA) to be invested as a pension fund. The annual contributions are not taxed as income in the year they are earned and are subject to tax only when they are withdrawn, usually after retirement when the recipient is in a lower tax bracket. Self-employed professionals can establish a tax-deferred savings plan to fulfill their pension needs. Under such a savings plan an individual can set aside up to $7,000 annually, free of income tax in the year earned.

Teachers at more than 3,000 educational and research institutions contribute to the Teachers' Insurance and Annuity Association (TIAA) with contributions also made by the employing institution. Like many individual retirement programs, TIAA provides a choice of pension funds for the worker. One fund is invested entirely in fixed income securities: corporate or government bonds, mortgages, or insured savings accounts. It is practically risk free. The other is invested in common stocks, and its performance depends on the performance of the market as a whole. Because its returns are subject to greater risk, the second fund is more appropriate for aggressive investors: young and financially secure professionals who are not imminently dependent on pension benefits.

The most generous pension plans are available to government employees. Almost all public sector workers are covered. Military personnel can retire early and receive substantial payments immediately, even while they may be working at other jobs or receiving other pension benefits. The benefits given by state and local governments average one-third more than those of private industry, and police and firemen's benefits are even higher. Federal civilian employees receive similar benefits, with early retirement option, regular cost-of-living adjustment, and death and disability benefits.

Questions for Discussion

1. What are the implications of a fully developed pension system for the level of private saving in the United States?

2. What are the implications for the behavior of securities markets?

Credit Allocation and Financial Intermediaries

The financial intermediaries described thus far play an important role in channeling the funds of savers into active use by investors. They help keep the nation's supply of money working and reduce the fraction of income held idle. They have another function that has to do with the allocation of credit toward particular uses.

Today in the United States financial intermediaries remain relatively specialized, although specialization is rapidly breaking down. Specialization is a result of different tax treatment and of legal restrictions on their sources of funds. As we have seen, the character of their liabilities limits the types of investments financial intermediaries may purchase. In fact, most financial intermediaries can be described as hedgers: they match the maturities of their assets to the maturities of their liabilities. Only S&Ls and mutuals can be described as speculators, because they typically borrow rather short and lend long.

Specialization among financial intermediaries has the effect of allocating credit toward particular sectors of the economy. Flows of savings into a particular type of financial intermediary may mean prosperity for a particular sector. Of course, the reverse is also true. Savings flows tend to respond to interest and dividend earnings in particular institutions. This is especially true with respect to short-term, irregular savings—the type of savings that normally flow into S&Ls and mutual savings banks. When interest and dividend earnings at other financial intermediaries rise above interest rates paid at S&Ls and mutuals, savings are likely to flow out.

Rising market rates of interest perform an important function in our economic system. Like rising prices for any good or service, they are a means of rationing scarce resources and channeling them toward where they are most needed. Too, rising interest rates and rising prices are a means of discouraging purchases that exceed the economy's capacity for producing goods and services.

The Dilemma Regarding Housing

Fluctuations in market interest rates create a dilemma for policymakers. On the one hand, policymakers want to allow interest rates to perform their rationing function and to slow down excessive growth in spending. But on the other hand, they regret imposing severe restraints on the housing industry. Housing and all its supplying industries comprise a major part of the nation's economy. Together they employ more people and generate more income than any other sector of the economy. To restrain the housing sector may be necessary in a period of too rapid growth, but it may also cause widespread economic distress, many small business failures, and a loss of skilled personnel from the industry. And it may mean a nationwide failure to provide decent living space for many people.

The housing dilemma seems to call for special policies to deal with special problems. Certain public institutions and public programs have been established to smooth the flow of funds into financial intermediaries for mortgage lending. The aim of these institutions and programs is to moderate somewhat the harsh results of free markets and to reduce a tendency toward boom and bust in the housing sector.

Public Financial Intermediaries

Three important public financial intermediaries serve to moderate the effects of market conditions on mortgage credit: the Federal National Mortgage Association (Fannie Mae), the Government National Mortgage Association (Ginnie Mae) and the Federal Home Loan Mortgage Company (Freddie Mac—established in 1970). As described in Chapter 4, these institutions have fundamentally the same function; they provide a secondary market for home mortgages. The existence of a secondary market makes mortgages more liquid. Like short-term debt instruments, they can be readily converted to cash without substantial loss of value. The ease of converting long-term mortgages to cash increases the ability of S&Ls and mutuals to extend such mortgages. When S&Ls are loaned up and the demand for mortgages is high, mortgage rates will tend to rise so as to ration out the scarce mortgage money. In times like these, S&Ls can sell some of their mortgage loans to FNMA, GNMA or FHLMC. Selling their mortgages frees up funds to use for new lending and keeps mortgage interest rates from rising so high.

When S&Ls have excess funds and low mortgage demand is reducing interest earnings, they can use their excess funds to purchase mortgages from the portfolios of these public institutions. This time the effect is to keep mortgage interest rates from falling sharply and to protect the earnings of S&Ls. In general, the existence of FNMA, GNMA and FHLMC helps to ease interest rate pressures in mortgage markets.

There is another interesting result. Fannie Mae is now a privately owned, profit-seeking institution. Carrying out the function described helps to increase its profit. Fannie Mae buys mortgages when interest rates are high. Abnormally high interest rates have the effect of reducing the market price of existing long-term debt instruments. (Recall our discussion of the inverse relationship between interest rates and bond prices in Chapter 4.) Thus, Fannie Mae buys mortgages at low prices and later resells them at higher prices. Because mortgages are sold back to S&Ls when interest rates are low, their market prices are higher. Fannie Mae makes a profit.

Ginnie Mae is not compelled to earn a profit because its function is to serve the public rather than to satisfy stockholders. When demand for mortgage loans is high, Ginnie Mae also buys mortgages from S&Ls, but frequently at higher prices than paid by Fannie Mae. And Ginnie Mae may also resell mortgages at a loss. Moreover, Ginnie Mae can guarantee additional borrowing by S&Ls when their mortgages are used as collateral.

Freddie Mac performs essentially the same functions as FNMA and GNMA with one difference. Whereas FNMA and GNMA deal only in FHA and VA mortgages, FHLMC purchases conventional mortgages as well.

Public Lending Programs

The federal government operates two programs for subsidized lending to home buyers. Mortgage loans to veterans are guaranteed under the Veterans' Administration. A loan guarantee increases the willingness of lenders to make such loans. The VA also may extend a limited quantity of mortgage loans directly. The Federal Housing Administration provides insurance on mortgage loans. If the home buyer defaults on an FHA-insured loan, the FHA pays off the lender and takes possession of the home. The property is often resold at a loss. Both VA and FHA loans may be exchanged in secondary markets.

The Federal Housing Administration imposes a maximum interest rate ceiling on its insured mortgages. When market rates rise above the allowed maximum, lenders may refuse to make FHA loans, so that mortgage money dries up. Some lenders get around the problem of a rate ceiling by charging points. The term *points* refers to a single payment that makes up the difference between the FHA maximum interest rate and the market rate. Paying points along with a down payment may enable home buyers to secure mortgages at a low nominal rate, but in fact the payment of points increases the effective rate they actually pay.

In recent years, some state and local governments have developed new mortgage lending programs for stimulating home ownership and home improvements in urban areas. Special *housing districts* have been formed and given the power to issue revenue bonds. Proceeds from the sale of bonds are loaned to home buyers at low rates of interest. In general, subsidized loans are made only to persons with incomes below a stated amount. Then their interest and principal payments are passed on to bondholders. The bonds are an attractive investment because interest income is exempt from federal taxation. Furthermore, the Department of Housing and Urban Development may guarantee payments to bondholders, should borrowers default.

MONEY AND BANKING IN PRACTICE: INSURING THE DREAM

The FHA made the American dream of home ownership come true for many Americans. By insuring the mortgage loans of qualified young, low-income home buyers the FHA promises to pay the mortgage lender if the borrower defaults.

Government-insured mortgages began in the 1930s in response to defaults and foreclosures that ran nearly 1,000 a day during the Great Depression. Before the FHA, a home buyer typically paid a down payment amounting to half the home's price, with full repayment due in five to ten years. Afterward, down payments fell as low as 10 percent, and repayment periods extended to as long as 30 years. The spectacular increase in homebuilding in the decades following World War II fueled a tremendous expansion in the U.S. economy as a whole.

Supporters of FHA contend that government-sponsored mortgage insurance made lending more efficient, because it made lenders more willing to hold mortgages. In 1968 Congress extended the FHA's power to subsidize construction of inner-city apartment buildings for renting to low-income tenants.

The Reagan administration has proposed changes in the nation's housing programs. One change would be to sell all or part of the FHA to private investors. Private firms say they can handle the job of making and insuring mortgages without government help.

Another change would give families *housing vouchers* for purchasing housing. Families could "spend" their vouchers for any kind of housing they want, and the landlord would be reimbursed from government funds.

Critics object to the sale of the FHA because the agency earns profit for the government every year. They wonder if private mortgage insurers would have the financial backing to survive a period of heavy defaults, and they conclude that the government would still be left with the riskiest mortgages. They point out that vouchers cannot guarantee that suitable housing will be available for low-income families.

Question for Discussion

1. Discuss the arguments for and against government involvement in home mortgage lending. Consider the issue in terms of efficiency, equity and externalities.

MONEY AND BANKING IN PRACTICE: NEW TYPES OF MORTGAGES

Savings and loan associations were once the major source of mortgage loans, but competition from other lenders has encouraged them to develop new types of mortgages. Variable rate mortgages are an example. Long-term lending for home mortgages tends to lock in interest income at rates prevailing in the past. When current rates on savings deposits rise, S&L profits decline or disappear. With variable rate mortgages S&Ls can raise rates charged on existing mortgages when current market rates rise and reduce rates when market rates fall.

Regulations limit the frequency and the amount of interest rate changes allowed, but the result has provided some profit protection for S&Ls. Variable rate mortgages have also helped many borrowers who might not be able to get long-term mortgage loans otherwise. Some S&Ls offer graduated payment mortgages, calling for low mortgage payments in the early years of home ownership and higher payments later.

These mortgages are attractive to young families whose income might be expected to rise throughout the term of their home mortgage.

In the late 1970s an old type of mortgage lending suddenly became respectable again: *second mortgages*, in the form of home equity loans. In years past, second mortgages were generally made to homeowners who were having financial difficulties and who needed to use their home as collateral for a new loan. In the 1970s many homeowners were facing a more pleasant situation. Inflation had increased the market value of existing homes far above the mortgage loan initially borrowed to purchase them. This left substantial *equity* in the hands of borrowers. (In this sense, equity is the difference between current market value and the remaining balance on the existing mortgage.)

Banks, mortgage companies and even finance companies began to offer home equity loans to these fortunate homeowners. Interest rates were higher and payback time shorter than for a first mortgage. But still home equity loans were a popular device for making use of inflation-generated gains in property values and for providing funds for workers whose incomes were lagging behind inflation. Some first-time home buyers used home equity loans to help with the initial purchase of their home. A home equity loan provided the cash to buy out the current owner and assume the existing first mortgage at the lower interest rates prevailing in past years.

Question for Discussion

1. What are the disadvantages of home equity loans?

Efficiency, Equity and Externalities

To involve governments in financial markets is a form of artificial credit allocation that may or may not benefit the economy. Government lending institutions and programs should be evaluated in terms of their efficiency and equity.

In general, free markets are believed to allocate resources more efficiently when they are allowed to operate without government interference. Free markets adjust price and output according to supply and demand:

1. High prices serve to ration scarce resources toward users whose needs are most urgent. Also, high prices encourage greater production of scarce goods and services.
2. Low prices make it possible for less urgent needs to be satisfied and discourage production of relatively plentiful goods and services.

Just as is true in the markets for goods, interest rates work to make financial markets more efficient. High real interest rates discourage excessive borrowing and encourage greater lending. The result is to allocate the available supply of financial capital efficiently according to the urgency of borrowers' needs. When government institutions intervene in the allocation of financial capital, the result may be a decrease in efficiency.

Government intervention in credit markets may affect equity as well. Equity refers to fairness in the distribution of the benefits and costs generated by our economic system. Many of us believe that persons who enjoy benefits should pay the costs. To a great extent, free markets achieve this kind of equity, because goods cannot be purchased unless the buyer is willing to pay the cost. When government intervenes in markets, however, this is no longer necessarily true. Governments use revenues collected from all taxpayers to provide subsidized loans to persons in particular groups. The result is a distribution of costs and benefits different from that in free markets—and a possible decrease in equity.

The decrease in efficiency and equity has been a basis for criticism of government-sponsored financial intermediaries and lending programs. Critics believe that financial markets should be allowed to operate freely without government intervention. Supporters of the present arrangement, however, argue that government intervention in credit allocation produces some positive externalities that might not be achieved in free markets. Positive externalities are extra benefits the community receives in addition to the actual goods or services exchanged in the market. (Negative externalities are the extra costs a community pays in addition to costs paid in the market: noise, traffic congestion, loss of woodlands and wildlife and so forth.) Widespread homeownership, for instance, is believed to convey certain benefits to the community as a whole: civic pride, family stability, respect for law and property, and economic incentives. For these benefits, some say, the community should be willing to subsidize through its tax payments greater home ownership among all classes of income earners.

Cyclical Instability

A more serious criticism of government-sponsored financial intermediaries and public lending programs arises from the dilemma policymakers face when designing policy for mortgage lending. Because housing construction involves so many small business firms and employs so many workers, it is especially hard hit by lack of credit. But for these same reasons, home construction is an appropriate sector for restraining total spending when the economy is approaching a boom. Policymakers must restrain homebuilding without severely damaging the industry—a difficult, if not impossible, job.

Government-sponsored financial intermediaries and lending programs represent an attempt to soften the impact of a credit crunch. Occasionally they do their job too well, offsetting completely the effect of high interest rates. Housing may continue to receive too much credit, and total spending may continue to grow too fast. Critics complain that housing is protected too well, and that the protection given to housing worsens inflationary pressures and increases the dangers of a future collapse.

MONEY AND BANKING IN PRACTICE: FINANCIAL INTERMEDIARIES AND ECONOMIC DEVELOPMENT: REDLINING

A healthy system of financial intermediaries is a necessary part of economic development. As a nation moves from a primitive economy to a modern industrialized economy, it must channel the idle funds of savers toward investors who will spend them productively. Capital investments for transportation facilities, electric power plants, steel mills and so forth help a nation grow, adding new specialization and diversity to its economy. Sustained economic progress is not likely to occur without financial intermediaries.

Financial intermediaries affect not only a nation's potential for growth and development, but also its direction. The uses of lending power help determine the kinds of capital investment that can be undertaken. Those projects favored by financial intermediaries will receive plentiful financial resources that virtually ensure their success. Other, not-so-favored projects may fail in spite of their basic soundness.

The issue of the direction of lending has become an important one for U.S. cities, and it gives policymakers a difficult dilemma. On the one hand, financial intermediaries are the guardians of the community's money; depositors entrust them with their savings for safekeeping. On the other hand, financial intermediaries are expected to make loans and investments that satisfy the community's needs for financial resources. Naturally, financial intermediaries want to use their depositors' funds for safe and profitable ventures. They want to avoid lending for risky, money-losing projects.

The dilemma arises from the need in many communities for funds to rehabilitate decaying urban neighborhoods. The movement to suburbia has left crime-infested slums in the hearts of many American cities. Efforts to repair, modernize and beautify these areas are costly and depend on long-term loans.

It is hoped that rehabilitation will increase the value of urban property, enabling borrowers to repay loans with interest. Even more important, rehabilitation in one area is expected to encourage similar efforts throughout the city.

Probably financial intermediaries are sincere in their desires to see all these good results come about. But they remember also their responsibility as guardians of their depositors' savings. They are reluctant to lend in neighborhoods where vandalism and crime may make their loans uncollectible. Furthermore, they worry that a single isolated rehabilitation project in the midst of

ugly blight cannot remain successful for very long.

Many financial intermediaries have been accused of *redlining*; that is, drawing a red line on city maps setting off certain neighborhoods where rehabilitation loans will not be made. City officials have been understandably unhappy about such policies, and financial intermediaries have looked for ways to resolve their dilemma. In many cities they have joined together in syndicates building a fund for urban rehabilitation projects. In this way the risks of default are spread over a number of institutions, and depositors' money is safe. Financial intermediaries can fulfill an important obligation to the community without neglecting their responsibility to depositors and stockholders.

Questions for Discussion

1. What are the proper concerns of financial intermediaries that engage in redlining?

2. What government policies might help resolve this dilemma of a shortage of funds in urban neighborhoods?

3. What are the efficiency-equity-externalities arguments relevant to this issue?

MONEY AND BANKING IN PRACTICE: FINANCIAL SUPERMARKETS?

The growth in demand for consumer credit has produced new opportunities for other business firms, not typically regarded as financial intermediaries. Because these institutions are not actually banks or S&Ls, they escape some of the regulations that limit the activities

of true financial intermediaries. One such institution is Sears. Along with other giant retail establishments, Sears is beginning to offer some of the same services as banks and thrift institutions.

Sears already owns 45 S&L branches and numerous insurance subsidiaries. Its vast listings of retail customers provide the means for communicating with savers and borrowers across the country. Sears plans to offer its charge customers small-denomination bonds paying interest rates that keep pace with market rates. It already provides checkable deposits for employees through its credit union; expanding its deposit services and transferring funds to its S&L subsidiaries would be relatively easy. Sears credit cards provide consumer loans to holders across the United States and in other nations where Sears operates retail stores. Sears borrows from citizens in other countries, too, through the sale of bonds denominated in foreign currencies.

Merrill Lynch is also a complex financial intermediary. It carries on the functions of an investment bank, underwriting large blocks of securities for corporate borrowers and reselling them to the public. It is also a brokerage firm, holding *margin accounts* for individuals and trading securities in their names. Margin accounts constitute an individual investor's down payment for security purchases. The remaining portion of a security's purchase price is usually borrowed from the brokerage firm, which in turn borrows from banks. Stockholder dividends and gains from appreciation of stock prices are added to the owner's margin account. As long as the margin account represents the required fraction of the value of a customer's stock holdings, the customer may write checks against it. Or customers may use Merrill Lynch credit cards, in effect borrowing against these accounts. Services like these are so similar to those offered by banks that many banks are complaining of the competition.

Questions for Discussion

1. Could the services offered by nonbank financial intermediaries interfere with efforts of the monetary authorities to control the quantity of money in the nation's economy?

2. How might "financial supermarkets" affect the efficiency of the nation's financial system?

Glossary of Terms

conventional mortgage. a home loan made by a bank or savings and loan association to a home buyer without the intervention of a government agency

disintermediation. withdrawing funds from a financial intermediary for the direct purchase of securities

ERISA. The Employee Retirement Income Security Act, passed by Congress in 1976 to mandate standards of retirement plans

indexed funds. investment funds that own a portfolio of assets corresponding to those used in a particular market index

money market certificate. a short-term savings instrument issued by savings and loan associations in denominations of $10,000 and earning interest tied to the Treasury bill rate

NOW accounts. savings accounts in mutuals and savings and loans on which checks can be written

pensions. funds in which worker and employer contributions accumulate for investment

second mortgage. a mortgage whose collateral is the homeowner's equity

share drafts. check-like devices for making payments from shares held in credit unions

yield. the return on an asset including interest earned and increase in resale value

Summary of Important Ideas

1. Financial intermediaries stand between savers and spenders and aid the process of lending and borrowing. Their sources of funds are deposits, borrowings and capital accounts. Their uses include investment portfolios that provide a balance of yield, safety and liquidity appropriate to the needs of particular institutions.

2. Savings and loan associations acquire funds at interest rates, some of which are subject to legal ceilings; but shareholders may practice disintermediation when market rates rise higher than the ceiling. Higher costs of funds and savings outflows reduce profits on a portfolio of long-term mortgages earning stable rates.

3. Mutual savings banks are chartered in a few states and offer NOW accounts as well as traditional deposits.

4. Life insurance companies experience larger and more predictable premium payments and claims than casualty companies. Therefore they make larger and more risky investments.

5. Finance companies acquire funds from bank loans or sale of debt, and they lend to consumers. Loans are relatively risky and interest rates relatively high.

6. Credit unions acquire funds from members' savings and make consumer and real estate loans. Their costs are low and risks are low, helping to keep interest rates low also.

7. Investment companies enable small savers to purchase shares in a diversified portfolio of corporate or government securities.

8. Funded pension funds purchase income-earning assets with regular employee and employer contributions.

9. Specialization among financial intermediaries is a result of different sources of funds and different tax treatment. Most intermediaries behave as hedgers. Savings flows through financial intermediaries respond to expected yield and have the effect of allocating financial capital to sectors of greatest demand.

10. Rising market rates of interest may reduce savings flows to housing, causing painful adjustments. The Federal National Mortgage Association, the Government National Mortgage Association, and the Federal Home Loan Mortgage Company purchase existing mortgages from primary lenders, providing funds for new lending when needed. Mortgage loans are guaranteed and insured by the Veterans' Administration and the Federal Housing Administration. Housing districts may also acquire low interest funds for mortgage lending.

11. Government intervention in financial markets may reduce the efficiency and equity associated with free markets, but intervention may be appropriate when there are positive externalities. Government credit programs may contribute to cyclical instability, however.

Questions for Discussion and Research

1. Discuss the significance of financial intermediaries for national economic growth. How do they contribute to stability or instability? What is their role in the allocation of resources?

2. What considerations affect selection of a financial intermediary's portfolio? How do these considerations differ among institutions?

3. Does disintermediation result in more efficient or less efficient allocation of capital resources? Defend your answer.

4. Explain the limitations of S&Ls in dealing with the problem of disintermediation.

5. Distinguish between the goals and limitations of each of the following pairs: life insurance companies and casualty insurance companies, finance companies and credit unions, investment companies and pension funds, funded and unfunded pension plans.

6. Define: NOW accounts, share drafts, ERISA.

7. Explain the statement that most financial intermediaries are hedgers. What dangers accompany speculation by financial intermediaries?

8. Illustrate the process by which FNMA, GNMA and FHLMC make mortgage funds available to S&Ls. Why would private investors be willing

to purchase the securities of government-sponsored or quasi-government institutions like these? Consult recent issues of *The Wall Street Journal* for information on current returns on these securities.

9. Discuss the important externalities involved in a healthy homebuilding sector. To what extent should positive externalities govern decisions to subsidize the housing sector? How is the housing sector currently affecting the nation's economic activity?

10. What are the problems and opportunities associated with shareholder participation in management of S&Ls? How much participation is likely? What may be the results in terms of S&L policy?

11. Before 1980, ceilings on interest paid on savings and time deposits enabled S&Ls to provide home mortgages at low rates. In effect, savers were subsidizing home ownership. Is this equitable? What information would be necessary before answering this question?

Additional Readings

Bray, Howard. "The FHA: Selling Off a Dream. *Across the Board* (June 1986): 8–14.

Cooper, Kerry and Donald R. Fraser. *Banking Deregulation and the New Competition in Financial Services,* Student Edition. Cambridge, Massachusetts: Ballinger Publishing Co., 1986.

Gilbert, R. Alton, and Jean M. Lovati. "Disintermediation: An Old Disorder with a New Remedy." *Federal Reserve Bank of St. Louis Review* 61 (January 1979): 10–15.

"Home Equity." *Business Week*, February 9, 1987, cover story.

MacLaury, Bruce K. "Federal Credit Programs—The Issues They Raise," *Issues in Debt Management Conference Series* 10. Federal Reserve Bank of Boston, June 1973.

Massaro, Vincent. "The Expanding Role of Federally Sponsored Agencies." *The Conference Board Record* (April 1971): 14–20.

"The Best Mutual Funds." *Business Week*, February 23, 1987, cover story.

CHAPTER

7

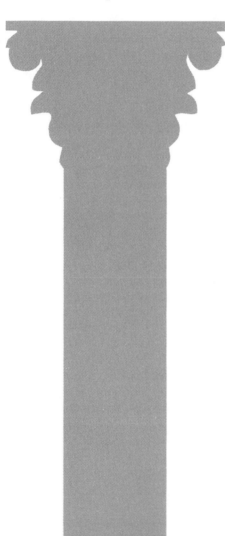

LEARNING OBJECTIVES

■ To understand the global benefits
that come from international
specialization and trade

■ To show how the internal terms of
trade and global demand for a
nation's speciality determine the
external terms of trade

■ To explain how changing demand
or changing national policies can
affect the terms of trade

■ To demonstrate the determination
and functioning of exchange rates

The Use of Money in International Trade

"Global interdependence is a reality. There is no alternative to international collaboration if growth is to be sustained."

Henry Kissinger

One of the important parts of the U.S. Constitution is the part that forbids barriers to trade among the states. The farmers and merchants who wrote the Constitution understood the benefits of the free flow of goods. In contrast to Europe, where national boundaries separated markets, the United States was assured a large free trade area.

Free trade means that regions are not forced to be self-sufficient. Each region can specialize in the types of production it does best and sell to the entire market. Producing for a larger market brings the benefits of *economies of scale*. Economies of scale are the lower unit costs that frequently result from using larger quantities of capital resources—together with land, labor and entrepreneurial resources—to produce a larger volume of output. Furthermore, specialization enables a region to develop technologies and improve worker skills for still greater productive efficiency over time. When the growth of industry as a whole brings lower costs to individual firms, we say there are positive externalities. An example of a positive externality is the development of supplying industries that sprang up to serve the auto manufacturing industry in Michigan.

Specialization for trade brings one disadvantage. When regions give up their self-sufficiency, they become dependent on each other for those goods produced elsewhere. Thus specialization has two results: greater total production, which comes from developing special skills and capabilities, and interdependence, which comes from a loss of self-sufficiency. Interdependence makes trade necessary, and greater total production increases living standards.

We have freely enjoyed the benefits of trade within the United States, and we enjoy to a degree the benefits of trade with other nations. International trade involves the same loss of self-sufficiency, the same interdependence and even greater gains from specialization as trade within the nation. But it involves also different money systems among nations, different cost and tax structures, and different government policies with respect to trade, all of which make international trade more complicated than trade within a single nation.

In this chapter we will examine the use of money in international trade. We will show how supply and demand in global markets determine the terms of trade among nations and how national currencies are used to finance trade. Then we will look at some of the problems and opportunities that follow changes in trade patterns.

Specialization

Specialization and trade are based on regional differences that give particular production advantages: Washington state produces apples, and the valley around Palo Alto in northern California produces integrated circuits. The advantage in the first case has to do with climate; in the second, with an abundance of electrical engineers. We say that Washington state and northern California have *absolute advantage* in these kinds of production.

Absolute Advantage

A region that has absolute advantage can produce a particular good or service at lower cost than it can be produced elsewhere. We have seen that lower costs can result from climate or from the abundance of particular labor resources used in production. Land resources may also provide absolute advantage, as sheltered harbors provide the shipbuilding industry in New England and coalfields the mining industry in Appalachia. Technology and capital resources can provide absolute advantage if a region devotes its research and development efforts toward improvements in the production of, say, automotive equipment in Michigan and chemical products in New Jersey and Delaware. (Does your region enjoy absolute advantage in any particular kind of production?)

With absolute advantage a region can trade its low-cost products for low-cost items produced elsewhere; citizens of both regions can live better as a result. But it is not necessary for a region to have absolute advantage to enjoy the benefits of trade. Trade yields benefits even when a region does not produce any good or service at lowest cost. In this case specialization and trade involve producing the good in which the region has *comparative advantage*.

Comparative Advantage

To understand comparative advantage, it is necessary to understand opportunity costs. Remember that most resources can be used to produce a variety of goods and services: land can be used for agriculture or modern factories, labor can build automobiles or write computer software, and capital equipment can produce cloth or aircraft parts. Whenever resources are allocated to one kind of production, the economy sacrifices the other kinds of goods and services that could have been produced. The sacrifice in other goods and services is called *opportunity costs*.

Specialization according to comparative advantage means that the nation produces those goods and services with lowest opportunity costs relative to their opportunity costs in other nations. Suppose there are two regions, East and West, with different resource endowments and technologies. For each year of labor available for production, East and West can produce the following quantities of food and machines:

	Food	*Machines*
East	100 bushels	60 machines
West	150 bushels	75 machines

Notice that West has absolute advantage in the production of both food and machines. This is the result of particular climate, resource or technological features that enable West to produce more with each labor–year.

Lacking absolute advantage in the production of either food or machines, East still has comparative advantage. To determine comparative advantage, calculate the opportunity cost of each bushel of food and each machine. Because a single labor–year could produce 100 bushels of food or 60 machines, the opportunity cost of a single bushel of food is: $60/100 = .6$ machine. The opportunity cost of a machine is: $100/60 = 1.7$ bushels. Opportunity costs per unit in both countries are:

	Food	*Machines*
East	.6 machine	1.7 bushels
West	.5 machine	2 bushels

Now compare opportunity costs in the two countries. Because East's opportunity costs are lower in the production of machines, East should specialize in machine production. West has lower opportunity costs in the production of food and should specialize in producing food.

Now suppose both nations have 100 labor–years to use in production, and they specialize according to comparative advantage. With specialization, total world production is:

	Food	*Machines*
East		60 × 100 = 6,000
West	150 × 100 = 15,000	

In order for both nations to enjoy some quantity of both goods, trade is necessary.

Establishing the Terms of Trade

Specialization requires an end to self-sufficiency and the beginning of international interdependence. An arrangement must be found for exchanging East's machines for food produced in West. The quantity of goods received per unit of goods paid out is called the *terms of trade*. The terms of trade by which goods are exchanged depend on opportunity costs of production in the producing nation and global demand for the nation's speciality.

The Internal Terms of Trade

To illustrate, East will be willing to trade its machines for food for a price that at least covers the cost of producing machines, expressed in terms of the opportunity cost of not producing food. Remember that the opportunity cost of machines in East is 1.7 bushels of food. Therefore, one machine must sell for at least 1.7 bushels of food: 1 machine equals 1.7 bushels of food. Otherwise, East could not afford to forego production of 1.7 bushels of food to produce each machine. It would be better not to produce the machine and to produce its own food instead.

What is the highest price West will pay for machines? The answer depends on the cost in West of producing its own machines. Remember that in West the opportunity cost of each machine is 2 bushels of food. Therefore, West will pay no more than 2 bushels of food for each machine: 1 machine equals 2 bushels of food. If West must pay more than 2 bushels of food for 1 machine, then it should produce machines and trade them for food. The ratios are:

(East) 1 Machine = 1.7 Bushels of Food

and

(West) 1 Machine = 2 Bushels of Food

The ratios are the *internal* terms of trade within East and West taken separately. They reflect the relative costs of producing two goods *inside* each nation, and they represent the limits within which exchange can take place *between the nations*.

The External Terms of Trade

We know that East will exchange one machine for no less than 1.7 bushels of food and West will exchange no more than 2 bushels of food for one machine. Thus, the values 1.7 and 2 are the minimum and maximum prices for machines, when price is expressed in terms of bushels of food. The actual ratio for which machines are exchanged for food must fall within this range.

The actual price ratio is called the *external* terms of trade and depends on the strength of demand for the two goods. The region producing the good in greatest demand will enjoy more of the gains from trade. If machines are in greater demand than food, for example, the external terms of trade will lie near the high limit of the range; say, 1 machine equals 2 bushels of food. The region producing machines (East) will enjoy more of the gains from trade.

Once the price of machines is established, the corresponding price of food is the inverse. Suppose West pays 2 bushels of food for 1 machine. If a machine costs 2 bushels of food, then food costs $1/2 = (.5)$ units of machines.

Now suppose food is in greater demand than machines, so that the external terms of trade lie near the low limit of the range, with 1 machine equal to 1.7 bushels of food. If a machine costs 1.7 bushels of food, then food costs $1/1.7 = (.59)$ units of machines. Thus, the price of a bushel of food can lie between .50 and .59 machines, depending on the strength of global demand for the two goods.

In this way, the gains from trade are divided among producing nations according to demand for their speciality.

The Effect of Changes in Costs of Production

This simple model of comparative advantage and trade can be expanded to include all nations in the world and all varieties of traded goods. The fundamental principles are the same:

1. Comparative advantage occurs when a nation produces a good or service at lower opportunity costs compared with those of other nations.
2. Nations specialize according to comparative advantage.
3. The limits of the terms of trade are the internal cost ratios for producing a nation's speciality.
4. The external terms of trade depend on global demand for particular specialities.

Some changes must be made in the simple model, however, to make it more realistic. One change involves production costs. By assuming constant opportunity costs for each good, we have also assumed that production costs are constant, regardless of the quantity the nation produces.

Economies of Scale

Constant production costs are possible only if the nation can continue to increase production of a particular good or service without experiencing changes in resource productivity. This is not a very realistic assumption for several reasons. First, we have noted that producing a large volume may yield economies of scale. Thus, specialization may initially bring increasing resource productivity and lower unit costs. On the other hand, when production reaches a very large volume, resource productivity may fall and costs rise. This suggests that total specialization in a particular kind of production may bring on *diseconomies of scale*.

Diminishing Marginal Product

Another basis for changing costs of production is the principle of *diminishing marginal product*. Diminishing marginal product occurs when resources are combined in various proportions.

In the short run, some of a nation's resources are said to be *fixed* in terms of quantity and function; their flexibility in production is limited as a result. Quantities of other resources are said to be *variable*; various amounts of these resources can be used together with a nation's existing stock of fixed resources. Factories and farmland are fixed resources in the short run. To use these fixed resources, various quantities of labor and equipment are added to produce goods for trade. There is some optimum combination of variable and fixed resources that yields the greatest output per unit of resource. To add more variable resources than this amount results in smaller additions to total product.

The principle of diminishing marginal product states that, beyond some optimum combination of variable and fixed resources, each additional unit of variable resources adds fewer units of output than the one before. The principle of diminishing marginal product has another side: If additional units of variable resources add fewer units of output, then the cost of each additional unit of output increases. When costs of production increase, the effect is an increase in the internal terms of trade for producing that good. The result is to narrow the range within which the actual terms of trade will occur. Transportation costs also have this result.

The optimum proportion of fixed and variable resources places limits on the degree of specialization in all nations. To attempt to use all resources in a single type of production would certainly exceed the optimum proportion and involve higher than minimum unit costs. Therefore, nations allocate their resources toward a variety of products. Instead of specializing completely, they continue to produce some goods because lack of comparative advantage is offset by the availability of certain fixed resources and by the costs of transporting the goods from abroad.

The Effect of Trade Restrictions

The terms of trade among nations may not depend exclusively on internal cost ratios and the strength of demand. Nations may impose restrictions on trade in an attempt to reduce the price paid for foreign goods and make their external terms of trade more favorable. We will have more to say about this possibility later.

Affecting the Terms of Trade

A nation's external terms of trade are significant in three fundamental ways:

1. The terms of trade determine the quantities of imports a nation receives for its exports and thereby affect living standards for its people.
2. The ability to trade makes possible new investments in capital resources, increasing the nation's capacity for producing its speciality.
3. Growth in productive capacity creates jobs to employ the nation's growing labor force.

The importance of its terms of trade for a nation's welfare has led to efforts to modify them for domestic advantage. To achieve more favorable terms of trade, some nations have established *commodity agreements* or *cartels*.

Commodity Agreements

Commodity agreements are international agreements to sell specific quantities of a particular export commodity. The effect is to limit and stabilize supply so as to keep the price of the export from falling and to maintain favorable terms of trade for the producing nations. The International Coffee Agreement is an example of a commodity agreement. Coffee-producing nations agree to hold excess coffee off the market when crops are good, to keep price from falling. They sell coffee from accumulated stockpiles when crops are poor, so that prices won't rise as steeply. Maintaining a stable supply in world markets protects coffee producers from drastic changes in terms of trade that would endanger their domestic economies. Similar agreements among producers of tin, sugar and copper also have this objective.

Commodity agreements are frequently difficult to enforce. When a surplus exists, a single producer has a strong incentive to throw excess supplies on the market, eventually depressing price for other producers. When a shortage exists, members may object to selling from stockpiles to keep price from rising. Commodity agreements often fall apart from conflicts like these.

Cartels

Cartels are more formal organizations for control of supply, but they are subject to the same internal conflicts. The Organization of Petroleum Exporting Countries (OPEC) is the world's most powerful cartel. Its purpose has been to improve the terms of trade for petroleum producers for the sake of domestic security and economic growth. OPEC's strategy has been to limit export quantities and keep price high. Conflict within the cartel has been the result primarily of different capacities for growth among OPEC nations, with different import needs. Nevertheless, their common interest in maintaining favorable terms of trade for the group as a whole has overcome these internal differences.

Tariffs

Terms of trade may also be changed by imposing a *tariff* on imports. A tariff is a tax on an imported good, raising the price of the import and encouraging purchase of domestically produced goods instead. The purpose of a tariff may be to protect local jobs, to encourage domestic industrial development, or to allow some strategic industry to operate without international competition.

When a tariff is paid to customs agents, the amount remaining to pay the foreign producer is less than it would be in the absence of a tariff. Thus, the price actually paid for imports falls relative to the price of exports, and the terms of trade improve. Needless to say, it is not possible for all nations to improve their terms of trade by imposing tariffs. The chief result of tariffs is to raise domestic prices, reduce specialization, reduce international competition and reduce the benefits of trade in general. Therefore, most nations now engage in regular negotiations to reduce tariffs. (We will have more to say about tariff negotiations in Chapter 19.)

Exchange Rates

Our discussion thus far has looked at trade as a barter arrangement in which goods are exchanged for other goods. Of course, trade seldom takes place without exchanging money. International currencies used for trade are called *foreign exchange*. Different values for international currencies make international trade more complex than domestic trade. The values of currencies must be clearly established in terms of each other before trade can take place.

For many years currency values were measured in terms of gold. In Chapter 2 we described how the gold standard worked. Where

$$\$1 = 0.029 \text{ ounce of gold and}$$

$$\pounds1 = .1 \text{ ounce of gold}$$

then

$$\$1/\pounds1 = 0.029 \text{ oz.}/.1 \text{ oz.}$$

$$\$1 = \pounds0.29.$$

Currency values remained stable because of gold shipments. A rise in the dollar price of pounds, for example, would lead U.S. importers to buy gold instead, shipping gold to Britain where it could be exchanged for currency at the guaranteed price. A fall in the dollar price of pounds would lead U.S. exporters to exchange pounds for gold in Britain, shipping gold to the United States where it could be exchanged for dollars at the guaranteed price.

The gold standard limited the quantity of currency a nation could print. Limits were necessary because paper currency might be brought to the Treasury for conversion to gold at any time. As national economies developed and trade expanded, more currency was needed, and the gold standard was finally abandoned. In 1945 in Bretton Woods, New Hampshire, representatives of trading nations agreed to establish a new standard for international currencies, the Gold-Exchange Standard. Under the new system, only the dollar would be denominated in terms of gold, and other currencies would be denominated in terms of the dollar. Instead of redeeming their currencies in gold, nations could redeem in other foreign exchange. The currency most often used in exchange was the dollar, making the new standard, in effect, a Gold-Dollar Standard.

Under the Gold-Dollar Standard, currency values were determined as follows:

$$1 \text{ oz. Gold} = \$35 = \pounds10.$$

Therefore:

$$\$1 = \pounds.29.$$

It was expected that currency values would remain stable so that prices of traded goods would not fluctuate widely and disturb markets.

Fixed exchange rates for international currencies were difficult to maintain. The reasons were different rates of economic growth among nations and changing currency values in the domestic economies. The United States, in particular, experienced strong growth during the 1940s and 1950s; the money supply grew to accommodate the needs of business, and its domestic purchasing power declined. Growth in U.S. imports was financed by rising exports and by the income from U.S.-owned investments abroad. Imports grew faster than exports, however, so that more U.S. dollars were paid out than the United States earned in foreign exchange. Excess supply of dollars in foreign exchange markets gradually depleted our stocks of gold and foreign exchange, as many foreign holders of dollars redeemed them for currencies to be spent elsewhere.

Whenever other nations experienced similar losses, a remedy was available. When holdings of gold and foreign exchange began to be depleted, a nation could reduce its currency's value in terms of gold and the dollar. A decrease in value meant that fewer units of gold or foreign exchange would be paid out per unit of domestic currency brought in for redemption. For a government to reduce the value of its currency is called *devaluation*; to increase the currency's value is called *revaluation*. Under the Bretton Woods agreement, devaluation greater than 10 percent could take place only in conditions of extreme emergency and after consultation with other parties to the agreement.

Because the U.S. dollar was the cornerstone of the Gold-Dollar Standard, monetary authorities in the United States believed the United States should not independently devalue its currency. Devaluing the dollar would have meant a higher dollar price for gold but would not necessarily have changed the dollar price of all other currencies. In fact, to change the dollar price of gold would have no effect on relative currency values if other nations continued to exchange their currency for the dollar according to the old relationships. *To devalue the dollar against other currencies required that other nations agree to revalue theirs.* Revaluing other currencies relative to the dollar would have raised dollar prices of other currencies and made goods priced in these currencies more expensive in trade. At first other nations resisted the U.S. proposal to raise their currency values relative to the dollar. Finally, however, in 1973 agreement was finally reached to allow foreign exchange values to move up or down in response to market forces without systematic actions by governments to maintain fixed rates.

Floating Exchange Rates

When market supply and demand determine currency values, the result is *floating exchange rates*. Since 1973 most currencies have been allowed to float, with only minor actions by governments to interfere with market processes. Floating rates can be illustrated graphically.

FIGURE 7–1   The Market for Pounds

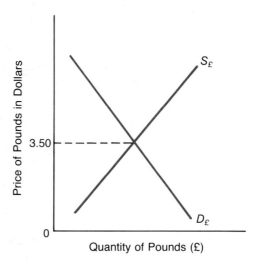

The equilibrium price for pounds occurs
where demand is equal to supply. The
market for dollars is the reverse of the
market for pounds, with demand for
pounds equivalent to the supply of dollars
and the supply of pounds equivalent to the
demand for dollars. The price of dollars in
terms of pounds would be $1 = £1/3.50,
or £.286.

Figure 7–1 represents the market for foreign exchange, where pounds
are bought with dollars. The horizontal axis measures the quantities of pounds;
the vertical axis measures price in dollars. The demand curve marks the
quantities of pounds that will be bought at various prices.

The demand for pounds arises out of the desire to purchase British
goods, to make investments in Britain or to lend to British borrowers. The
higher the dollar price of pounds, the less urgent is the desire to buy pounds
for these purposes. The lower the price, the greater is the desire for pounds.
Thus, the demand for pounds is a typical demand curve, sloping downward
from left to right.

Similarly, the supply curve is the quantities of pounds that will be sold
for various prices. The supply of pounds arises out of the desire of Britons
to exchange their pounds for dollars when they need dollars to purchase
U.S. goods, to make investments in the United States, or to lend to U.S.
citizens or businesses. If the price of pounds is high, more pounds will be

supplied; if the price is low, fewer pounds will be supplied. Therefore, the supply of pounds is drawn as a typical, upward-sloping supply curve.

The market exchange rate is determined at equilibrium, where the supply of pounds is equal to demand. For any higher price, there would be a surplus of pounds and price would fall. For a lower price, there would be a shortage and price would rise. In Figure 7–1 supply is equal to demand at an exchange rate of $3.50. Thus, £1 equals $3.50.

Note that the reverse of Figure 7–1 would be the market for dollars. The supply of pounds would be the demand for dollars in the reverse market, and the demand for pounds would be the supply of dollars. This is because a supplier of pounds is at the same time a demander of dollars, and vice versa. The exchange rate is the reverse also: $3.50 = £1 and $1 = (£1 ÷ $3.50) = £.29.

Arbitrage

Exchange rates between currencies tend toward equal values in all markets. This is because of currency *arbitrage*. Arbitrage is the simultaneous purchase and sale of two currencies with the aim of making a profit. Suppose, for example, that £1 was selling for $4.00 in the United States and $3.00 were selling for £1 in Great Britain. An arbitrager could make an immediate profit of $1 by buying a pound for $3 in Britain and reselling it immediately for $4 in the United States.

In this example, an arbitrage profit is possible because pounds are cheaper in Britain and dollars are cheaper in the United States. By buying pounds in Britain the arbitrager pushes their price up; by selling pounds in the United States (buying dollars) the arbitrager pushes their price down. Whenever currency values are out of line in various markets, arbitragers can be expected to move in for a quick, no-risk profit. The result is to bring market exchange rates back toward a single equilibrium level in all markets.

Changes in Exchange Rates

Changes in trading, investment, and lending plans shift currency demand and supply curves and change the equilibrium exchange rate. An increase in demand for pounds might result from the increasing popularity of British goods and vacations in British nations, an improved outlook for British investments, or a greater willingness to make loans to British firms or make deposits in British banks. Whatever its source, an increase in demand shifts the demand curve to the right and raises the exchange rate for pounds. Remember that demanders of pounds are also suppliers of dollars (or yen, marks, francs or zlotys). An increase in demand for pounds and a higher exchange rate implies an increase in supply of another currency (or currencies) and a correspondingly lower exchange rate. In Figure 7–2 the increased

FIGURE 7–2　The Market for Pounds

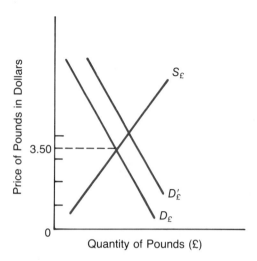

An increase in demand for pounds raises
the pound's exchange rate (and reduces
the exchange rate for dollars).

demand for pounds causes their price to rise so that $4.00 equals £1. In the
reverse market, the price of dollars falls to £1/$4, or £.25.

Changes in currency demand and supply may result also from the actions of currency speculators. Speculators buy and sell various currencies
with the goal of making a profit. Speculators differ from arbitragers because
they do not simultaneously buy and sell. They may take a *long position—*
buying more of a single currency than they really want—or a *short position—*
selling quantities of a currency they do not yet own. Whether a speculator
makes a profit depends on which currencies rise in value and which currencies fall. If a speculator is long in a currency that rises in value, he or
she makes a profit. Or if a speculator is short in a currency that falls, he or
she can buy the currency at a lower price to satisfy the sale contract at a
profit. If a reverse change takes place, the speculator loses. Clearly, speculation is more risky than arbitrage.

Speculation also has an effect on a currency's exchange rate, often on
the basis of what speculators expect to happen to a currency's value. Thus,
if speculators expect a currency to rise in value, they will tend to buy,
increasing demand and increasing its exchange rate. As buyers in one market,
speculators are also sellers in another, increasing the supply of a currency
whose value they expect to fall. This type of speculation is said to be *de-*

stabilizing because the effect is to worsen whatever tendencies speculators expect for exchange rates.

Exchange Rates and Purchasing Power Parity

Exchange rates reflect the relative values of currencies used in international transactions. Under a floating system, they fluctuate with supply and demand in foreign exchange markets. Underlying the value of a currency's exchange rate is its usefulness for purchasing goods, services and investments or for making loans in the nation that issued it. Thus, the domestic purchasing power of a currency helps determine its value in international trade.

Suppose a representative collection of goods, services and investments costs $350 in the United States and the same collection costs £100 in Great Britain. With a price ratio of

$$P_{US}/P_{GB} = \$350/\pounds100,$$

the exchange rate for pounds would be $350/£100, so that $3.50 equals £1. Because costs of producing particular goods differ in the two nations, it is not likely that individual price ratios will precisely equal the exchange rate. After all, it is differences in prices that yield the benefits from trade. If identical pairs of shoes cost $50 in the United States and £14.29 in Great Britain, there would be no need for trade at all (because a U.S. consumer would have to pay £14.29 times $3.50, or $50, for the British product).

Still, relative purchasing power—and, specifically, changes in purchasing power—are important for determining exchange rates. Relative purchasing power of currencies varies with inflation rates in various countries. To illustrate, suppose 10 percent inflation in the United States pushes the price of the collection of goods and services to $350 times 1.10, or $385. Zero inflation in Great Britain keeps the British price at £100. With a price ratio of $385/£100, the exchange rate for pounds becomes $385/£100, so that $3.85 equals £1. The dollar price of pounds should rise to offset the reduced purchasing power of the dollar. Alternatively, the value of a dollar falls from £100/$350 (with $1 equal to £.29) to £100/$385, so that $1 equals £.26. Ten percent greater inflation in the United States should produce a 10 percent drop in the dollar's exchange rate.

When exchange rates correctly reflect purchasing power in the two nations, there is *purchasing power parity*. Purchasing power parity means that the exchange rate for two currencies equals the ratio of their domestic purchasing power. Purchasing power parity seldom exists in the real world, because many unrelated factors influence supply and demand in foreign exchange markets. Movements of speculative currency holdings are an important example. But over the long run, and in the absence of repeated shocks in currency markets, we might expect exchange rates to tend toward the value that reflects the ratio of their purchasing power.

Let us consider again the representative collection of goods, services and investments in the two nations. The $350 price in the United States might include $90 worth of food, $140 of clothing and $120 of gasoline. In Great Britain the £100 price includes £50 of food, £40 of clothing and £10 of gasoline. Compare the price ratios for particular goods with the total price ratio:

$$\$90/\pounds50 \neq \$140/\pounds40 \neq \$120/\pounds10 \neq \$350/\pounds100.$$

Differences between individual price ratios and the total ratio suggest cost differences and comparative advantage. Thus, with a U.S. price level 3.5 times that of Great Britain ($350/£100, or 3.5), the United States sells food comparatively cheaply at $90/£50, or 1.8 times the price in Great Britain. Gasoline is much more costly at $120/£10, or 12 times the price in Great Britain. Clothing is priced no differently from the aggregate U.S./G.B. price ratio: $140/£40, or 3.5. We might conclude that the United States should import gasoline from Britain and export food. Both nations may become self-sufficient in clothing manufacture.

Dynamic Aspects of Trade

We have shown how comparative advantage determines specialization, how opportunity costs and demand determine external terms of trade, and how currency exchange rates reflect all these variables and allow trade to take place. Our discussion has been static: as if all conditions remain constant long enough for us to describe and analyze the forces affecting international exchange. Of course, this is not true in the real world. Conditions in the real world are dynamic, with constantly changing production costs, changing demand and changing exchange rates as traders and speculators react to these fundamental changes. New circumstances bring disruption to existing markets, often requiring painful readjustments by domestic consumers and producers. Some examples are familiar.

1. Commodity agreements raise coffee prices, force a drop in consumption and cause consumers to shift to other beverages. The oil cartel raises petroleum prices and forces changes in where we live, how we dress and how we work. In both cases, U.S. consumers live less well as we export more of our nation's wealth for each unit of foreign product we import.

2. Apparel manufacturers lose comparative advantage as low-wage producers abroad gain in this labor-intensive industry. Steel mak-

ers are inefficient because of the use of obsolete equipment, but the loss of profits to more technically advanced producers abroad makes new capital investment impossible. In both cases, U.S. workers lose job security, and business firms face heavy losses.

3. The United States develops personal computers, but producing and assembling computers become simplified to the extent that low-wage manufacturers in Japan capture markets formerly controlled by U.S. firms. Resources in the United States shift from production of computers to computer software.

The changing pattern of U.S. exports and imports over the recent decade is shown in Table 7–1. Our largest exports continue to be capital goods, constituting about a third of total exports. Exports of other industrial supplies and materials and food commodities have declined as a portion of total exports.

TABLE 7–1 Merchandise Trade of the United States (totals in billions of dollars)

	Percent of Total							
	Exports				*Imports*			
	1970	*1975*	*1980*	*1986*	*1970*	*1975*	*1980*	*1986*
Foods, Feeds, and Beverages	17%	21%	19%	9%	16%	10%	7%	6%
Industrial Supplies and Materials	29	25	29	27	31	24	22	18
Capital Goods, except Automotive	35	34	33	36	10	10	12	19
Auto Vehicles, Parts, etc.	9	10	8	11	14	12	11	20
Other	10	10	11	15	22	16	16	28
Petroleum and Products	NA	NA	NA	NA	7	27	32	9
Total Trade	$42.5	$107.1	$224.3	$217.0	$39.9	$98.2	$249.8	$373.3

The greatest changes have occurred in U.S. imports. The total value of imports has increased faster than exports, and imports of petroleum products, capital goods and auto vehicles constitute larger shares of imports. Food imports have declined sharply.

Changes in trading relationships impose hardships on U.S. consumers and workers. We would call these effects *microeconomic* effects, because they disrupt individual markets. All the individual microeconomic effects of changing trade relationships combine to yield *macroeconomic* effects. Macroeconomic effects are reflected in a trading nation's total output and employment and the general price level. Our concerns here are primarily macroeconomic, because we are focusing on the money supply and its relationship to total production. We will be interested in how changing trade patterns affect the nation's money supply and, in turn, the level of economic activity.

MONEY AND BANKING IN PRACTICE: CHANGING THE NATION'S TERMS OF TRADE

Over the past 15 years the United States has undergone a fundamental change in trading relationships that threatens our nation's prosperity. Unless U.S. industries can regain their comparative advantage in highly valued manufactured goods, we will continue to lose markets to foreign competition. As our terms of trade continue to decline, we will be able to import fewer goods and services for every unit of goods and services we export. The result will be that our own standards of living will eventually suffer.

During the years when U.S. manufacturing firms dominated major markets around the world, advances in the quality of U.S. products fell behind the great advances that were occurring in Japan and in other newly industrializing countries (NICs). Today, many U.S. manufacturers spend as much as 20 to 30 percent of production costs to locate and correct product defects. Most modern manufacturing processes require hundreds of separate operations, any one of which could malfunction and cause a product defect. It takes sophisticated statistical tools to identify the

source of problems before the problems become costly.

U.S. engineers have pioneered in quality control, but U.S. industries have been slow to implement their programs. Early in the 1980s, U.S. auto manufacturers discovered that the Japanese were building better cars, and soon after, manufacturers of semiconductors made the same discovery. Textiles, steel and major appliance manufacturers had learned the same lesson a decade earlier. Today, all these industries are pushing hard to cut costs and improve product quality.

Computer-based management is a key ingredient of the drive to improve quality. Computer information systems can identify design flaws and control purchasing and inventory.

Computerized statistical programs and the use of worker teams have succeeded in narrowing the quality gap for some U.S. autos. The use of automated robots has reduced labor costs and increased precision on auto assembly lines. Major appliance manufacturers have spent hundreds of millions of dollars to automate factories and improve product design. Production workers have been invited to participate in programs to evaluate production processes and suggest product improvements.

All of these efforts help to reduce costs of production and enhance comparative advantage in goods for which global demand is high. As consumers the world over regain their respect for the quality of U.S. products, we may expect the terms of trade to increase.

Question for Discussion

1. Explain how a decrease in a nation's terms of trade could lead to a "vicious cycle" of further decreases. How does your answer explain the need for a major effort to reverse tendencies in terms of trade?

Glossary of Terms

absolute advantage.   the ability of a producing unit to produce a good or service more cheaply than the good or service can be produced elsewhere

arbitrage.   the simultaneous purchase and sale of two currencies with the aim of making a profit

cartel.   an organization of producers for controlling the supply of an export good

commodity agreement.   an agreement to export specific quantities of a good

comparative advantage.   the ability to produce a good or service more cheaply in terms of its opportunity costs

devaluation.   reducing the value of one nation's currency in terms of other currencies

diminishing marginal product.   the principle that describes the decline in additional output as larger quantities of variable resources are added to fixed resources

diseconomies of scale.   the rising unit costs that result from producing a larger volume

economies of scale.   the lower unit costs that result from producing a larger volume

fixed resource.   a resource whose quantity is fixed in the short run

floating exchange rates.   exchange rates that fluctuate according to supply and demand

foreign exchange.   currency issued by a foreign government

purchasing power parity.   a condition in which exchange rates reflect the real domestic purchasing power of different currencies

revaluation.   increasing the value of one nation's currency in terms of other currencies

tariff.   a tax on imported goods and services

terms of trade.   the quantity of goods imported per unit of goods exported

variable resource.   a resource, various quantities of which can be added to available fixed resources

---

Summary of Important Ideas

1. Specialization in production leads to economies of scale and creates externalities that allow goods to be produced more efficiently. But specialization makes nations interdependent and makes trade necessary. Trade is based on the existence of absolute or comparative advantage.

2. The terms of trade determine the quantity of imported goods a nation receives per unit of goods it exports. External terms of trade depend on internal production costs and global demand. Changes in costs and demand affect a nation's gains from trade and require adjustments in production. Nations may manipulate their terms of trade through commodity agreements, cartels and tariffs.

3. International currency values were once denominated in gold. In 1945 the gold standard was modified to the Gold-Dollar Standard, and other currencies came to be denominated in dollars.

4. The outflow of U.S. dollars caused problems when conversion of dollars to gold and foreign currencies depleted our supply. In 1973 we devalued the dollar, other nations revalued their currencies, and currency values were allowed to float.

5. Changes in supply and demand affect a currency's value, and arbitrage brings values in line worldwide.

6. Under the purchasing power parity doctrine, international currency values should reflect their relative domestic purchasing power.

7. Exchange rates among currencies are determined in markets by supply and demand. Changes in trading, investment, and lending plans shift currency demand and supply curves and change the equilibrium exchange rate. Changes in demand and supply may also be the result of currency speculation.

Questions for Discussion and Research

1. Discuss the basis for the belief that trade leads to increasing world production of goods and services. What are the accompanying disadvantages?

2. Use the hypothetical information below to answer the questions that follow:

Output per Labor–Year		
	Wheat	*Trucks*
U.S.	200	25
U.S.S.R.	120	20

How would you describe the two nations with respect to absolute advantage and comparative advantage? How should each nation specialize? What are the limits to the terms of trade? Explain how the actual terms of trade would be determined.

3. What factors determine whether or not specialization will be complete? Explain the effect of external economies and diminishing marginal product.

4. To what extent does increased productivity in its speciality improve a nation's ability to trade? What other strategies are often used to enhance terms of trade?

5. Suppose the following relationships are true:

$$100 \text{ Fennings} = 1 \text{ oz. Gold}$$
$$1 \text{ Kira} = 5 \text{ oz. Gold}$$

What is the exchange rate between fennings and kira? Illustrate the process by which gold shipments ensure a stable exchange rate.

6. In what ways was the Gold-Dollar Standard an improvement over the gold standard? What new problems did it create?

7. Distinguish between stabilizing and destabilizing speculation. Show how speculators can profit from a fall in a currency's value.

8. How does purchasing power parity reduce or enhance efficiency in world trade and resource allocation? What factors may operate against purchasing power parity?

Additional Readings

Balback, Anatol B. "The Mechanics of Intervention in Exchange Markets." *Federal Reserve Bank of St. Louis Review* 60 (February 1978): 2–7.

Drucker, Peter F. "The Changed World Economy." *Foreign Affairs* (Spring 1986): 768–91.

Friedman, Milton. "The Case for Flexible Exchange Rates." In *Essays in Positive Economics*, Chicago: University of Chicago Press, 1966, 157–203.

The International Economic Report of the President. Washington: U.S. Government Printing Office, various years.

Luttrell, Clifton B. "Rising Farm Exports and International Trade Policies," *Federal Reserve Bank of St. Louis Review* 61 (July 1979): 3–10.

Mudd, Douglas R., and Geoffrey E. Wood. "Oil Imports and the Fall of the Dollar." *Federal Reserve Bank of St. Louis Review* 60 (August 1978): 2–6.

Wallich, Henry C. "What Makes Exchange Rates Move?" *Challenge* 20 (July/August 1977): 34–40.

Whalen, Richard. "No American Business Is an Island," *Across the Board* 17 (July 1980).

Wood, Geoffrey E., and Douglas R. Mudd. "The Recent U.S. Trade Deficit—No Cause for Panic." *Federal Reserve Bank of St. Louis Review* 60 (April 1978): 2–7.

PART II

How Much Money
Should There Be?

How much money should there be? How fast should money grow? Who should decide?

In Part I we discussed money in all its forms—from giraffes' tails to electronic impulses. We saw how the use of money brought economic growth and prosperity but also how the emergence of new money forms has complicated the job of managing money. Managing money efficiently is necessary if the nation is to enjoy stable growth and dependable purchasing power.

Because most of our money is created by commercial banks, much of our attention in Part II will be directed to banks. Understanding how commercial banks create money will help us understand the increasing money-creation powers of nonbank financial intermediaries. The nation's monetary policymakers must understand how banks operate and how the independent decisions of bankers are likely to affect the economy as a whole. Then they must establish procedures for helping all financial intermediaries operate more efficiently.

All this must be accomplished within a free economic system, where financial intermediaries are free and independent business firms. Deciding on a healthy level of individual freedom versus government control is a fundamental dilemma of our democratic system. We Americans want to ensure maximum freedom for creative effort, and we have been reluctant to impose controls, especially in the important area of finance. The following chapters will focus on this issue: how financial intermediaries influence the supply of money and how government regulation of credit can affect the efficiency, equity and positive externalities associated with our financial system.

CHAPTER

8

LEARNING OBJECTIVES

- To understand how changes in bank lending create or destroy money
- To calculate a money multiplier that shows the relationship between bank reserve accounts and the nation's money supply
- To see how the actions of banks may at times conflict with the goals of full employment and price stability

Banks and the Money Supply

Bank Manager: Where did you learn to count money so fast?
New Employee: Yale.
Bank Manager (impressed): Really! And what is your name, young man?
New Employee: Yim Yohnson.

Deciding on the correct quantity of money *and achieving it* are difficult in a complex economy like ours. In part, the reason is the variety of forms money can take. Whenever there have been restraints on the quantity of money, banks and nonbank financial intermediaries have cleverly created other credit instruments to serve as money. The result is a multitude of moneys, near moneys, and other liquid claims that perform the four functions of money: a medium of exchange, a standard of value, a store of value and a medium of deferred payments. It is difficult to measure or control the quantity of something that cannot be precisely defined.

Another problem with regulating money has to do with the various groups that actually decide and carry out decisions regarding the money supply. In the United States the chief responsibility for deciding monetary policy rests with the Federal Reserve System. We will have more to say about the structure and functions of this institution later. In addition to the Federal Reserve, the U.S. Treasury affects the money supply. Contrary to popular opinion, the Treasury does not normally print new money for its own use. Nevertheless, policies of the Treasury do influence the quantity of money available for spending. Remember that money is defined as cash and checkable deposits *in the hands of the public;* this definition excludes money paid in taxes to the Treasury. The effect of taxes is to reduce the quantity of money until tax revenues are paid out to some other individual or business firm. Policies of the Treasury may reinforce the policies of the Federal Reserve to increase or decrease the money supply. Or the two institutions may move in opposite directions, partially offsetting each other. And finally, the U.S. money supply is strongly influenced by international money flows among consumers and investors in the United States and those of other nations with which we trade.

The primary responsibility for actually creating money rests with the nation's commercial banks. Whatever money supply policy is decided by the Federal Reserve, it must ultimately be carried out by the banks themselves and the banks' customers. Banks must be willing to lend, and individuals or business firms must be willing to borrow. The power actually to create money must be exercised before new money can come into existence. Money cannot simply be passed out on street corners; creating it requires a conscious decision of banker and borrower.

In this chapter we will focus on the process of money creation: what determines a bank's lending ability and how bank lending affects the money supply.

Bank Loans and Investments

Bank lending creates assets for the bank. Bank loans and investments have value because they are the borrowers' promises to pay, with interest, when due. Loans constitute about 60 percent of a typical bank's assets and earn interest that varies according to the type of loan. Investments constitute about 20 percent and generally earn interest at lower rates because they are considered less risky and more liquid.

When a bank makes a loan or investment, it normally pays by creating a new deposit in the name of the borrower. Because the deposit is payable to its owner on demand, it is called a *demand deposit*. The borrower's demand deposit is a liability to the bank, offset by the borrower's own promise to pay. In the example that follows, we will demonstrate the process of lending step by step.

Required Reserves

Remember that commercial banks are able to make loans because of the fractional reserve system of banking. Under the fractional reserve system, commercial banks hold a fraction of their deposits in vault cash and in reserve accounts in other banks. They make loans and investments on the basis of excess reserves only. State and federal banking regulations require that they do so. *Required reserves* vary with the size of the bank, but we will use the fraction one-fifth, or .20, as a convenient fraction in this example. We will assume that commercial banks must hold at least .20 of deposits in cash and reserve accounts.

Suppose a commercial bank is holding cash, reserves and demand deposits in the amounts shown on the balance sheet in Figure 8–1. The bank's deposits come from its customers, both in the United States and in other nations with which we trade.

FIGURE 8–1

HYPOTHETICAL BANK BALANCE SHEET

Assets		Liabilities	
(R) Cash and Reserve Accounts	$ 25,000	(D) Demand Deposits	$100,000
Loans and Other Assets	$100,000	Other Liabilities and Capital Accounts	$ 25,000

The required reserve ratio is: $r = R/D = .20$. With demand deposits (D) of $100,000, the bank is required to hold in cash and reserve accounts: $rD = .20$ ($100,000) $= $20,000. The equation ($rD = R$) just satisfies the reserve requirement. Alternatively, the equation ($r = R/D = .20$) satisfies the reserve requirement.

Excess Reserves

With actual reserve holdings of $25,000, our hypothetical bank has *excess reserves*:

Total Cash and Reserve Accounts	$25,000
Less: Required Reserves	− 20,000
Excess Reserves	$ 5,000

This commercial bank can make loans by creating new demand deposits in the amount of excess reserves. Then, if the borrower draws out his or her newly created demand deposit in cash, the bank is still in compliance with reserve requirements.

To illustrate the effects of bank lending, we will record the changes that occur in the bank's balance sheet on T-accounts. T-accounts are useful because they require only that we record changes in accounts. However, in order that the balance sheet as a whole remain in balance, it is necessary that we make equal changes on both sides of the T-account or opposite changes on the same side. We show the effect of (a) making a $5,000 loan and creating a new deposit account in Figure 8–2 and (b) paying out cash and reserves in the amount of the loan in Figure 8–3.

FIGURE 8–2

HYPOTHETICAL BANK: T-ACCOUNT

| Reserves | No Change | Demand Deposits | + $5,000 |
| Loans | + $5,000 | | |

FIGURE 8–3

HYPOTHETICAL BANK: T-ACCOUNT

| Reserves | − $5,000 | Demand Deposits | − $5,000 |
| Loans | No Change | | |

With reserves of $20,000 and deposits of $100,000, the bank is precisely in compliance with reserve requirements and can create no more loans.

Lending by a Second Bank

The effect of a loan is, first, to increase the money supply by the amount of the loan—either in the form of a checking account or in the form of cash paid out to the borrower. Thus, the effect of the loan in the preceding example is to increase the money supply by $5,000. Normally the borrower will use the loan to purchase goods or equipment, paying for the purchase by check or cash. Very likely the receiving merchant will deposit the check or cash in another bank. Figure 8–4 shows changes in the balance sheet of the second bank. When the second bank receives the new deposit, it can increase its lending as well. In Figure 8–5 the second bank holds

$$R/D = r = .20$$

of the new deposit in its reserve account and makes another loan equal to excess reserves of $4,000. By lending only an amount equal to excess reserves, the second bank also remains in compliance with reserve requirements.

FIGURE 8–4

SECOND BANK: T-ACCOUNT

| Reserves | + $5,000 | Demand Deposits | + $5,000 |

FIGURE 8–5

SECOND BANK: T-ACCOUNT

| Reserves | No Change | Demand Deposits | + $4,000 |
| Loan | + $4,000 | | |

Lending by Other Banks

Again, the borrower will probably use the bank loan to purchase goods or equipment. The result for the second bank is shown in Figure 8–6.

FIGURE 8–6

SECOND BANK: T-ACCOUNT

| Reserves | − $4,000 | Demand Deposits | − $4,000 |
| Loans | No Change | | |

The receiving merchant deposits the payment in still another bank, providing excess reserves on which that bank can make another loan. We might expect this process to continue, involving a series of deposits in a series of banks, with the result that each new deposit forms the basis for new loans and new deposits. Each successive bank receives a smaller deposit and a smaller addition to its reserve account. Likewise, excess reserves and new lending are smaller at each successive stage. Ultimately, the original $5,000 in excess reserves will result in new lending of:

$5,000	(1st bank)	1,310	(7th bank)
4,000	(2nd bank)	1,050	(8th bank)
3,200	(3rd bank)	840	(9th bank)
2,560	(4th bank)	670	(10th bank)
2,050	(5th bank)	—	(all other banks)
1,650	(6th bank)	$25,000	Total New Loans

The Total Change in Bank Lending

Each bank in the series above creates loans and deposits equal to $(1 - r)$ times its new deposit. The total of new loans and deposits made by all banks is the sum of a *geometric progression*. The formula for the sum of all new lending is:

$$\text{Change in Bank Lending} = \text{Excess Reserves} \times [1/r],$$

where $[1/r]$ is the reciprocal of the required reserve ratio. Through the process of borrowing and spending borrowed funds, the excess reserves of

$5,000 in the first bank become distributed among many banks, providing the basis for further new lending. Finally, the total of new loans and deposits in all banks is $25,000.

There is an important point to remember here. In this example we assumed that all new lending returns to the banks as demand deposits. If no cash is held outside the banks, then all will remain as reserves to support the maximum amount of new lending. In this case, all bank excess reserves contribute to the creation of new deposits and, hence, the maximum possible increase in new lending. We will call the equation that measures the change in bank lending Equation 1:

(1)   Change in Bank Lending = Excess Reserves × [1/r]

or

$$\Delta L = ER \, [1/r].$$

With excess reserves of $5,000 the banking system creates new deposits of $25,000. As new deposits are withdrawn and spent, excess reserves shrink to zero, but the banking system as a whole remains in compliance with reserve requirements:

$$r = R/D = 5,000/25,000 = 0.20.$$

The Effect of a New Cash Deposit

New cash deposited in the banking system affects bank deposits differently. In this case, the first bank receives both a new deposit and an equal addition to its cash and reserve account. Of the additional reserves, only the fraction r is required reserves under state and federal law. The remainder $(1 - r)$ is excess reserves and can serve as the basis for new lending.

New lending is as measured in Equation 1, but total deposits are larger by the initial cash deposit.

It is important to distinguish between a new cash deposit and created deposits. In our first example, the deposits created by bank lending are called *derivative deposits*. In our second example the new cash deposit is a *primary deposit*. Thus Equation 1 measures derivative deposits. In our second example the total change in deposits is the sum of the initial primary deposit *plus* derivative or created deposits and is measured by Equation 2:

(2)   Total Change in Deposits = Change in Reserves (1/r)

or

$$\Delta D = \Delta R \, [1/r],$$

where ΔR is the change in reserves that results from a new cash deposit.

In 1987, commercial banks in the United States held about $50 billion in cash and reserve accounts. Under the simplified assumptions in this example, a new cash deposit of $10 million would increase total reserves by $10 million and excess reserves by

$$ER = \$10 \ (1 - .20) = \$8 \text{ million.}$$

Excess reserves of $8 million could serve as the basis for new lending according to Equation 1:

$$\Delta L = ER \ [1/r] = 8 \ [1/.20] = \$40 \text{ million.}$$

As a result of the cash deposit of $10, total bank deposits are larger by Equation 2:

$$\Delta D = \Delta R \ [1/r] = 10 \ [1/.20] = \$50 \text{ million.}$$

The initial $10 million cash deposit is a primary deposit; the $40 million in deposits created by new lending are derivative deposits. Total primary plus derivative deposits are $50 million.

Using the Deposit Multiplier

These relationships would be easier to see if there were only one large bank in the nation holding all reserves and all deposit accounts. Any increase in reserves would permit the giant bank to hold a higher level of deposits, always making sure that reserves remain the required ratio of deposits. Thus, holding total reserves and deposits ($R = rD$), an increase in reserves would permit the giant bank to increase its deposits by Equation 2:

$$\Delta D = \Delta R \ [1/r].$$

It is only slightly more difficult to think of total reserves (R), excess reserves (ER), and total deposits (D) as the sums of amounts held by many banks. For all banks taken together, receipt of new reserves would permit the banks to hold additional deposits according to Equation 2:

$$\Delta D = \Delta R \ [1/r].$$

Derivative deposits for all the banks would be determined by Equation 1:

$$\Delta L = ER \ [1/r].$$

The factor in brackets determines the maximum allowed change in derivative deposits expanded from a given level of excess reserves. And it determines the maximum allowed change in total primary plus derivative deposits resulting from a change in total reserves. In our example:

$$[1/r] = 1/.20 = 5.$$

By Equation 1 the banking system as a whole may create derivative deposits up to five times its excess reserves. And by Equation 2 a new cash deposit can cause total deposits to increase by five times the new cash deposit.

Whenever the banking system is maintaining precisely the required reserve ratio, any increase in reserves (R) becomes the basis for a new round of lending such as the one we have described. The result is a potential increase in bank lending according to Equation 1:

$$\Delta L = ER \,[1/r]$$

and increase in total deposits according to Equation 2:

$$\Delta D = \Delta R \,[1/r].$$

A *decrease* in cash reserves (R) would have the opposite effect, *reducing* bank lending by $ER \,[1/r]$ where ER has a negative sign. This time the factor in brackets $[1/r]$ determines the quantity of money that must be destroyed. Money is destroyed when banks *reduce* their lending. With negative excess reserves, banks must stop creating new loans and collect old loans without renewal. In our example, negative excess reserves (ER) of $-\$5$ million would require banks to destroy deposits of $25 million.

The Drain of Excess Reserves

To this point, our explanation has been simplified by the assumption that banks always lend amounts equal to their excess reserves and that individuals deposit all their cash in commercial bank checking accounts. Relaxing these assumptions changes our computations somewhat.

First, let us suppose that banks hesitate to lend the full amount of their excess reserves, fearing credit risks among prospective borrowers or expecting more favorable lending terms in the future. We will call the ratio of the additional excess reserves that banks elect to hold relative to total deposits: $E/D = e$. The decision to hold excess reserves increases the ratio of actual reserves to deposits to:

$$R/D + E/D = r + e.$$

Thus, a required reserve (r) of .20 and excess reserve holdings (e) of .05 raises total reserves to .20 plus .05, or .25, of deposits. Under these assumptions, new lending is less than in our previous example. Equation 1 becomes:

$$\Delta L = ER \,[1/(r+e)]$$

and the factor in brackets is:

$$[1/(r+e)] = 1/(.20 + .05) = 1/.25 = 4.$$

Likewise, the change in total deposits is less. Equation 2 becomes:

$$\Delta D = \Delta R \, [1/(r+e)].$$

The Drain of Public Cash Holdings

Now let us change our assumptions again to allow for public holdings of cash. When the public leaves cash in the banking system, reserves can be used fully to support bank lending. Deposits can expand to the maximum amount allowed by reserves and reserve requirements. Furthermore, if the public holds no cash, the change in total deposits is identical to the change in the money supply:

$$\Delta D = \Delta R \, [1/(r+e)] = \Delta M1.$$

(For this explanation we use the first definition of the money supply: M1 equals currency plus checking accounts in commercial banks plus travelers checks plus other checkable accounts in thrift institutions. The latter is a growing component of the nation's total spending power, increasingly significant for guiding monetary policy decisions. However, because the money-creating ability of thrifts is small, we will refer to the institutions that create money as commercial banks.)

A decision to withdraw cash from demand deposits affects the results of our analysis. We will see that a drain of reserves into public cash holdings affects not only the amount of excess reserves available at each stage of new lending, but also the factor by which total deposits can grow.

Suppose individuals decide to hold cash equal to .15 of their demand deposits. We may call the cash drain

$$C/D = c$$

where c is the ratio of public holdings of cash relative to demand deposits. When the public draws out cash reserves, the effect is to reduce bank lending ability and to reduce the change in deposits that results from new reserves. Equation 1 becomes

$$\Delta L + ER \, [1/(r+e+c)]$$

and the factor in brackets is:

$$[1/(r+e+c)] = [1/(.20+.05+.15)] = 1/.40 = 2.5.$$

Equation 2 becomes:

$$\Delta D = \Delta R \, [1/(r+e+c)].$$

Note that the tendency to hold cash reduces the factor in brackets in our example from 4 to 2.5. The reason is simple. When the first bank extends a new loan, some cash is drawn out and held outside the banking system. The result is to reduce the new deposit going to a second bank and to reduce its excess reserves. With lower excess reserves, the second bank—and similarly all other banks—can make fewer loans. The maximum allowed change in derivative deposits is smaller than before. (When the public withdraws money as cash, any injection of new reserves ends up partially as reserves and partially as public cash holdings. The total of bank reserves and public cash holdings constitutes the quantity known as the money base, a topic to be discussed shortly.)

Notice that the new circumstances also change the money supply. A cash deposit causes derivative deposits to grow by

$$\Delta L = ER[2.5]$$

for total new deposits of:

$$\Delta D = \Delta R[2.5]$$

but this amount does not constitute the total money supply. Cash holdings of the public must also be taken into account. To compute the change in the money supply, Equation 2 must be revised to:

$$\Delta M1 = \Delta D + \Delta C = \Delta D + c\Delta D = \Delta R[1/(r+e+c)] + cR[1/(r+e+c)].$$

Rearranging terms yields:

(3) $\Delta M1 = \Delta R[(1+c)/(r+e+c)].$

Under these assumptions we should call the factor in brackets the *money multiplier*. Changing the numerator to $(1 + c)$ ensures that cash holdings will be included in the money supply, according to the M1 definition.

Now let us use the new versions of Equations 1, 2 and 3 to trace the effects of a primary cash deposit of $10 million. With r of .20 and e of .05, excess reserves (ER) are .75(10), or $7.50, million, and the change in bank lending can be as much as:

$$\Delta L = ER[1/(r+e+c)] = 7.5[1/(.2+.05+.15)] = 7.5[2.5] = \$18.75 \text{ million.}$$

After all new lending, the change in deposits can be as much as:

$$\Delta D = \Delta R[1/(r+e+c)] = 10[2.5] = \$25 \text{ million.}$$

The money supply, including cash and checkable deposits, will grow by:

$$\Delta M1 = \Delta R[(1+c)/(r+e+c)] = 10[2.875] = \$28.75 \text{ million.}$$

With:

$$C/D = c = .15$$

the public holds an additional .15(25), or $3.75, million in cash. Cash holdings reduce the factor in brackets to 2.5 and yield a money multiplier of 2.875.

A T-account for the banking system as a whole is shown in Figure 8–7.

FIGURE 8–7

BANKING SYSTEM: T-ACCOUNT

Reserves		Deposits	+25
Required	+ 5		
Excess	+ 1.25		
Loans	+18.75		

The Money Base

Once we acknowledge the public's tendency to hold cash, it is no longer appropriate to consider only bank reserves as sources of money. True, reserves provide banks the basis for making new loans. But the monetary authorities realize that reserves can change independently of any actions by policymakers. In fact, decisions by the public to hold more (or less) cash have the effect of decreasing (or increasing) bank reserves. This means that the total of reserves currently held by banks *plus* cash in the hands of the public is potentially available as a basis for making new loans—and potentially significant for determining the nation's money supply.

The total of bank reserves plus cash held by the public is called the *money base*:

Money Base (B) = Reserves (R) + Cash Held by Public (C)

When we correct our previous equations to allow for public cash holdings, we get for Equation 2:

$$\Delta D = \Delta B[1/(r+e+c)]$$

and for Equation 3:

$$\Delta M1 = \Delta B[(1+c)/(r+e+c)]$$

The multipliers in the brackets remain the same, but the multipliers are applied to changes in the money base, whether added to bank reserves or to public holdings of cash.

The Drain of Savings and Time Deposits and Money Market Fund Shares

Let us change our assumptions once again to make our model even more realistic. This time we will allow for the fact that the public wants to hold some of its wealth claims in the form of savings or time deposits or in money market funds. The ease of withdrawing these deposits and the interest they earn have increased their attractiveness to customers of banks and thrift institutions.

Including savings and time deposits and money market shares changes our computations in several ways. First, because savings accounts have lower reserve requirements than demand deposits, the flow of funds into these accounts increases the level of excess reserves. But second, because some part of each newly created loan flows into savings accounts, the change in demand deposits is not as great as before. Finally, the change in the $M1$ supply of money is less than before, but the change in the $M2$ supply of money (including savings and time deposits and money market fund shares) is greater than before.

Suppose the public wants to hold twice as much in these kinds of savings accounts as in demand deposits. We will call the ratio of these holdings to demand deposits:

$$T/D = t = 2.$$

The reserve requirement for these accounts is about .05. Thus:

$$R/T = r_t = .05.$$

Required reserves against these accounts change the factor in brackets to:

$$\left[\frac{1}{r + e + c + r_t t} \right]$$

In the denominator the reserve requirement r_t must be multiplied by the ratio of t to account for twice as many savings and time deposits as demand deposits. The factor in brackets becomes:

$$\frac{1}{.20 + .05 + .15 + .05(2)} = \frac{1}{.5} = 2$$

Likewise Equation 2 must be changed to:

$$\Delta D = \Delta B \left[\frac{1}{r + e + c + r_t t} \right]$$

and Equation 3 to:

$$\Delta M1 = \Delta B \left[\frac{1 + c}{r + e + c + r_t t} \right]$$

FIGURE 8–8

BANKING SYSTEM: T-ACCOUNT

Reserves		Demand Deposits	+ 20
Required for Demand			
Deposits	+ 4		
Required for Time		Savings and Time	
Deposits	+ 2	Deposits and Money	
Excess	+ 1	Market Shares	+ 40
Loans and Investments	+ 53		

Including savings and time deposits and money market fund shares in the *M2* definition of money yields a new money equation:

(4) $$\Delta M2 = \Delta B \left[\frac{1 + c + t}{r + e + c + r_t t} \right]$$

Changing the numerator to $(1 + c + t)$ ensures that savings and time deposits and money market fund shares are included in the *M2* definition of the money supply.

Again assume an initial cash deposit of $10 million. Demand deposits can grow by:

$$\Delta D = \Delta B \left[\frac{1}{r + e + c + r_t t} \right] = 10[2] = \$20 \text{ million.}$$

Total cash and demand deposits can grow by:

$$\Delta M1 = \Delta B \left[\frac{1 + c}{r + e + c + r_t t} \right] = 10[2.3] = \$23 \text{ million.}$$

Total new cash, demand deposits, savings and time deposits, and money market fund shares might be as much as:

$$\Delta M2 = \Delta B \left[\frac{1 + c + t}{r + e + c + r_t t} \right] = 10[6.3] = \$63 \text{ million.}$$

The public is holding additional cash of

$$c(D) = .15(20) = \$3 \text{ million}$$

and savings deposits and money market shares totaling

$$t(D) = 2(20) = \$40 \text{ million.}$$

The final T-account for the banking system as a whole is shown in Figure 8–8.

Implications for the Money Supply

Compare these results with those of the previous example. The differences between the money multipliers in the two examples depend on the values of r_t and t. The lower the reserve requirement on time deposits and the smaller the quantity of time deposits relative to demand deposits, the greater is the factor in brackets and the greater the potential expansion of the money supply. As r_t and t become very small, the factors in brackets from the two examples become almost identical. Moreover, with a very small value of t the quantity of M2 becomes almost the same as M1.

The opposite characteristics are true of our modern economy. With an increase in the ratio t, the measured value of M2 has increased significantly relative to the value of M1. The implications of this change are serious for money managers. It is no longer sufficient to control the growth of money according to the M1 definition. True, only cash and checkable deposits are immediately available for spending. But converting savings and time deposits and money market shares to cash or checking accounts is becoming more and more convenient, especially where automatic tellers are provided. This means that holders of the $40 million in new savings deposits and money market shares in the example above might quickly decide to convert them, increasing M1 money significantly and complicating the process of controlling spending power. Too much spending power could create inflationary pressures before banks could act to reduce their loans and bring down the level of total deposits.

There is another problem associated with an abrupt movement of savings and time deposits into demand deposits or cash. If the $40 million in savings deposits and money market shares were to be converted into demand deposits or cash, many banks would face liquidity problems. Total reserves would be insufficient to support demand deposits at the higher required ratio (r) of .20 and would be quickly depleted by a major currency drain. Many banks would be forced to call in loans and stop new lending entirely, with disastrous effects for their customers.

To summarize, banks acquire deposits from their customers, both in the United States and abroad. Banks are required to hold a fraction of deposits in reserves. When banks receive additional reserves, the banking system as a whole may expand total deposits to a multiple of reserves. The value of the multiple depends on banks' decisions to hold excess reserves and the public's decisions to hold cash and savings deposits. Holdings of cash and savings deposits are added to demand deposits to determine the various measures of the money supply.

Changes in any of these factors yield changes in banks' ability to create money and may lead to changes in spending, prices and economic activity.

Equations Measuring the Total Money Supply

Changes in reserves produce changes in the money supply according to the money multipliers described in this chapter. The same equations can be used to measure the total stock of money at any time. Thus, if the potential *change* in deposits is

$$\Delta D = \Delta B \left[1/(r + e + c + r_t t)\right]$$

then *total* deposits may be as much as

$$D = B \left[1/(r + e + c + r_t t)\right].$$

And if the potential *change* in M1 is

$$\Delta M1 = \Delta B \left[(1+c)/(r + e + c + r_t t)\right]$$

then *total* M1 may be as much as:

$$M1 = B \left[(1+c)/(r + e + c + r_t t)\right].$$

And if the potential *change* in M2 is:

$$\Delta M2 = B \left[(1+c+e)/(r + e + c + r_t t)\right]$$

then total M2 may be as much as

$$M2 = B \left[(1+c+e)/(r + e + c + r_t t)\right].$$

Predicting correctly the values of the variables in the money equations can help policymakers regulate the supply of money in line with the needs of the economy. Frequent changes in the variables that constitute the money equations make predictions more difficult and may lead to wider fluctuations in the money supply.

MONEY AND BANKING IN PRACTICE: CASH AND THE UNDERGROUND ECONOMY

What determines public holdings of cash? This is a significant question because the preference for cash c can affect the money multiplier. A larger value for c in the denominator will reduce the value of $[(1 + c)/(r + e + c + r_t t)]$ and reduce the impact of a change in reserves on the nation's money supply.

Several factors have been tending to reduce cash holdings. First, abnormally high interest rates have encouraged more efficient *cash management.* Funds are left to earn interest until they are actually needed for spending. Second, new credit devices have made it possible to carry on many transactions without the use of cash at all. And finally, the possibility of loss or theft makes holding cash risky. In spite of all these disincentives to carry cash, the value of *c* has actually increased in recent years—from only 25 percent of demand deposits in 1959 to 34 percent of all checkable deposits in 1987. This amounts to average cash holdings of $2,885 per family.

Some economists have come up with a disturbing explanation for the increase in cash holdings. It is that more cash is needed for operating in what may be called the underground economy. Illegal activities such as gambling, drug dealing and loan sharking require large amounts of cash. (The Miami Federal Reserve Bank is said frequently to experience a surplus of cash because of the large amounts of money generated by the import of Colombian "grass.") Cash is also used to pay wages to persons who do not want to report their income for tax purposes. Part-time service workers, repair persons, moonlighters and some professionals may receive income as cash and fail to pay the proper tax. This is a growing problem in many industrial countries, when inflation pushes workers into higher and higher tax brackets.

Economists estimate the total level of underground income in either of two ways. One way is to apply past ratios of cash holdings to income to current cash holdings. Another is to estimate the number of times a bill is spent before it deteriorates completely and must be replaced. Such measures have produced estimates of the underground economy amounting to as much as one-quarter of total production for the year.

The movement of vast amounts of our nation's productive resources into illegal activities has serious implications for the national economy. To artificially stimulate one sector and retard another through tax disincentives reduces the efficiency of resource allocation and may worsen our competitive position internationally. Underground activities probably absorb substantial numbers of workers who are incorrectly reported as unemployed, thus overstating the unemployment rate. Because taxes are not paid on illegal incomes, the actual tax rate for the nation is lower than the legislated rate. Finally, because the effect of the underground economy is to reduce the reported value of national income and its growth over time, it may cause policymakers to recommend faster growth than is actually needed to stimulate production. The result may be a tendency to accelerating inflation and even greater incentives to illegal activities.

Question for Discussion

1. Cite other reasons for holding large amounts of cash in today's economy.

The Growth of the Money Supply Over Time

Policymakers agree that the money supply should grow fast enough to satisfy the needs of the economy but not so fast as to exceed growth in the nation's capacity to produce goods and services. Enough money will help ensure stable, noninflationary growth in production with full employment of the nation's resources.

What has been the actual experience with money growth? In 1987, the money supply by the *M*1 definition reached almost $750 billion. Between 1959, when comparable data became available, and 1987 the *M*1 supply of money had grown at an average annual rate of about 6 percent. The fastest growth in money forms has occurred in savings and time deposits, both in commercial banks and in nonbank thrift institutions. With annual growth of almost 11 percent, these deposits caused the *M*2 and *M*3 money stocks to grow at about 9 percent a year.

Figure 8–9 traces money growth over the years for which comparable data are available. Notice the faster growth of *M*2 and *M*3 relative to *M*1 over the period shown. Notice also an apparent increase in the growth rate over recent years. For the decade ending December 1979, *M*1 grew at an annual rate of 6.2 percent compared with 3.8 percent over the previous decade and 1.8 percent over the earliest period shown. In the first seven years of the 1980s, *M*1 grew at an average rate of 9.4 percent annually. The other money values behaved similarly, with substantially increased growth rates over the previous decade.

The factors responsible for faster money growth are (1) demographic changes, (2) changes in banking structure, (3) increases in capital needs and (4) tendencies toward inflation.

Demographic Changes

We have become an increasingly urban and suburban society. Nowadays, more activities take place in the market than in earlier periods when we were a nation of small towns and farmers. The growth of market activity has increased our need for money as a medium of exchange. At the same time, the variety of credit devices available in many cities enables us to function with less cash relative to other money forms. Thus, more of the money base remains in bank reserve accounts, and the money supply can grow faster.

Banking Structure

The number of banks has increased over the period, with the greatest increase occurring in states that strictly limit or prohibit branch banking. States permitting limited or statewide branching experienced an increase in

FIGURE 8–9 Growth of the Money Supply, 1960–1985

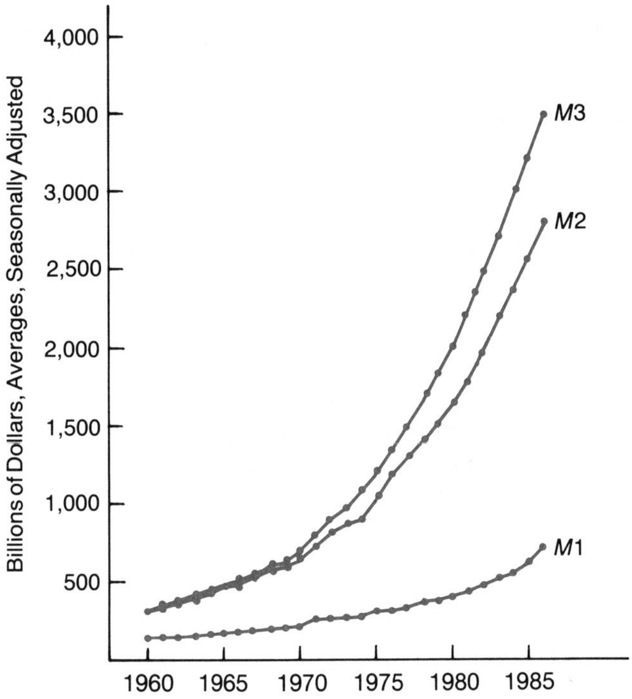

the number of bank offices, even though the number of independent banks declined. Growing numbers of small unit banks in convenient shopping centers have meant increasing competition for consumer and business loans and more efficient use of bank reserves.

Capital Needs

The expansion of economic activity over the past several decades has called for financial capital provided by bank lending. The need for capital has also stimulated the growth of new nonbank financial institutions, increasing the growth of M2 and M3.

Inflation

A tendency toward price inflation has increased the need for money for carrying on all transactions. This was especially true during the 1970s when prices increased 6.5 percent annually compared with less than 2 percent annually during the previous decade. Whether the more rapid growth of money caused the higher level of inflation or whether inflation brought on money growth is a subject for debate. In any case, the higher level of inflation increased the need for money for carrying on all transactions.

The Composition of Bank Credit

Throughout this discussion we have concentrated on the process of bank lending through deposit creation. We have seen the effect of excess reserves on bank lending and how total reserves affect the various measures of the money supply. But we have not yet looked specifically at the character of bank lending itself.

The total of bank loans and investments is called *bank credit*. Bank credit constitutes the earning assets on a bank's balance sheet. It is the value of total assets less cash and reserve accounts as shown in Figure 8–10.

FIGURE 8–10

Assets	Liabilities

Cash and Reserve Accounts
Bank Credit:
  Loans
  Investments
	Demand Deposits
	Savings and Time Deposits
	
	Capital Accounts

Looked at another way, bank credit is demand, savings and time deposits less reserves held against these deposits. (This is precisely true only if we ignore capital accounts. Because capital accounts are a relatively small source of funds for lending, it may be appropriate to exclude them from our analysis at this point. It would be simpler to include them later.)

This relationship allows us to develop another factor we will call the *bank credit multiplier*. It is the change in bank credit that could result from a change in the money base. The numerator of this multiplier is excess reserves: total deposits less required reserves held against deposits. And the denominator is the denominator of the factor we have called the deposit multiplier. Thus:

$$\Delta L = \Delta BC = \Delta B\left[\frac{(1+t) - (r+r_t t+e)}{(r+e+c+r_t t)}\right] \text{ and } BC = B\left[\frac{(1+t) - (r+r_t t+e)}{(r+e+c+r_t t)}\right]$$

Note that this equation is basically the same equation with which we began. The numerator is a measure of excess reserves: total demand deposits and time deposits $(1+t)$ less reserves against deposits $(r + r_t t + e)$. Thus, $B[(1+t)-(r+r_t t+e)]$ is the excess reserves associated with any change in the money base, when demand deposits are created according to the familiar deposit multiplier $1/(r+e+r_t t+c)$.

Under our assumptions in the example, a $10 million increase in the money base would increase bank credit by:

$$\Delta BC = 10\left[\frac{(1 + 2)-(.20 + .10 + .05)}{.20 + .05 + .15 + 2(.05)}\right] = \$10[5.3] = \$53 \text{ million.}$$

The $53 million in bank credit may be in the form of loans or investments. Remember that bank loans are typically made to the bank's customers. Such loans include commercial, industrial, real estate, consumer and broker loans. Loans are generally made face-to-face to borrowers, while investments are securities issued by a party that may not deal regularly with the bank. The issuing party may be a state or local government, the U.S. Treasury, or a private corporation. A typical bank portfolio would be composed about 65 percent of loans and 20 percent of investments.

The bank credit multiplier tells us only the quantity, but nothing about the composition of bank credit. The composition may have important implications for the economy, however. In general, economists believe that loans are respent more rapidly than investments. Commercial, industrial and consumer borrowers, for instance, probably put their funds back into the spending stream more readily than persons who receive payments from the sale of investments. As a result, a heavy concentration of bank credit in loans stimulates more spending than a heavy concentration of bank credit in investments. On the other hand, a shift of bank credit from loans to investments has a contractionary effect on economic activity in the local community.

The decision as to the proper combination of loans and investments is based on considerations of return and risk in the lending bank. Managers of a bank's portfolio compare the relative advantages and disadvantages of both types of bank credit. Individual commercial banks differ in the trade-offs they assign to expected return and risk. Some prefer a portfolio dominated by less liquid, high-yielding loans, and others a portfolio of safe, lower yielding investments. Most banks reevaluate their portfolio decisions frequently as market conditions change. A change in the economic climate—from optimistic to pessimistic, for example—could cause a bank to shift its portfolio from loans toward a higher concentration of investments.

Policymakers whose concern is the quantity of spending power and its effect on economic activity may occasionally find such actions of banks inappropriate. A pessimistic business climate might seriously depress economic activity, particularly if at the same time banks are contracting the total level of bank credit.

Conclusion

In this chapter we have focused on the process of creating money. In the United States, money is created primarily by the independent acts of privately owned commercial banks, operating within the limitations established by state and federal banking regulations and subject to the budgetary policies of the Treasury. Commercial banks can create demand deposits because of two fundamental features of our financial structure: (1) banks hold only a fraction of their deposits in cash and reserve accounts and (2) the deposits they create remain largely within the banking system. As a result, available reserves can satisfy the fractional reserve requirements of many banks.

Until recently, nonbank financial intermediaries lacked these characteristics and thus lacked the ability to create money. Because they could not create checking accounts, they could lend only the amounts they received from savers. Today, savings and loan associations, mutual savings banks, insurance companies, credit unions and investment companies offer checkable deposits so similar to commercial bank demand deposits that they also have a role in creating money. From practically zero ten years ago, by 1987 the checkable deposits of nonbank financial intermediaries amounted to almost a third of the M1 money supply.

As still more institutions assume the role of creating money substitutes, the job of regulating the supply becomes even more difficult. With so many new wealth forms, policymakers must look more closely at the M3 definition of money: cash, all checkable deposits, savings and time deposits at all depository institutions, as well as money market fund shares.

Glossary of Terms

bank credit.   the total of bank loans and investments

bank credit multiplier.   a ratio that determines the effect on bank credit of new reserves

cash management.   the practice of minimizing idle cash balances so as to increase yields on financial assets

demand deposits.   commercial bank deposits that may be withdrawn on demand

derivative deposit.   a deposit created by bank lending

excess reserves.   reserve accounts in excess of the required fraction of deposits

money base.   the total of bank reserves and cash held by the public

money multiplier.   a ratio that determines the effect on the money supply of new reserves or excess reserves

primary deposit. a deposit of new funds from outside the banking system
required reserves. accounts that represent a fraction of total deposits, required by state and federal chartering institutions

Summary of Important Ideas

1. The primary responsibility for creating money rests with the nation's
   commercial banks. Banks create demand deposits when they make loans
   in the amount of their excess reserves. By maintaining fractional reserves,
   a series of banks can make loans equal to a multiple of excess reserves:
   $$\Delta L = ER[1/r].$$
   The total change in the money supply from a new deposit is:
   $$\Delta M1 = \Delta R[1/r].$$

2. Bank holdings of excess reserves, currency holdings of the public, and
   public holdings of savings deposits change the factor in brackets so that
   $$\Delta D = \Delta R[1/(r+e+c+r_t t)] \text{ and } \Delta M2 = R[(1+c+t)/(r+e+c+r_t t)].$$

3. Changes in bank holdings of excess reserves (e) or in public holdings
   of cash and time deposits (c and t) change the factors in brackets and
   complicate the job of regulating the money supply.

4. When reserves (R) are combined with total cash holdings of the public
   (C), the result is the money base (B). The size of the money base is of
   concern to policymakers because cash holdings represent potential bank
   reserves.

5. Total bank credit is bank loans plus investments. The distribution of
   assets between loans and investments affects the rate of spending. During periods of slow growth, banks may collect old loans and purchase
   investments instead, with the result that total spending declines.

6. Until recently, only commercial banks could create money, because the
   money substitutes issued by other financial intermediaries were not generally acceptable for spending. However, new money substitutes increase claims to real wealth and make controlling the money supply
   more difficult.

Questions for Discussion and Research

1. Explain why the fraction (r) is included in the multiplier for measuring
   money created by banks. How would changes in r affect bank lending?

2. Use the following hypothetical data to compute total demand deposits,
   $M1$, $M2$ and the money base:

Commercial bank reserves: R	$57 billion
Reserve requirements:	
Demand deposits r	.12
Savings and time deposits: r_t	.05
Average bank holdings of excess reserves as a fraction of demand deposits: e	.02
Public cash holdings as a fraction of demand deposits: c	.12
Savings and time deposits as a fraction of demand deposits: t	2.50

Suppose new reserves of $8 billion enter the banking system. Show the effect on demand deposits, $M1$ and $M2$. What is the effect on the money base, and why is this significant?

3. What considerations affect a bank's decision to purchase loans versus investments? What are the likely effects in terms of economic activity?

4. Discuss the effects of inflation on bank lending. What effect would more efficient use of reserves have on the money multiplier?

5. Consult *The Wall Street Journal* for information about the recent behavior of the money supply. Compute the current deposit and money multipliers.

6. A top executive of a major bank once observed: Traveling through many of the towns of Middle America, one discovers that the shabbiness of the local community is directly proportional to the size of the local bank's portfolio of government bonds. What are the implications of this statement, what conditions helped bring it about, and how might it be changed?

7. Discuss the various factors that continue to operate toward increasing money growth. What would be the arguments in the debate over whether money growth causes inflation or results from inflation?

Additional Readings

Garcia, Gillian, and Simon Pak. "The Ratio of Currency to Demand Deposits in the United States." *Journal of Finance* 34 (June 1979): 703–715.

Gutmann, Peter M. "Statistical Illusions, Mistaken Policies." *Challenge* 22 (November/December 1979): 14–18.

Humphrey, Thomas M. "The Theory of Multiple Expansion of Deposits: What It Is and Whence It Came." *Economic Review, Federal Reserve Bank of Richmond* (March/April 1987): 3–11.

Kopcke, Richard W. "How Erratic Is Money Growth?" *New England Economic Review* (May/June 1986): 3–20.

Tatom, John A., and Richard W. Lang.   "Automatic Transfers and the Money Supply Process." *Federal Reserve Bank of St. Louis Review* 61 (February 1979): 2–10.

Tobin, James.   "Commercial Banks as Creators of 'Money.' " In *Banking and Monetary Studies,* edited by Deane Carson. Homewood, Ill.: Richard D. Irwin, Inc., 1963.

Weintraub, Sidney.   "Wall Street's Mindless Affair with Tight Money." *Challenge* (January/February 1978): 34–39.

CHAPTER

9

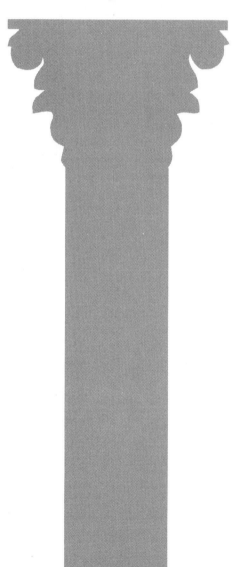

- To begin to explore the relationship between money and economic activity
- To see how theories of banking have changed along with changes in the world economy
- To understand the basis for laws regulating banking
- To consider the relative advantages of a policy of "rules" versus a policy of "discretion"

Theories of Banking

"As banking developed from the seventeenth century on, so, with the support of other circumstance, did the cycles of euphoria and panic. Their length came to accord roughly with the time it took people to forget the last disaster—for the financial geniuses of one generation to die in disrepute and be replaced by new craftsmen who the gullible and the gulled could believe had, this time but truly, the Midas touch."

John Kenneth Galbraith

Since the beginning of economic society, those who have money and those who lack it have been in fundamental conflict. Those who have money prefer to limit its quantity so as to preserve its value. Those who lack it want the supply increased so that they can enjoy its benefits. This fundamental conflict is the basis for two theories by which banking policy has at times been governed.

Supporters of both sides in the argument would answer the question "How much money should there be?" with the same response: Enough. Enough to satisfy the needs of the economy. Not so much as to exceed the nation's capacity to produce goods and services, but not so little as to retard spending and economic growth. Their answers would be the same, but their definitions of "enough" would be different.

The Currency School of Banking

The views of the first group dominated our nation's early experience with banking. Commercial banks were expected to be merely depositories of the public's money, holding the assets of their customers and making payments but creating no additional money. The money supply would consist of paper currency, fully backed by specie. In effect, banks would serve as currency warehouses and middlemen between lenders and borrowers. Because of their emphasis on limiting the supply of currency, this group of economists was called the *Currency School of Banking*.

The Currency School required no monetary policy at all. A nation's money supply would depend at all times on its supply of specie—monetary gold and silver. Whenever new gold or silver was discovered, the supply of money would increase. Consumers would purchase more goods and services, stimulating local production and increasing imports. Some of the new specie would flow abroad into other nations for purchasing imports. In this way, the global stock of gold and silver would come to be distributed among nations according to their ability to produce goods and services. Thus, the supply of money would always be "enough" to satisfy the needs of trade, but it would never be so much as to suffer a decrease in value.

Critics of the Currency School questioned whether the supply of so vital a commodity as money should be determined solely by nature's gifts of gold. They feared that wide extremes of wealth would persist, dividing the world into the very poor and the very rich. The lack of money in some regions would depress economic activity and reduce living standards; too much money in others might encourage wasteful exploitation of global resources. International specie flows would probably not work according to theory. In actual fact, nations that lost gold often avoided facing a decline in spending and simply issued more paper currency, so that the assumptions of the Currency School finally broke down.

The Banking School

Without substantial supplies of gold and silver, the United States was especially constrained by the Currency School of Banking. Quickly we came to accept the *Banking School's* theory of the proper role of banks. Under the Banking School, the nation would not be tied to its specie holdings as a basis for creating money. Banks would create credit money in the form of new loans equal to the community's growing capacity to produce real goods and services. The creation of bank credit money would ensure that the quantity of spending power would be "enough" for stable, noninflationary growth at full employment.

The Real Bills Doctrine

To accomplish the proper rate of money growth, banks were encouraged to follow a rule called the *real bills doctrine*. Under the real bills doctrine loans would be made only for real, productive purposes—purposes that would ultimately result in the production of new goods and services. Normally, bank loans would be short-term commercial, industrial or agricultural loans.

Borrowers would use their newly created money to purchase raw materials or tools for use in production. Then, selling the finished goods would provide the funds for repaying the loan with interest.

Short-term commercial, industrial or agricultural loans would have two important characteristics. They would be *self-liquidating* because the borrowed money would be used to earn the funds to pay off, or liquidate, the loan. A bank that made these kinds of loans would not have to worry that borrowers would be unable to pay and that they would be left with worthless paper. The loans would also be *self-regulating* because the quantity of money would be precisely equal to the value of new production. Lending only for real productive purposes would ensure this result.

Under the real bills doctrine, there was no lending for real estate or for long-term capital investment. Such loans were not clearly self-liquidating, at least during the short term when banks could count on holding their depositors' funds. Long-term investments like these were expected to be made from the long-term savings of the community, generally through direct sales of securities to the public.

The real bills doctrine persuaded policymakers that banks would never create too much or too little money. Stable money growth would accommodate the legitimate needs of merchants, manufacturers and farmers. Claims to real wealth would grow in accordance with annual production of real goods and services.

Weaknesses of the Theory

You will probably not be surprised to learn that some of the confidence in the real bills doctrine was misplaced. In a very simple economy, short-term commercial loans might truly be self-liquidating. In a more complex economy with many stages of processing, they might not. For a loan to be self-liquidating, production must take place precisely in time with the loans. Unless new money is spent precisely as goods are completed, there will at times be too much or too little money, with a tendency for prices to rise or fall. Furthermore, the goods produced with borrowed money must be sold at prices high enough to liquidate the loan. This might not be possible if too many banks make too many loans for producing too many goods for a market that is already satisfied. U.S. automobile manufacturers and dealers are painfully aware of this possibility.

Whether short-term commercial loans are self-regulating may depend on whether bankers are optimistic or pessimistic regarding the legitimate needs of merchants, manufacturers and farmers. If many bankers become overly optimistic, they may extend too many loans, increasing the supply of money faster than the potential growth in real goods and services. Some borrowers may be unable to pay, changing bankers' optimism to pessimism. Too much money in one period might be followed by a severe credit crunch in the next.

The real bills doctrine ignored another necessary basis for creating new money: the consumer. If consumers are to buy the goods produced as a result of bank loans, they may need consumer loans. In fact, to liquidate a commercial or industrial loan might require a series of consumer loans, but the real bills doctrine considered consumer loans to be unproductive.

All these problems might be worked out if there were just one bank and one policy-making body. But when many independent banks are competing for loans, the healthy results of the real bills doctrine may not occur. This was certainly true of banking during the 1800s. Throughout the 1800s the money supply varied widely—increasing sharply when business looked good and falling just as sharply when business looked bad. In bad times—when credit was most needed—bank lending dropped practically to zero.

In the 1900s another problem developed that complicated even more the process of keeping the supply of money in balance with total production. Whatever the process policymakers devised for restricting the amount of credit, lenders and borrowers found ways to get around it. Where profits could be made, banks "invented" new types of credit instruments. They made loans on top of loans, where paying off one loan depended on being able to borrow again. When the lending stopped, the borrower defaulted. When many borrowers defaulted at once, banks saw a substantial part of their assets melt away. Banks—and their depositors' money—simply disappeared.

The Continuing Debate: Unit Banking versus Branch Banking

We haven't settled the debate over bank credit. We still disagree on the question of how banks can best serve our economic system: increasing efficiency in the allocation of resources, increasing equity in the way we share the benefits and costs of production, and increasing positive (and reducing negative) externalities associated with production.

The debate over banking is similar to a fundamental debate over what kind of economic system works best. One side of the debate wants to keep firms small and competitive and believes in keeping government out of business decisions. The other side worries that small competing units lack any sort of central coordination and create cycles of too much and too little economic activity. In this view, larger firms are more efficient and better able to survive a financial crisis. But, counters the first view, large firms use their market power unfairly to the advantage of certain groups at the expense of others. In this case, replies the second, government must step in and regulate them to protect the public interest.

For most of our history the first position has dominated the thinking of Americans. In general, we want to keep decision-making units small and retain power as much as possible in the hands of individuals and local institutions. Our faith in competition has generally governed our national policy for chartering banks. As a result, the United States has many independent banks—in contrast with Great Britain, France and Germany, which have a few large banks, each operating many branches.

The U.S. Constitution places much of the responsibility for setting bank policy in the hands of state governments. States may establish their own banking rules and rules with regard to bank branching. Almost a third of the states forbid branching entirely, and another third limit branching to the same or adjacent county. National banks follow the laws of the state in which they operate. Thus, our banking system remains primarily a system of small, unit banks.

There are some advantages of dealing with small neighborhood banks. Locally owned and operated banks probably have a clearer understanding of local needs than a branch bank managed by a parent company in a distant city. Small, independent banks may compete more vigorously for local borrowers than if they had substantial interests in other communities. Many of us feel more comfortable when people we know (or know about) control our money rather than people far away that we don't know.

There are some disadvantages with our unitary system of banking. Larger banks might have access to greater resources to satisfy a wider variety of their customers' needs. They could establish separate departments for providing research and information to business firms and local governments. Their personnel could become more expert in particular banking functions. Probably a small-town branch of a large city bank would be just as competitive as an independent bank, because it would face competition from other banks' branches. And it might be even more sympathetic to local needs than an independent bank that has enjoyed a monopoly of the local market for a long time. Most important, perhaps, is the greater financial stability of a system of large banks with many branches. In such a system, problems of illiquidity and insolvency in a single branch can be dealt with through the parent bank, so that bank failure is less likely.

Over time, Americans have gradually come to accept the idea that large banks have some advantages and that banks should be allowed to grow. As our fears of market power have diminished, more states have become willing to permit branch banking. Still, applicants for a bank charter must prove that the new branch will not reduce competition in the community or exert market power. Like other business firms in our economy, banks can be prosecuted under the antitrust laws if they become too large and powerful. Information regarding banking laws in the various states is given in Table 9–1.

TABLE 9–1   State Banking Laws

States with Statewide Branch Banking

Alaska	Maryland	South Carolina
Arizona	Nevada	South Dakota
California	New Jersey	Utah
Connecticut	New York	Vermont
Delaware	North Carolina	Virginia
Hawaii	Oregon	Washington
Idaho	Rhode Island	Washington, D.C.
Maine		

States with Limited Branch Banking

Alabama	Kentucky	New Mexico
Arkansas	Louisiana	Ohio
Florida	Massachusetts	Pennsylvania
Georgia	Michigan	Tennessee
Indiana	Mississippi	Wisconsin
Iowa		

States with Unit Banking

Colorado	Missouri	Oklahoma
Illinois	Montana	Texas
Kansas	Nebraska	West Virginia
Minnesota	North Dakota	Wyoming

Bank Holding Companies

Bank holding companies have been one way to get around laws against branching in many states. A holding company typically produces no good or service. It exists only to hold stock in other firms and manage them for profit.

A bank holding company can own stock in one or more banks and perhaps other financial institutions as well: finance companies, mortgage companies, insurance companies and leasing companies. Initially, holding companies could operate in more than one state, thus getting around laws against branching across state lines. Although this is no longer permitted, BankAmerica in California and Citicorp in New York are permitted to keep banks in other states that they acquired when the practice was legal.

Federal laws now limit the amount and types of firms a holding company can own. Some holding companies can own a limited number of banks alone but no other types of financial institutions. Others can own only one bank and an assortment of other institutions related to banking. The aim appears to be to allow a small bank to diversify, the better to weather a financial crisis in any one of its markets.

A bank holding company has some advantages. The parent company can borrow from the public by issuing short-term commercial paper or long-term corporate bonds. Then the parent company can relend the proceeds of the loans to any of the subsidiary companies, including the bank or banks. The result is to increase the banks' lending ability and to increase profits for the holding company. The largest bank holding companies in the nation are Chase Manhattan, BankAmerica, Citicorp, J.P. Morgan, Manufacturers Hanover, First Chicago, Chemical, Security Pacific, and Bankers Trust.

MONEY AND BANKING IN PRACTICE: THE REITs

An important subsidiary company of many bank holding companies is a Real Estate Investment Trust (or REIT). REITs became popular in the 1970s when building construction was enjoying a boom and interest rates were high. REITs acquire funds through sale of stock or commercial paper and from bank loans. They invest their funds in real property: apartment and office buildings, shopping centers, hotels and so forth. Rental income and appreciation of property values provide a return to stockholders and creditors.

REITs also make various types of mortgage loans. A *land development loan* finances necessary improvements on raw land before construction. Then a *construction loan* may be made to finance various stages toward a project's completion. Finally, a *long-term mortgage* may be made or a short-term mortgage to tide the developer over until credit conditions are most favorable for borrowing long-term.

The severe recession of 1975 took a heavy toll of REIT earnings. Building costs soared in the inflation of the 1970s, energy grew scarce and costly, interest rates rose to new heights and long-term mortgage money dried up. One major REIT, Great American Mortgage Investors, lost as much as $2 million a month. Even worse, the boom in construction produced such a surplus of commercial properties that many could not be rented or sold. As short-term commercial paper came due, REITs were unable to sell new issues, and many were forced out of business.

The problems of the REITs illustrate a common mistake in banking. When banks make substantial loans to any single activity, the lenders, in a sense, become hostages of the borrowers! If borrowers are unable to pay interest and principal when due, banks may feel pressured to extend more loans and perhaps even reduce interest charges on existing loans. The alternative might be bankruptcy for the borrower, in which case the affairs of the borrower are placed in the hands of outside management, and interest payments stop entirely. Banks did not want to foreclose on real property because of the heavy additional costs foreclosure would place on the bank, e.g. property taxes, maintenance and construction expenses and management costs.

To avoid foreclosure, many lending banks joined together in an attempt to help REITs recover from their financial problems. Chase Manhattan, Continental Illinois, First National City Bank of New York and First National of Chicago were major lenders to REITs. The profits of these banks suffered severely from the drop in earnings on their loan portfolios. When the nation's economy began a strong recovery in the mid-1980s, building construction picked up, and REITs began lending again. But presumably their experience in the 1970s made them more cautious regarding the quality of their loans.

Questions for Discussion

1. What are the advantages and disadvantages of central control of the kinds of loans banks are permitted to make?

2. How is question 1 related to other fundamental questions of our economic system?

3. How is question 1 related to the efficiency and equity of our financial sector?

MONEY AND BANKING IN PRACTICE: ARE LARGE BANKS MORE EFFICIENT?

How well do banks use our resources to produce the financial services we need? Does competition among small, unit banks work to cut costs and the prices of services? Or do large banks with many branches enjoy economies of scale that enable them to provide better service at lower cost?

Most bankers argue that all banks—large and small—face competition. They face competition not only from other banks but from other types of financial intermediaries: consumer finance companies, savings and loan associations, insurance companies, investment companies and even large retail stores. All these institutions make loans and pay interest on savings, as we have seen. This kind of competition keeps bank charges and bank profits low. Moreover, it keeps banks alert to community needs for new financial services. If competition is vigorous, large banks should be just as efficient as small ones.

Large banks may or may not enjoy economies of scale. Economies of scale result when fixed costs of operation are spread over larger and larger quantities of output. The cost of a bank's building or main office, its administrative staff, its legal and financial officers, its computer and communications equipment—all these represent substantial financial outlays that must be included in the bank's costs of production. For a bank that performs a large volume of service, each unit of service bears only a small part of the burden of fixed costs, and the average cost of bank services is lower.

Economies of scale occur in any economic activity, as fixed costs are spread over a larger quantity of output. Certain other costs generally rise with quantity of output. When a firm grows very large, coordinating activities among the various departments becomes more difficult. Communications between levels of authority become slow and incomplete. Often work effort declines in very large firms; low-level employees feel separated from decision making and may be less productive than in small firms. These kinds of problems cause the average cost of bank services to increase as volume increases, and we say there are diseconomies of scale. The important question is at what quantity of output are the gains from lower fixed cost per unit of service fully offset by other rising costs: In other words, at what size are economies of scale replaced by diseconomies?

Studies suggest that economies of scale outweigh diseconomies over a wide range of bank size; that is, large banks appear to have significantly lower unit costs than small banks. However,

the advantages enjoyed by very large banks are not substantially greater than those of medium-sized banks. This suggests that in the absence of any legal restrictions on bank size, the nation might expect a system of large and medium—but no small—banks to develop. The somewhat greater efficiency of large banks would be offset by the greater accessibility of medium-sized banks and perhaps their greater responsiveness to customers' needs.

Another feature of large banks probably increases their efficiency. Markets are more efficient when goods and services can move freely out of areas where demand is low relative to supply and into areas where demand is high. Free and easy movement among markets helps equalize prices and brings prices in all markets in line with the true cost of producing the good or service. This is particularly true of financial markets. For a large bank with many branches, deposits in one market may be more than enough to satisfy loan demand. The price of a loan (and the yield to the lender) would be rather low. If the bank operates a branch in another market where deposits are low relative to loan demand, it can draw funds out of the first market for lending in the second. This brings interest rates closer to equality throughout all markets. The result is a more efficient allocation of the nation's financial resources, with more balanced economic growth in all markets.

Questions for Discussion

1. What are the advantages and disadvantages to the local community when a large bank shifts funds around according to supply and demand for financial capital?

2. What economies and diseconomies of
   scale might apply to a bank holding company?

Loan Defaults, Bank Failures and Financial Panics

Banks want to make loans. Their business is to allocate the funds of savers to borrowers who will use the money for building new capital resources. The spread between the interest paid the saver and the interest charged the borrower determines bank profit. Profits are paid to bank stockholders or are kept in the bank as a basis for making more loans.

Occasionally bank lending is not profitable. Borrowers default on their loans; savers become concerned about the safety of their funds and draw deposits out of the bank. Bank stockholders lose their asset. Like any other business, banks face the risk of loss.

The risks of banking depend in part on the way banks are organized. At times in our history setting up a bank was a fairly simple matter. A few investors would purchase stock and invite savers to bring in their deposits. Soon many small banks would be offering loans to local firms. New businesses would be established, and old businesses would expand. Total spending would rise, bringing higher incomes and improved standards of living. Growth in economic activity would encourage new investments, and higher incomes would provide the savings for making still more loans.

A high rate of economic growth cannot be sustained forever. At some point, all worthwhile projects are already underway, and banks may begin making loans to less creditworthy borrowers. Beyond this point, continuing to increase bank credit may cause spending to rise above the productive capacity of the economy. Too much money leads to rising prices, rising costs of production, lower profits and loan defaults. When banks are unable to collect their loans, new lending is cut back. Spending and incomes fall, reducing investment and reducing saving for future investment.

Throughout the 1800s money growth fluctuated widely in the U.S. economy. One reason was the fragmented structure of our banking system. Small unit banks competed vigorously for loans when times were good and faded sadly out of sight when times were bad. The real bills doctrine could not eliminate bank risk or ensure stability for our economic system. Without any sort of centralized authority to regulate the money supply, we had to depend on the self-interest of many small banks to determine the nation's money.

Wide fluctuations in money growth are not efficient—either for the individual banks or for the economy as a whole. Wide swings in money are

TABLE 9-2 Commercial Bank Failures

Period	Number
1921–1929	5,711
1930–1933	9,096*
1934–1939	397†
1940–1949	115
1950–1959	43
1960–1969	57
1970–1979	81
1980–1985	309
1986	145

* Before deposit insurance.
† After deposit insurance.
SOURCE: Adapted from Milton Friedman and Anna Jacobson Schwartz, *A Monetary History of the United States, 1867–1960* (Princeton, N.J.: Princeton University Press, 1963), and FDIC.

typically associated with wide swings in economic activity, with rampant inflation followed by collapse and financial panic.

The severest collapse of economic activity in recent history was the Great Depression of the 1930s, when economic activity in the United States fell by about one-third. Unemployment rose to one-quarter of the labor force, and ten years passed before production again reached the level of 1929. In the financial panic that accompanied the depression, bank loans fell by more than half. Interest rates fell, reducing bank profits and reducing returns to savers. During 1930 to 1933, more than 9,000 U.S. banks simply disappeared, taking $2.5 billion of their depositors' and stockholders' savings and destroying confidence throughout the economy for years to come. The magnitude of bank failures during the period, relative to more recent decades, is shown in Table 9-2.

The depression hit small banks the hardest. Small banks were less able to diversify their loan portfolios. Frequently they had concentrated their lending in the local area, lending to farmers and merchants well-known to the bank. Among such borrowers, hard times spread fast. Farmers who were unable to sell their crops were unable to pay local merchants. Unemployed farm workers were forced to cut their spending, and local merchants cut their orders and laid off workers. For many depressed communities, economic activity ground slowly to a halt.

Larger banks or banks with branches would have been more able to diversify. They would have made loans to a variety of businesses in many different communities. Loan losses in one area would have been offset by profits in another. A large bank would have been less likely to make risky loans, because if creditworthy borrowers were scarce in one community, a large bank would have found them in another.

The Great Depression brought on changes in the structure of our financial system and the policies that regulate it. Gradually we have come to accept the idea that large banks may reduce the risks of loan defaults, bank failures and financial panics. At the same time we want to restrain the banking system from too much lending during periods of economic expansion; and we want to encourage lending in recession when new spending is most needed.

MONEY AND BANKING IN PRACTICE: INTERSTATE BANKING

Banking regulations in the United States allow a state to forbid banks to expand across state lines, and many states do so. One reason is pressure from small local banks to keep out out-of-state competition.

In the mid-1980s some states began to relax restrictions on interstate banking. They allowed banks from four or five neighboring states to buy into the local banking system. In some states, the monetary authorities have brought in large out-of-state banks to rescue failed local banks.

Freedom to open banks anywhere in the country has some advantages and some disadvantages. Profits on bank operations depend on efficiency, which may increase with size, because large banks use the most modern technologies for communicating financial information. But large size may reduce efficiency if size makes it more difficult to coordinate bank operations.

Citicorp of New York has purchased banks and thrifts in California, Florida, Illinois and Texas. It already accepts deposits in many states as a result of its purchases of failed savings and loan associations, and it operates credit-card businesses in others. BankAmerica of California owns branches up and down the West Coast and would like to establish branches in major cities like New York, Chicago, Atlanta, Washington, Miami and Boston.

Chase Manhattan of New York wants to set up medium-sized banks and thrifts in the major regions of the country and coordinate them with electronic and direct-mail services. Manufacturers Hanover owns 1,000 offices in 44 states outside New York, its home state. The offices are not banks but finance companies, mortgage companies, and other kinds of loan offices. Chemical Bank of Chicago is interested primarily in banking in its own region. Security Pacific is one of the nation's most profitable large banks and is less interested in acquiring more banks than in obtaining permission for banks to carry on more different types of financial services, like lending for real estate development and marketing corporate stocks and bonds. Marine Midland Bank, which is controlled by the Hongkong and Shanghai Banking Corporation, aims to establish a network of banks across the country, each of which will operate fairly independently.

Question for Discussion

1. What are some other advantages and disadvantages of interstate banking?

MONEY AND BANKING IN PRACTICE: BASIC BANKING

Over the past ten years, changes in banking regulations have brought fundamental changes in how banks do business. The result has been still more fundamental changes in how people and communities use banks. Some economists acknowledge that the changes may have brought greater efficiency, but they worry that they may also have brought some inequity.

One result of changes in bank regulations has been more competition among financial intermediaries. Increasing competition forces all intermediaries to cut costs. One way to do that is to eliminate services that were formerly provided free. An example is free checking, which many banks provided to all customers whether or not their average balances yielded enough income to pay the costs. Another example is extensive branching: Depositors could establish a close relationship with a neighborhood bank whether or not their deposits were large enough to pay the cost of the branch.

With competition, banks have set prices on all bank services according to the cost of service, and they have closed unprofitable branches. Changes like these have had their greatest impact on low-income families and their communities. Low-income families are less able to afford the minimum balances now required on deposit accounts. Furthermore, without a neighborhood branch, low-income families are less able to obtain bank credit than when they were personally known to the bank.

Some economists believe banks have an obligation to choose policies that increase equity as well as efficiency in financial services. They point out that banks are awarded their charters by government, and they receive benefits from government agencies: in particular, deposit insurance and regulatory supervision. These economists are encouraging a move to "basic banking" by all depository institutions. The Federal Reserve Bulletin defines basic banking as "the minimum level of financial services that should be available to all citizens, regardless of income."

Minimum financial services include "a safe and accessible place to keep money, a way to obtain cash and a way to make payments to third parties." Lacking these services, low-income families may be forced out of the financial system entirely, a result that discourages saving and requires greater reliance on cash. It may also deprive low-income families of access to credit. The Federal Reserve estimates that 12 percent of U.S. families, or roughly 9.5 million families, hold neither a checking nor a savings account. The majority of these families fall into the lowest income families and include disproportionate numbers of nonwhite women heads of households and nonwhite families.

Some banks are providing basic banking services to certain customers: checking accounts with low minimum balance requirements and reduced fees, free checking accounts with all deposits and withdrawals made through automated teller machines, and savings accounts with low or zero minimum balances and a limited number of deposits and withdrawals.

Questions for Discussion

1. Should banks be treated differently from other business firms, with respect to production of services for low-income families? Why or why not?

2. What other approaches might be made toward the issue of equity in banking?

Policies for Money Growth

Throughout this chapter we have been concerned with the supply of money: how the banking system affects the money supply and how the money supply affects economic activity. In general, we have focused on the elasticity of the money supply. An elastic money supply is one that expands or contracts along with the needs of the economy.

Population growth and the advance of technical knowledge practically ensure growth of economic activity over the long term. An *elastic currency* provides an increase in purchasing power, in line with the nation's growing capacity to produce goods and services. A unitary, fragmented banking system can produce a money supply that is *too* elastic: expanding above the economy's real needs in good times and contracting below the economy's needs in bad times. An objective of policy should be to help banks provide just enough money to satisfy the nation's needs, without contributing to inflation or financial panic.

Economists and monetary policymakers do not always agree on the correct way to achieve this objective. The basis for the debate is the proper level of government regulation over the activities of banks. A free market system seeks to accomplish its economic objectives with a minimum of government interference. It is not always clear that government officials have the necessary information for guiding the actions of the private sector in the most efficient way. Without correct knowledge and proper tools for carrying out decisions quickly, government intervention may produce results more harmful than those that flow from private decisions.

The Monetarists

Economists who worry about too much government intervention favor a fairly automatic and regular increase in the money supply. Because population growth and technological progress together increase our productive capacity by about 4 percent every year, they propose a regular 4 percent increase in the money supply. The *4 percent rule* would provide enough money for economic growth without relying on either the independent decisions of banks or the fallible decisions of government. Allowing the money supply to grow by a fixed percentage a year, they say, reduces the tendency toward alternating periods of inflation and financial panic.

Economists who favor a money-supply rule call themselves *Monetarists*, and their leader is Milton Friedman of Stanford's Hoover Institution. Friedman's chief concern is to preserve maximum freedom for individuals to pursue their own economic objectives, without interference by government. Functions that can be performed well by the private sector, says Friedman, should remain the responsibility of private individuals and institutions. Unnecessary interference by government will only destabilize and weaken the free market economy.

Real and Nominal Money

An important part of monetary theory is a distinction between the *nominal money supply* and the *real money supply*. The nominal money supply is its value in current dollar amounts; the real money supply is its value in dollars of constant purchasing power. To determine the real money supply, it is necessary to deflate (or inflate) the nominal money supply by dividing by a price index.

To illustrate, the nominal money supply in December 1985 was $626.6 billion, and the price index was 1.115 (with base year 1982). Thus the real money supply was:

Nominal Money Supply/Price Index = $626.6/1.115 = $561.97 billion

when measured in terms of constant dollars of 1982. In December 1986 the nominal money supply was $730.4 and the price index was 1.145, making the real money supply:

$$\$730.4/1.145 = \$637.90.$$

Nominal money grew by almost 17 percent in 1986, but inflation reduced real money growth to less than 14 percent.

Varying rates of inflation change steady nominal money growth to *varying* growth in real money. In fact, variations in real money growth help moderate a tendency toward inflation and financial panic. To see why, suppose spending begins to grow too fast, faster than 4 percent annually and beyond the real productive capacity of the nation's resources. With spending increasing faster than real production, prices begin to rise. If the nominal money supply continues to grow at the rate of 4 percent, however, growth of the real money supply will fall. The decrease in real money growth works to limit the increase in spending and slows down the increase in prices.

The opposite change in the real money supply helps increase spending to correct a slowdown in economic growth. When economic growth slows to less than 4 percent, incomes and spending fall off, unemployment increases, and price inflation levels off or declines. If the nominal money supply continues to grow as before, the real money supply grows faster. The increase in real money stimulates spending and income, increases investment, and reduces unemployment.

Rules versus Discretion

Some economists think all this sounds too good to be true. They worry about the time it might take for all these results to take place. They say that the economy must already be experiencing inflation or deflation—possibly for a considerable length of time—before the real value of the money supply changes. There may be a long, painful business crisis before spenders adjust to the change in the real money supply. In fact, prices may never fall in recession, so that the real money supply does not grow, and automatic recovery cannot take place.

These economists prefer flexibility in money management rather than rigid rules. They recommend money growth policies that vary according to the *discretion* of policymakers. In their view, the money supply should be allowed to grow at a rate consistent with the needs of the economy. Discretion allows for steady growth during periods of healthy economic growth and slower growth if inflation accelerates. During a slowdown in economic growth, money growth could be speeded up so as to encourage new spending.

Discretionary monetary policy can be completely effective only if policymakers have immediate information about economic conditions and reliable forecasts about future developments. Their decisions must be made and carried out promptly if they are to be consistent with current economic problems. Without prompt action, a policy to increase money growth to avoid a slowdown in economic activity might finally take place after the economy has moved into expansion. On the other hand, decreasing money growth to moderate inflation might come too late and worsen the financial panic that follows.

Glossary of Terms

Banking School.   economists who belived banks should create credit money in line with growth of production of goods and services

Currency School.   economists who believed banks should be merely depositories of the public's money

discretion.   the use of judgment to determine the appropriate changes in the money supply

elastic currency.   a money supply that expands and contracts along with the needs of the economy

4 percent rule.   a rule that the money supply should grow at a steady rate equal to average annual increases in productive capacity

Monetarists.   economists who place the greatest importance on the supply of money for determining economic growth and deciding economic policy

nominal money supply.   the money supply measured in terms of current dollars

real bills doctrine.   a principle that loans should be made only for productive activity

real money supply.   the money supply measured in terms of dollars of constant purchasing power

REIT.   Real Estate Investment Trust, a subsidiary of a bank holding company organized for lending for commercial construction

self-liquidating.   the characteristic of a loan through which productive activity earns the funds for paying the lender

self-regulating.   the characteristic of a loan through which the supply of credit money parallels the growth of production

Summary of Important Ideas

1. The Currency School believed banks should be storehouses of the community's gold and silver money. Banks should not create money; instead, the production and distribution of specie around the world would respond automatically to the needs of trade.

2. The Banking School believed banks should create additional credit money, but only for production of real goods and services. Bank credit would be self-liquidating and self-regulating, so that money creation would never contribute to economic instability. Nevertheless, the real bills doctrine was found to work badly in a complex economy with many stages of processing and with the need for consumer credit.

3. The community may exercise control over banking in either of two ways: (1) banks can be kept small so as to preclude the growth of market power or (2) banks can be allowed to grow and then be regulated by a central authority. Many state banking laws restrict bank size, and national banks are regulated.

4. The question of bank size involves consideration of efficiency and equity. Bank holding companies increase the variety of services and probably the efficiency of banks.

5. In past centuries, a proliferation of small, state-chartered banks frequently contributed to excessive money growth and business cycles. An elastic money supply expands or contracts along with the needs of the economy.

6. Monetarists favor steady growth in nominal money, believing that accompanying variations in real money will moderate business cycles. They believe information on economic conditions is too unreliable to guarantee correct decisions on money growth. Other economists recommend discretionary changes in the money supply to accommodate credit needs.

Questions for Discussion and Research

1. Illustrate the weakness of the real bills doctrine in a modern economy. Show how the doctrine might be destabilizing.

2. How is the question of bank size related to other fundamental questions of our economic and political system? Why is the question becoming more important now than in the past?

3. What are the advantages and disadvantages of bank holding companies in terms of their efficiency and equity?

4. What are the implications of bank failure for economic efficiency, stability and economic growth? (Are there any favorable implications?) Consult the *Readers' Guide* for sources of information on bank failures in the 1970s and 1980s.

5. How is the debate over rules versus discretion significant in other areas of national economic activity? How do advances in technology bear on the debate?

6. What would be the results of 100 percent reserve banking? Defend positions supporting and opposing such a policy.

7. A study in 1976 revealed that banks in a unit-banking state (Oklahoma) earned 1.18 percent on assets. How does this return compare with the national average for banks? How would you account for the difference?

8. Some of the nation's large banks are opening loan offices in other states. Some of the loan offices also sell their own notes. What are the implications of this development?

9. Some inner-city residents complain that local savings, deposited in local banks, are used for lending to suburban homeowners. Does this represent a conflict between efficiency and equity? How are such conflicts resolved?

Additional Readings

Bowsher, Norman. "Have Multibank Holding Companies Affected Commercial Bank Performance?" *Federal Reserve Bank of St. Louis Review* 60 (April 1978): 8–15.

"Interstate Banking Developments." *Federal Reserve Bulletin* (February 1987): 79–92.

Jessee, Michael, and Steven A. Seelig. *A Bank Holding Company and the Public Interest: An Economic Analysis.* Lexington, Mass.: Lexington Books, 1977.

Korobow, Leon, and George Budzeika, "Financial Limits on Interstate Bank Expansion." *Federal Reserve Bank of New York Quarterly Review* (Summer 1985): 13–27.

Palash, Carl J. "The Household Debt Burden: How Heavy Is It?" *Federal Reserve Bank of New York Quarterly Review* 4 (Summer 1979): 9–11.

C H A P T E R

10

- To understand the problems that led to creation of the Federal Reserve System
- To learn the structure and functions of Federal Reserve Banks
- To see the tools Federal Reserve Banks use to affect money creation

The Federal Reserve System

"For those who do not believe in socialism it is very hard to accept this proposed action on the part of government."

The American Bankers Association

Commercial banks provide services that stimulate economic activity and improve economic efficiency. They hold deposits of individuals, business firms and governments, and they make payments for their depositors. They accept financial capital from stockholders. They use their funds to make loans and investments that earn a return for depositors and stockholders; and they create additional deposits to satisfy our nation's growing need for money.

The importance of these functions gives banks tremendous power over our economic lives and gives rise to efforts to curb and direct that power. Bank power can be regulated in either of two ways. Banks can be kept so small as to prevent the use of market power. Whereas small size may threaten economic stability and may reduce bank efficiency, we may prefer these disadvantages to the dangers associated with market power. Or banks may be allowed to grow and then be regulated by a central authority. The regulatory authority would interpret the needs of the economy and offer the appropriate incentives and limitations for banks to satisfy those needs. The disadvantages associated with large banks may be offset by the greater co-ordination between economic objectives and banking practices.

In the United States we have used both approaches to limit the power of banks: legal restrictions that have kept banks relatively small, on the one hand, and government regulation of bank practices, on the other. The result is a dual system of banks, with some sacrifice of economic efficiency and with less-than-perfect coordination of bank policies.

Early Banking in the United States: State Banks and the Bank of the United States

The U.S. Constitution gave the states the power to charter banks, a power they began to exercise rather quickly. As early as 1791, the nation had about 18 state banks, each accepting deposits and issuing loans in the form of state bank notes. Some of the Founding Fathers were already worried about the overissue of bank credit, however, and Secretary of the Treasury Alexander Hamilton persuaded Congress to charter a national bank, the first Bank of the United States.

The Bank of the United States helped limit bank credit in several ways. It limited its own currency to the value of its paid-in capital, which at the time was $10 million. When its bank notes were deposited in state banks, state banks would redeem them for specie at the Bank of the United States. Then the state banks would hold specie and other national bank notes as reserves against their own issue of state bank notes. If the Bank of the United States reduced its lending, it reduced the flow of national bank notes to state banks and reduced their ability to issue state bank notes.

The Bank of the United States had an even more effective tool against overissue of state bank notes. When state bank notes were deposited in the Bank of the United States, the Bank would present them to the issuing bank for redemption in specie. This could be an unhappy experience for state banks whose note issue far exceeded their specie reserves.

The Bank of the United States also served as banker for the U.S. Treasury, accepting deposits of tax revenues and making payments. And it helped the Treasury borrow when tax revenues fell short of spending needs.

To some early Americans, the Bank of the United States seemed too powerful. They feared any sort of central authority, allied with the Treasury and able to control borrowing and lending. Their opposition and a revival of support for states' rights led to a lapse of the Bank's charter in 1811.

Without the limitations imposed by the Bank of the United States, many state banks went back to their old habits. They made too many loans, issued too many bank notes, and brought on a banking crisis. Many banks gave out all their specie and were forced to suspend convertibility. The Treasury continued to accept state bank notes in payment of taxes, however, partly because of its own financial problems. The War of 1812 with Britain was becoming expensive and was forcing the government to borrow. In 1816, Congress chartered the second Bank of the United States to carry on the same functions as the first and to assist the Treasury in borrowing.

The second Bank of the United States was no more popular with the public than the first. The nation's political balance was slowly shifting to farmers of the West and South, as reflected in the election of President

Andrew Jackson in 1828. Western and Southern voters did not trust the Eastern financial "monopoly," and they opposed the Bank's restrictions on state bank notes. The Bank itself was found to be guilty of mismanagement and unethical practices. In 1831, President Jackson withdrew the Treasury's deposits from the Bank, and soon after that its charter was allowed to expire for the last time.

Between 1836 and 1863, there was little centralized regulation of banks. For a time, the Treasury kept its funds in "pet banks" scattered around the country, but it soon became clear that many banks were using Treasury deposits (and the accompanying reserves) to make too many loans. Eventually independent sub-Treasuries were set up in certain cities so that the government's deposits could be held outside the banking system entirely. With no regulation of their lending, state banks were free to expand their note issue. The result was several decades of wildcat banking, particularly in the less settled areas of the country where it was difficult to present bank notes to the issuing bank for redemption in specie. There followed successive periods of, first, overissue of currency, then inflation and suspension of convertibility, and finally the collapse of many banks.

State Banking Regulations

Some states tried to regulate banks at the state level. New York established the Safety Fund System, requiring state-chartered banks to contribute a percentage of their loans to a kind of insurance fund that would guarantee payment to the depositors and noteholders of failed banks. The system worked fairly well as long as bank failures were few. But when banks in nearby states failed and their notes became worthless, New York banks holding such notes faced insolvency, too. Financial panics and bank crises spread rapidly and depleted the fund, wiping out the assets of many bank depositors.

In Massachusetts, a different system proved more successful. The Suffolk Bank in Boston accepted deposits of notes issued by country banks. Often these notes circulated at less than par, or face value, because of the difficulty of redeeming them in specie. The Bank "invited" state banks to deposit specie in the Suffolk Bank for redeeming their notes at par. If they refused, the Suffolk Bank would collect their notes and present them for redemption. This turned out to be a reasonably effective way to discourage overissue.

The strictest state control of banks was established in Louisiana. Louisiana law required state banks to hold specie reserves equal to one-third the value of their deposits and outstanding bank notes. Bank loans were to be limited to short-term commercial loans only—no real estate loans or loans described as speculative. All bank notes received on deposit in any bank were to be returned to the issuing bank for redemption in specie. Such restrictions effectively limited note issue in that state.

The National Banking System

Frequent cycles of heavy lending and inflation followed by loan defaults, bank failures and financial panic continued in the United States until the time of the Civil War. By then, more voters had come to support some form of government regulation. Meanwhile, the war was increasing Treasury borrowing needs. For both these reasons, Congress passed the National Banking Act of 1863 setting up a new system of nationally chartered banks.

National banks were chartered by the U.S. Comptroller of the Currency, an official of the Treasury. The Comptroller set minimum capital requirements for national banks, with the highest requirements for banks in large cities. A national bank was required to purchase U.S. government securities equal to some fraction of its total liabilities. It was allowed to issue notes up to 90 percent of the value of these securities, but never more than the value of its own capital stock. In addition, national banks were required to maintain a fund with the Treasury for redemption of their notes. Total national bank notes were initially limited to $300 million.

National banks were also required to hold reserves against their deposits and outstanding notes. Small country banks held reserves in the form of specie, Treasury currency, or in accounts in the larger reserve city banks. Reserve city banks held reserves in the form of vault cash and reserve accounts in still larger central reserve city banks. For central reserve city banks, reserves were specie and Treasury currency only. The reserve requirements placed effective limits on currency issue for nationally chartered banks.

Some Problems

The National Banking System was not completely successful in stabilizing economic activity and achieving efficiency in the nation's financial system. The government's tax and spending policies were partly to blame. After the Civil War, the U.S. government decided to reduce the amount of outstanding currency issued during the war. So much currency had been issued that it could not be redeemed in specie, and the nation was, in effect, on a paper money standard.

Restoring convertibility required years of higher taxes and lower government spending until convertibility was finally restored in 1879. Tax money was paid in to the Treasury and removed from the money supply. As a result, bank reserves declined, and bank lending collapsed. Spending slowed, and economic activity declined as well. Slow growth and economic distress led to growing public demand for use of the more plentiful silver along with gold as a money standard. Financial panics and bank failures occurred fairly regularly, and existing banking laws were inadequate to prevent them.

The shortcomings of the National Banking System were in part a result of the structure of the system itself. One problem was the absence of a central clearinghouse for checks. Banks were forced into temporary arrangements among themselves, a practice that was especially difficult over long distances and that made financial transactions slow and cumbersome. The arrangement for holding reserves was a problem, too. Periodically, country banks would call upon reserve city banks for currency to satisfy their depositors' needs. As their reserve accounts were drawn out, reserve city banks had to cut back their own lending or call in their loans. If the reserve city banks looked to central reserve city banks for currency, these banks would experience the same problems.

The plan for holding reserves caused crises to spread quickly. Deposit withdrawals placed all banks in a liquidity crunch. Then banks put pressure on borrowers, forcing them to cut back their own spending and causing some to default. Under the National Banking System there was no "lender of last resort" to step in with additional funds in a credit crunch. Because holders of reserves were themselves commercial banks, they were all subject to the same contractionary forces.

The regulations governing note issue created other problems. Remember that national banks could issue notes equal in value to 90 percent of the value of their U.S. government securities. The effect of this rule was to tie note issue to the size of the federal debt. Normally, as the economy expands, tax revenues increase and the Treasury reduces its borrowing. Under the National Banking Act, a reduction in Treasury borrowing meant a reduction in banks' ability to issue notes. When banks were unable to issue additional notes, a general scarcity of money and credit caused a slowdown in economic activity. In fact, over the period 1881 through 1896—fifteen years of potentially vigorous economic growth—there was no appreciable increase in the public's holdings of currency. The accompanying decline in prices probably contributed to a lower level of real growth than would have occurred otherwise.

During the half century from 1863 to 1913, the shortcomings of the National Banking System became more and more apparent. To achieve healthy economic growth and to improve efficiency in the nation's financial system, certain changes seemed necessary: (1) a central clearinghouse for checks, (2) a system of reserve deposits that would be less vulnerable to financial crisis, (3) a "lender of last resort" when banks needed liquidity and (4) note issue tied to the legitimate needs of the economy. In 1913, following the most severe financial crisis to date, Congress passed new banking legislation to provide for these needs.

The Federal Reserve Act of 1913

The law that created the Federal Reserve System took account of voters' concerns about too much centralization of power. Thus, it divided the nation into 12 districts, each with its own Federal Reserve Bank. The 12 Federal

Reserve Banks were expected to consult regularly and coordinate their policies to achieve healthy growth of credit. Federal Reserve Banks were to hold no individual deposits but were to act as "bankers' banks" and banker for the U.S. Treasury. They would hold required reserve accounts for commercial banks and use these accounts for clearing checks. They would hold Treasury accounts and make payments for the Treasury; and they would assist the Treasury in issuing new U.S. government securities. Federal Reserve Banks would also hold deposits of foreign central banks for use in clearing checks used in international trade. The individual Federal Reserve Banks were to be privately owned institutions, selling shares of stock to the commercial banks in their district.

The Federal Reserve System was given power to issue Federal Reserve notes, which were to take the place of notes formerly issued by national banks. Federal Reserve notes are liabilities of the Federal Reserve System, which holds, in turn, U.S. government securities, gold certificates, Special Drawing Rights (issued by the International Monetary Fund) and certain other types of assets. About 90 percent of the nation's currency is Federal Reserve notes, the remainder being a small quantity of Treasury notes and coins. Commercial banks acquire currency when needed by drawing down their reserve accounts at the Federal Reserve Bank.

The Federal Reserve Act marked an important shift in emphasis from that which governed the National Banking System. Under the National Banking System, the primary objective was to maintain currency convertibility; national banks exerted their various powers to limit note issue so as to prevent overexpansion and collapse. Little attention was paid to establishing the appropriate quantity of money—appropriate in terms of the legitimate needs of a growing economy. The Federal Reserve Act stated as an objective of the new system to provide for an elastic currency, one that would respond to the nation's goals of full employment, stable economic growth and price stability.

The Board of Governors

Although the Federal Reserve Act called for decentralized bank regulation, providing for an elastic currency is more properly the responsibility of a central authority. The central governing body of the Federal Reserve System is the Board of Governors, headquartered in Washington, D.C. The Board has broad powers for making policy in accordance with national objectives. Seven Governors are appointed to the Board by the President (and approved by Congress) to serve terms of fourteen years. (Members cannot be reappointed after serving a full term.) Because they are appointed for long terms, the Governors are less subject to political pressures than elected officials; they are free to use their own training, experience and judgment as guides to policy decisions. Furthermore, their terms are arranged to expire every second year, making it generally impossible for a president to appoint more than two Governors during a single term of office. Thus, no President can achieve a quick majority of the Board and influence its decisions.

One member of the Board of Governors is designated by the President to serve as Chairman for a term of four years, not coincident with the President's own term of office but eligible for reappointment. The Chairman represents the Board before the public and in regular appearances before Congress. The Chairman also meets with the President, the Secretary of the Treasury, the Chairman of the President's Council of Economic Advisors, and the Director of the Office of Management and Budget. Together, these officials assess current and future needs of the economy and coordinate policies to fill these needs. The Board of Governors is assisted in this function by the Federal Advisory Council: a council of representatives from each Federal Reserve district.

The Politics of the Federal Reserve Act

Passage of the Federal Reserve Act did not eliminate the public's concerns about too much government interference in the control of the nation's money. The law aimed at preserving decentralization of the banking system and independence of the Federal Reserve—independence from Congress and the President. Independence would ensure that decisions would be based on the public interest rather than on political considerations. It was expected that the Federal Reserve System would coordinate its actions with policy decisions of the legislative and executive branches, but cooperation was not guaranteed. In fact, it was hoped that the Federal Reserve would use its independence to restrain what might be improper actions of the two branches.

Coordination and cooperation have generally prevailed. There have been some exceptions, which we will discuss in time. The exceptions have strengthened the role of the Federal Reserve in influencing economic activity, but they demonstrate also that the system must move cautiously when it acts in opposition to Congress. Congress passed the law that created the Federal Reserve, and it could pass a new law destroying it or curbing its powers. This is not likely to happen, because many legislators remain opposed to greater centralization of economic power. Still, in 1975 Congress directed the Chairman of the Board of Governors to report regularly to Congress on the intended policy actions of the system. At these reporting sessions the Chairman is subject to intensive questioning about the goals of the Federal Reserve System and its success in meeting these goals.

The Federal Reserve Banks

The 12 Federal Reserve Banks are located in Boston, New York, Philadelphia, Cleveland, Richmond, Atlanta, Chicago, St. Louis, Minneapolis,

Kansas City, Dallas and San Francisco. Twenty-four additional cities have Federal Reserve branches, and the Federal Reserve also operates 36 automated clearinghouses for clearing checks at other locations. Commercial banks have no voice in determining Federal Reserve policy, but they are permitted to vote for members of the district Bank's Board of Directors. Three directors are designated Class A directors and may be engaged in banking; three are designated Class B directors and may not be engaged in banking. The Board of Governors in Washington appoints three Class C directors in each district and designates one chairman. The nine directors carry out Federal Reserve policy within their district according to guidelines established by the Board of Governors.

Profits earned on Federal Reserve Bank assets—primarily U.S. government securities—are used to pay a 6 percent dividend return to stockholder banks, with the remainder paid to the Treasury. The Banks have generally been profitable, returning 80 percent of earnings to the Treasury. Returning profits to the Treasury removes the profit-seeking incentive from Bank operations and helps ensure that policy will be made in the public interest alone. Financial independence also helps the Federal Reserve avoid political pressure and pressures from the President or Congress.

Rules and Regulations

The Garn–St. Germaine Depository Institutions Act of 1982 requires all depository institutions to hold reserves against their deposits. The term "depository institutions" includes commercial banks, savings and loan associations, mutual savings banks, credit unions and international branches of these institutions.

Required reserves may be in the form of vault cash or deposits in the district Federal Reserve Bank. Reserve accounts earn no interest and therefore tend to reduce a bank's profits. Banks are also required to observe certain rules with respect to adequate capital stock, mergers with other banks or establishment of branches, relationships with holding companies, and limitations on loans and investments. All commercial banks are examined regularly—national banks by the Comptroller of the Currency and state banks by the Federal Reserve.

The Federal Reserve provides certain benefits to the nation's commercial banks. These benefits include check clearing and the use of the Federal Reserve's wire transfer for dispatching funds and securities among cities, the privilege of borrowing reserves under certain restrictions established by regulation, currency when needed, use of Federal Reserve research facilities for obtaining economic information, and the opportunity to participate in selection of Class A and Class B directors and to receive dividends on Federal Reserve stock.

MONEY AND BANKING IN PRACTICE:
THE FEDERAL RESERVE: INDEPENDENCE OR CONTROL?

The Constitution of the United States established a government in which each branch was to be independent of the others. The authors of the Constitution believed that such a division of power was "essential to the preservation of liberty." (Alexander Hamilton, quoted by Arthur F. Burns, "The Independence of the Federal Reserve System," *Federal Reserve Bulletin*, June 1976.) The Federal Reserve Act of 1913 was designed to maintain this division, insulating board members from political considerations and encouraging actions to serve the public and the general welfare. Independence was necessary if the system was to avoid pressure from voters and, more especially, from the legislative and executive branches of government itself.

Federal Reserve independence from the legislative and executive branches was intended to prevent excessive money growth. Especially since the Employment Act of 1946, the federal government has become increasingly committed to policies of full employment, economic growth, and improved opportunities for the nation's poor and disadvantaged. In general, Congress and the President support programs with these objectives, but they resist tax increases to finance the increased expenditures. The result is a tendency toward budget deficits, which must be financed by Treasury borrowing. If the Federal Reserve were subordinate to the wishes of the President and Congress, the result might be excessive money growth and worsening inflation.

The Federal Reserve is not completely independent, nevertheless. It was created by Congress to be independent *within* the government—not independent *of* government. Independence was to be assured by the fact that the system itself is financially self-supporting. It does not have to apply to Congress for appropriations to meet its annual budget, and therefore it does not have to justify its policies before Congress.

Still, the Federal Reserve cannot afford to ignore the objectives of Congress. Since 1975, the Federal Reserve Chairman has been required to meet with Congress twice a year to discuss policy. In February the Chairman is expected to discuss the President's economic goals for the year and how the system will perform with respect to those goals. Then in July he is asked to evaluate progress toward the administration's goals. In regular conferences with Congress and the President, the direction of influence probably goes both ways: Congress and the President seek the system's cooperation toward their objectives, but the Chairman also attempts to guide administration policy in ways he believes to be healthy for the economy. (As yet there has been no "she.")

What about Federal Reserve independence from voters? Some critics of the system's independence believe that the public should indeed have some influence in making Federal Reserve policy. Unless voters are allowed a voice in policy, these critics say, there is a danger that organized special interests may come to dominate the system. In particular, they worry that members of the financial community itself may impose their attitudes on the Federal Reserve, causing money growth to increase or decrease in line with their own interests.

In fact, the original legislation took account of the need for some public influence on the Federal Reserve System. Establishment of 12 district Banks, each with its own separate shareholders and directors, was expected to guarantee local control. District Bank directors are representatives of the local banking and business community. One director from each bank is designated a member of the Federal Advisory Council (FAC), which meets four times annually with the Board of Governors. The original purpose of the FAC was to consult on regional economic issues and make recommendations to the Board on economic policy. In practice, neither district Bank directors nor the Federal Advisory Council exercises substantial influence on policy.

The Issues: To what extent should the Federal Reserve cooperate with the objectives of Congress and the President and with the interests of voters? Should the Federal Reserve increase commercial bank reserves to assist in financing the Treasury's deficit?

The primary responsibility of the Federal Reserve is to regulate money growth within a range that allows spending to increase in line with the nation's capacity to produce goods and services. Too-fast money growth tends to encourage too much spending and lead to inflation. Throughout history, rapid inflation typically is followed by financial panic and bank failures. Without independence from political pressure, the Federal Reserve might be subject to excessive demands to increase money growth.

There is another side to the question of money growth. Congress and the President are correct in advocating money growth fast enough to provide for new capital investment. Slow money growth keeps interest rates high and discourages business and private investment spending. A decrease in the rate of capital investment reduces productivity growth and creates fewer new jobs. High mortgage interest rates reduce homebuilding. In both cases, the result may be a lower level of total production and higher prices someday in the future. Thus Federal Reserve policies to reduce inflation may end by actually increasing inflation.

An End to Independence? The question of political pressure creates a difficult dilemma for the Federal Reserve System. If the Federal Reserve deviates too far from the growth rate desired by Congress and the President, there could be a change in its status. Under the influence of Presidential pressure the Congress could pass new legislation placing the Federal Reserve under more complete control.

This is not likely, however. Although Congress puts on frequent displays of displeasure with the Federal Reserve, legislators probably welcome an outside restraint on their actions. If the Federal Reserve were subservient to Congress, members of Congress could not "run against the Fed." (In election years, legislators want an independent scapegoat to take the blame for policies that their voters don't like). Congress more likely will continue to require regular reports from the Board of Governors as to its intentions and its success in achieving past objectives. Such conferences are not only helpful to Congress, but they also supply information to the general public. This information plays an important role in increasing voters' awareness of the policies of the Federal Reserve and how those policies affect their own lives.

Questions for Discussion

1. To what extent should the Federal Reserve be responsive to the wishes of Congress? the President? the voters?

2. How might members of the financial community differ in their preferences regarding money supply growth? Consider the interest-rate implications (both short-term and long-term) of changes in money growth.

3. How seriously should one take Congressional threats to change the independent status of the Federal Reserve? Why?

MONEY AND BANKING IN PRACTICE: ALAN GREENSPAN AS FEDERAL RESERVE CHAIRMAN

Alan Greenspan was Chairman of President Ford's Council of Economic Advisors. He was an economic consultant for most of his subsequent career. He was nominated Chairman of the Board of Governors of the Federal Reserve System at a particularly difficult time for monetary policymaking.

In 1987 the nation had been enjoying a long period of economic expansion, with rising economic activity, rising incomes and falling unemployment. A significant factor in the expansion was the increase in the money supply that began under former Chairman Paul Volcker in 1982. Until 1982, Volcker had resisted pressure to increase money growth, reasoning that faster money growth without substantial increases in productivity would eventually lead to inflation.

Some investors were worried that Greenspan would be less able to resist similar pressure and that rising inflation would ultimately bring on rising interest rates. Rising interest rates would mean falling prices on existing securities sold with fixed interest rates. Immediately after Greenspan's nomination, many investors sold securities from their portfolios, and prices did fall. Prices rebounded fairly quickly, however, suggesting that investors had regained their confidence in Greenspan.

Greenspan is generally described as a conservative economist, one who resists abrupt short-run changes in policy and favors policies to ensure long-run economic stability. He opposes much of government regulation and is likely to favor policies that ease restrictions and increase competition among financial intermediaries.

Other members of the Federal Reserve Board are likely to agree. Manuel Johnson is Vice Chairman and has close ties with President Reagan's conservative economic advisers. Wayne Angell and Edward Kelley were also appointed by President Reagan and generally share his conservative economic philosophy. Martha Seger frequently disagreed with former Chairman Volcker about money growth, along with other members tending to favor faster money growth than Volcker was willing to allow. Among the present Federal Reserve Board members, Robert Heller has the broadest experience in international trade and finance, an area that is growing increasingly important. (The seventh seat on the Board of Governors is currently vacant.)

Like Volcker, Greenspan will probably be more cautious than other Federal Reserve Board members. He tends to oppose radical moves that may destabilize the economy. Unlike Volcker, however, he is highly political and may be inclined to adjust his policies to achieve political goals.

Questions for Discussion

1. Why do you suppose economists described as conservative favored faster money growth during the administration of President Reagan?

2. Compare the position of economists during the Reagan administration with that of the neoclassical economists.

Federal Reserve Functions: Check Clearing, Bank Borrowing and Cash Withdrawals

Federal Reserve Banks provide three important services to commercial banks: check clearing, bank borrowing and currency withdrawals.

Check Clearing

Check clearing involves the transfer of funds from one financial institution to another and can be illustrated with T-accounts showing changes in balance sheets. As "bankers' banks," the Federal Reserve Banks hold reserve deposits for commercial banks in their district. Like other banks, they also hold assets in the form of cash, loans and investments. An outline of a balance sheet for a Federal Reserve Bank is shown in Figure 10–1.

FIGURE 10–1 Federal Reserve Bank

Assets	Liabilities

Currency
Loans
Investments
	Reserve Accounts
	  Lombard Bank
	  Peachtree Bank
	  Wall Street Bank
	Capital Accounts

As a central clearinghouse for checks, the Federal Reserve handles checks written against accounts in one bank and paid into accounts in another. It uses commercial bank reserve accounts to transfer funds from the paying bank to the receiving bank. Then it notifies both banks of the change in their reserve accounts.

To illustrate, suppose a depositor of Lombard Bank writes a $10 check to a depositor of Peachtree Bank. When the Peachtree Bank receives the check, it sends it along with many others to the Federal Reserve Bank or branch in the district. Check-sorting equipment helps separate checks drawn against various banks, and the Federal Reserve adjusts bank reserve accounts accordingly. The T-account in Figure 10–2 shows the changes made at the Federal Reserve.

FIGURE 10–2

FEDERAL RESERVE BANK

	Reserve Accounts
	  Lombard Bank − 10
	  Peachtree Bank + 10

The Federal Reserve notifies Peachtree Bank of the increase in its reserve account. Then it returns the check to Lombard Bank to be deducted from its reserves and from its depositor's own checking account. Changes in commercial bank balance sheets are shown in Figures 10–3 and 10–4.

FIGURE 10–3

LOMBARD BANK

Reserves	− 10	Deposits	− 10

FIGURE 10–4

	PEACHTREE BANK		
Reserves	+ 10	Deposits	+ 10

Often the paying and receiving banks are in different Federal Reserve districts. In this case, reserve funds must be transferred from one Federal Reserve Bank to another. All Federal Reserve Banks have asset accounts on deposit with the *Interdistrict Settlement Fund* in Washington, D.C. When one Federal Reserve district loses reserves to a bank in another district, the Interdistrict Settlement Fund transfers assets from one account to the other, as shown in Figure 10–5.

FIGURE 10–5

INTERDISTRICT SETTLEMENT FUND	
	Asset Accounts
	District 1 Bank − 10
	District 2 Bank + 10

Then, the individual Federal Reserve Banks must adjust their balance sheets accordingly.

Bank Borrowing

Once a week commercial banks are required to count their deposits and compute their required reserves. Then they compare actual reserves with required reserves. Any excess reserves may be loaned overnight to another bank whose own reserves are less than required reserves; but if excess reserves continue, the bank might decide to increase its own loans and investments. (Reserves are computed on the basis of deposits held two weeks earlier, but this regulation is being reviewed and may be changed.)

If a bank's actual reserves are less than required reserves, it may borrow reserves from the Federal Reserve Bank. It must have suitable collateral for the loan, and it must pay an interest rate (or discount rate) that is slightly below other borrowing rates. A $10 loan from the Federal Reserve changes balance sheets as shown in Figures 10–6 and 10–7.

FIGURE 10-6

FEDERAL RESERVE BANK			
Loans to Banks	+ 10	Reserve Accounts Wall Street Bank	+ 10

FIGURE 10-7

WALL STREET BANK			
Reserves	+10	Borrowing from Federal Reserve	+10

Frequent borrowings are discouraged by the Federal Reserve and may lead to closer examination of the borrowing bank's lending policies. Still, the borrowing privilege probably reduces the amount of excess reserves banks would otherwise need to hold to meet a liquidity crisis.

Currency Withdrawals

In addition to check clearing and lending, the Federal Reserve Bank also provides currency for commercial banks. Needs for currency tend to occur seasonally, as depositors draw out funds for holidays, vacations, and so forth. If a bank's vault currency is insufficient for current needs, it can request additional currency from the Federal Reserve, drawing down its reserve account in the process. The T-accounts in Figures 10–8, 10–9 and 10–10 illustrate currency withdrawals.

FIGURE 10-8

FEDERAL RESERVE BANK			
Currency	− 10	Reserve Accounts Lombard Bank	− 10

FIGURE 10-9

LOMBARD BANK (1)		
Reserves	− 10	
Currency	+ 10	

FIGURE 10-10

LOMBARD BANK (2)			
Currency	− 10	Deposits	− 10

Normally after a period of heavy withdrawals, holders spend their currency, and it is quickly returned to bank deposits, so there is no permanent change in reserves or deposits. Because the Federal Reserve supplies most of the nation's currency, the only limit to the availability of currency is bank reserves and collateral for borrowing additional reserves.

Determining Commercial Bank Reserves

Bank reserves are the raw material from which money is created. Creating and managing bank reserves is the responsibility of Federal Reserve Banks. Other institutions also play a part, however, in creating bank reserves and in drawing down the level of reserves. Thus, other institutions influence the nation's money supply. It is helpful to classify the actions of all these institutions as: (1) actions that supply reserves to commercial banks and (2) actions that absorb funds that would otherwise become reserves. Primary responsibility for (1) rests with the Federal Reserve. Responsibility for (2) is more diffused among private individuals and foreigners and the U.S. Treasury. We will look first at Federal Reserve actions that supply reserves to banks.

Actions That Supply Reserves

Every time a commercial bank purchases an asset it acquires an offsetting liability or addition to capital. We have demonstrated, in particular, how commercial bank purchases of loans or investments are offset by increases in deposit liabilities. The same is true for Federal Reserve Banks: A net increase in assets requires an offsetting increase in liability or capital accounts. Federal Reserve Banks acquire assets similar to those acquired by commercial banks: domestic and foreign currency, loans and investments. Acquisition of any of these assets by Federal Reserve Banks can increase reserve accounts of the nation's commercial banks.

Currency. Currency holdings of Federal Reserve Banks include small quantities of U.S. Treasury currency and coins and Federal Reserve notes issued by other Federal Reserve Banks. Because one Federal Reserve Bank's holdings of another's notes constitute a liability for the second bank, Federal Reserve notes cancel each other out and are not counted as assets for the system as a whole. The Federal Reserve's largest holdings of currency are gold certificates, representing a claim against the Treasury's holdings of gold. The Federal Reserve was once required to hold gold certificates equal to a stated percentage of its notes and deposits, but laws passed in 1965 and 1968 ended that requirement.

New gold certificates may be issued whenever the Treasury acquires more gold through international transactions or whenever the value of the existing gold stock increases. The partial balance sheets in Figures 10–11 and 10–12 show changes in accounts at the Federal Reserve Bank and a commercial bank following the Treasury's purchase of gold. A $100 purchase of gold is paid for (a) by a check drawn against the Treasury's account at the Federal Reserve. The Treasury then (b) issues new gold certificates in the amount of the purchase and deposits them in the Federal Reserve Bank. In the meantime, the seller of the gold (c) deposits the Treasury's check in his or her personal account in a commercial bank. When the check clears at the Federal Reserve, funds are (a) deducted from the Treasury's account and (d) added to the receiving bank's reserve account.

FIGURE 10–11

	FEDERAL RESERVE BANK	
(b) Gold Certificates	+ 100	(a) U.S. Treasury	− 100
		(b) U.S. Treasury	+ 100
		(d) Bank Reserve Account	+ 100

FIGURE 10–12

	COMMERCIAL BANK	
(d) Reserve Account at Federal Reserve	+ 100	(c) Deposits	100

The end result of this transaction is that the Federal Reserve has increased its assets in the form of gold certificates and increased commercial bank reserve accounts by an equal amount. What is the effect on the nation's money supply? With an equal increase in deposits and reserves, the commercial bank has excess reserves and may begin creating new deposits through lending. Thus, the increase in holdings of gold certificates can increase the money supply by a multiple of the initial amount.

Other Federal Reserve Bank currency includes Special Drawing Rights (SDRs) issued to the Treasury by the International Monetary Fund. SDRs are deposited at the Federal Reserve when the Treasury wants to increase its deposits. The transaction would be shown on the Federal Reserve balance sheet in the same way as a transaction involving gold. Federal Reserve currency assets in 1987 were:

Gold Certificates	$11.1 billion
Special Drawing Rights	5.0 billion
Other Domestic and Foreign Currency and Coins	.6 billion

Loans. The Federal Reserve makes loans to commercial banks in either of two ways. *Discounts* are outright purchases by the Federal Reserve of commercial bank holdings of short-term agricultural, commercial or industrial loans. Purchases are made at a discount that reflects the Federal Reserve's current discount rate. In April 1987 the discount rate was 5.5 percent. Thus, a $100 loan maturing in 90 days could be sold[1] to the Federal Reserve for:

$$C = FV/(1+r) = 100/(1+.06/4) = 100/1.014 = \$98.64$$

More frequently, loans are made by granting *advances*, loans for which government securities, federal agency securities, or other riskless investments are used as collateral. Advances are made at the prevailing discount rate and require the borrowing bank to repay when the loan comes due.

Again, the acquisition of an asset by the Federal Reserve Banks is offset by an equal liability. The T-accounts in Figures 10–13 and 10–14 illustrate bank lending to a commercial bank and an addition to the commercial bank's reserve account.

FIGURE 10–13

FEDERAL RESERVE BANK

Discounts and Advances	+ 100	Reserve Accounts	+ 100

FIGURE 10–14

COMMERCIAL BANK

Reserves	+ 100	Borrowings from Federal Reserve	+ 100

Commercial banks may borrow against certain other collateral for an additional one-half percent interest charge. And other individuals, partnerships and corporations may also borrow at the higher rate in certain extraordinary circumstances. In either case, bank reserve accounts increase, and excess reserves are available for lending, so that the money supply can expand by a multiple of the initial loan. In 1987 Federal Reserve Banks were holding $.5 billion in discounts and advances to commercial banks.

Investments.   U.S. government securities and federal agency securities are classified as investments of the Federal Reserve. The Federal Reserve purchases investments at discount from commercial banks or through dealers operating in New York City. Federal Reserve holdings of investments in 1987 were:

U.S. Government Securities	$202.5 billion
Federal Agency Securities	8.6 billion

Investments represent the largest single category of Federal Reserve assets and have the greatest power to affect commercial bank reserves. We will have more to say about Federal Reserve holdings of government securities in Chapter 11.

Float.   Currency, loans and investments constitute the types of assets acquired by the Federal Reserve in the process of creating commercial bank reserves. A fourth item on Federal Reserve balance sheets affects reserve accounts too, but is generally less significant than these other assets. *Float* is the name given to the artificial increase in reserve accounts that results from time delays in check processing.

Federal Reserve Banks normally wait about two days after receiving checks before increasing the receiving bank's account. The two-day wait is to allow checks to reach the paying bank and to be deducted from that bank's reserves. Often the actual collection process takes longer than two days, and the value of the check is included in reserve accounts for both banks. Float is the difference between checks not yet deducted from reserve accounts (Cash Items in Process of Collection) and checks being held for 48 hours before being added to reserve accounts (Deferred Availability Cash Items). Float ranges from relatively small to rather large amounts, depending on the season and the weather. Abrupt changes in float can cause wide fluctuations in commercial bank reserves, with accompanying changes in the money supply.

U.S. Treasury Currency Outstanding.   When Federal Reserve Banks acquire assets, they supply reserve funds to commercial banks. The U.S. Treasury has also been a source of commercial bank reserves by supplying coins in response to the public's needs. Whenever the Treasury deposits new currency or coins in a bank, the effect is to increase commercial bank deposits and reserve accounts. Treasury currency was only $17.6 billion in 1987 and had only grown by $4 billion over the previous six years. Thus, although the Treasury plays a role in supplying reserve funds, its role is a small one. Primary responsibility rests with the Federal Reserve.

Factors supplying reserves in January 1987 are summarized in Table 10–1. Notice the relative significance of the various sources.

TABLE 10–1 Factors Supplying Commercial Bank Reserves, January 1987 (millions of dollars)

Federal Reserve Assets:	
Gold Stock	$ 11,059
SDRs	5,018
Loans and Acceptances	979
U.S. Government Securities	211,774
Float	4,324
Other Federal Reserve Assets	17,123
Treasury Currency Outstanding	17,611
Total	$267,888

Factors That Absorb Reserves

Funds supplied to commercial banks may become reserves, or they may be absorbed in other nonreserve functions. A result of nonreserve functions is to reduce the total level of reserve accounts. We saw that reserves are supplied primarily through actions of the Federal Reserve to acquire assets. Now we will see that nonreserve liabilities of the Federal Reserve are important uses that draw down the quantity of reserves available to support new lending. The Treasury and the public also play a part in absorbing reserve funds.

Nonreserve Liabilities of the Federal Reserve. Some of the funds supplied to banks find their way into accounts at the Federal Reserve that are not counted as bank reserves. In particular, Federal Reserve Banks hold accounts for the U.S. Treasury and for foreigners. The Treasury's accounts are generally small, because frequent payments are made from them. The Treasury has to borrow regularly to make its payments; therefore, to keep a large idle balance would be unwise. Treasury balances in 1987 amounted to almost $16.9 billion. Foreign balances were only $.23 billion. These are primarily deposits of foreign central banks and are used to clear international trade balances. Again, because they earn no interest they are generally small. Other nonreserve deposits and Federal Reserve capital accounts amounted to $9 billion in 1987.

Treasury Currency Holdings. Currency that is withdrawn from circulation and held in Treasury vaults reduces funds available for bank reserves.

TABLE 10–2 Factors Absorbing Commercial Bank Reserves, January 1987
(millions of dollars)

Nonreserve Deposits at the Federal Reserve:	
Treasury	$ 16,853
Foreign	230
Other (including Capital Accounts)	9,094
Treasury Cash Holdings	443
Currency in Circulation	205,945
Total	$232,565

Treasury currency holdings were only $.44 billion in 1987. Because this amount is small and remains fairly stable, it has little effect on bank reserves.

Currency in Circulation.   The most important factor absorbing bank reserves is currency in circulation. Public holdings of cash tend to vary according to long-term economic growth and short-run cycles in economic activity. Moreover, within a single year currency holdings vary with changes in the seasons, rising during holiday seasons and falling at other times. In particular, November and December usually experience increased currency holdings ($196 billion in December of 1985) followed by substantially reduced holdings ($190 billion in January of 1986).

When the Federal Reserve was established, a major goal was to moderate the effect on bank reserves of seasonal variations in currency holdings. Without flexibility in those factors supplying additional reserves, many banks would face regular seasonal crises as their reserves drain out into public currency holdings.

Factors absorbing reserves in January 1987 are summarized in Table 10–2. Again notice the relative significance of the various uses.

The difference between factors supplying reserves and factors absorbing reserves is bank reserves. Therefore:

Factors Supplying Reserves	$267,888
Less: Factors Absorbing Reserves	−232,565
Reserves at Federal Reserve Banks	$ 35,323

This relationship can be stated in the form of an equation:

(Federal Reserve Assets + Treasury Currency Outstanding)
− (Nonreserve Liabilities of the Federal Reserve + Treasury
  Currency Holdings + Currency in Circulation)
= Reserves at the Federal Reserve

The Federal Reserve has direct control only of its own assets; acquisition of assets provides the funds that increase commercial bank reserve accounts. Other nonreserve uses of funds have the effect of reducing funds available for reserves, reducing the raw material from which money is created.

The balance sheet in Figure 10–15 is a consolidated balance sheet for all 12 Federal Reserve Banks and their branches. Note especially the asset accounts that supply reserves to commercial banks and the liability accounts that absorb them.

FIGURE 10–15 All Federal Reserve Banks, January 1987

Assets (in millions)		Liabilities (in millions)	
Gold Certificate Account	$ 11,075	Federal Reserve Notes	
		Outstanding	$188,763
SDR Account	5,018	Deposits	
Coins	553	Reserve Accounts	34,588
Loans and Acceptances	513	U.S. Treasury	15,746
Federal Agency Securities	8,576	Foreign Accounts	226
U.S. Government Securities	202,486	Other Accounts	453
Cash Items in Process		Deferred Availability	
of Collection	5,947	Cash Items	5,231
Bank Premises	665	Other Liabilities	2,268
Other Assets	17,375	Capital Accounts	4,933
Totals	252,208		252,208

The Money Base

Factors supplying reserves contribute to commercial banks' ability to create money; other factors absorb reserves and draw down banks' money-creating ability. The largest factor absorbing reserves is currency in the hands of the public. Although public currency holdings draw down total reserves, they are a part of the money base:

$$\text{Money Base} = B = R + C.$$

In January 1987 the money base was the sum of reserves and currency in circulation:

$$R + C = 35,323 + 205,945 = 241,268 \text{ billion dollars.}$$

When the Federal Reserve purchases assets, the result is to increase reserves. Then, as banks purchase loans and investments, currency is drawn out and held by the public. The effect of Federal Reserve policy on the money base depends on decisions of the banks and the public. If the Federal Reserve can predict accurately the behavior of these groups, it may be able to select policy for achieving the desired changes in the money base.

Defensive and Dynamic Operations of the Federal Reserve

With reserve accounts of $35 billion and vault cash of $23 billion in 1987, commercial banks were making loans and investments and creating deposits that were included in the various definitions of the money supply. Banks' capacity to create money depended on: the public's decisions to hold currency, checking, and time deposits (c, D, and t); reserve requirements on particular kinds of deposits (r and r_t); and commercial bank reserves (R). Frequent shifts in public holdings of liquid assets and changes in the other factors that affect reserves require changes in bank loans and investments. The result may be wide swings in the availability of credit and in the money supply.

A major responsibility of the Federal Reserve is to offset unwanted shifts in the factors affecting reserve accounts so as to minimize the effects of such shifts on the nation's economic activity. Federal Reserve actions to offset short-run decisions in the private or government sector may be called *defensive operations*: They are responses to what may be unwanted actions on the part of the public or the Treasury. Another type of Federal Reserve actions may be called *dynamic operations*: These are independent actions specifically designed to cause fundamental changes in reserve accounts over the long run. Dynamic operations are aimed at providing money for a healthy level of economic growth without inflation or unemployment. In general, the Federal Reserve acts to reduce the growth of reserves when too rapid money growth appears to be creating inflation. And it acts to increase the growth of bank reserves when a scarcity of credit is causing unemployment, low investment and business failures.

In Chapter 11 we will explore in detail the tools used by the Federal Reserve for conducting its defensive and dynamic operations. If you will refer back to the section in this chapter on actions that supply reserves, you will see that the principal means for supplying reserves is the acquisition of assets, particularly U.S. government securities. We will begin with a description of the process and the results of Federal Reserve actions to acquire (or to sell) assets.

MONEY AND BANKING IN PRACTICE:
THE FEDERAL DEPOSIT INSURANCE CORPORATION

Bank failures were a regular event during the 1800s. To guard against bank failures in the future, a section of the Banking Act of 1933 established a permanent deposit insurance plan to be administered by the Federal Deposit Insurance Corporation (FDIC). After passage of the law, bank failures dropped to 66 annually during the 1930s, 11 during the 1940s, and only 4 annually during the 1950s. Between 1960 and 1970, failures averaged about 4.5 annually. During that entire period, more than $7.33 billion of depositors' money was recovered and only $14.7 million lost. Uninsured deposits now amount to less than 1 percent of total commercial bank deposits.

Why do banks fail? A common cause has been ill-considered loans to the bank's own management or to friends of management. In some cases, bad loans were based on "brokered money": Deposits were brought in from a savings and loan association, labor union, or other institution in return for a fee paid to a broker; then funds were loaned out to favored borrowers who were unable to obtain credit elsewhere. When losses on bad loans exceeded the banks' capital cushion, the bank faced insolvency.

Some banks fail as a result of embezzlement or improper activity of bank employees. Occasionally, a bank employee may cooperate in a *check kiting* scheme. Check kiting involves the deposit in one bank of a bad check drawn against another and using the deposit to make payments. The kiter depends on a long time lag between the time the original bank informs the second bank that the deposit is no good and the time his or her own checks are returned to the second bank for payment. A bank employee may cooperate in this scheme by holding up payment of checks and thus increasing the time lag. In the meantime, the second bank will have paid out substantial sums on the basis of worthless checks.

Less frequently, bank failure is a result of more blatantly illegal activity. Bank cashiers or bank managers accept payment for falsely adding to an account or creating false assets for a borrower to use as loan collateral at another bank. Or a bank employee may use Treasury bills held for the bank's customers for his or her own purposes. Illegal activity is often accompanied by poor record keeping, lax collection standards and other forms of manipulation by bank employees.

Insured banks must maintain high lending standards and submit to regular examination by federal or state authorities. If a bank gets into trouble and must be closed, officers of the FDIC physically take over the bank premises and all its branches. Depositors may be paid off directly by the FDIC from the sale of the bank's assets. Or the failed bank's liabilities and acceptable assets may be sold at auction to the highest bidder, who is then responsible for operating the bank. The new owner is guaranteed acceptable assets equal to the value of deposits assumed. Unacceptable assets are transferred to the FDIC, which then attempts to collect on the loans and investments. All this can take place within the space of about 24 hours and with no loss to bank depositors. Stockholders of failed banks generally lose their entire investment, however.

A spectacular bank failure was the failure of Franklin National Bank in April 1974. Franklin National was located in New York City and was the nation's 20th largest bank. The high bid was $125 million for the bank's liabilities and assets of $1.5 billion. The failure of Franklin National followed several years of declining earnings from loan losses, low-yielding long-term municipal bonds, and high personnel and overhead costs. The immediate cause, however, was substantial losses on speculation in foreign currencies. Franklin National was unable to cover its losses through loans of federal funds and eventually borrowed $1.7 billion from the Federal Reserve. All this bad publicity led holders of Franklin National's CDs to draw their funds out of the bank and ultimately precipitated the collapse.

The FDIC keeps a list of problem banks, which included more than 1,600 banks in 1987. Many of the problem banks were victims of losses on energy and agricultural loans, which threatened to absorb their capital cushion. Most are small banks. Since 1973, about 30 percent of the "serious problem" banks have actually failed. The FDIC may take steps to assist a fundamentally healthy bank if its failure would endanger the quality of banking services in the community.

Currently the FDIC operates an insurance fund of about $10 billion on insured deposits of about $1 trillion. Each year the fund grows by about $900 million in insurance premiums and $700 million in interest earned on investments in government securities.

Questions for Discussion

1. Discuss the advantages and disadvantages of placing the responsibility for deposit insurance in the hands of a government-sponsored corporation as opposed to a privately owned one.

2. In what ways does bank size affect the safety of deposits and the quality of bank operations?

Glossary of Terms

advances. loans from the Federal Reserve to commercial banks on the basis of suitable collateral

check kiting. the practice of depositing a bad check in a bank and using the deposit to make payments

defensive operations. Federal Reserve policy actions designed to correct short-run changes in the supply of money

discounts. sales of commercial bank loans and investments at discount to the Federal Reserve Bank

dynamic operations. Federal Reserve policies designed to produce long-run changes in the money supply and in economic activity

float. the difference between checks not yet deducted from reserve accounts and checks being held for 48 hours before being added to reserve accounts

Interdistrict Settlement Fund. a fund of central bank assets used for transferring payments among Federal Reserve districts

Summary of Important Ideas

1. Because the money-creating power of commercial banks gives them the ability to influence economic activity, some regulation is called for.

2. The dual system of banking in the United States includes state-chartered and nationally-chartered banks. In the early years of our nation, state banks extended loans through issue of bank notes; the resulting fluctuations of the money supply caused frequent financial crises. Until 1836, the first and second Banks of the United States attempted to correct this problem by restricting the issue of state bank notes.

3. For several decades after 1836 there was no centralized regulation of money growth, although several states established local systems of control. During the Civil War, Congress established the National Banking System to regulate money growth and assist in Treasury borrowing.

4. National banks were required to hold reserves in amounts determined by their status as country bank, reserve city bank or central reserve city bank. There was no coordinated system of check clearing, however, and the fact that reserves were held as deposits in other commercial banks led to frequent liquidity problems. There was no "lender of last resort," and national banks' money-creating powers were tied to the Treasury's outstanding debt.

5. To correct these problems was the objective of the Federal Reserve System, established in 1913. Commercial banks may draw cash from the Federal Reserve, use Federal Reserve check clearing, and borrow at the Federal Reserve discount rate. In 1982, all depository institutions became subject to the Federal Reserve's reserve requirements.

6. The 12 district Federal Reserve Banks are governed by a seven-member Board of Governors whose appointment and tenure remove them from the nation's political processes. This gives the Federal Reserve broad powers for influencing economic activity, although extreme deviation from Congressional goals might bring on new legislation to curb that power.

7. The Federal Reserve's influence on the money supply depends on differences between factors supplying reserves and factors absorbing reserves. Federal Reserve acquisitions of cash, loans and investments supply reserves, as does Treasury issue of new currency. Nonreserve deposits in the Federal Reserve Banks, Treasury cash holdings, and currency in circulation absorb reserves.

8. The money base is the sum of reserves and currency in the hands of the public.

9. The Federal Reserve supplies reserves to fulfill its defensive and dynamic policy objectives.

Questions for Discussion and Research

1. Distinguish among the various systems for regulating state bank note issue. What are their common characteristics? Why do you suppose the state of Louisiana enacted such strong regulations for state banks?

2. One of the shortcomings of the National Banking System was said to be "pyramiding" of reserves. Explain the system for holding reserves and tell why it was inadequate.

3. Describe the services the Federal Reserve provides commercial banks. What particular problem does each service address?

4. Use T-accounts to show the effect on bank reserves of a Federal Reserve purchase of $50 of government securities from a depositor in a commercial bank.

5. What are the major factors in public decisions to hold cash and how do these factors affect the money supply?

6. Define: float, defensive and dynamic Federal Reserve policy.

7. An economist in the office of the Comptroller of the Currency has said: "Since the regulator gets the blame whenever a bank fails, he starts with a hypothesis that one should always be suspicious of attempts to gain entry to the market. Indeed, too many regulators, victims of a depression mentality and fearful of outside criticism, have usually been opposed to freedom of entry." Comment.

Additional Readings

Canterbery, E. Ray. "The Awkward Independence of the Federal Reserve." *Challenge* (September/October 1975).

"Chairman Greenspan." *Business Week* (June 15, 1987): cover story.

D'Antonio, Louis J., and Ronald W. Melicher. "Changes in Federal Reserve Membership: A Risk-Return Profitability Analysis." *Journal of Finance* 34 (September 1979): 987–997.

Morris, Frank E. "The Changing World of Central Banking." *New England Economic Review* (March/April 1986): 3–6.

Endnote

[1]With C = current price, FV = face value, and r = discount or interest rate, $C(1+r) = FV$ and $C = FV/(1+r)$. A 90-day bill earns interest of $r/4$; therefore, $C = FV/(1+r/4)$.

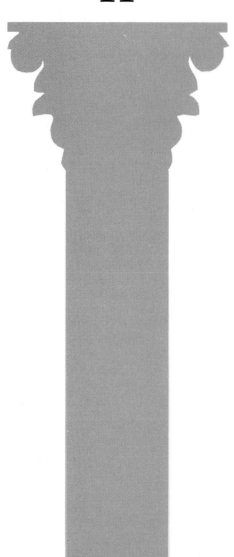

C H A P T E R

11

- To understand how the Federal Reserve accomplishes its money-supply objectives
- To learn some of the advantages of open market operations
- To understand the reactions of financial markets to Federal Reserve policies
- To understand the conflict between Federal Reserve objectives and those of the Treasury
- To learn how discount rate policy affects the money supply and its relative advantages and disadvantages
- To understand reserve requirements and their impact on the money supply
- To evaluate quantitative money controls relative to qualitative controls
- To understand the purpose of interest rate ceilings, margin requirements and selective credit controls

Instruments for Monetary Control

"Who e'er aspiring, struggles on, For him there is salvation."

Goethe

The Federal Reserve System is charged with the responsibility of providing an elastic supply of money consistent with the nation's economic objectives. Changes in the supply of money produce broad effects throughout the economy, providing credit on roughly equal terms to the various regions and sectors that comprise the total. To accomplish its money supply objectives, the Federal Reserve has three *quantitative* instruments of control. The use of either of the quantitative controls affects the money-creating powers of commercial banks, withholding or expanding credit according to the nation's needs.

We have seen that the quantity of money depends on decisions of the Federal Reserve, commercial banks, the public and the U.S. Treasury. Actions by these groups affect the values in the money-supply equation:

$$M1 = (R + C)\left[\frac{1 + c}{r + e + c + r_t t}\right]$$

Of the variables in the money-supply equation, only three are within the regulatory power of the Federal Reserve: R, r, and r_t. Two of the Federal Reserve's quantitative instruments deal with the level of reserves R: open market operations and discount rate policy. The third, reserve requirements, deals with the ratios r and r_t. We begin this chapter with a discussion of the three quantitative instruments of control: how they are implemented, how their effects spread through financial markets, and their relative effectiveness.

Qualitative instruments of control are aimed at the allocation of credit among particular sectors. We will discuss qualitative controls and evaluate controls in general later in the chapter.

Open Market Operations as a Quantitative Instrument

Open market operations are a quantitative instrument of monetary control aimed at affecting bank reserves (R) and the money base ($R + C$). In Chapter 10 we saw that commercial banks receive reserves when Federal Reserve Banks acquire assets. This is true regardless of the asset acquired: gold certificates, SDRs, loans, securities and even Federal Reserve Bank buildings. In practice, the most convenient asset for affecting bank reserves and the money base is U.S. government securities. Government securities constitute the largest single type of financial asset in the nation, so that moderate purchases by Federal Reserve Banks will not seriously disrupt markets. (Marketable securities totaled about $1.5 trillion in 1987.) Moreover, government securities are quite liquid, easily bought and sold in accordance with the Federal Reserve's objectives. The Federal Reserve also acquires federal agency securities and bankers' acceptances, but in much smaller amounts than U.S. Treasury securities.

Open market operations are the most flexible tool for influencing reserve accounts, and they are the tool most constantly in use. Just about every working day, you might expect open market purchases and sales to be conducted on behalf of Federal Reserve Banks. This was not always the case, however. The Federal Reserve Act of 1913 made no provision for open market operations as a tool of monetary control.

In the beginning, individual Federal Reserve Banks bought or sold securities for their interest income only. Often banks in neighboring districts followed contradictory policies. The Federal Reserve Bank in one district might be buying government securities while the bank in another might be selling. Commercial banks in the buying district would gain deposits, as their depositors received checks from the Federal Reserve Bank. Their reserve accounts would also increase, increasing the money base and the supply of credit in that district. In the meantime, commercial banks in the selling district would be losing deposits and reserves, as their depositors wrote checks to the Federal Reserve in payment for securities. These banks would be forced to contract credit; some might need loans from the Federal Reserve to keep their reserve accounts in line with reserve requirements. The result of uncoordinated purchases and sales of government securities was easy credit among banks in one district and tightness in another.

Not until 1920 and 1921, when the nation was experiencing the post–World War I recession, did the monetary authorities realize the advantages of coordinated open market operations for controlling reserves. Policymakers noted that purchases of securities in certain districts reduced commercial bank requests for loans in those districts. They realized that coordinated purchases and sales would affect bank reserves and influence the nation's total supply of credit. When the nation moved into another serious business depression in 1929, the monetary authorities were better prepared to use this new tool.

The Federal Open Market Committee

A formal procedure for deciding open market policy and coordinating action was needed first, however. The Federal Open Market Committee (FOMC) was set up to meet regularly for this purpose. The FOMC consists of the seven Federal Reserve Governors and five district bank presidents, who serve as members on a rotating basis with the other district bank presidents. The Committee meets every third or fourth week. At the meetings, staff researchers from the banks and from the Board of Governors present data describing current and expected future economic conditions: changes in productive activity, trade, employment, prices, and stocks of industrial commodities. The FOMC evaluates the evidence and decides the appropriate direction of policy.

Some care is taken to keep secret the Committee's deliberations. In part, this is a result of a natural tendency toward secrecy in financial matters. The FOMC is afraid that a person with advance notification of a policy change might use the information improperly for personal profit. Too, awareness of an imminent change in policy might cause individual savers and investors to overreact in some way that might complicate the Federal Reserve's job.

The Account Manager

After each meeting, the FOMC summarizes its decision in a directive, stating the basis for the policy decision and recommending ways to accomplish it. The recommendations are usually sufficiently vague as to allow some flexibility in carrying them out. The Committee sends the directive to the Federal Reserve Bank of New York, where one vice president is designated the Federal Reserve's Open Market Account Manager. The Account Manager is instructed to weigh the Committee's recommendations carefully and use good judgment in carrying out actual purchases and sales day by day.

New York City is an appropriate location for the Open Market Account Manager. In New York there are about 20 firms for which a major activity is trading U.S. government securities. These dealer firms hold inventories of securities, and they buy and sell securities among individuals, business firms, governments and financial institutions. Transactions are easy and quick, averaging about $3 billion a day. Dealers earn a profit by selling securities for a higher price than they pay or by borrowing against their securities and relending the proceeds for a higher rate of interest.

By 11:00 each morning the Account Manager has decided on the day's buying and selling objectives and has communicated with Committee members for authority to go ahead. Federal Reserve traders then place calls with dealers who state their price for buying or selling securities of various maturities. When the Federal Reserve is buying securities, it seeks the lowest price; when it is selling, the highest.

Outright Purchases and Repurchase Agreements

Federal Reserve purchases of government securities can take either of two forms. Outright purchases involve the transfer of ownership to the Federal Reserve, with the assumption that the transfer is to be permanent. Sellers of securities receive deposits or reserves in accordance with FOMC policy goals. Often, however, conditions call for a temporary injection of reserves, perhaps for three or four days only, after which reserves should return to their former level.

Temporary injections of reserves are appropriate to offset certain developments outside the banking system. An increase in public holdings of currency over the 4th of July weekend and a withdrawal of deposits on April 15, for example, reduce bank reserves temporarily and call for a temporary injection of reserves. In times like these, the Account Manager purchases government securities under a *repurchase agreement*. A repurchase agreement, or *repo* (RP), includes the seller's obligation to repurchase the securities after some specified time, usually less than a week.

Repos are used also when the Federal Reserve wants to reduce bank reserves temporarily. In this case, they are called *reverse repos*, and they involve a temporary sale of securities with the obligation to repurchase after a certain period of time. The sale of reverse repos is appropriate when commercial banks are experiencing an unwanted increase in reserves; a rise in float due to a snowstorm, for instance, would cause a temporary surge in reserves and call for the sale of reverse repos.

Changes in Bank Balance Sheets

The effect of Federal Reserve purchases can be shown on a T-account. Suppose the Account Manager offers to purchase $250 million in Treasury bills maturing in three weeks. The New York Federal Reserve Bank writes checks to dealers, who deposit them in commercial banks; thus reserves increase (Figures 11–1 and 11–2).

FIGURE 11–1

FEDERAL RESERVE BANK

U.S. Government Securities	+250m	Reserves	+250m

FIGURE 11–2

COMMERCIAL BANKS

Reserves	+250m	Deposits	+250m

Note that commercial banks now have excess reserves and can increase their lending.

Some securities dealers are commercial banks. If the Federal Reserve purchases $250 million of securities from commercial banks, excess reserves increase by the full amount of the purchase (Figures 11–3 and 11–4).

FIGURE 11–3

FEDERAL RESERVE BANK

U.S. Government Securities	+250m	Reserves	+250m

FIGURE 11–4

COMMERCIAL BANKS

Reserves	+250m		
U.S. Government Securities	−250m		

When commercial banks acquire excess reserves, they increase their lending, and total deposits grow by a multiple.

A Federal Reserve sale of government securities produces the opposite results, reducing the deposits of the dealers who purchase the securities and reducing reserve accounts of commercial banks. A decrease in reserves may mean negative excess reserves for some banks, with a cutback in loans and investments and a decrease in the money supply.

Responding to Changes in Reserves

Open market purchases and sales change bank reserves, often creating positive or negative excess reserves. Positive excess reserves provide commercial banks the opportunity for new lending to increase the banks' portfolios and, they hope, increase bank earnings. Negative excess reserves have less pleasant consequences. Commercial banks respond to negative excess reserves in either of two ways: They may try to increase their reserves to bring them in line with current deposits; or they may reduce total deposits by collecting old loans and reducing new lending. Although commercial banks prefer the first alternative, it is not generally possible for all banks. This is because total reserves for all banks together are limited, and actions to increase one bank's reserves have the effect of reducing another's.

There is another problem with the first alternative. Attempts to increase reserves send many banks to secondary markets to sell their existing loans and securities. The increased supply of securities for sale in secondary markets tends to reduce their prices. If securities are sold at prices lower than their purchase price, banks suffer a capital loss. As a result, some commercial banks become locked in to their current holdings. The *lock-in effect* is the tendency of banks to retain certain assets when selling them would involve a capital loss. And the lock-in effect forces banks to accept the second alternative: to reduce deposits and reduce the supply of bank credit.

An illustration may be helpful. Suppose the Federal Open Market Committee interprets current economic conditions as potentially inflationary and directs the Account Manager to act to slow money growth. Daily sales of government securities to the public would be increased, withdrawing reserves from commercial banks as shown in Figures 11–5 and 11–6.

FIGURE 11–5

FEDERAL RESERVE BANK

| U.S. Government Securities −250m | Reserves   −250m |

FIGURE 11–6

COMMERCIAL BANKS

| Reserves   −250m | Deposits   −250m |

As buyers pay for the securities, they draw down their deposits, and bank reserves fall. If banks were formerly loaned up, they will now have negative excess reserves.

Notice that the decrease in deposits reduces banks' required reserves also, so that negative excess reserves are not the full amount of the $250 million change in reserves. If we assume required reserves (r) of .20, negative excess reserves are $250(1 - r)$:

Change in Total Reserves	−$250
Less: Change in Required Reserves: $0.20(\Delta D) = 0.20(-250)$	−(−50)
Excess Reserves	− $200 .

With negative excess reserves of $200 million, commercial banks must reduce their lending, accepting checks in payment of old loans and failing to issue new ones. Throughout the banking system, bank lending will contract by a multiple of negative excess reserves, according to Equation 1 derived in Chapter 8:

$$\Delta L = ER[1/(r + e + c + r_t t)] = -200(1/0.5) = - 400.$$

The money supply will decline by

$$\Delta M1 = \Delta R[(1 + c)/(r + e + c + r_t t)] = -250(2.3) = - 575$$

according to Equation 3 in Chapter 8. The scarcity of credit will reduce spending and moderate inflationary tendencies. If the sale of securities is handled smoothly and in proper amounts, the desired results can take place gradually without severe distress to banks or their customers.

Portfolio Adjustments, Interest Rates and Arbitrage

We have demonstrated the effect of open market purchases and sales on commercial bank reserves. Changes in bank reserves affect bank lending and the quantity of money available for spending. There is another result that acts to reinforce the Federal Reserve's economic policy objectives. The result has to do with securities prices and interest rates.

Again, let us suppose current economic data suggest an increasing rate of spending with too rapid growth in economic activity. The Federal Open Market Committee decides to reduce the supply of money, expecting to slow the rate of spending and avoid inflation. In order to find buyers for the Federal Reserve's holdings of government securities, the Account Manager must reduce the price. The lower price for government securities increases their attractiveness relative to similar securities issued by private institutions, and securities dealers shift their purchases away from corporate bonds, mortgages and industrial or consumer loans. When business firms are unable to sell their securities at satisfactory prices, they must reduce their own spending, helping to achieve the Federal Reserve's goals.

Now suppose the FOMC believes economic growth is slowing and wants to increase spending. When the Account Manager enters the market to buy government securities, the effect is to increase demand for securities and push their prices up. This time the rise in price will lead securities dealers to shift their purchases away from government securities toward other loans and investments with lower prices. Among business firms the ease of selling their own securities encourages new investment spending and helps achieve the Federal Reserve's goals.

In both cases described above, changes in securities prices produce an opposite change in their interest yield. Purchase of a high-priced security is equivalent to lending at a low interest rate. (Remember that a 90-day $100 security priced at $97 yields a return of 12.4 percent, but if its price rises to $98 the yield falls to only 8.2 percent.) Thus, the *buy* decision above has the effect both of increasing commercial bank reserves and reducing borrowing costs for individuals and business firms. Similarly, the decision to *sell* securities reduces commercial bank reserves and increases interest rates in securities markets. (A 90-day $100 security priced at only $96 implies an interest yield of 16.7 percent.) Thus, a decision to contract commercial bank reserves is reinforced by a tendency toward higher borrowing costs throughout the financial community.

The spread of price changes through a market is helped by arbitrage. When an arbitrager sells one security for a high price and purchases another at a lower price, the effect is to reduce the price of the first security and raise the price of the second. Arbitrage thus moderates all price movements and spreads them throughout the market. Arbitrage in financial markets shifts the entire spectrum of interest rates up or down in response to the Federal Reserve's open market operations.

Twisting the Yield Curve

Different kinds of open market operations affect selected interest rates differently—in particular, long-term versus short-term rates. The effect is to change the shape of the yield curve.

Remember that a yield curve shows the interest rates on securities of different maturities. In Chapter 4 we discussed four theories explaining the shape of a yield curve: the liquidity preference theory, the risk premium theory, the expectations theory and the segmented markets theory.

A yield curve usually slopes upward to show higher interest rates on longer term securities. An upward-sloping yield curve has some disadvantages. Low short-term rates affect the interest earnings of international investors: multinational corporations, foreign banks, and central banks with temporary stocks of excess funds. These investors are highly sensitive to interest rates, pulling cash out of low-interest countries in favor of higher rates elsewhere. Abrupt outflows of "hot money" cause distress among U.S. banks and reduce the value of the U.S. dollar in foreign exchange markets. (We discussed the dollar's exchange rate in Chapter 7.)

High long-term rates present other problems. Because most capital investment requires long-term loans, real investment spending responds to long-term rates. High long-term rates discourage construction of homes and business plant and equipment and even research and development spending. The effect of high long-term interest rates may be to slow technological progress and reduce our nation's competitiveness in international markets.

On a few occasions, the Federal Reserve has attempted to arrange its open market operations to influence the yield curve. During the 1960s, the nation was experiencing substantial drains of short-term funds abroad. Banks were suffering a loss of reserves, and the dollar was subject to downward price pressure in exchange markets. Foreign central banks bought up the excess dollars to keep the actual price from falling. In the meantime, capital investment spending was sluggish, and our nation's productivity growth appeared to be slowing.

The Federal Reserve attempted to *twist* the yield curve: that is, to raise short-term rates and reduce long-term rates. To accomplish this, the Federal Reserve decided (1) to sell short-term securities, driving their price down and increasing their yield, and (2) to buy long-term securities, driving price up and reducing yield. The Treasury cooperated with the objective by borrowing funds short-term and paying off long-term debt.

Actual results of the "twist" operation turned out to be somewhat less than expected. Many variables other than interest rates influence international money flows and domestic capital investment: political factors, economic factors, and psychological factors are important, too. Unless actions in financial markets are strong enough to offset these other factors, private decisions will continue as before.

Open Market Operations and the U.S. Treasury

The use of open market operations as a countercyclical tool developed slowly. Although in the early 1930s some purchases were made to increase bank reserves, by the mid-1940s new concerns were emerging. It had become obvious that Federal Reserve purchases and sales of government securities would affect not only commercial bank reserves and the availability of credit to private borrowers, but also the costs of borrowing for the U.S. Treasury.

As the nation's largest borrower, the Treasury suffers most when interest rates rise. Treasury expenditures have risen sharply in recent decades, particularly during war years. Increased spending for defense during World War II pushed government outlays far above the amount that could be financed from tax revenues. Total budget deficits for 1940 to 1946 approached $200 billion. The wartime emergency made it necessary to finance the Treasury's needs quickly and, it was hoped, with minimum interest costs.

Supporting the Government Bond Market.   To finance the Treasury's needs, the Federal Reserve decided on a policy to "support the government bond market." Federal law limits the quantity of securities the Federal Reserve can buy directly from the Treasury, but Federal Reserve open market purchases can provide enough new reserves that banks and the public can buy new government securities. Without open market purchases by the Federal Reserve, the Treasury would be competing with private borrowers—business firms and consumers—for a fixed supply of credit. The increased supply of Treasury securities would force their prices down. Interest rates would rise, impairing the Treasury's ability to finance needed military equipment and personnel. Federal Reserve open market purchases supported their price and kept Treasury borrowing costs down.

Supporting the government bond market during and after the war had other effects. Purchases of securities from the public increased bank deposits directly and added to bank reserves. Purchases from commercial banks increased reserves only, in both cases substantially increasing the ability of commercial banks to create new money. Substantial money creation is likely to be inflationary, particularly during wartime when the production of military goods leaves fewer resources available for civilian production. Price controls and rationing were put in place to hold prices down, and scarcities of many consumer goods kept private spending from rising. But the liquid claims created during the war were stored for use in peacetime, contributing to a great burst of consumer spending and accelerating inflation after controls were removed.

The Accord of 1951.   After several years of worsening inflation, the Federal Reserve reviewed its policy of supporting government bond prices. Needless to say, the Treasury opposed any policy to reduce open market purchases and allow interest rates to rise. The Treasury was borrowing heavily to pay off maturing debt and was hoping for easy credit terms. Finally, in 1951 the Treasury and the Federal Reserve came to an agreement that the appropriate responsibility of the Federal Reserve is to promote stable economic growth: to reduce bank reserves when spending is growing too fast and to increase reserves when spending slows. The appropriate rate of spending growth ensures full employment without inflation. The *Accord of 1951* forced the Treasury to moderate its own credit demand when private credit demand is high, if it is to avoid high interest charges on Treasury debt.

The Discount Rate as a Quantitative Instrument

A second quantitative tool of monetary policy is used less often and is less effective in achieving money supply goals than open market operations. The second tool is the Federal Reserve Banks' power to set discount rates on discounts and advances to commercial banks.

Remember that a serious defect of the national banking system (1863–1913) was the absence of a "lender of last resort." One of the important functions of the Federal Reserve is to fill this need. Commercial banks use the "discount window" for temporarily increasing reserves to meet unexpected currency withdrawals or to ease the process of monetary restraint.

Borrowing for certain purposes is considered inappropriate. Borrowing to make speculative loans and investments or to relend at higher rates to other banks are examples. Borrowing as a substitute for raising capital is discouraged. Borrowing to purchase other loans and investments at a profit or to refinance other borrowings is also inappropriate.

Loans from the Federal Reserve may take either of two forms: Discounts are the sale of securities to the Federal Reserve, and advances are loans secured by adequate collateral. Securities eligible for discounts or advances include U.S. government or federal agency securities and high grade commercial, industrial or agricultural loans. The latter must mature in at most 90 days or, in the case of agricultural loans, nine months. Loans judged to be speculative are not acceptable. Certain other collateral may at times be accepted, but interest charges are one-half a percentage point higher.

Because Federal Reserve lending was originally in the form of discounting (or rediscounting) previously issued commercial bank loans, the interest rate was called the discount (or rediscount) rate. In the beginning, it was assumed that each of the 12 Federal Reserve Banks would review economic conditions within its own district and establish a discount rate appropriate to local needs. The Board of Governors would have to approve each bank's decision, but there was no feeling that discount rates would necessarily be uniform among the 12 districts. Over the years since the original legislation, the nation's economy has become more fully integrated, so that today's economic objectives are more clearly national goals. The result is a tendency toward consistent nationwide policy for discount rates.

The discount rate is set every two weeks according to Federal Reserve policy objectives for the period. A policy of credit expansion calls for a reduction in the rate, pushing the rate below the cost of other sources of bank reserves. A policy of credit contraction calls for an increase, raising borrowing costs above expected returns on bank lending. The expected result is an increase in bank borowing and bank reserves in the first case and a decrease in the second. Whether the expected results actually take place depends on commercial bank policies with respect to their own asset portfolios.

In general, commercial banks prefer to obtain additional reserves from sources other than Federal Reserve discounts and advances. They are reluctant to face the added scrutiny frequent borrowing may bring on, particularly when they can borrow reserves from other banks (federal funds), sell securities from their portfolios, or issue large certificates of deposit. Unlike discounts and advances, these alternative sources do not change total bank reserves but affect only the distribution of reserves among banks. This makes the other sources more desirable also from the standpoint of the Federal Reserve, which would like to avoid abrupt changes in the total quantity of reserves.

In 1973, the Board of Governors became concerned that larger commercial banks might have freer access to borrowed reserves than small banks. This is particularly distressing for banks in agricultural or resort areas where credit demand fluctuates widely throughout the year. Without the borrowing privilege, such banks would be forced to accumulate substantial holdings of short-term securities as a source of liquidity for heavy seasonal loan demand. The need for liquidity may prevent these banks from satisfying local credit needs at other times during the year. To deal with this inequity, the Federal Reserve set up a special seasonal borrowing privilege to provide regular loans for these banks.

Changing the Discount Rate

The Federal Reserve changes discount rates frequently in response to two types of events: changes in market rates of interest (defensive operations) and changes in Federal Reserve policy with respect to the availability of credit in general (dynamic operations). When interest rates change on federal funds and on short-term commercial paper, the discount rate is often changed, too. In general, the discount rate is set between one-half and one percentage point below these market rates. If the spread between the discount rate and these market rates increases substantially, banks might feel tempted to increase their discounts and advances and use their borrowings to profit from other lending.

A change in the discount rate can have two effects: the *direct* effect of changes in banks' borrowing costs and an *indirect* effect of the announcement of the change. To illustrate, suppose the Federal Reserve decides to tighten credit by increasing the discount rate; commercial banks will cut back borrowed reserves and reduce their own lending. These direct effects might be reinforced by indirect announcement effects in the financial community. Investors would look upon the rate increase as a signal of a change in Federal Reserve policy, with greater credit restraints and open market sales expected for the future. To prepare for tighter credit, investors would reduce their security holdings to acquire additional liquidity. Heavy sales of securities would push their prices down and increase their yields, aggravating the general scarcity of credit. Indeed, the announcement effects alone might be sufficient to accomplish the Federal Reserve's objective.

You might expect bank borrowings to respond inversely to changes in the discount rate. During a period of inflation, a rise in the rate to discourage borrowing and reduce reserves for making loans might be expected; in recession, you might expect a reduction in the rate to encourage borrowing for

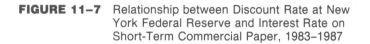

FIGURE 11-7   Relationship between Discount Rate at New York Federal Reserve and Interest Rate on Short-Term Commercial Paper, 1983–1987

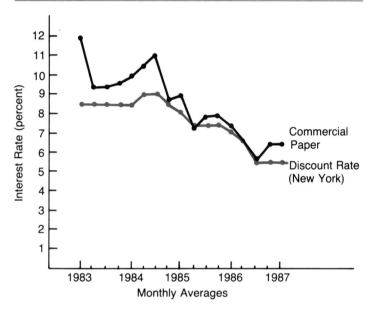

new lending. Frequently this has not been the case, perhaps because the rate has not moved far enough in either direction. When demand for business and consumer loans is high and profits can be made, banks have generally been willing to pay a relatively high discount rate to borrow from the Federal Reserve. On the other hand, when loan demand is low, low interest yields on bank loans make borrowing from the Federal Reserve unattractive, whatever the discount rate.

The result has been a tendency for bank borrowings to rise and fall along with the discount rate, making the discount rate a poor tool for regulating bank credit. Figures 11–7 and 11–8 illustrate the relationship. Note first the close relationship between the discount rate prevailing at the New York Federal Reserve and the interest rate on short-term commercial paper. Only once over the period shown was the discount rate higher, and the spread averaged less than one percentage point. Total bank borrowings also followed closely the behavior of the discount rate. During the strong expansion of 1984 the discount rate rose, but member bank borrowing rose also. As the expansion slowed, the discount rate fell, accompanied by further decreases in bank borrowing.

Another explanation for the positive correlation between bank borrowing and the discount rate is that the discount rate tool is performing its job.

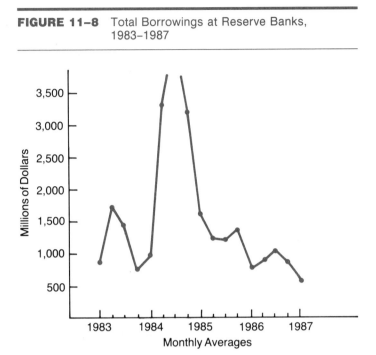

FIGURE 11-8 Total Borrowings at Reserve Banks, 1983–1987

The discounting privilege is providing a safety valve for banks during periods of inadequate reserves. When the Federal Reserve is using open market operations to draw reserves from the system, the discount window can sustain banks temporarily until they can reduce their loans in an orderly manner. Without the borrowing privilege, banks would be forced to liquidate substantial quantities of assets and face heavy capital losses. Their customers would experience severe credit problems that might disrupt financial relationships for years to come.

The Discount Rate and the Money Multiplier

The discount rate may have a significant effect on commercial bank holdings of excess reserves (e) in the money multiplier:

$$\left[\frac{1 + c}{r + e + c + r_t t}\right]$$

A liberal discount policy means that banks need to hold fewer excess reserves. With a smaller fraction of reserves held idle, the money multiplier increases. The result is an increase in the money supply, because the existing money base serves as a basis for more bank lending.

A more restrictive discount policy produces the opposite results. Without liberal borrowing privileges, banks must maintain sufficient excess reserves to guard against short-term liquidity problems. When the fraction e increases, the money multiplier shrinks, and the money supply falls.

Effectiveness of the Discount Tool

As a temporary source of reserves to moderate a credit crunch, the discount rate tool serves its function well. At some point in any business expansion, however, the discount window will finally be closed to banks that have used this privilege too often. Further borrowing will be cut off, and banks must deal with a shortage of reserves by liquidating assets or by finally reducing their total deposits. Such activity by many banks will have the expected results: reduced availability of bank credit and higher interest charges. Discount rates can ultimately be moved high enough and the discounting privilege can be tightened sufficiently to force a slowdown in money growth.

Action in the opposite direction may not be as effective. One reason is the obvious fact that there is a limit below which discount rates cannot be reduced; loans cannot be offered at discount rates less than zero. Furthermore, whereas banks can be refused loans in periods of credit contraction, they cannot be forced to borrow in periods of recession. During a recession, banks may even increase their excess reserves rather than make loans in an uncertain business climate. The risk of default and the expectation of higher interest rates in the future may discourage the active use of available reserves.

Economists describe the discount rate tool as *cyclically asymmetrical*: Its effects are more strongly felt on the upswing of a business cycle than on the downswing. The asymmetry results from the fact that banks can be prevented from borrowing in expansion but they cannot be forced to borrow to spur recovery from recession. Furthermore, with the development of the federal funds market, banks can avoid use of the discount window altogether.

The announcement effects of discount rate changes may also cause problems. Announcement of an increase, for example, may produce fears of further credit tightening, even when the action is purely defensive: a move to keep the discount rate in line with other market rates rather than a decision to reduce the availability of credit. Critics of discount rate policy recommend more frequent, smaller adjustments of the discount rate so that eventually the *announcement effects* disappear. Some suggest tying the discount rate to some widely known market rate such as the rate on 90-day Treasury bills or the current rate on federal funds, so that changes would be purely automatic. A rigid discount rate formula of this kind would further limit its effectiveness as a discretionary policy tool.

Reserve Requirements as a Quantitative Instrument

The Federal Reserve's third quantitative tool for regulating money is the reserve requirement. This tool differs from the first two in an important respect. Whereas open market operations and the discount rate affect mainly the quantity of reserves and excess reserves (R and ER), reserve requirements affect the multiplier that relates reserves to the money supply:

$$\left[\frac{1 + c}{r + e + c + r_t t} \right]$$

A change in r or r_t can be used *defensively* to offset opposite changes in other money variables or *dynamically* to produce certain policy objectives. The effect is to change banks' ability to make new loans and investments.

Current Reserve Requirements

Banking legislation of the 1930s gave the Board of Governors authority to set reserve requirements as follows: Reserves against demand deposits (r) can change from 7 to 22 percent. Since December 1976 reserve requirements have been 7 percent on the first $2 million of demand deposits, 9½ percent on the next $8 million, 11¾ percent on the next $90 million, 12¾ percent on the next $300 million, and 16¼ percent on demand deposits greater than $400 million. The result of graduated reserve requirements is that larger banks must hold on the average a larger fraction of deposits in reserve than smaller banks.

Reserves against time deposits (r_t) can range from 1 percent to 6 percent, with lower requirements for time deposits of four years or more. Reserve requirements on long-term savings and time deposits are only 1 percent, but ordinary savings deposits require 3 percent reserves. Reserves can be in the form of vault cash or reserve accounts in Federal Reserve Banks. Each bank prepares a weekly statement stating the quantities of demand and time deposits and the corresponding level of required reserves.[1] Currently, a bank has two weeks to ensure that actual reserves are sufficient to satisfy reserve requirements. Failure to maintain adequate reserves involves a penalty interest charge on the deficiency: two percentage points above the current discount rate. In general, banks arrange to have adequate reserves and avoid the penalty. Borrowing from banks with excess reserves (federal funds) is the most popular source of temporary reserves and relieves banks of the stigma associated with frequent borrowing at the discount window.

Changing Reserve Requirements

As a regulatory tool, changes in reserve requirements have several disadvantages. From the point of view of policymakers, changes in r and r_t produce significant announcement effects. Unlike open market operations, which can take place quietly and in small amounts, changes in r and r_t attract immediate attention and often cause overreaction from participants in financial markets. Indeed, when reserve requirements are increased, banks must react immediately to reduce deposits in line with their actual reserve holdings. Even a one-half percentage point change in r and r_t can cause a substantial gap between actual reserves and required reserves, leaving many banks with negative excess reserves.

The partial balance sheet in Figure 11–9 shows a hypothetical circumstance in which all commercial banks taken together are complying with reserve requirements of .20 (r) and .05 (r_t).

FIGURE 11–9

ALL COMMERCIAL BANKS			
Reserves	$ 30 b	Demand Deposits	$100 b
Loans and Investments	$280 b	Time Deposits	$200 b
		Capital Accounts	$ 10 b

A change in reserve requirements to .205 (r) and .055 (r_t) would leave banks with excess reserves of:

Total Reserves	$30 billion
Less: Required Reserves: .205(100) + .055(200)	− $31.5 billion
Excess Reserves	− $ 1.5 billion

All banks would experience a scarcity of reserves simultaneously, and all would feel the effects of the credit contraction.

As banks reduce their lending, total deposits would decrease by a multiple of the negative excess reserves according to the equations derived in Chapter 8. Using Equation 1:

$$\Delta L = ER[1/(r + e + c + r_t)]$$
$$= ER[1/(.20 + .05 + .15 + .05(2))] = ER(2).$$

Changing r and r_t to the values above yields a new equation:

$$[1/(.205 + .05 + .15 + .055(2))] = 1/.515 = 1.94.$$

Deposits would fall by
$$\Delta L = -1.5(1.94) = -2.91 \text{ billion.}$$

TABLE 11–1   Reserve Requirements of Depository Institutions

	Percent of Deposits	Effective Date
Net Transaction Accounts		
$ 0 to $ 36.7 million	3	12/30/86
Over $36.7 million	12	12/30/86
Nonpersonal Time Deposits		
(by original maturity)		
Less than 1½ years	3	10/6/83
1½ years or more	0	10/6/83
Eurocurrency Liabilities	3	11/13/80

SOURCE: Federal Reserve Bulletin, April 1987.

By Equation 3 in Chapter 8, the money supply would fall by

$$\Delta M1 = \Delta R[(1 + c)/r + e + c + r_t)]$$
$$= -1.5(1.15/.515) = -3.35 \text{ billion.}$$

Notice that changes in reserve requirements change both factors in the deposit equation: the quantity of excess reserves and the multiplier that produces new money. The effect is to cause massive and abrupt changes in the availability of bank credit, with serious disruptions in financial markets and wide fluctuations in the prices of financial assets. For these reasons, the Federal Reserve has generally avoided large changes in reserve requirements. Instead, the Federal Reserve makes slight changes in reserve requirements for one or more categories of deposits.

Table 11–1 shows bank reserve requirements in effect in 1987 and the effective dates of the requirements. The last major changes in reserve requirements occurred in 1980 when the Federal Reserve began phasing in reserve requirements for all banks and thrift institutions.

Changes in reserve requirements are rather blunt instruments of policy, inappropriate for effecting subtle changes in credit conditions. Their use is normally accompanied by open market operations and discount policy to ease the scarcity of reserves and prevent major disruptions in financial markets.

Evaluation of Quantitative Controls as Policy Tools

Some of the arguments favoring quantitative instruments of control are: their effects spread rather broadly throughout the economy, they produce indirect effects that may reinforce the desired results, arbitrage helps spread the effects of initial changes widely through financial markets, and some announcement effects act to reinforce particular policy objectives.

Other advantages have to do with the Federal Reserve's structure and procedures for making decisions. Independence from political considerations helps ensure that policy decisions are indeed in the long-run public interest—no matter how painful they may be in the short run. Decisions can be made quietly and carried out smoothly and gradually; they can even be reversed quickly when conditions change. Too, the variety of quantitative tools allows for considerable flexibility, with subtle changes of greater or lesser amounts to suit immediate goals.

A disadvantage of quantitative controls has to do with their questionable effectiveness. We have noted the relative ease with which the Federal Reserve can reduce commercial bank reserves and put a stop to new bank lending. An inflationary expansion can be stopped if the Federal Reserve acts ruthlessly. To cure a recession is not so simple. Banks cannot be forced to increase their lending, and bank customers cannot be forced to borrow. The result is a kind of cyclical asymmetry, with the result that monetary restraints are more effective than policies aimed at monetary expansion. (Some analysts say that trying to force banks to create money is like pushing on a string. You can pull money out of the economy during inflation, but "you can't push on a string" during recession.)

Other disadvantages involve the accompanying changes in interest rates. High interest rates may be necessary during inflation to ration scarce credit so that only the most urgent borrowers are satisfied. But high interest rates also retard capital construction and increase the U.S. Treasury's borrowing costs, all of which may ultimately worsen inflationary pressures. Low interest rates may be used to encourage expansion, but they may not be effective in this goal if low interest rates cause deposits to move out of the country in search of higher rates elsewhere. In fact, much of the Federal Reserve's quantitative policy actions may be offset by international flows of financial capital (as will be discussed in Chapters 18 and 19).

MONEY AND BANKING IN PRACTICE: THE FED's TWO JOBS

The Federal Reserve has two jobs, performing either of which successfully may make it difficult (or impossible) to perform the other.

One of the Fed's jobs is to be a "lender of last resort": to provide liquidity to the banking system when bank reserves are low. Performing this job successfully would protect solvent banks from failure and prevent the financial crisis that might result. But performing this job might also prevent the Fed from performing its other job: to provide a money supply adequate to the needs of the economy but not so great as to cause inflation. Protecting banks from failure could call for excessive money growth and build in strong inflationary pressures that eventually require strongly contractionary monetary policy.

The conflict between the Fed's two jobs has grown sharper in recent years, with more nonbank financial intermediaries offering checkable deposits classified as money. Providing liquidity to sustain all these new kinds of lending has called for massive increases in Federal Reserve holdings of government securities and massive increases in the money base (reserves plus outstanding currency).

Other factors have complicated the Fed's job. More and more, bank asset portfolios have come to be dominated by business loans, rather than government securities. Whereas government securities depend on tax revenues for payment, business loans depend on business profits. Increasing business profits often calls for increasing consumer loans, which may constitute a further drain on bank reserves unless the Fed conducts expansionary monetary policy.

The internationalization of banking has created other complications. Foreign holders of dollar-denominated assets (bank deposits, commercial paper or U.S. Treasury bills) expect to be able to convert their assets into dollars fairly quickly. This means that U.S. banks (and ultimately the Fed) must supply the funds for that purpose. If foreign holders of dollar-denominated assets come to doubt the ability (or willingness) of banks to provide needed liquidity, there will be a rush to liquidate these assets.

Some economists are particularly worried about the internationalization of banking. They say that foreign holdings of dollar-denominated assets give the Fed "responsibility without control": the Fed is responsible for providing liquidity but it has no control over the level of lending. Believing that the Fed will accept its responsibility to provide liquidity, more and more foreigners are holding their funds in dollar-denominated assets. The result is to increase the Fed's obligation to provide liquidity without increasing its power to limit lending.

The increase in the money-creating powers of nonbank financial institutions, the shift of bank assets from government securities to business loans, and the internationalization of banking may create long-term problems for the Fed. There are several proposals for dealing with the problems:

1. Banks could be required to maintain larger capital accounts relative to total assets. However, such a requirement would squeeze bank profits at a time when they are already suffering from competition from nonbank financial intermediaries.

2. Bank size could be limited so as to minimize the financial crises that might result from bank failures. Then the Fed could let some banks fail and concentrate more on the job of maintaining the appropriate money supply.

3. Monetary policy could be con- ducted more through discounts and advances than through open mar- ket operations. This would give the Fed greater supervisory power over bank lending and would tend to pre- vent excesses.

Question for Discussion

1. Which of the proposed remedies would you recommend? Why?

Qualitative Instruments

Quantitative instruments of monetary control affect various sectors of the economy equally, providing or withholding the means for creating credit without discriminating according to particular needs. In contrast, qualitative instruments of control focus on particular types of credit with the aim of influencing the allocation of credit among sectors. Thus, qualitative instruments involve greater government intervention into financial markets and require selective judgment as to the proper sectors for emphasis. In general, qualitative controls focus on credit for housing, for purchases of corporate stock and for consumer purchases during national emergencies. The Federal Reserve may allocate credit among these sectors by means of three types of qualitative controls: interest rate ceilings on savings and time deposits, margin requirements on stock purchases, and selective credit controls for real estate and consumer durables.

Interest Rate Ceilings on Savings and Time Deposits

Savings and time deposits are popular among small savers seeking convenient means for earning interest on short-term balances. These deposits are also important to commercial banks and S&Ls, because reserve requirements are low. A relatively stable level of savings and time deposits provides a valuable source of reserves for long-term lending, particularly for the housing industry.

Until 1980, Federal Reserve Regulation Q gave the Board of Governors the authority to set maximum interest rates banks pay on savings and time deposits. The Federal Home Loan Bank Board is a regulatory body for S&Ls comparable to the Federal Reserve. The FHLBB cooperated with the Board of Governors and set ceilings on savings and time deposits in S&Ls and mutuals one-quarter percent above interest rates payable by commercial banks.

There were two reasons for establishing ceilings on interest rates paid on these deposits. One was to protect small thrift institutions from excessive competition for funds. If all depository institutions were free to bid competitively for savings, some might be forced out of business. Institutions with high-yielding financial assets could afford to pay higher interest rates on savings and capture the entire market. Ultimately, a few monopoly institutions might control all the savings in the community. A second reason had to do with earnings of thrift institutions. Because their uses of funds are primarily long-term, interest earnings are relatively constant. To subject these institutions to periods of rising interest costs on their deposits would reduce profitability and impair stability.

The goal of protecting thrift institutions is closely related to the goal of protecting the housing sector. Because most funds for homebuilding come from S&Ls and mutual savings banks, instability among these institutions can reduce credit for housing and all those other industries that depend on housing. Similarly, ceilings on interest paid by commercial banks were intended to reduce the cost of funds for lending to small business firms. Such firms may not be able to issue securities and are dependent on commercial banks for financing.

Ceilings on interest rates payable on these important sources of funds caused serious disruptions in the flows of savings to financial institutions. In periods when demand for credit was increasing relative to bank lending ability, market interest rates would rise above the ceiling interest rate payable on savings. The result was disintermediation: a flow of funds out of financial intermediaries and into direct purchases of commercial paper and corporate bonds. The loss of funds for lending forced banks and thrifts to reduce their loans to housing and to other small business borrowers, with some business failures the result.

The danger of disintermediation forced the Federal Reserve to rethink the policy of interest rate ceilings on all savings and time deposits. In 1980, Congress began phasing out interest rate ceilings on savings and time deposits, and all ceilings were removed by 1987.

Margin Requirements

The Securities Act of 1934 gave the Federal Reserve Board of Governors authority to regulate bank lending for stock purchases. The Governors set a required *margin*, or down payment, for corporate stocks bought on credit when the stocks are to serve as collateral for the loan. A margin requirement of 60 percent, for instance, means that the investor must pay at least 60 percent of the purchase price and borrow no more than 40 percent. The stock serves as security for the loan.

Margin requirements are believed necessary to deal with the problem of excessive borrowing for stock speculation. During the late 1920s, heavy speculation, financed by credit, was largely responsible for the boom in stock prices and the subsequent financial panic. Speculators found they could buy a $100 stock by paying, say, $10 and borrowing $90. Then if the stock's price rose by only $1, they could sell, pay off the loan, and pocket a return of almost 10 percent (after paying interest on the $90 loan). Thus, a 1 percent increase in stock prices would mean a much larger return for a highly *leveraged investor*: one whose borrowings constitute a large fraction of the stock's value.

Profits like these drew many speculators into the stock market, and prices did rise. Profits made on stock purchases fueled even greater speculation, until many stock prices rose far above any realistic measure of their true value. At this point some speculators elected to take their gains and get out of the market. Their sales had the effect of driving stock prices down. Note that when the previously mentioned $100 stock bought for $10 falls by $1 in value, the 10 percent gain on the upside quickly becomes a 10 percent loss on the downside. Unhappily, losses cumulate more quickly than gains, as speculators rush to cut their losses and sell. The stock market crash of 1929 was the source of many personal and business tragedies and contributed to the severity of the Great Depression that followed.

Other Selective Credit Controls

When consumer spending grows too fast, other sorts of credit controls may be necessary. This is particularly true during wartime, when military and defense production is creating new jobs and increasing family incomes. Because resources are being used to produce military equipment, production of civilian goods may not be growing. Without limitations on consumer spending, prices would tend to rise. During World War II and the Korean War, the Federal Reserve was given authority to set borrowing conditions for certain types of consumer loans. In 1969, the President was given the power to ask the Federal Reserve Board to revive selective credit controls, should they be needed in the future.

Selective credit controls are generally used to discourage spending for consumer durable goods and real estate. Frequently, controls involve minimum down payments for homes or installment purchases and maximum time periods for repayment. An increase in the required down payment and a reduction in the payback period will increase monthly payments and discourage some buyers. The expected result is to reduce spending in line with the reduced production of civilian goods and homes.

Selective credit controls may also be used countercyclically to encourage consumer spending. In the early stages of recovery from recession, for example, auto sales tend to be weak. The result may be continued high levels of unemployment and stagnation for the automobile industry. The Federal Reserve may respond by lengthening maximum auto loan maturities to as long as five years. Lower monthly payments may encourage increased sales, but some economists fear that longer loan periods might have the effect of reducing auto sales in the future.

Moral Suasion

The Federal Reserve is often said to exert moral suasion to influence bank credit policies. Moral suasion includes the implicit threat of more substantive policy actions if banks fail to cooperate with Federal Reserve objectives. An example of moral suasion was the Board's request in 1979 that banks lend only for productive—and not speculative—purposes. To the extent that commercial banks believe the Federal Reserve might eventually back up its request with the use of quantitative controls, they may be expected to cooperate.

Evaluation and Conclusions

The main criticism of qualitative controls is that they involve excessive government intervention in free markets. Critics prefer that the nation's financial resources be allocated according to market supply and demand rather than according to the decisions of government regulators. Direct controls tend to distort resource allocation and alter the distribution of financial resources according to the subjective judgment of policymakers. Because policymakers are fallible, critics say, qualitative controls should be used only as a last resort in a national emergency.

Qualitative controls may have other harmful effects. Adding selective controls to the more general quantitative controls increases the complexity of money management. Greater complexity increases the likelihood that various policy instruments might be used inconsistently: the effects of one detracting from or even offsetting entirely the effects of another. Too, controls give rise to efforts among financial intermediaries to evade controls by developing new credit devices. The probable result may be still more controls to deal with new credit devices and a further expansion of a costly regulatory bureaucracy.

Often, selective credit controls lead to the formation of interest groups organized to ensure continuation of favorable policies. Needless to say, interest group pressures do not guarantee that actions will be taken in the public interest. Moreover, the presence of interest groups adds rigidity to policy making and prolongs existing distortions in resource allocation.

Some economists question whether qualitative controls actually accomplish their stated purpose. In particular, it is difficult to control certain types of credit when borrowers are free to shift their own funds around. Borrowers might arrange loans for purposes normally satisfied by their own money holdings, then use their money for a purpose the qualitative control was designed to prevent. In this view, qualitative controls add bureaucratic complexity and encourage evasive behavior without producing substantial gains in money management. (This point of view was tested in 1980 when the Federal Reserve imposed controls on certain types of credit in an effort to reduce inflationary pressures.)

Glossary of Terms

Accord of 1951.   an agreement between the Federal Reserve and the U.S. Treasury that the Federal Reserve would no longer "support the government bond market"

announcement effect.   the reactions in the financial community that frequently follow the announcement of a change in Federal Reserve policy

cyclical asymmetry.   the fact that Federal Reserve policy is more effective during one phase of the business cycle than the other

lock-in effect.   the tendency to hold securities whose value has fallen, so as to avoid a capital loss

margin requirements.   minimum down payment requirements for purchases of securities, when the security is to serve as collateral for the loan

repurchase agreement.   the purchase of a government security with the condition that the seller will buy it back after a certain time; also called a repo

reverse repos.   the sale of securities under an agreement to repurchase

Summary of Important Ideas

1. Quantitative controls affect the supply of reserves (R) or the money multiplier through reserve requirements (r and r_t).

2. Open market operations involve Federal Reserve purchase and sale of U.S. government securities. Changes in the Federal Reserve's asset portfolio change bank reserves and may change the rate of money growth. The Federal Open Market Committee uses information on current economic conditions to decide the appropriate direction of policy. The Fed-

eral Reserve Bank of New York buys and sells securities outright or engages in repurchase agreements with dealers and commercial banks. Commercial banks respond to changes in reserve accounts by changing their credit policy; the lock-in effect limits banks' ability to acquire additional reserves during periods of credit stringency.

3. Federal Reserve open market operations affect security prices and interest rates. Arbitrage works to spread the effects throughout credit markets. Interest rate effects tend to reinforce the intended results of security dealings. Selective purchases and sales can affect short- and long-term rates differently, for the sake of other policy objectives.

4. Credit stringency with high rates may be detrimental to the interests of the U.S. Treasury; but since the Accord of 1951, the Federal Reserve has attempted to govern its actions solely for the sake of healthy levels of economic activity.

5. Access to discounts and advances assures commercial banks a lender of last resort. The discount rate reflects current credit conditions and the direction of Federal Reserve policy. Frequently, the indirect announcement effects of changes in the discount rate cause investor reactions that may reinforce Federal Reserve goals or may contradict actual intentions. Contrary to first expectations, total commercial bank borrowing tends to move up or down along with the discount rate. Moreover, this tool is inadequate for stimulating borrowing and money growth during recession.

6. Changes in reserve requirements produce significant announcement effects and may involve overreaction from market participants. Furthermore, their effects may be too large for achieving smooth adjustments in the money supply. Consequently, this tool is seldom used.

7. Qualitative tools have the disadvantage that they involve government intervention in specific sectors of the economy and, thus, greater government control over the allocation of credit. Interest rate ceilings on savings and time deposits were intended to reduce ruinous competition for savings among financial intermediaries and to assure a dependable source of credit for the housing industry. Margin requirements limit lending for purchase of stocks so as to guard against speculative excesses. Selective credit controls may be appropriate during wartime or in similar periods of extreme scarcity. In general, qualitative controls have questionable effectiveness and increase bureaucratic complexity and inefficiency.

Questions for Discussion and Research

1. Use T-accounts to demonstrate the effects of open market purchases from private dealers and from commercial banks. In what way are the results different? Similar?

2. Explain the lock-in effect. Are institutions other than commercial banks subject to the lock-in effect? Are individuals?

3. Show how arbitrage operates in the markets for commodities (like wheat) as well as for credit instruments. What factors might prevent equality of prices in all markets? How does modern technology affect the results of arbitrage?

4. What circumstances probably act to reduce the effectiveness of Federal Reserve operations to "twist" the yield curve? How might individual investors react to the policy? What does your answer imply about the basis for the term structure of interest rates?

5. Illustrate graphically the market for securities, showing the effects of Treasury bond sales on the supply of securities. Then illustrate Federal Reserve actions to "support the government bond market." Explain and critically evaluate.

6. Explain the paradox that commercial bank borrowings tend to rise and fall along with the discount rate. Why is this tool cyclically asymmetrical?

7. Use the hypothetical data in Question 2 of Chapter 8 to demonstrate the effect on the money supply of a one percentage point increase in reserve requirements on demand and time deposits. Explain the process by which the change in the money supply takes place.

8. Outline the arguments for and against maximum interest rates on savings and time deposits.

9. Demonstrate the process by which leveraged investors can experience large gains or losses when interest rates change. Is this true of investments other than financial investments?

10. Evaluate the advantages and disadvantages of quantitative and qualitative controls of the Federal Reserve. What changes in the controls might enhance their effectiveness?

11. Explain why government securities are a proper instrument for regulating bank reserves. What problems would result from the use of other assets: gold, corporate bonds and real property, for instance?

12. How would widely fluctuating interest rates affect New York's securities dealers? Why do economists at the New York Federal Reserve Bank sometimes jokingly call their Open Market Account Department the "Dealers Protection Association"?

Additional Readings

Gilbert, R. Alton. "Benefits of Borrowing from the Federal Reserve When the Discount Rate Is Below Market Interest Rates." *Federal Reserve Bank of St. Louis Review* 61 (March 1979): 25–31.

Gilbert, R. Alton. "Access to the Discount Window for All Commercial Banks: Is It Important for Monetary Policy?" *Federal Reserve Bank of St. Louis Review* 62 (February 1980): 15–24.

Mengle, David L. "The Discount Window." *Economic Review of the Federal Reserve Bank of Richmond* (May/June 1986): 2–10.

Endnote

[1]A bank with demand deposits of $150 million and four-year time deposits of $100 would be required to hold in reserve: 7%(2) + 9½%(8) + 11¾%(90) + 12¾%(50) + 1%(100) = $18.86 million.

C H A P T E R

12

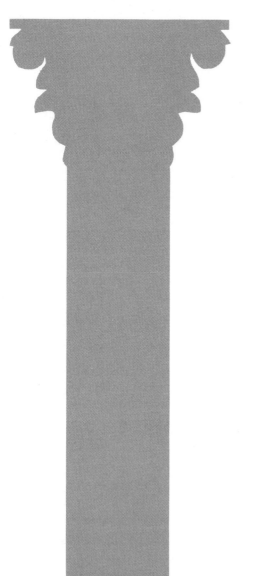

International Transactions and the Supply of Money

"Not because our own prices, in terms of dollars, had risen nor because our products were of inferior quality, not because we did not have sufficient products to export. But because, in terms of foreign currencies our products had become so much more expensive, we were not able to maintain our fair share of the world's trade. It was, therefore, necessary to take measures which would result in bringing the dollar back to the position where a fair amount of foreign currency could again buy our products."

Franklin D. Roosevelt

For a nation like the United States, open to international trade, answering the question "How much money should there be?" is difficult. The reason is the massive flows of money into and out of the nation in payment for traded goods and services. Whatever U.S. monetary authorities decide about the quantity of money, international money flows can work to offset their decisions.

This is not to say that international money flows should be prohibited. In Chapter 7 we discussed the gains in efficiency that come from a nation's move from self-sufficiency in production to specialization. Specialization and trade based on comparative advantage increase world production and stimulate technical progress. Restraints on trade retard growth and limit a nation's opportunities to consume a wide variety of goods and services.

If international trade is to promote efficiency, equity and the production of positive externalities, there must be a system for measuring money flows and balancing money flows with the flows of goods and services. Within a single nation, balancing the flows of money and goods is relatively straightforward. Buyers know they must produce goods and services equal in value to those they consume. The process is symbolized by the transfer of money: currency, checking accounts and various other claims to liquid wealth. Those who receive payments are entitled to purchase consumer goods and services or invest in capital goods or financial assets.

Among nations, flows of money and goods are not as straightforward, but the fundamental circumstances are the same. Nations that consume goods and services must produce goods and services of equal value. Buyers use international currencies to transfer purchasing power, so that sellers can choose their purchases. As world trade expands, buyers and sellers become accustomed to international exchange, and the process becomes less mysterious. Still, the arrangements by which transfers of purchasing power take place are more complex than domestic buying and selling.

A nation's Balance of Payments statement summarizes international flows of money, goods and services for the year. This chapter will describe how international payments are recorded and how the Balance of Payments statement is brought into balance. Then we will consider the problem of disequilibrium, when a nation experiences continuing Balance of Payments deficits or surpluses. We will look at some causes of disequilibrium and some of the resulting problems the United States has faced in recent years.

The Balance of Payments Statement

The Balance of Payments statement is divided into three parts according to the types of transactions included in each. Parts 1 and 2 include all independent transactions involving trade and international investment. Together, Parts 1 and 2 constitute the autonomous part of the Balance of Payments. *Autonomous transactions* result from the individual decisions of buyers and sellers around the world. We will look at Parts 1 and 2 in detail, using Table 12–1 for reference.

Part 1: The Current Account

The largest and most important part of the Balance of Payments is the Current Account. This is where exchange of goods and services is recorded.

The United States exports large quantities of agricultural products, industrial machinery, transportation equipment and other products, which totaled almost $219 billion in 1986. Merchandise exports are recorded on line 1 of the Balance of Payments; exports are classified as *credit transactions* because they result in an inflow of payments to U.S. citizens.

Merchandise imports are *debit transactions* because they result in an outflow of payments by U.S. citizens to foreigners. The largest single import item for the United States is petroleum, which accounted for about 10 percent of total imports in 1986. Industrial supplies and other goods and services completed merchandise imports, for a total of more than $365 billion in 1986. Notice that in 1986 outflows for imports were greater than inflows for exports, so that the United States had a debit balance of more than $146 billion on merchandise trade. That is the net value of unsatisfied claims

TABLE 12–1 Balance of Payments: 1986 (estimated) (millions of dollars)

	Credits	Debits	Balance
Part 1: Current Account			
Merchandise Exports	218,837		
Merchandise Imports		−365,233	
Merchandise Trade Balance			−146,396
Military Transactions		− 3,180	
Investment Income (net)	23,135		
Other, including Unilateral Transfers		−13,200	
Balance on Current Account			−139,641
Part 2: Capital Account		−35,159	
Direct Investment	11,923		
Portfolio Investment		−10,179	
Long-term	106,392		
Short-term	−7,402	− 8,124	
Bank Claims			
Owned by U.S. Citizens Abroad		−38,081	
Owned by Foreigners in U.S.	58,899		
Balance on Capital Account			78,269
Balance on Current and Capital Account			− 61,372
Part 3: Compensatory Transactions			
Gold Reserves Paid Out	0		
Foreign Currencies Received		1,096	
Other Assets Received by U.S. Government		2,407	
Official Borrowing of U.S. Government	44,016		
Borrowing through IMF	1,337		
Statistical Discrepancy	19,522		

against the United States held by foreign sellers after all foreign buyers had paid for their purchases of U.S. exports.

A nation can have a trade deficit with some of its trading partners and a surplus with others. Whether its total trade account is in balance depends on the relative size of deficits and surpluses. Over the past decade the United States has consistently been in deficit with Japan and Canada, and occasionally in deficit with other American countries and developing countries in Asia and Africa (not including OPEC countries). Petroleum deficits alone totaled $35 billion in 1986. The United States has been in surplus with Western European nations and Communist bloc nations, but the surpluses have not been great enough to offset our other deficits.

Other transactions on Current Account are: military transactions, government grants, income from investments owned abroad and unilateral transfers. Military transactions and grants are generally *debit* transactions, or net outpayments. Investment income is generally a *credit*, because Americans own more investments abroad than foreigners own in the United States. Income from foreign investments is a major inflow into the U.S. Balance of

Payments. Unilateral transfers are one-way payments, frequently from one member of a family to another or from a business firm to an individual. Unilateral transfers are generally *debit* amounts in the U.S. balance.

When all debit outflows are subtracted from credit inflows, the result is the Balance on Current Account. This is the net value of claims outstanding from all transactions during the year. In 1986 the excess of outpayments (debits) over inpayments (credits) produced a debit balance on Current Account of almost $140 billion.

Part 2: The Capital Account

Aside from purchases of goods and services, international transactions include purchases of investments. Investments can be classified as direct or portfolio investment and as long- or short-term investment.

Direct investments are purchases of physical facilities used for producing goods or services: textile mills, automobile factories, farms, mines and resort hotels. Direct investment responds to expected profitability in various nations over the world. In 1986 U.S. investors purchased direct investments worth $35,159 billion abroad, and foreigners purchased $11,923 billion of direct investments in the United States. Portfolio investments are corporate stocks or government securities. As can be seen in Table 12–1, U.S. investors purchased $10,179 billion and foreigners purchased $106,392 billion in long-term portfolio investments.

Direct investment and much of portfolio investment are long term; that is, holders expect to keep the investment at least a year before selling. Short-term investments include claims that mature within a year; examples of short-term claims are bank balances, bank borrowing and trade acceptances denominated in one nation's currency and owned by citizens of another. Short-term investments amounted to $8,124 plus $38,081, or $46,205, billion owed to U.S. investors and $58,899 less $7,402, or $51,497, billion owed to foreigners. Short-term investments are sometimes called *"hot money,"* because their liquidity makes it convenient to shift them from one country to another in search of higher interest income. The result of such shifts may be abrupt changes in bank reserves, with changes in banks' money creating powers and the level of liquidity in the nation as a whole. The Federal Reserve may be forced to conduct defensive operations to offset the effects of international flows of "hot money."

Total new U.S. investments abroad (debits) are subtracted from foreign investments in the United States (credits) to yield the balance on short- and long-term capital: a credit balance of $78,269 billion for 1986.

Combining the Balance on Current Account with the Balance on Capital Account yields the net balance of all autonomous transactions between U.S. citizens and citizens of other nations. This is the figure that many people mean when they talk about a deficit or surplus in the Balance of Payments.

It is the net change in unsatisfied claims held by citizens of one country against citizens of another. In 1986 the United States had a deficit on Current and Capital Account of $61,372 billion, indicating that foreigners accumulated more than $61 billion in claims against the United States. The balance of claims resulting from autonomous transactions may be settled by transactions classified as *compensatory transactions*. Compensatory transactions comprise Part 3 of the Balance of Payments statement.

Part 3: Compensatory Transactions

The Balance of Payments statement must always balance; payments made by U.S. citizens establish claims abroad that must be satisfied. If foreign holders of claims against the United States choose not to satisfy their claims by purchasing goods, services, investments or bank balances, their claims may be satisfied by compensatory transactions among their respective governments. Compensatory transactions offset autonomous transactions and bring the Balance of Payments into balance.

Outstanding claims may be satisfied by government in three ways. There are limits to the use of each, however.

Gold Shipments.   Until 1972, outstanding claims against the United States could be satisfied by shipment of official holdings of gold. Today, official gold holdings of the Treasury amount to only $11 billion, when gold is valued at the official price of $42.22 an ounce. To satisfy outstanding claims through shipments of gold would quickly deplete U.S. official gold holdings; therefore, gold is no longer shipped abroad to satisfy outstanding claims against the United States.

Payments of Foreign Currency.   Outstanding claims can be satisfied by paying out official U.S. holdings of foreign currencies. Foreign currency holdings arise from currency exchanges made by banks around the country, with deposits finally arriving at the Federal Reserve Bank. In 1987 official holdings of foreign currencies were $18 billion. Again, it is clear that shipments of foreign currencies to satisfy outstanding claims would quickly deplete the Federal Reserve's holdings.

Borrowing.   A third method of settling international balances is by borrowing. The U.S. government can borrow foreign exchange through its membership in the International Monetary Fund; the IMF is an international financial institution that we will discuss in more detail in Chapter 19. The U.S. Treasury may also sell government securities to foreign central banks. In this way, foreign banks can earn interest on holdings of dollar-denominated assets. Foreign central banks may also purchase U.S. corporate stocks and securities of state and local governments, and they may make deposits in U.S. financial institutions.

There are limits to government borrowings, too. The IMF will lend only under certain restrictions, and foreign central banks prefer to limit their holdings of assets denominated in particular currencies. Moreover, even government borrowing cannot continue forever. Like any other borrowing, it must eventually be repaid. For these reasons, it is important that a nation avoid piling up international debt year after year.

Every year, some international transactions fail to be recorded. Some merchandise imports and exports and tourist expenditures will not appear in the total debits and credits for settlement. This means that necessary official transactions may not precisely equal the Balance on Current and Capital Accounts. A statistical discrepancy is included to bring these figures into balance.

Changes in Exchange Rates

If a government exhausts all its official sources of funds for settling outstanding claims, there is a fourth alternative. The fourth alternative is for government to abandon the foreign exchange market and allow outstanding claims to be settled by individual traders and investors. In this case, outstanding claims are satisfied by supply and demand in markets for particular currencies. A deficit on Current and Capital Account produces an abundance of outstanding claims in that nation's currency; when the supply of the currency is greater than the demand, the currency's value falls. A surplus on Current and Capital Account implies an increase in demand for a particular currency, and its exchange rate increases. Thus, the nation's Balance of Payments comes into balance through changes in its currency's exchange rate.

Changes in exchange rates affect the value of one nation's claims against the real wealth of another. Deficits reduce the value of outstanding claims and discourage foreigners from holding the currency as an asset. At the same time, the currency's lower exchange rate reduces its value in trade and tends to reduce imports. Surpluses yield the opposite result. They increase the value of the currency and encourage its use for trade and investments, thus tending to increase imports. In all these cases, changes in exchange rates have the effect of moving the Balance of Payments back toward balance.

To summarize, the Balance of Payments is simply a method of measuring the process we talked about at the beginning of this chapter; that is, the process of producing and consuming goods and services from current production. When U.S. citizens consume goods and services, they must contribute goods and services—or claims to goods and services— of equal value. Foreigners can satisfy their claims against U.S. citizens immediately, or they may hold them for use in the future. Their willingness to postpone satisfying their claims enables U.S. citizens temporarily to consume more than we produce. But eventually all claims must be satisfied by the transfer of real wealth.

Balance of Payments Disequilibrium

Satisfying outstanding claims requires that a nation produce goods and services or offer investment opportunities attractive to citizens of other nations. Under ideal circumstances, a nation that consumes more than it produces in one year would produce more for sale than it consumes in the next. Over a period of several years, claims for goods and services would eventually be balanced by real production. Circumstances do not generally work this way in the real world.

We have said that the Balance of Payments must always balance. This is literally true because outstanding claims must somehow be settled. While in balance, the Balance of Payments may be in *disequilibrium*. Disequilibrium refers to either of two conditions: a condition of continuing deficits on Current and Capital Account that must be satisfied by repeated borrowing; or a condition of continuing surpluses that are satisfied by repeated lending. Whatever the source of disequilibrium, a nation finds itself adding to its own stock of claims or to others' claims against it year after year. A fundamental disequilibrium means that one nation (or nations) is continuing to consume more than it produces. World trade is increasingly one-sided, creating distortions that eventually must be corrected.

Since 1981 the U.S. Balance on Current Account has been in deficit. Surpluses on Capital Account have offset about three-fourths of the Current Account deficit; that is, foreigners have used the dollars they earned in merchandise trade to purchase direct and portfolio investments in the United States. These conditions have reduced the net investment position of the United States from $140 billion in 1981 to −$107 billion in 1986. The remaining outstanding claims have been satisfied through transfer of U.S. official holdings of foreign exchange.

Continuing deficits on Current and Capital Account represent a fundamental disequilibrium in the U.S. Balance of Payments and call for actions to correct the disequilibrium. In the sections that follow we will discuss some of the reasons for disequilibrium and suggest some of the processes by which disequilibrium can be corrected.

Deficits on Current Account

We will begin with consideration of the balance of trade, as recorded in the Current Account. Trade takes place because nations have comparative advantage. A nation specializes in producing the goods or services it produces at lower cost relative to other goods. When a nation exports its specialty, it earns income that can be used for purchasing needed imports. The relationship between the quantity of imports and the quantity of exports is a nation's *terms of trade*. The greater the world demand for a nation's exports, the more favorable are its terms of trade and the more goods it can reasonably expect to import.

The terms of trade refer to import quantities per unit of exports: in terms of the Balance of Payments, this is debit items per unit of credit items. It reflects the relative prices of imports and exports. In addition to the price of imports, a nation's trade balance depends on *total quantities* bought and sold: total debits and total credits. As conditions of world demand and conditions of production change, the prices and quantities of traded goods tend to change as well. Some of the sources of change are: changes in productivity growth among producing nations, changing levels of income in consuming nations, and changes in the prices of currencies used for international payments. Unfavorable changes in any of these conditions worsen a nation's export prospects and make paying for imports more difficult.

Productivity Growth. Productivity depends on the quality of a nation's productive resources: its labor, land, capital and entrepreneurial skills. Fertile land and climate, highly skilled and motivated workers, and technically advanced capital equipment enhance productivity and reduce costs. A decrease in productivity growth raises the costs and may reduce the quality of a nation's exports. Both these problems have affected U.S. exports in recent years and have contributed to the growing disequilibrium in the U.S. Balance of Payments.

In a world of free international trade, U.S. producers must continue to seek ways of improving productivity, to reduce the costs and increase the quality of the goods they sell. Only in this way can the United States be assured export trade sufficient to offset our imports of needed goods and services.

Income Growth. The growth of incomes among nations depends on productivity growth, resource growth and government policies. Higher incomes lead to rising demand for many imports, as more affluent consumers purchase cameras, stereo equipment, jewelry and works of art, fine clothing, and trips abroad. Irregular growth of incomes among consuming nations means irregular export demand for producing nations.

Differing growth rates among our trading partners have significantly affected the U.S. trade balance in recent years. The United States recovered more quickly from the 1981–1982 recession than did our European trading partners. Our rising incomes have enabled us to increase our imports, stimulating employment and production in other nations. Relative slow income growth abroad has slowed U.S. exports and worsened export prospects for the United States.

Faulty Exchange Rates. Productivity in producing nations and demand in consuming nations determine the terms of trade in real terms; that is, the real quantities of exported goods the nation must give up per unit of imported goods. Actual quantities of goods exchanged depend on their prices in terms of international currencies. Currency exchange rates should reflect the relative purchasing power of currencies, so that their international prices correctly reflect the real terms of trade.

Exchange rates are subject to many supply and demand factors that distort their values and affect the terms of trade. When other factors influence the exchange rate, a nation's currency may become *overvalued* or *undervalued*. A currency is overvalued if its price in foreign exchange markets is higher than its domestic purchasing power. If foreigners must pay more for a currency than it is worth in purchasing power, they are not likely to buy. In fact, an overvalued currency is likely to diminish a nation's export sales. One reason for declining U.S. exports in recent years has been an overvalued dollar, which made U.S. goods too costly for foreign consumers.

To summarize, we have identified the sources of merchandise trade disequilibrium as: differences in productivity growth among nations, changes in incomes and consumer demand, and exchange rates that incorrectly reflect the real purchasing power of international currencies. To correct a fundamental disequilibrium in a nation's Current Account requires changes in any or all of these conditions.

Deficits on Capital Account

A fundamental disequilibrium in the Balance of Payments may also be the result of uneven flows of international investments. Like domestic investment, investment spending among nations responds to expected rates of return and expected risk. Investors will accept lower returns on direct and portfolio investments in nations with stable political and economic systems than in those subject to frequent turmoil. Another important consideration has to do with expectations of a change in the value of the currency itself. If an expected decrease in a currency's exchange rate offsets the yield on investments, there will be no incentive to invest. On the other hand, an expected increase in a currency's exchange rate increases the investor's net return and reduces the yield that is necessary to encourage U.S. investments.

Forward Transactions. Traders and investors protect themselves against changes in currency exchange rates by hedging in foreign exchange markets. *Forward transactions* are the purchase or sale today of something for actual delivery in the future. For example, traders (European importers) who expect to need dollars to pay for merchandise at some time in the future buy dollars today for delivery when needed. At the same time, holders of short-term investments in the United States sell today for delivery in the future the dollars they expect to receive when their investments mature.

In this explanation, traders are demanders of forward exchange and investors are suppliers, but the reverse is also possible. Traders (European exporters) who expect to receive dollars from sales are suppliers of forward dollars, and U.S. holders of short-term investments in other countries are demanders of forward dollars (to replace the foreign currencies they expect to receive when their investments mature). In both these cases, hedging enables traders and investors to avoid risks associated with changes in a currency's value. Buyers and sellers can determine today the selling price of the currency that will change hands at some future date.

Hedging takes place in *forward markets* because actual exchange takes place in the future. The price of forward exchange depends on demand and supply. As we have seen, demand and supply are the result of hedging by traders and investors. An increase in demand relative to supply reflects increased demand for a nation's exports and investments and tends to push its currency's exchange rate up. An increase in supply relative to demand reflects increased imports and purchases of foreign investments and tends to push the exchange rate down.

International Currency Speculation.   Trends in demand and supply of forward exchange reflect fundamental trends in autonomous trade and investment decisions and determine trends in exchange rates. But demand and supply are also the result of actions by currency speculators. Speculators make their buy and sell decisions on the basis of expected changes in a currency's value. They buy forward exchange (go *long*) when they expect the exchange rate to rise; their demand helps push the forward rate up. When speculators expect the exchange rate to fall, they sell forward exchange (go *short*), expecting to buy the currency at lower prices before the date of delivery. This time, their added supply helps push the forward rate down.

Investors around the world compare exchange rate trends and interest rates for various currencies. By using the forward markets, they estimate the potential gain or loss on international currencies and their net return: the sum of interest and exchange rate effects. If an expected interest gain is precisely offset by an exchange loss, no investment will be made. Expected gains in both cause investment funds to move into the high-yielding currency. Expected losses in both cause funds to move out. In either case, the nation may experience disequilibrium in its Capital Accounts.

Changes in Interest Rates.   Some monetary effects of investment flows help to correct disequilibrium in investment accounts. Heavy inflows of investment funds increase a nation's money supply and push interest rates down. Moreover, inflows increase the supply of the nation's forward currency and push its price down. The effect is to reduce the potential gain from investments in that nation's currency and slow the inflow of investment funds. Heavy outflows of investment funds have the opposite effect. They reduce the nation's money supply, push interest rates up, and increase the demand (and the price) for forward currency. The result is to increase the potential gain from new investment in that nation and encourage additional investment inflows.

These market conditions help regulate the flow of direct and portfolio investment, encouraging or discouraging investment according to the supply of money and credit in particular nations. Market forces may not bring about equilibrium, however, because of all the many factors that influence domestic interest rates and forward exchange rates. The actions of speculators, in particular, and the decisions of monetary authorities around the world strongly influence the attractiveness of international investment.

MONEY AND BANKING IN PRACTICE: A PLAN FOR INTERNATIONAL MONETARY REFORM

The dollar's exchange rate reached bottom in 1980. Then, between 1980 and 1985 the dollar's value almost doubled, to a value economists estimate at 30 percent to 50 percent above purchasing power parity with our trading partners.

By 1985 the disadvantages of a strong dollar were becoming painfully obvious. The dollar's high value was encouraging U.S. consumers to spend dollars abroad and discouraging foreigners from buying dollars to spend in the United States. U.S. manufacturing firms were losing sales to foreign manufacturers, and some were going out of business. Moreover, a high dollar was reducing the value of earnings of U.S.

investments abroad; when the dollar is high, converting yen, pounds or marks earned abroad to dollars yields fewer dollars than when the dollar is low.

There were also advantages, of course. The high dollar value of U.S. investments was bringing in dollars from abroad and helping to keep U.S. interest rates from rising. The variety of U.S. financial instruments was another reason for the attractiveness of U.S. investments.

President Reagan's Secretary of the Treasury James Baker wanted to retain some of the advantages of the strong dollar and correct some of the disadvantages. To accomplish this,

Baker proposed that the governments of our major trading partners agree to hold their currency exchange rates within secret ranges agreed on in advance. If exchange rates move outside the range, he said, central banks should buy or sell the affected currencies until their prices move back into the range. To ensure success, the governments should also adjust their domestic economic policies to keep purchasing power relatively stable within each nation.

The first step in Baker's plan occurred in the fall of 1985, when the finance ministers of Japan, West Germany, France and Britain (the Group of Five, or G5) met in New York and agreed to reduce the value of the dollar. To accomplish this, the other nations agreed to increase their own interest rates so as to attract investors into their currencies and away from the dollar. By the end of 1986, the dollar had dropped by 15 percent against a market basket of other currencies.

One problem with Treasury Secretary Baker's scheme was the difficulty of containing the dollar's fall. In fact, the dollar reached its desired level and continued to plummet. By mid-1987 Baker was worried about the continuing fall of the dollar. To curb the dollar's fall, he urged Japan and Germany to increase their domestic money supplies so that spending would increase and increase the demand for dollars. Neither nation was willing to cooperate—at least to the extent desired by Baker.

This problem reflects the chief difficulty with programs to influence exchange rates. To maintain exchange rates at a level not dictated by the market requires coordinating economic policies in the affected nations. To agree to consult on domestic economic policies requires a certain sacrifice of national sovereignty, which many nations are reluctant to make.

Questions for Discussion

1. What problems may continue to plague U.S. manufacturing firms after they have lost customers to lower priced firms abroad? Can you think of other disadvantages of bringing the dollar's value down?

2. What should determine the range within which currency values lie? Why is it important to keep the range secret?

Multinational Corporations

The kinds of investment flows described here are carried out routinely by *multinational corporations*. Multinational corporations are private enterprises that own production or distribution facilities in more than one country. Often they distribute production processes among countries according to relative production costs; that is, they carry on labor-intensive operations in a low-wage country, most profitable operations in a low-tax country, and so forth. Of course, they also borrow in low-interest countries for investment in high-interest countries. And they constantly receive payments from sales, giving them funds for short-term investments in securities or bank deposits. Interest rate differentials and forward exchange rates are important for making many of their investment decisions.

When multinational corporations shift funds, the result is often a substantial change in debit or credit flows in a nation's Balance of Payments. In fact, the actions of multinationals may magnify tendencies toward deficits or surpluses. A nation with a trade deficit experiences a currency outflow and the expectation that its currency will decrease in value. The forward exchange rate tends to fall, because few buyers want to purchase an asset whose value is expected to fall but many speculators will want to sell it forward. (They go short, expecting to buy the currency at lower prices in the future and deliver it when promised.) A falling forward rate reduces the net yield on investments and encourages an outflow of investment funds. At the same time, surplus countries experience a rising forward rate (speculators go long), a rise in net yield, and an inflow of investment funds. Deficits increase in the first country and surpluses in the second.

Interest rate effects may be damaging also. The deficit nation loses more spending power, so that interest rates tend to rise. Higher interest rates may attract funds (if rates are higher than the expected decrease in exchange rates), but higher interest rates also discourage capital investment, retard productivity growth and may aggravate domestic inflation. The more fortunate surplus country enjoys the benefits of lower interest rates, greater capital investment and lower price inflation. The result of interest rate changes may be to reduce further the relative trade competitiveness of deficit nations and worsen their deficits.

Eurodollars

Over recent decades United States trade and investments have funneled more and more dollars into the hands of Europeans. Individuals, business firms and banks abroad have held dollars as short-term assets and sources of liquidity for trade. Dollars owned by foreigners came to be called Eurodollars. For European banks, Eurodollars became reserves against which new lending could take place. The new lending magnified the original dollars and increased the money supplies of the nations involved.

Eurodollars eventually were joined by Euromarks, Euroyen and any number of other currencies. By 1986 the total of all Eurocurrencies had mushroomed to about $1 trillion, about 80 percent of which was in dollars.

The large quantity of Eurodollars creates some problems for the U.S. Balance of Payments, primarily because of its effect on short-term investments, including bank balances. During the 1980s relatively high U.S. interest rates and a strong dollar have encouraged foreigners to retain their short-term dollar investments. But for the long run, large dollar holdings hang over foreign exchange markets and threaten to push the exchange rate down. Once the dollar begins to fall, expectations of further reductions in the exchange rate will encourage speculators to go short in forward markets. Falling forward rates will reduce the net return and discourage investment in the United States. Foreigners will sell their short-term investments and withdraw their bank balances. The result will be increased autonomous debit transactions and greater deficits. The danger is that official borrowing must increase to compensate for the increase in autonomous outpayments.

MONEY AND BANKING IN PRACTICE: EURODOLLARS

The Eurocurrency market is not new. In fact, as far back as Medieval times traders held currencies on deposit in various parts of the world for earning interest and making payments. The market began its recent growth spurt in the 1950s, in part because of the Cold War between the United States and the Soviet Union. The Soviet Union did not want to leave dollar holdings on deposit in U.S. banks for fear the U.S. government might freeze or nationalize them. So it established correspondent relationships with banks in Paris and London for holding dollar balances. The Soviet Union borrowed dollars for spending the world over and began encouraging other savers to bring their dollars in for profitable returns.

United States policy also worked perversely to encourage the growth of the Eurodollar market. During the 1960s policymakers in the United States at-tempted to curb the dollar outflow by placing a tax on foreign earnings and urging a voluntary reduction in foreign investments. Additionally, the Federal Reserve took steps to reduce money growth and restricted the amount of credit available to corporate borrowers. Both actions had the effect of encouraging multinational firms to keep their earnings abroad and to borrow from foreign sources.

The tremendous growth of the Eurocurrency market has some troubling aspects. There is no international regulatory power to impose reserve requirements and control its growth, so it has mushroomed. Moreover, the sophistication of Eurocurrency depositors and their access to electronic funds transfer make this a particularly volatile market. Funds move instantaneously from country to country, often offsetting entirely the policy actions of central banks. When Eurodollars are loaned to local borrowers and converted to domestic currency, the result is to increase the domestic money supply as well as the dollar reserves of central banks.

What are its probable long-run effects? One positive result emanates from the market as a source of financial capital. As U.S. and foreign borrowers use funds productively, global income should rise. Along with higher incomes should come an increase in demand for globally traded consumer goods. The result will be a more fully integrated world economy, with greater opportunities for specialization and greater total trade.

Questions for Discussion

1. Evaluate the Eurodollar market in terms of efficiency and equity. What particular difficulties does this market impose on the United States?
2. How would freely fluctuating exchange rates affect the Eurocurrency market?

3. Given that central banks intervene occasionally to maintain stable currency values, what has been the effect on international capital flows?

International Money Flows and the Domestic Money Supply

Equilibrium in a nation's Balance of Payments means that the nation is withdrawing from total production goods and services equal in value to those it produces. In that sense, international equilibrium ensures equity in the distribution of total world output and minimizes the potential for international conflict. It helps promote free trade and the advantages that follow from international specialization.

Disequilibrium in the Balance of Payments means the reverse. When trade and investment flows are one-sided, money flows are also one-sided, and production and consumption arrangements are out of balance.

Under the Gold Standard, it was assumed that automatic forces within free markets would correct a Balance of Payments disequilibrium without need for any government policy at all. Remember that the Gold Standard established a nation's money supply on the basis of its supply of gold reserves. A Balance of Payments deficit meant an outflow of currency redeemable in gold and a reduction in the domestic money supply. As the reduced money supply worked to reduce income, prices and wages would fall also, until exports again became attractive and the deficit was eliminated.

In contrast, nations with trade surpluses would experience gold inflows, rising employment and rising prices. As domestic prices rose, imports would increase relative to exports and the balance of trade surplus would diminish. Note that in both cases Balance of Payments disequilibrium was corrected automatically as a result of natural forces at work within the system. Whenever a nation experienced a deficit or a surplus, gold flows would work to correct it.

The theory behind the Gold Standard was more acceptable than the fact. In fact, even under the Gold Standard prices seldom fell far enough to bring trade accounts into balance.

The main problem with the Gold Standard was the requirement that paper money be convertible to gold. Tying a nation's money supply to its gold stock imposed spending limits on governments and required that government expenditures be financed by taxes. Both restrictions were unacceptable to governments increasingly subject to election by popular vote. The result was predictable. The restraints of the Gold Standard were ignored, money supplies were increased in deficit as well as surplus nations, and the self-correcting forces of the Gold Standard failed to go to work.

Overissue of currency finally brought an end to the Gold Standard after World War I. Currency convertibility had been suspended during the war, as governments spent heavily for defense. After the war, Britain attempted to regain her position as financial leader of the world by restoring the pound's convertibility at the prewar gold price. To return to the pound's prewar value meant that millions of pounds had to be withdrawn from circulation. To do this required high taxes and low government expenditures, slow money growth, and high interest rates. Such policies succeeded in raising the pound's value, but in doing so they damaged British export industries and sharply reduced domestic production and employment. Similar policies throughout Western nations contributed to the Great Depression of the 1930s. The Gold Standard was finally abandoned.

The Gold-Dollar Standard

World War II brought more government spending for military purposes and heavy gold flows to the United States. After the war, finance ministers of Western nations met at Bretton Woods, New Hampshire, to plan new trade arrangements for the postwar era. They agreed that gold alone could no longer finance the expected increased volume of world trade. Great Britain was unable to accept the responsibility of financing trade because of her seriously weakened economy. The only really strong economy—backed by substantial gold reserves and an intact industrial capacity—was that of the United States. The nations agreed on a Gold-Dollar Standard in which gold and U.S. dollars would be held as reserves in central banks, to be used in settlement transactions in Balance of Payments accounts.

The dollar was evaluated in terms of gold, and other currencies were pegged to the dollar. Thus, other currencies could be redeemed in dollars, and dollars redeemed in gold. Central banks agreed to maintain the pegged values of their currencies by buying and selling currencies in foreign exchange markets. Because dollars were needed for trade, the United States expanded the money supply and allowed more currency to flow out to reserve accounts around the world. A healthy revival of world trade and new industrial development followed.

The dollar served three purposes during these years. It was a *transactions currency*: the means by which importers paid for goods and services. It was a *reserve currency*: the stored assets of central banks for settling payments deficits. And it was an *interventionist currency*: the means by which central banks paid for the currencies they purchased to maintain their pegged rates. For a single currency to fulfill all these responsibilities is difficult, if not impossible. This is because widespread holdings will eventually threaten a currency's value. Maintaining a stable value is necessary if it is to continue to serve these important functions.

By the late 1960s, this problem was becoming apparent. Moreover, heavy conversion of dollars to gold had severely reduced U.S. gold stocks. The United States sought new arrangements to relieve some of the pressures on the dollar. Specifically, the United States wanted to reduce the dollar's value relative to gold and relative to all the other currencies pegged to it.

Correcting Disequilibrium under the Bretton Woods Agreement

During the 25 years of the Bretton Woods agreement, it was acknowledged that a nation might need to change its currency's value. But it was hoped that other means to achieve external balance would be used first. We have shown how an overvalued currency makes a nation's exports costly in terms of world prices and makes imports cheap. The result is excess imports relative to exports and continuing trade deficits. An undervalued currency creates imbalance in the opposite direction: trade surpluses.

To reduce an overvalued currency's pegged value is called devaluation; to increase an undervalued currency's pegged value is revaluation. It was expected that nations would not take these steps lightly, that internal policies would be used first to correct disequilibrium. For the overvalued currency this would mean policies to reduce money growth and reduce prices on exports (to offset the high exchange rate for the currency). Such policies would raise the purchasing power of the currency to the level of its exchange rate. For the undervalued currency correcting disequilibrium would require policies to increase the money supply and reduce its value (by raising domestic prices).

In other words, the Bretton Woods agreement required nations to accept painful changes in domestic prices in order to achieve external balance. It is understandable that nations avoided such measures until, finally, pegged currency values had to be changed: Overvalued currencies had to be devalued, and undervalued currencies revalued. During the time leading up to the change, financial markets were often disrupted, as speculators bought currencies whose pegs were expected to rise and sold those whose pegs were expected to fall. In order to maintain the pegs, central banks paid out millions of the strong currency and purchased millions of the weak currency. The unhappy result was a decline in the value of their foreign exchange reserves.

The dollar was under pressure to devalue for more than a decade. With their overvalued dollars U.S. consumers bought many foreign goods and investments and traveled widely abroad. Exports rose more slowly, not only because of the overvalued dollar but also because of the revival of industrial production in many of our trading partners. We experienced fundamental disequilibrium in international payments, but we avoided policies to reduce money growth and reduce domestic prices.

External disequilibrium created problems internally as well. Export industries and those competing with imports suffered rising unemployment and business failures. Examples are electronics, industrial equipment, steel, textiles and automobiles. To achieve external balance would have required slower money growth to encourage exports. But high domestic unemployment called for increased money growth to stimulate economic activity.

To devalue the dollar was a serious step. Friendly nations had held dollars as reserves, confident of their stable value in terms of gold. Following devaluation, investors around the world would never again hold dollars as confidently as before. Furthermore, devaluation might not correct the problem of external disequilibrium. If other nations continued to peg their currencies to the dollar at the old rate, there would be no improvement in the dollar's relative position. Other nations had to agree to revalue their currencies relative to the dollar.

Devaluation and Floating Rates

New currency arrangements were established in the early 1970s. The dollar's value was reduced in terms of gold; that is, the official price of gold was increased from $35 an ounce to $42.22 an ounce. But the Treasury announced it would no longer redeem dollars in gold for private citizens, and it asked foreign central banks to refrain from presenting dollars for redemption. Other currencies were revalued against the dollar at rates consistent with their domestic purchasing power.

At the same time, the parties to the Bretton Woods agreement decided to let their currency values float. Floating currency values are determined by supply and demand in foreign exchange markets. Some advantages were

FIGURE 12–1 Temporary Payments
Deficit

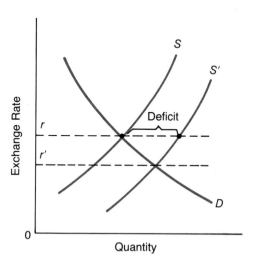

The supply curve shifts to the right as
currency flows out to foreign exchange
markets. The exchange rate *(r)* floats
down.

expected to flow from floating currencies, particularly with respect to external
balance. If currency values were allowed to move in response to supply and
demand, it was reasoned, there would be no payments deficits or surpluses.

To see why, consider a nation that is experiencing a temporary payments
deficit. More currency is flowing out to foreign exchange markets, and its
supply curve shifts to the right as shown in Figure 12–1. At the current
exchange rate the deficit is the difference between currency demanded (for
making credit transactions) and currency supplied (for making debit transactions). But if the exchange rate is allowed to float down to its equilibrium
value, the quantity demanded will increase; more of the currency will be
used to purchase the nation's exports and domestic investments. Moreover,
the quantity supplied will fall; less of the currency will be used to purchase
imports and foreign investments. The Balance of Payments will return to
balance.

Elsewhere in the world other nations would be experiencing temporary
surpluses, with excess demand for their currencies for purchasing their exports. In their cases, the exchange rate would float upward until the surplus

FIGURE 12–2 Temporary Payments Surplus

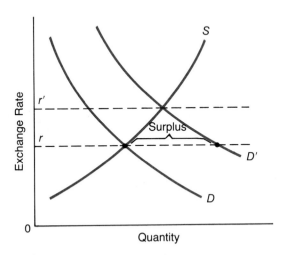

As the demand curve shifts to the right,
the exchange rate *(r)* floats upward.

disappears and balance is restored. Figure 12–2 illustrates this situation. The expected result of floating exchange rates was that continuous adjustments would take place to correct disequilibrium. Freely floating exchange rates would avoid the problem of pressure slowly building for a change, with currency speculation and finally a massive and abrupt change, disrupting markets and damaging financial relationships.

Floating rates were expected to have another important advantage. Nations would conduct their own money growth policies independent of the need to adjust domestic prices to international exchange rates. No longer would central banks have to buy foreign currencies and issue their own in exchange, threatening domestic inflation. Nor would central banks have to borrow foreign currencies to settle international trade imbalances. In both cases, central banks would be free to increase or decrease money growth on the basis of internal considerations only.

Note that freely floating exchange rates would remove the need for Part 3 of the Balance of Payments entirely. Nations would not need to hold reserves for settling accounts nor borrow for that purpose. Part 3 was necessary only for a system of pegged rates. (Because all currencies do not float freely even now, Part 3 is still in use.)

Some Continuing Problems

You may not be surprised to learn that floating exchange rates have not solved all the world's trading problems. Deficit nations have experienced declining exchange rates, but accounts have not moved into balance. Frequently deficits have worsened. There are two reasons for this result.

Elasticity of Demand

One reason has to do with inelasticity of demand for imports and exports. A declining currency value implies that imports will decrease and exports increase. But if the need for imports continues at the same level, and if needed imports cost more in terms of domestic currency, the currency outflow may actually increase. Moreover, unless demand for exports is price elastic, export sales will not increase, and earnings from exports will probably fall. Unfortunately, demand for traded goods is often price inelastic, because there are few substitutes. (If there were substitutes freely available at home, international trade might not have begun at all.)

The "J" Effect

Even if demand is price elastic, deficits may increase—at least in the short run. This is because orders for traded goods take months to fill. Imports ordered before currency values fell will cost more in the cheaper currency. Exports priced in domestic currency will earn dollars of lower value. The resulting fall in the trade balance is an example of what economists call the "J" effect. A period of even larger deficits may be necessary before trade accounts finally come into balance.

Vicious Cycles and Virtuous Cycles

Of course, worsening deficits in one country imply accumulating surpluses in another. The result has been what some economists call vicious cycles for deficit nations and virtuous cycles for surplus nations. With only floating rates to bring about equilibrium, disequilibrium has worsened.

The principal reason for cumulating imbalance has been the effect of floating rates on domestic prices. Deficit nations have experienced downward floating exchange rates and rising prices for needed imports. When imported materials constitute a major input for industrial production, production costs must increase. The result is domestic inflation and reduced ability to sell exports abroad. The "virtuous" nation experiences the opposite price effects and increased exports. For many nations, floating rates have made economic development more costly and have stifled domestic production and employment, aggravated inflation, and worsened living standards. For others, floating rates have brought prosperity and stable prices.

Another problem with floating exchange rates has been the uncertainty they bring to international trade. Traders may hesitate to enter into international transactions if they are uncertain of the final cost. Some economists have concluded that floating rates reduce the total level of trade and, therefore, the potential benefits of global specialization.

What further means remain by which nations can correct Balance of Payments disequilibrium? The old answer is just as correct today as it was during the period of the Gold Standard—and just as painful. Nations with deficits must increase exports and reduce imports. To accomplish this, it may be necessary to slow money growth to reduce prices and slow the growth of imports.

Nations with surpluses must reduce the growth of exports and increase imports. It may be necessary to increase money growth to increase domestic incomes. Barriers to imports should be removed and government subsidies to promote exports should be stopped. Japan and occasionally Germany have been urged to adopt these measures.

In both cases, domestic political considerations sometimes work against pursuit of external balance and contribute to continued disequilibrium.

MONEY AND BANKING IN PRACTICE: THE ENERGY CRISIS AND THE PROBLEM OF PETRODOLLARS

Short of war, no event has disrupted the world economy so much as the continuing energy crisis. The Arab oil embargo of 1973 and subsequent price increases have thrown most industrial nations into painful disequilibrium, pressing less developed nations deeper into poverty. Years—and perhaps decades—will be required for adjustments to moderate the unsettling effects of the energy crisis.

The problems of affected nations can be described in terms of internal and external disequilibrium. Internally, the energy crisis produced both extremes of economic hardship: inflation and unemployment. Not only have soaring oil prices themselves exacerbated inflation, but the higher costs have been built into every other consumer good and service. High oil prices have pushed up prices of other substitute sources of energy, and lower profits have reduced funds available for investing in modern capital equipment.

Higher energy prices should work to reduce quantity demanded, and to a certain extent this has occurred. But short-run demand for energy was relatively inelastic, so that a high level of consumption continued. The result was a reallocation of consumer purchases, with reduced spending for other goods and services. Rising unemployment in the affected industries has worsened a tendency toward recession throughout the economy.

Less developed countries (LDCs) suffer even more deeply from inflation and unemployment than the industrialized nations. For many, imported oil is a necessary element of their development plans—both for development of manufacturing capacity and for bringing scientific procedures to agriculture. The energy crisis condemned more generations of their people to ill health, unrealized potential and even starvation.

In terms of external disequilibrium, oil-importing nations experienced a vast transfer of income to oil exporters. The income transfer has made future production difficult for two reasons. First, it has reduced the capacity in both industrialized nations and LDCs to produce goods and services, as we have seen. Second, the immense transfer of purchasing power has changed spending patterns and reduced production incentives. If future production is to grow, the dollars paid out for oil must be *recycled* back into the spending stream.

Recycling petrodollars was a major concern of the 1970s. Oil-importing nations encouraged exporting nations to use their oil revenues for trade and in-

vestment. Spending their billions of dollars proved to be difficult, in part because oil-exporting nations themselves were at such a low stage of development that many consumer goods would not be useful to their people at all. Investing on such a large scale frequently meant purchase of unfamiliar and unprofitable properties. Wasteful spending aggravated inflation in exporting nations and worsened domestic tendencies toward social unrest.

How could petrodollars be used to correct problems of internal and external balance in importing nations in ways favorable to oil exporters? One solution was to deposit petrodollars in international banks for lending to LDCs. However, there were some problems with this solution. The banks were faced with the age-old problem of mismatch between the maturities of their assets and liabilities. Petrodollar deposits were subject to quick withdrawal in response to interest incentives the world over, while LDC loans tended to be very long term. Moreover, many banks quickly reached legal limits on their lending to a single borrower. As the 1980s began, new oil price increases worsened the recycling problem; many commercial banks worried about their exposure to losses in particular LDCs. Some borrowing nations were allowed to stretch out their interest and principal payments so as to avoid default, but in general, banks were reluctant to continue carrying the major burden of the recycling problem. They hoped that an international organization would assume the responsibility of holding short-term petro-deposits and allocating investment according to expected profitability.

Regional banks like the Asian Development Bank and the World Bank and International Monetary Fund (to be discussed in Chapter 19) began to assume this role. An international organization can diversify holdings and minimize risks. Investments can be made in facilities needed for long-term growth, helping to bring about a convergence of growth rates between Western industrialized nations and LDCs (both oil and non-oil). Improved capacity for production and consumption should reduce problems of external balance in the future.

Oil-exporting nations face a situation common to that faced by banks throughout history. Accepting the debts of others makes the lender, in effect, a hostage to the borrower. The lender's own prosperity depends on the healthy progress of the borrowing nation.

Question for Discussion

1. In general, fluctuating exchange rates are recommended as a means of correcting Balance of Payments disequilibrium. Why are exchange rate adjustments likely to be slow to bring about the recycling of petrodollars?

Correcting Disequilibrium Through Exchange Control

One further way to correct Balance of Payments disequilibrium is exchange control. Exchange control requires exporters to turn over all foreign exchange earnings to government and allows government to pay out foreign exchange only for government-approved imports.

Exchange control ensures that valuable foreign exchange is used only for purchases that serve the purposes of government. This may mean that foreign exchange earnings are used only for purchases of capital equipment; or it may mean that importers with influence in government can acquire foreign exchange for purchase of luxuries. Whatever the goals of exchange control, there is substantial room for abuse, with bribery and extortion the possible results.

Control of foreign exchange may enable government to establish *multiple exchange rates*: high rates for currency to be used for imports of consumer goods and low rates for imports of capital goods. Multiple exchange rates are illustrated in Figures 12–3a to 12–3c. Supply and demand would establish an equilibrium exchange rate of r_e, as shown in Figure 12–3a. But the available supply at S is allocated to consumer goods (S_c) and capital goods (S_k) in Figures 12–3b and 12–3c. Demand for these two classes of imports establishes a high rate (and thus high prices) for consumer goods and low rates (and low prices) for capital goods.

FIGURE 12–3a   Equilibrium Exchange
                    Rate (r_e)

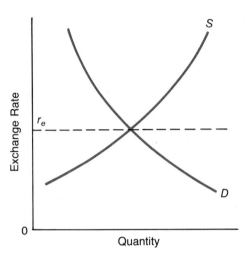

Available supply is allocated to consumer
goods and capital goods, as shown in
Figures 12–3b and 12–3c.

FIGURE 12–3b   Allocation of Supply to
                    Consumer Goods (S_c)

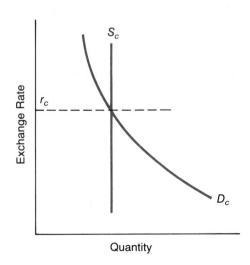

FIGURE 12–3c   Allocation of Supply to
                    Capital Goods (S_k)

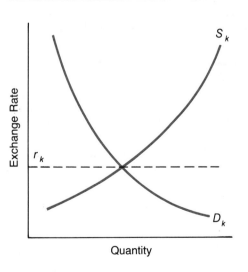

The Soviet Union maintains strict exchange control, with severe penalties for violators. The result is to limit the use of foreign exchange for imports of blue jeans and rock recordings and to preserve foreign exchange for imports of computers, oil-drilling equipment and feed grains.

MONEY AND BANKING IN PRACTICE: STABILIZING CURRENCY EXCHANGE RATES

After decades of a positive balance on current account, the U.S. Balance of Payments moved into deficit in 1971. One reason was the great increase in U.S. imports and the slower growth of income from U.S. investments abroad. Exporters around the world used their earnings from sales in the United States to purchase U.S. investments, including entire business firms, corporate stocks and bonds and bank balances. In the years following 1971 the U.S. Balance of Payments continued to deteriorate, and in September 1985 U.S. Secretary of the Treasury James Baker called a meeting of representatives of major trading nations to seek a solution of world trade problems.

Secretary Baker's objective was to allow the dollar's exchange rate to fall. High interest yields in the United States relative to interest yields abroad had increased the demand for dollars and pushed its exchange rate 50 percent above its rate in 1980. The high dollar discouraged purchases of U.S. exports and encouraged imports. Reducing the dollar's value would require foreign central banks to sell dollars from their foreign exchange reserves; this would increase the supply of dollars and push the dollar's exchange rate down. Selling dollars is the same as buying other currencies, which increases their demand and pushes their exchange rates upward.

Other nations agreed (reluctantly) to help push the dollar's exchange rate down. They were reluctant because of the expectation that their own currencies' higher exchange rates would discourage their own exports and encourage imports. Thus, by helping to reduce the United States' Balance of Payments deficit, they would create deficits (or smaller surpluses) in their own Balance of Payments.

In fact, the dollar's exchange rate declined throughout 1986. By the middle of 1987 Treasury Secretary Baker was worried that the dollar had fallen too far. The lower dollar had the effect of increasing the dollar cost of U.S. imports, so that the monthly trade deficit had not improved very much. The objective of U.S. policy then became to stop the dollar's fall and allow a small increase.

Japanese investors helped accomplish this objective. Interest rates on U.S. government securities were about twice those on comparable Japanese investments, which encouraged an inflow of investment funds from Japan. Foreign central banks also helped by buying dollars to add to their foreign exchange reserves. Both these actions increased demand for dollars and helped raise the dollar's value. In one sense, the world's major trading nations returned briefly to the Bretton Woods system for stabilizing exchange rates.

Economists were worried that maintaining the dollar's value would require fundamental improvements in U.S. trade: increased competitiveness for U.S. exports in global markets and reduced U.S. purchases of oil imports. Unless the U.S. Balance of Trade improves, exchange rate manipulations to stabilize the Balance of Payments will become increasingly difficult.

Questions for Discussion

1. What are the advantages and disadvantages of international conferences for stabilizing exchange rates?

2. What fundamental actions may yield more enduring results?

Glossary of Terms

autonomous transactions. international transactions initiated by private individuals or business firms

compensatory transactions. official transactions made to settle outstanding claims from autonomous transactions

credit transactions. international transactions that result in an inflow of payments to the United States

debit transactions. international transactions that result in an outflow of payments from the United States

disequilibrium. a condition in which a nation experiences repeated deficits or surpluses in international payments

forward transactions. contracts to purchase or to deliver foreign exchange at some specified date in the future

"hot money". short-term financial capital that moves freely from nation to nation in response to differences in interest rates

interventionist currency. a currency used to purchase other currencies for the purpose of influencing relative values

multinational corporation. a corporation that conducts operations in more than one nation

multiple exchange rates. a schedule of exchange rates based on the expected use of the foreign exchange

overvalued currency. a currency whose exchange value exceeds its domestic purchasing power

reserve currency. a currency held as a financial asset

terms of trade. the quantities of goods and services a nation is willing to export per unit of imports

transaction currency. a currency used for exchanging goods and services

undervalued currency. a currency whose exchange value is less than its domestic purchasing power

Summary of Important Ideas

1. The Balance of Payments statement records the value of all international spending and investment flows. Parts 1 and 2 list autonomous transactions: private decisions to purchase goods and services, private income flows, government grants and military expenditures, and private investment expenditures. The difference between all outpayments for debit transactions and inpayments for credit transactions indicates a net deficit or net surplus.

2. Part 3 records compensatory transactions for balancing the deficit or surplus. Settlement may be through payments of gold or foreign currencies or through borrowing and lending.

3. Although the Balance of Payments will always balance, it may experience disequilibrium: a chronic condition of deficit or surplus, so that debts or debt claims accumulate year after year. Disequilibrium might be the result of changes in comparative advantage, changing world demand for traded goods, differences in income growth among nations, or a failure of exchange rates to reflect real purchasing power of currencies.

4. Investment flows may be perverse because of speculators' expectations about future currency values or because of hedging operations on the part of multinational corporations.

5. Large outstanding holdings of Eurodollars represent a threat, because the resulting downward pressure on the dollar's value probably encourages an outflow of short-term investment.

Questions for Discussion and Research

1. Distinguish between the following pairs: autonomous and compensatory transactions, debit and credit transactions, current and capital account, direct and portfolio investment.

2. Explain what is meant by a chronic disequilibrium in the Balance of Payments. How would you distinguish between corrective measures for disequilibrium and those for imbalance?

3. Consult the current *Economic Report of the President* for data on trends in U.S. trade. Comment on your findings and note the industries that are most strongly affected.

4. Explain how faulty exchange rates can improve or worsen a nation's trade. Consult *The Wall Street Journal* for information on dollar exchange rates and show how recent trends have affected U.S. trade.

5. Illustrate mathematically the relationship between expected future exchange rates and short-term investment. How might investment flows help change the forces that initially caused them?

6. Discuss the impact of multinational corporations on Balance of Payments statements. Consider both the current and capital accounts, long- and short-term.

Additional Readings

Aliber, Robert Z. *The International Money Game.* New York: Basic Books, 1976.

Bergstrand, Jeffrey H. "Exchange Rate Variation and Monetary Policy." *New England Economic Review* (May/June 1986): 3–20.

Cooper, Richard N. "Dealing with the Trade Deficit in a Floating Rate System." Brookings, 1986: 1, 195–207.

Feldstein, Martin. "Why the Dollar Is Strong." *Challenge* (January/February 1984): 37–41.

Fellner, William, et al. *Maintaining and Restoring Balance in International Payments.* Princeton, N.J.: Princeton University Press, 1966.

Little, Jane Sneddon. *Euro-dollars.* New York: Harper and Row, 1975.

Machlup, Fritz. *International Payments, Debts, and Gold.* 2nd ed. New York: New York University Press, 1976.

Maital, Shlomo. "The Mad Mad World of Currency Trading." *Across the Board* (December 1986): 10–21.

Resler, David H. "Does Eurodollar Borrowing Improve the Dollar's Exchange Value?" *Federal Reserve Bank of St. Louis Review* 61 (August 1979): 10–16.

Roosa, Robert V. *The Dollar and World Liquidity.* New York: Random House, 1967.

"Treasury and Federal Reserve Foreign Exchange Operations." *Federal Reserve Bank of New York Quarterly Review* (Winter 1985–1986): 45–48.

"U.S. International Transactions in 1986." *Federal Reserve Bulletin* (May 1987): 322–29.

Wallich, Henry C.   "Reflections on the U.S. Balance of Payments." *Challenge* 21 (March/April 1978): 56–58.

"William E. Brock on International Trade." *The Brookings Review* (Spring 1984): 26–31.

PART III

How Does Money Affect Our Economic Goals?

How does money affect our economic goals involving efficiency in the allocation of resources, equity in the distribution of output, and the production of positive externalities? How can government in a free society help private financial institutions create a healthy climate for achieving our economic goals?

Scholars have pondered these questions for centuries, adding to or rejecting answers that came before. Thus, the study of money has evolved along with changes in the forms of money and changes in the nation's financial intermediaries. New developments continue to call for new theories to explain the changing role of money. Today's advancing technology of information makes possible more scientific measures of money and more accurate predictions of its effects on our economic goals.

Government has a major role to play in a modern economy, collecting taxes and spending for public projects. To moderate the effects of government borrowing on private financial markets, new financial arrangements may be needed. The goals of efficiency and equity become more elusive in complex economies like ours. Policymakers continue to experiment with new strategies for increasing prosperity and enhancing opportunity.

Part III is a critical part of this course of study. It brings together the scholarly thinking of monetary economists with the real world of day-to-day monetary policymaking. Understanding the material in Part III can help today's citizens evaluate current policy in terms of its effects on their own well-being. And it can help individuals plan their own economic activity in the light of current policy.

Proceed with care!

CHAPTER

13

- To explore the relationship between money and economic activity
- To learn how monetary theory has evolved with changes in the economic environment
- To understand how people use money

Theories of the Role of Money

"To err is human, to live by rules divine."

Walter Heller

Money matters. Not many people would disagree with that. Precisely how money matters may be difficult to explain, however.

Every day we see around us examples of how money matters. Economists look below the surface effects to examine the deeper, more fundamental and abiding consequences of money and the ways we manage it. The most fundamental consequence has to do with how we allocate productive resources. Under one monetary system, resources may be allocated primarily toward production of goods for export; under another, luxurious palaces; another, industrial capital. Decisions on how to manage money reflect a nation's priorities with respect to the proper use of productive resources.

In democratic societies like ours, citizens have a voice in making such decisions. The result is a tendency toward decisions that increase the well-being of the majority. In general, the majority favors decisions that achieve the fullest possible use of resources along with price stability. These are not simple goals, and they may be incompatible. Policies that achieve one or the other may create unwanted side effects. As a nation, we try to choose policies with the greatest benefits—in terms of the ways we use resources—and the lowest costs—in terms of other uses we give up.

Economists can help us choose. They help by developing theories to explain how money affects other variables in the economic environment. No theory is perfect, however; the economic environment is too complex. Furthermore, the political implications of any theory make agreement difficult. One theory may emphasize the fullest possible use of resources, and another, price stability. Political interest groups tend to favor the theory that best promotes their special goals.

An example of differences in political goals is the conflict over the proper role of government in the economy. Some economists recommend a policy of laissez-faire. They believe the economy is basically stable and requires little or no government intervention. In fact, they believe that government interference destroys automatic tendencies in the economy toward stability. Other economists recommend government intervention to offset tendencies toward business cycles. They believe that without government intervention the economy tends toward periods of high unemployment alternating with periods of unstable prices. In their view, no automatic forces exist to restore stability in the absence of government intervention.

As you read this chapter, consider how the various theories of money deal with the issue of resource allocation, how various theories serve particular political interests, and how theories have evolved to serve broader interests. Note especially the relative importance the various theories give to the goals of full employment and price stability.

The Quantity Theory of Money

The first major theory of the role of money was born in the sixteenth century and dominated economic theory until the early 1900s. Sixteenth-century explorers returning to Europe from Mexico and the Orient brought back splendid gold and silver treasures, which they melted down and made into coins. The increase in the money supply caused noticeable changes in certain economic variables. Most obvious was the effect on prices. Holders of the new gold and silver coins increased their spending, causing prices of consumer goods to rise. Higher prices led to workers' demands for higher wages, which increased manufacturing firms' costs of production and pushed prices up still higher. Generally, the initial increase in prices continued until much of the new gold and silver had flowed out to other nations through trade. The final result was a generally higher level of prices proportionate to the larger supply of money.

The theory that prices would be proportionate to the supply of money became known as the *quantity theory of money*. The quantity theory can be expressed algebraically. Begin with an expression *(MV)* for total spending for new goods and services over some period, where:

$$M = \text{quantity of money and}$$
$$V = \text{velocity of turnover.}$$

Velocity of turnover is the number of times money is spent during the period.

Then write an expression for total output:

$$\text{Total Output} = \Sigma \, pq$$

where

p = the price of every good or service sold and
q = the quantities of every good produced during the period.

The sum of all prices times quantities is total output for the period. Total output can be expressed:

$$\Sigma \, pq = PQ$$

where

P = the general price level (or price index) and
Q = the total quantity of goods and services produced.

Finally, combine the two expressions:

$$\text{Total Spending} = \text{Total Output}[1]$$
$$MV = PQ.$$

The expression ($MV = PQ$) is an identity, in which the two sides of the equality measure essentially the same thing. An identity is shown this way: $MV \equiv PQ$. The expression is also an identity between total spending (MV) and current income from production of new goods and services (which is often written as Y). Thus, $MV \equiv Y$.

The Equation of Exchange

The expression ($MV \equiv PQ$) is called the equation of exchange. It expresses simply and correctly the necessary equality between spending and income.

In 1986, the supply of money ($M1$) was $730 billion and output of new goods and services was $4,208 billion. Substituting these values in the equation of exchange yields:

$$\text{Total Spending} \equiv \text{Total Output} \equiv \text{Income}$$
$$(M)\,(V) \equiv 4{,}208$$
$$(730)\,(V) \equiv (P)\,(Q)$$
$$(730)\,(V) \equiv (1.145)\,(3{,}675)$$
$$(730)\,(5.76) \equiv (1.145)\,(3{,}675)$$

Velocity of turnover was almost six times in 1986. The price index (P) for 1986 is 1.145 when 1982 is the base year, and real production (Q) in terms of 1982 dollars was $3,675 billion.

Under these conditions, we might expect that a $10 billion increase in the money supply (M) for the next year would cause total output to increase by:

$$(\Delta M)\ (V) = \Delta\ (P)\ (Q) = 10(5.76) = \$57.6 \text{ billion}$$

for total output of \$4,265.6 billion. A \$10 billion decrease would cause a \$57.6 billion decrease in output. (Note that the distribution of the \$57.6 billion—between prices and quantity of output—is not yet known. This is a point to be addressed shortly.)

The Assumptions

To some economists, the equation of exchange became a useful guide to policy regarding the money supply. Whether they were correct or not depends on whether their assumptions were correct. Three fundamental assumptions underlie the earliest (and most extreme) view of the quantity theory and its role in deciding economic policy. They are: (1) the assumption of stable V and Q, (2) the assumption of full employment, and (3) the assumption of causality from money to prices.

Assumption 1: Stable V and Q.   The first assumption is that V and Q are basically stable and unaffected by changes in M. Over the long term, V and Q may change in response to changes in other economic conditions. But if changes are gradual and predictable, the equation of exchange can be used to project the economy's need for money.

In fact, in recent years velocity (V) has appeared to be on an upward trend. The reason may be certain changes in many of our economic institutions: (a) New types of financial intermediaries have made credit readily available for emergencies or unexpected spending needs. It has become less necessary to set aside funds for such purposes, so that people can spend their money faster. (b) Our modern economy employs more workers in industry than in agriculture. When workers receive regular and frequent paychecks, it is less necessary to hold idle currency, so that incomes are spent faster. (c) Over time, business demand for financial capital has increased, pushing up interest rates on borrowed funds. When interest rates are high, it becomes costly to hold idle currency. Savers quickly lend funds to borrowers, who spend them quickly.

Quantity of output (Q) has been increasing, too. Our labor force has increased and become more productive, and new capital and new technology have increased our capacity to produce goods and services. All these changes have had the effect of increasing V and Q, but the changes have been fairly gradual and predictable.

Assumption 2: Full Employment.   In the most extreme version of the quantity theory, the second assumption is the assumption of full employment. Under this assumption, the value of Q will tend always to be the maximum amount that can be produced.

The assumption of full employment depends on wage rates that fluctuate according to supply and demand in labor markets. According to the extreme version, if there were to be any unemployment, the excess supply of workers would drive wages down. Firms would move down their demand curves and hire all workers willing to work at the equilibrium wage. Thus, employment would quickly return to the full employment level and Q to its long-term trend.

The important thing about assumptions (1) and (2) is that with a stable V and the full employment level of Q, only M and P can vary. In fact, with assumptions (1) and (2), M and P will remain roughly proportional to each other. If M doubles, P will also double. If M falls by one-tenth, P will fall by one-tenth, and so forth.

The modern version of the quantity theory acknowledges that during a business cycle assumptions (1) and (2) may not hold. In recession, employment and output (Q) may fall below the full employment level. In recovery, employment and output may grow faster than normal, as production moves back up to the long-term trend. Business-cycle changes in Q will not destroy the proportional relationship between M and P, however. This is because velocity (V) will also change with the business cycle. As output and employment fall, workers will spend their incomes more slowly so as to accumulate funds for a possible future emergency. Later, when employment and output begin to increase, business firms and workers will spend faster for the purchases they postponed earlier. If Q and V rise and fall together in a business cycle, M and P will remain the same proportion.

Assumption 3: Causality.   The assumptions of a stable V and the full employment level of Q are fundamental if the quantity theory of money is to be used to guide monetary policy. Still, one additional assumption is necessary before the theory is complete. The quantity theory assumes that the chain of causality runs from money to prices; that is, a change in M must cause a change in P—rather than the reverse. Under the quantity theory, there can be no independent change in prices, which *itself* leads to a proportional change in the money supply.

The third assumption rules out the possibility that causality might lead from prices to money. In the quantity theory, a rise in certain prices would have to be offset by a fall in others. Increased spending in some markets would be offset by lower spending in others. As long as there are offsetting price changes, the general price level stays the same. In fact, unless the money supply changes, there can be no change in the price level.

The Money Supply Rule

The most extreme version of the quantity theory led to a very simple monetary policy rule. Because irregular changes in the supply of money produce only changes in prices, the supply of money should grow at a steady rate. The appropriate rate of money growth depends, first, on long-range growth in productive capacity and, second, on long-range trends in velocity. If the supply of money grows so that the combined growth of MV is equal to the potential growth of Q, prices (P) will remain stable.

Some Problems

We have shown that the strictest version of the quantity theory called for fairly steady growth in M, based on expected long-term trends in Q and V. For this policy to be effective, the theory and the related assumptions must correctly describe economic behavior. The problems with the theory and the assumptions we have outlined have to do mainly with distinctions between the short and the long run.

Although V and Q have grown at a fairly stable rate over the long run, they have been wildly erratic in the short run. During business cycles, fluctuations in V and Q have made it difficult to predict their behavior and to adjust M accordingly. Abrupt changes in V and Q can cause severe economic distress, and steady growth in M may not correct the problem. To see why, imagine first a decrease in velocity, with a drop in spending, production and employment. As the economy moves into recession, the monetary policy rule calls for a steady increase in the money supply to increase spending and speed recovery. The problem is that in a recession steady growth in M may not be possible. In recession when business conditions are bad, it may be difficult to persuade banks to create the money and borrowers to make new loans. The actual growth in M may fall below the intended rate, and the economy may stagnate indefinitely at a low level of production and employment.

Now imagine the opposite problem, with an increase in velocity, too rapid growth in output, and a tendency for prices to rise. The money supply rule would call for steady money growth to prevent further increases in spending and prevent an economic boom. Unfortunately, during periods of prosperity with rising prices it may be just as difficult to discourage banks from lending and borrowers from spending. In order to maintain steady money growth, it might be necessary to cut bank reserves drastically, forcing some banks into a liquidity crisis and many borrowers into default. In both these cases, a different money supply rule might be sorely needed. Even if it could be agreed on, however, short-run variations in M might be difficult, painful and possibly even ineffective.

The assumption of full employment has proved to be unrealistic, too. In the extreme version of the quantity theory, the automatic tendency toward full employment depends on wage flexibility—in the downward direction as well as up. Today's labor contracts generally permit only upward movement in wages. Unless wages fall, unemployment may continue, so that Q fails to grow over long periods. With M continuing to increase at a steady rate, prices would have to rise too, pushing wages up another notch and perhaps worsening unemployment.

Probably the most difficult assumption to justify in all of economics is the assumption of causality: Does a change in M cause a change in P, or does a change in P cause a change in M? Or are there complex feedbacks between cause and effect that make a definite answer impossible? It would be difficult to argue that the oil price increases of the 1970s were caused solely by money growth. Moreover, to follow the quantity theory and assume that rising prices in one sector of the economy will be offset by falling prices in another is no longer realistic. If the general price level increases, the money supply will tend to increase too, as business firms seek larger bank loans to finance more costly production and higher priced inventory. If no new money is available, business firms will find ways to increase velocity, mobilizing idle funds and speeding the turnover of the existing money supply.

The Cash-Balance Theory of Money

Problems with the quantity theory of money (the extreme version) increased during the Great Depression of the 1930s. Q and V behaved differently from policymakers' expectations, money grew at unpredicted rates, and monetary policy was generally ineffective in restoring full employment. As part of a major change in economic theory, there was a change in the theoretical explanation of the role of money.

The new approach was to focus on *holding* money rather than *spending* it. Whereas V refers to the rate money is spent, k was used to measure money held. The values V and k are necessarily the reverse of each other; if V (the spending rate) is high, then k (the holding rate) must be low—and vice versa.

The advantage of measuring k is to focus attention on the demand for money, the desire of the public to hold money in the form of cash and checkable deposits. The focus on demand makes it possible to compare supply with demand and to predict what will happen when supply and demand get out of balance.

Expressed algebraically the *cash-balance theory of money* is:

$$\text{Supply of Money} = \text{Demand for Money}$$
$$M = k(P)(Q).$$

Again, the expression $(P)(Q)$ measures output and income; k is the fraction of income that the public wants to hold as money. In 1986, with $M1$ of \$730 billion and PQ of \$4,208 billion, the expression became:

$$M = k(P)\,(Q)$$
$$730 = k\,(4,208)$$

and

$$k = .17.$$

The expression ($k = .17$) tells us that the public wanted to hold .17 of income as money in the form of cash and checkable deposits. The decimal fraction .17 is the reciprocal of velocity (V) of 5.76; that is:

$$1/V = 1/5.76 = .17.$$

Thus: $k = 1/V$.

We will not express the equation ($M = kPQ$) as an identity, because demand for money may not always be identical to supply. When demand and supply are different, adjustments will take place that bring demand and supply toward equilibrium. The reason is simple. Although the demand for money may not be *identical* to supply, the amount of money actually held must necessarily be *equal* to supply. This is because money is by definition that which is held by the public. All the nation's money is being held at any time by persons or business firms (not commercial banks or other financial intermediaries).

Changes in M

Recognizing that supply and demand may not be identical allows us to make some general observations. Suppose the supply of money increases, so that the public is actually holding more money than the desired fraction of income. Supply greater than demand is shown as an inequality: $M > kPQ$. The difference between supply and demand leads to a series of adjustments to push the two sides of the inequality into balance.

First, the excess money increases idle money balances beyond the fraction (k) that the public wants to hold. Excess money balances will prompt people to put their idle dollars to work. Some will increase their spending, causing P and Q to increase and increasing incomes. Others will increase their lending, pushing interest rates down and encouraging new investment spending; again the result is to increase income, PQ. At some point, lower interest rates will reduce the willingness to lend and increase the desire to hold money balances, k. These adjustments will continue, increasing the demand side of the inequality until M equals kPQ at a higher level of PQ and a lower interest rate.

Now suppose the supply of money is less than the demand for idle money balances, so that M is less than kPQ. Can you trace the reverse adjustments that would take place until a lower level of PQ and higher interest rates bring the inequality into balance?

Changes in k

Similar adjustments would follow an independent change in k. Suppose the public decides to increase its currency and checking account balances (k) from .17 to .20 of income. In a year like 1986 this would require money balances of

$$kPQ = .20(4{,}208) = \$842 \text{ billion.}$$

With an available money supply (M1) of only \$730 billion, it is not possible for all of us to increase the fraction of income we hold as money. In this case, demand for money would exceed supply: $M < kPQ$.

Whenever the demand for money exceeds supply, people attempt to build up their money balances by reducing their spending and lending. Income PQ tends to fall and interest rates to rise. At the lower income and higher interest rates, the quantity of money the public wants to hold idle falls, until kPQ is again equal to M. The opposite result would follow a decision to reduce money balances. With k equal to .10 of income in 1986, for instance, the public would be holding excessive cash balances. In this case, supply would exceed demand: $M > kPQ$. Spending and lending would increase, and income PQ would rise and interest rates fall until M equals kPQ.

Changes in *P* or *Q*

Increases in P or Q would also increase the demand for money. Growth in real output (Q) would call for larger money balances to finance a higher level of spending. If an increased money supply is not available for satisfying the higher demand, the public may reduce the fraction k instead. (Remember that to reduce idle holdings k is the same as to increase turnover V in the quantity theory of money.) An increase in the general level of prices (P) would have the same effect. A higher level of P would call for additional money or for a reduction in k. If neither of these events takes place, there must be a decrease in Q, so that the existing supply of money can finance a smaller quantity of output at higher prices.

Long-Run Changes in the Demand for Money

The cash-balance theory of money is a more useful explanation of economic behavior than the simple quantity theory. Focusing on k helps us notice some long-range changes in our financial intermediaries and in the effects of new financial services on money demand.

Probably the most fundamental new service provided by today's financial intermediaries is credit cards. Wallets bulging with plastic have turned out to be even more satisfying to most of us than wallets bulging with currency. Armed with Visa, MasterCard, and BankAmericard, U.S. consumers can get along with less money. We can use our incomes to purchase securities and earn interest until the bill for our credit purchases arrives. Smaller holdings of currency and checking account balances reduce the fraction k. With less of our money held idle, the existing quantity of money can work harder to stimulate production.

Other changes in U.S. industry have also helped reduce k. Whereas once many small firms produced component parts for sale to other firms, today large, integrated firms carry out entire production processes from raw materials to finished products. When firms produce their own raw materials and component parts, they make fewer payments to suppliers, and they need to hold smaller money balances. Also, today many firms provide services for their employees that reduce their need to hold idle money. Firms pay frequent, regular paychecks; they provide health insurance and retirement programs for workers' families; and through company credit unions they make employee loans for emergencies and for installment purchases.

In all these cases, smaller money balances (k) imply greater velocity (V). Thus the cash-balance theory allows for the effects of changes in financial intermediaries and in industrial organization that change the public's desire to hold money (or to spend it).

Change is continuing, of course, and we might expect further changes to affect the cash-balance equation in the future. When changes take place in money supply or demand, the cash-balance theory of money allows us to trace the adjustments that bring supply and demand back into balance.

The Real-Balance Theory of Money

Following the cash-balance theory of money leads to some of the same policy conclusions as the quantity theory. With Q expected to grow in the long run and k falling, keeping P stable requires sufficient growth in M to keep the equation in balance.

Still, the cash-balance theory needed a basis for dealing with short-term fluctuations around long-term trends: a way to deal with business cycles. That basis was provided by the Italian economist, A.C. Pigou. Pigou argued that even short-run business cycles could be corrected automatically through steady money growth. While the money supply continued to grow at a steady rate, he said, the real value of the money supply would change to offset short-run changes in Q. The real value of the money supply is its value corrected for changes in prices.

An illustration may be helpful. First suppose the economy moves into recession, with decreasing output (Q) and employment. Income begins to fall, and the lower rate of spending leaves merchants with unsold inventories. Many merchants reduce prices in an attempt to increase sales. Falling prices increase the real value of the money supply, increasing the wealth of money holders and stimulating new spending. The result is to increase spending and production, so that prices return to normal without any change from steady money growth.

The Pigou effect is also called the *real-wealth effect* because it focuses on the real value of accumulated wealth. In theory it would work also to correct the problem of inflation. If the general level of prices should begin to rise, the real value of money balances would fall, leaving people poorer than before. In an attempt to rebuild their wealth, individuals and business firms would reduce their spending, and prices would tend to fall. Again, no change in money growth is necessary if markets are free to adjust the real money supply toward the appropriate level of real purchasing power.

The Political Implications

The quantity theory and the cash-balance theory of money gave support to economists who favored laissez-faire: the reduced role of government in the economy. There are two ways to look at the results.

One way focuses on the concern of the theories with price stability. It suggests that the primary goal of policy should be to maintain money as a stable store of value and a dependable medium of exchange. It implies that the problem of maintaining full employment will take care of itself.

The other way focuses on concern with the power of government. It suggests that relying on government to stabilize economic activity could lead to government's increased power over citizens' personal lives. Excessive government power could interfere with the workings of the market system and damage the efficiency of resource allocation. Government might even be a party to reduced equity in our economic system.

These are significant issues—beyond the power of economists to resolve. Citizens who help resolve them should understand their implications for the economy and for our political system.

The Portfolio Theory of Money

The modern theory of money uses elements of both the quantity theory and the cash-balance theory and considers money as a part of a larger portfolio of assets. Whereas the earlier theories emphasized the money supply, modern theory focuses on money demand: the reasons the public wants to hold assets in idle money balances rather than in the form of interest-earning financial instruments or real wealth.

We have said that money is valuable in use. It is a means of linking producers with consumers. This is true, and yet it suggests that money is always in motion. We know that this is not possible but that money comes to rest (however briefly) in the hands of someone. Someone is holding every piece of money at any point in time. Understanding why people hold money rather than interest-earning assets is essential before designing policies to manage money.

Motives for Holding Money

The most obvious reason for holding idle money balances is liquidity: money is immediately usable as purchasing power. As a nation, we tend to hold a fairly stable portion of our income in liquid form, suitable for making transactions. This includes pocket money as well as checking accounts for paying bills. Most of us even keep a little extra money handy in case of some emergency when we might need cash in a hurry: an illness, car repairs or the need to travel.

Economists call these motives for holding money the *transactions motive* and the *precautionary motive*. The transactions motive includes currency and checking accounts for making normal transactions, and the precautionary motive includes money held for unforeseen emergencies.

Holding idle money balances involves two kinds of sacrifice—the sacrifice of the real assets we might have bought with it and the sacrifice of the interest we might have earned by purchasing financial assets. Idle pocket money and many checking accounts earn no interest. The last $10 of your paycheck that you spend on the 30th day of the month may have lain idle in your account since the first day of the month. Of course, the interest you did not receive is rather small, and most of us believe that having the money available for transactions and emergencies is worth the sacrifice.

The actual amount of money held for transactions and precautionary purposes depends primarily on income. Some of us have greater transactions needs because our incomes are greater and our lifestyles more costly. Some of us get by with smaller money holdings because our needs are smaller and our capacity to satisfy those needs is less.

On the average, the economy as a whole might decide to hold 20 percent of income for transactions purposes and 5 percent for precautionary purposes. We would say that the demand for transactions and precautionary balances depends on income:

$$L_t = lY$$

where

$$L_t = \text{demand for money for transactions,}$$
$$l = \text{fraction of income held as money, and}$$
$$Y = \text{income in dollars.}$$

Because the precautionary motive for holding money is small, we can include precautionary demand along with transactions demand in the fraction l, so that l equals .25 and L_t equals .25Y.

Note that transactions and precautionary motives for holding money focus on money as a medium of exchange. To hold money as a store of value depends on other considerations. We have seen that holding money in idle balances involves sacrifices, primarily the sacrifice of the interest our money might earn for us if we should purchase financial instruments. To purchase financial instruments involves a sacrifice, too—the sacrifice of liquidity. Moreover, purchasing financial instruments involves the risk of loss or default. Deciding whether to hold money idle requires that we balance off the sacrifice of foregone interest earnings against the sacrifice of liquidity and the risks of purchasing financial instruments.

Economists call the third motive for holding idle money balances the *speculative motive*. The most important (and most easily measured) determinant of speculative demand is the interest rate. The interest rate is the sacrifice, or *opportunity cost*, of holding money in its liquid form. Stated differently, it is the reward for giving up liquidity and accepting the risks of purchasing financial instruments. (An opportunity cost is the cost of any economic decision; it is the result of giving up one alternative use of resources in favor of another.) Because the interest rate is the cost of holding idle money, we would expect the amount of money held for speculative purposes to vary inversely with interest rates. Low interest rates would mean low opportunity costs and larger speculative holdings. Furthermore, because low interest rates reward lenders poorly for sacrificing liquidity and accepting the risks of purchasing financial instruments, low interest rates encourage holders of speculative money to increase their idle money balances. They expect more profitable lending opportunities in the future, and they want to keep their funds liquid to take advantage of higher future interest rates.

The reverse is likely to be true when interest rates are high. The high opportunity cost of holding idle money and the high interest earnings make the purchase of financial instruments more attractive. High interest rates offset the risks of default and the sacrifice of liquidity. Furthermore, because high interest rates may not last for long, holders of idle money would want to take advantage of current conditions, so that their speculative money balances fall.

We might express the demand for money for speculative purposes as:

$$L_s = l_s / i$$

where

$$L_s = \text{demand for speculative money balances,}$$
l_s = the coefficient that describes the relationship between speculative balances and the interest rate and
$$i = \text{interest rate.}$$

The term (l_s/i) is written as a ratio to indicate the inverse relationship between interest rates and speculative demand: a rise in interest rates means a fall in speculative balances, and vice versa. The size of the coefficient l_s depends on the responsiveness of the public to changes in interest rates: a relatively large l_s means that a one-point change in the interest rates causes a relatively large change in speculative balances (in the other direction). We might expect a modern, sophisticated public to be highly sensitive to interest rates, with many savers varying their money holdings frequently to take advantage of favorable conditions for purchasing financial instruments or to avoid unfavorable conditions.

Combining the transactions, precautionary and speculative motives for holding money yields the total demand for idle money balances in the community:

$$\text{Demand for Money} = L = L_t + L_s = lY + l_s/i.$$

Portfolio Adjustments

We have suggested that the supply of money may be greater than demand, that people and business firms might be holding more money than they want. Such a condition is difficult for most of us to imagine unless we remember that money is only one way among many ways to store wealth. We want to hold money for making regular purchases, and we want some amount for emergencies and speculative purposes. But in our complete portfolio of wealth we want to hold other assets as well as money: real goods and property and income-earning financial instruments. As more money piles up in idle money balances, we may find our portfolios heavy with money and lacking proportionally in other assets. (Of course, the reverse may also be true.)

When portfolios get out of balance with current preferences, their owners try to correct the imbalance. Too much money causes money holders to increase their spending for real goods, raising business profits and encouraging firms to increase production. Or too much money causes holders to purchase financial instruments at lower interest rates; they buy securities, pushing their prices up and interest rates down. These adjustments continue until portfolios are in balance with the preferences of the public, and money demand is precisely equal to money supply. (What adjustments would accompany a condition of too little money in asset portfolios?)

The portfolio explanation of the demand for money differs in an important respect from the quantity theory and the cash-balance theory. Those theories combined all money holdings into one—taking account of only one motive (the transactions motive) for holding money. Such an omission is understandable in view of the level of economic development during the 1800s, when the earlier theories enjoyed their greatest influence among economists and policymakers. More recently, as our economy has become more productive, more industrialized, more fully integrated and more complex, our reasons for holding money have changed too. Today a smaller fraction of income is needed for making normal transactions, and even the precautionary motive is largely satisfied by holdings of near money. All these developments have increased the importance of the speculative motive. Modern financial intermediaries and our individual desires to protect the value of our wealth claims against inflation have made us more aware of the effects of interest rate changes on the value of our portfolios. Our increased sensitivity to interest rates has made portfolio adjustments more volatile, more abrupt and less predictable than in simpler times. We might expect that changes in the actual supply of money would affect each of these money holdings differently and that our reactions to those changes will affect the results of policy.

MONEY AND BANKING IN PRACTICE: WHAT'S UP WITH VELOCITY?

Achieving the appropriate money supply for stable economic growth without inflation depends on a fairly stable rate of spending, or velocity of money turnover. Unless the monetary authorities can predict the rate of spending, money growth may be more or less than current requirements. During the 1980s, velocity has been less reliable for predicting economic activity than in earlier decades in the United States. One reason is deregulation of financial institutions, and another is the reduction in inflation.

Deregulation has allowed financial institutions to pay interest on deposit accounts normally used for making day-to-day transactions. Today, interest-bearing transactions accounts amount to nearly one-third of *M*1, compared with

less than one-tenth at the beginning of the 1980s. People tend to spend their interest-bearing accounts more slowly, so that the increase in the interest-bearing component of *M*1 has meant a decrease in the rate of spending.

Changes in the rate of inflation affect velocity by their effect on the value of money holdings. Rising inflation reduces the value of money holdings, reduces money demand, and increases velocity. Declining inflation, as has occurred since 1981, has the opposite effect. Thus, declining inflation allows people to hold money balances without significant loss of purchasing power and reduces velocity.

Figure 13–1 illustrates *M*1 velocity since World War II. Over the period as a whole, *M*1 velocity has followed a fairly stable upward trend, increasing an average of 3.4 percent a year from about 2 in 1947 to 7 in 1980. *M*1 velocity has fluctuated above and below its long-term trend during peaks and valleys of the business cycle. Since 1981, however, *M*1 velocity has behaved quite differently.

In addition to deregulation and lower inflation, the sharp decrease in velocity in the 1980s probably reflects increasing sensitivity to interest rates. Increasing sensitivity to interest rates makes the demand for money curve more elastic. Then, when interest rates

fall, as they did in the early 1980s, the quantity of *M*1 balances demanded increases, and people accumulate idle balances in anticipation of better investment opportunities in the future. An increase in the demand for money balances is the same as a decrease in the rate of spending. Thus, *M*1 velocity falls.

To make up for the decrease in velocity since 1981, the Fed has had to increase the money base by an average of 8 percent a year, compared with an annual average increase of 6 percent prior to 1981.

FIGURE 13–1   Velocity of *M*1: Ratio of Nominal GNP to *M*1

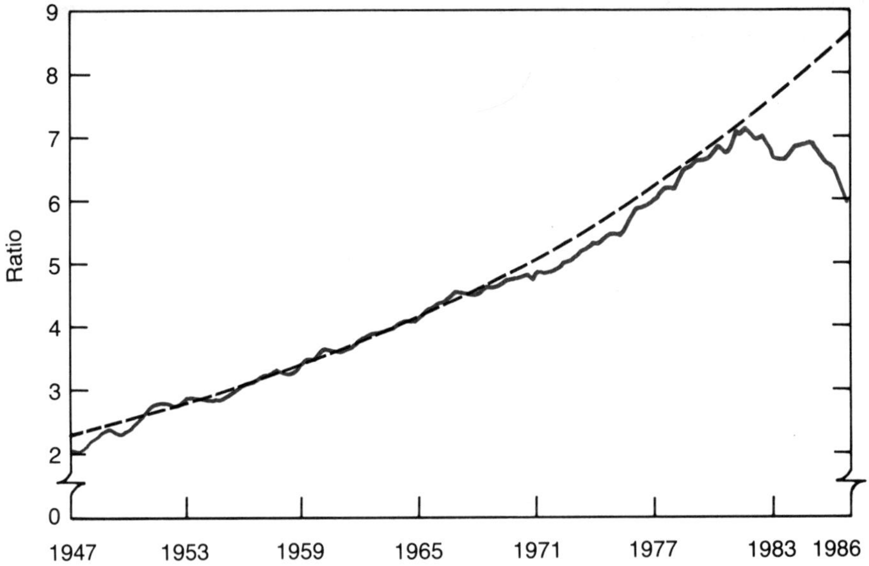

SOURCE: *Economic Report of the President*, January 1987.

Questions for Discussion

1. With a more elastic demand for money curve, would you expect increases and decreases in the money supply to affect primarily interest rates or income? Why? Explain the process by which policy would bring about the expected change.

2. How would you expect the changes de-
    scribed in this article to affect the *M*1
    money multiplier? What circumstances
    might offset the expected effect?

Historical Behavior of Money, Prices and Output

One way to judge the effect of money on prices and output is to observe the behavior of these variables in past years. Reasonably good statistics on the money supply in the United States go back as far as 1867. Then the public held about $585 million in currency—mostly Civil War Greenbacks, national bank notes and coins—and $729 million in commercial bank demand and time deposits. Nonbank thrift institutions held deposits of $276 million in 1867, so that the total $1,590 million corresponds roughly to our *M*2 definition of the money supply.

One hundred twenty years later, the *M*2 money supply had grown to almost $3 trillion, an increase of more than 600-fold. This represents average annual growth of about 6 percent. The 6 percent annual increase can be broken down as follows:

1. The population grew about 1.6 percent annually, increasing the need for currency.
2. Prices rose an average of 1.4 percent annually, increasing the nominal value of all transactions.
3. Output per capita increased almost 2 percent a year, increasing incomes and spending similarly.
4. The remaining 1 percent is the rate of increase in *M*2 money balances, expressed as the portion of total personal income that the public wished to hold as money. In 1867, the public held about one-fourth of income in *M*2 money balances. By 1987, *M*2 money balances were more than three-fourths of personal income.

Money Growth, Prices and Output

Professor Milton Friedman of Stanford's Hoover Institution is the nation's most prominent monetary economist. He has examined closely the behavior of money, prices and output between the end of the Civil War and 1960 for evidence to support his theory of the causal relationship between money and prices. Over the nearly 100 years in the study, severe price inflation occurred in only two periods: 1914–1920 and 1939–1948. Both periods were associated with world wars, and both experienced more than a doubling of the money supply. In the years since Professor Friedman's study, money growth and price inflation have continued to move roughly parallel to each other. During the 1960s, prices increased about 2.3 percent annually and the money supply about 3.8 percent. During the 1970s, price increases averaged 7 percent and money growth 6.3 percent. The close correlation between money growth and price inflation appears to confirm Friedman's belief in a significant proportional relationship between money and prices, at least in the upward direction.

Downward changes in money growth seemed to have had their greatest effect on output, however. Professor Friedman identified six severe economic contractions that caused widespread financial distress and unemployment: 1873–1879, 1893–1897, 1902–1908, 1920–1921, 1929–1933 and 1937–1938. Each of these periods was characterized by sharper contractions in the money supply than occurred in any other period. Each was accompanied by loan defaults, bank failures and financial panics. In contrast to all these periods, stable money growth was associated with relative price stability—again evidence to support Friedman's view of the causal relationship between money and prices.

The Question of Causality

Professor Friedman deals also with the direction of causality: Did changes in the money supply precede price and output changes or the reverse? In every case, he identifies independent sources of money supply changes: gold flows, silver purchases, or Federal Reserve policy decisions to change the money supply. Independent changes in the money supply, he says, brought on the price or output changes that followed. Friedman acknowledges that independent price changes may lead to similar changes in the money supply, which will in turn bring on more price changes. But he believes the primary responsibility for changes in prices rests with changes in the money supply.

Not only is Professor Friedman convinced of the important relationship between money, on the one hand, and output and prices, on the other; he is also convinced that the relationships have remained fairly stable over the years. Because of their relative stability, he sees these fundamental relationships as good predictors of future economic conditions and useful guides to economic policy.

Money Growth and Velocity

A stable relationship between M on the one hand and P and Q on the other implies also a constant level of velocity. Velocity has changed over time, but changes have occurred slowly. For most of the last century, the trend of velocity was downward, falling more sharply during recessions and less sharply during recoveries. In general, over the 100 years in Professor Friedman's study, more money went into idle balances, so that by 1960 the public was holding a larger fraction of income idle. With large idle money balances, money income grew more slowly over the period than did the money supply.

Since World War II, the downward trend of velocity has reversed. In recent decades, velocity has increased so that money income has grown almost twice as fast as the money supply. The relatively smaller supply of money has been turning over faster. Several explanations are possible for the new upward trend in velocity. Professor Friedman believes that one reason may be growing public confidence in national stability. During periods of concern about national welfare, he says, the public wants to hold enough money to meet emergencies. When the future seems safe and predictable, people reduce their idle balances, and velocity increases. Savers purchase new financial instruments to store wealth for the future. They look to new financial instruments to put their money to work. The result is greater spending with new incentives to increase the growth in output.

There is another side to the question of velocity. Should confidence in the future decline, there might be another reversal in the long-term trend of *V*. Idle money balances could begin to build up again and spending to slow. Unless money growth increases substantially, business firms would be unable to sell their securities. Declines in total spending would finally force a decrease in the growth of total production.

Some Conclusions and a Look Ahead

We close this chapter with a reminder of our fundamental objectives in this course of study: first, to understand money and its role in the economy and, second, to evaluate policies designed to help money perform its role more efficiently. Success in these objectives should help achieve the maximum level of production with stable prices.

Economists frequently disagree on their recommendations for policy. Disagreements are a result of different assumptions about behavior and different theoretical explanations of money's role. In the next chapter we will consider another approach to the determination of income, output, prices and employment. Then we will combine the two theories for a comprehensive explanation of the role of money and the other factors that contribute to the level of economic activity. Finally, we will explore policy tools for promoting stable growth with stable prices.

Glossary of Terms

cash-balance theory of money. the theory that the public's decisions to hold idle money balances determine the relationship between money and income

opportunity cost. a sacrifice experienced as a result of choosing one alternative over another

precautionary motive. holding money for taking care of emergencies

quantity theory of money. the theory that prices change proportionally to changes in the supply of money

real-wealth effect. the changes in the value of money holdings that result from price changes

speculative motive. holding money because current lending conditions are less favorable than expected future conditions

transactions motive. holding money for the purpose of making everyday transactions

---

Summary of Important Ideas

1. For two centuries, the quantity theory of money was used to explain the relationship between money (M) and total output (PQ). With a constant velocity of money turnover (V) and the full employment level of output (Q), changes in the money supply could only affect prices. Therefore, the appropriate monetary policy rule was to allow money to grow steadily in line with the productive capacity of the economy.

2. A more relaxed modern version of the quantity theory would allow short-run deviations from steady money growth to deal with cyclical changes in velocity and total production.

3. The weaknesses of such policy are: the difficulty of predicting short-run changes in V or Q soon enough to change money growth rates, the difficulty of expanding money during recession and the financial crises that result from severe contraction during inflation, and the possibility that price changes may occur independently of an increase in the money supply.

4. A twentieth-century version of the quantity theory shifts emphasis from the money supply to money demand and examines the motives for holding idle money. The fraction of income the public wants to hold as money is k, the inverse of the velocity of spending, V.

5. Whenever the actual supply of money (M) differs from the amount the public wants to hold (kPQ), there will be changes in spending and lending plans. The result will be a new level of income and interest rates.

6. Similar adjustments will follow a change in k, as changes in financial habits and institutions change the desire to hold idle cash. Again, the appropriate monetary policy rule was steady money growth, a recommendation consistent with Classical economists' belief in laissez-faire.

7. Pigou's real-wealth effect argued that short-run cycles in economic activity would be corrected by automatic changes in the real value of money balances.

8. Modern economists examine the reasons for holding money—the transactions, precautionary and speculative motives—and show how changes in the money supply lead to portfolio adjustments among money, financial instruments and real goods.

9. The nation's chief monetary economist is Milton Friedman, who has identified a causal relationship between money, on the one hand, and prices and output, on the other. Friedman also identified a long-term decline in velocity until World War II. Since then velocity has increased, and the ratio of money holdings to income has decreased.

Questions for Discussion and Research

1. Describe the difficulties associated with developing a definitive theory of the role of money in the economy. How has the focus of theory shifted over history? What adjustments in theory continue to be necessary today?

2. Explain the difference between an equality and an identity. What is the significance of the identity $(MV \equiv PQ)$? What values must remain constant or predictable if the identity is to be useful for guiding policy?

3. Discuss the factors that contribute to a rise or fall in velocity (V) over the short run and the long run. To what extent are these factors predictable or controllable?

4. Critically evaluate the Classical assumptions underlying the stability of output (Q). Distinguish between the short run and the long run in your answer.

5. Why is the direction of causality significant in the quantity theory of money?

6. Explain the significance of the shift in emphasis from V to k in the modern approach to monetary theory. Why is the cash-balance equation not an identity, and what are the implications for policymakers?

7. Illustrate the effects of a change in money (M) on individual portfolios. Describe the adjustments in particular financial markets: shifts in supply or demand and changes in prices and interest rates.

8. Discuss the policy implications of the Pigou effect and its weakness under today's economic conditions.

9. Discuss the motives and habits that affect the fraction k. Discuss in terms of individual portfolios.

10. Explain the pattern of behavior of velocity over the past century and over the past several decades. How is the behavior of *V* related to the development of financial intermediaries?

Additional Readings

Friedman, Milton. *Studies in the Quantity Theory of Money.* Chicago: University of Chicago Press, 1956, pp. 3–21.

Friedman, Milton, and Anna Jacobson Schwartz. *A Monetary History of the United States, 1867–1960.* Princeton, N.J.: Princeton University Press, 1961, especially Chapter 13.

Lekachman, Robert. *A History of Economic Ideas.* New York: McGraw-Hill, 1959.

Morris, Frank E. "Rules Plus Discretion in Monetary Policy—An Appraisal of Our Experience since October 1979." *New England Economic Review* (September/October 1985): 3–8.

Endnote

[1]The original expression was $MV = PT$, where T is total transactions for the period. Transactions would include the sale of assets produced in earlier periods. Because total transactions remain a fairly constant proportion of current production (Q), we will not consider other transactions explicitly in this simple explanation.

C H A P T E R

14

LEARNING OBJECTIVES

- To understand how Keynesian theory explains economic activity
- To explain the significance of saving and net saving, planned investment and unplanned investment
- To learn how changes in spending cause multiple effects on income
- To demonstrate all these relationships algebraically and graphically

The Keynesian Theory of Income Determination

"To understand my state of mind, you have to know that I believe myself to be writing a book on economic theory which will largely revolutionise—not, I suppose, at once but in the course of the next ten years—the way the world thinks about economic problems."

John Maynard Keynes

More than other courses of study, economics is an evolving science. In the physical sciences—like chemistry and physics—certain "truths" have been established that have remained true for centuries. New discoveries add to the body of knowledge every year, of course; but it is seldom necessary to "unlearn" facts proved true in years before.

This is not to say that economics changes willy-nilly from one generation to the next. Still, as a social science, economics changes with changes in the society, making it a continuously evolving course of study. New technologies call for new economic relationships; new opportunities lead to new kinds of behavior; new problems bring on new institutions. Some of the principles of economics must change, too, to reflect these changes in the society.

Modern economic thought began with the beginning of world trade more than 300 years ago. Conditions then focused attention on flows of money brought into Europe from trade with the New World and the Orient. Money stimulated production and enhanced the benefits of specialization and exchange. Employment increased, workers learned new skills, and growth in production brought improved standards of living. To attribute the increased economic activity to the larger supply of money was understandable. Using changes in the supply of money to regulate economic activity seemed a natural basis for economic policy—a "truth," you might say. Money was said to influence economic activity according to the identity ($MV \equiv PQ$). A steady increase in the supply of money (M) would ensure stable prices (P)

and allow production (Q) to grow in line with the economy's increasing capacity to produce.

Concern with total production, the general price level and employment constitutes the part of economics called *macroeconomics*. Macroeconomic issues dominated the thinking of seventeenth and eighteenth century economists. Nineteenth century economists turned to other issues. Having apparently solved the problem of stabilizing macroeconomic variables, they concentrated on *microeconomic* issues. Microeconomics involves the composition of output: the allocation of resources among individual markets for producing the goods and services consumers want.

Nineteenth century economists assumed that full employment would be the natural state for the economy. Total production (Q) would be the largest quantity possible using available resources and technology; the general price level (P) would depend on the supply of money. The prices (p) and quantities (q) of particular goods and services would depend on supply and demand in particular markets. For these economists, erratic fluctuations in the supply of money would affect the general price level only. For this reason, they applauded the establishment of the Federal Reserve System in 1913 as a means of regulating the money supply and promoting steady growth at stable prices.

After more than a century of the dominance of microeconomics, macroeconomic issues returned to the scene in the early twentieth century. The occasion was the Great Depression of the 1930s. Between 1929 and 1933, total production in the United States fell by one-third and the money supply fell by one-fourth. The general price level dropped 30 percent, and unemployment rose to one-fourth of the labor force. Finally, in the mid-1930s, attempts were made to increase money growth and stimulate economic activity, but they were not very effective.

The failure of monetary policy to restore the economy to stable growth raised new questions about the determinants of economic activity. The old "truths" seemed inadequate to explain behavior and guide policy. Some new answers were offered by the British economist John Maynard Keynes.

The Keynesian Theory of Income: Fundamentals

John M. Keynes developed a theory of production based not on the money supply but on individual decisions to purchase goods and services. In the Keynesian theory, total spending constitutes *aggregate demand*. Aggregate demand is the sum of spending by individuals and groups during a certain time period: consumers, business firms, governments of states and localities as well as the federal government, and foreign buyers. Total spending for all goods and services is equal to gross national product (GNP), the value of total production. And total spending is also equal to total income, because all amounts spent are simultaneously received by someone or some institution as income.

Table 14–1 summarizes the components of GNP from the spending side and the income side. The items on the spending side constitute aggregate demand for goods and services produced in the nation during the year. The items on the income side may be thought of as *aggregate supply*, because they measure the costs of producing (and therefore the value of) all the goods and services that make up GNP for the year.

TABLE 14–1   Gross National Product

Spending		*Income*	
1. Consumer spending	(C)	6. Wages and salaries	(w)
2. Business investment spending	(I)	7. Rental income	(r)
3. Government purchases	(G)	8. Interest income	(i)
4. Net foreign purchases	(F_n)	9. Profits	(π)
5. Government income from taxes (Incomes of Resources)	(T)	10. Capital consumption allowance	(CCA)
Aggregate Demand	(GNP)	Aggregate Supply	(GNP)

Components of Aggregate Demand: Spending

1. Consumption.   The largest component of aggregate demand is consumer spending: about 65 percent of GNP in 1986. Consumers spend for nondurable goods like food, fuel, clothing and school supplies. Spending for nondurables rises with population growth but is relatively stable from year to year. Spending for durable goods is more sensitive to year-to-year changes in incomes, falling in recessions and rising in more prosperous years. Families like to upgrade their autos and home furnishings when times are good but postpone major purchases when times are bad. The third category of consumer purchases is services: health and personal care services, education, travel and recreation. About half of consumer spending in 1986 was for services. *Consumption* of services has increased over time, along with rising consumer incomes.

2. Business Investment Spending.   Investment spending is an important component of aggregate demand because it provides the means for increasing production in the future. Investment refers to new capital goods, like factories and machinery, homes, and inventories. Inventories include raw materials and component parts, as well as finished goods. Business firms produce or purchase inventories so as to serve consumers' needs more effectively. They may also accumulate unplanned inventory investment when consumer spending falls short of expectations. We will have more to say about unplanned inventory investment later.

It is important to distinguish between *gross investment* and *net investment*. Gross investment (I_g) differs from net investment (I_n) by the amount of investment needed to replace equipment that depreciates during the year:

$$(I_g) - \text{Depreciation} = (I_n).$$

For computing total spending we use the value of gross investment, which together with other spending yields gross national product (GNP). To include net investment only would yield net national product (NNP).

3. Government Purchases.   Government purchases constitute about 20 percent of total spending. In 1986, state and local governments purchased $498 billion of goods and services, and the federal government $367 billion. Only government purchases are included in aggregate demand—not *transfer payments*, like welfare benefits, Social Security checks and other subsidies governments pay to individuals and businesses. Transfer payments do not constitute purchases until their recipients actually spend them, at which point they become a part of consumer spending or business investment.

4. Net Foreign Purchases.   Net foreign purchases are also called net foreign investment and include foreign purchases of U.S. goods and services less U.S. purchases of items produced abroad. In effect, this is our balance of trade. *Net foreign investment* is a growing part of aggregate demand in the United States and vital for our nation's economy. The importance and complexity of foreign transactions require that they be given special attention. Therefore, we will omit this component from much of our discussion at this point and discuss foreign purchases in detail in Chapter 19.

Aggregate demand is the sum of these four major components:

$$C + I + G + F_n = \text{AD}.$$

Total spending from these four groups is paid to business to be distributed among the classes of income recipients listed on the right side of Table 14–1. Receipts are characterized as income: to governments and to owners of resources in households and business firms.

Components of Aggregate Supply: Income

5. Net Taxes.   Before income can be paid to productive resources, taxes must be paid to governments. Governments collected tax revenues of $1,341 billion in 1986. State and local tax revenues come from income, property, sales and excise taxes. Federal tax revenues come from personal and corporate income taxes, estate and excise taxes, and customs duties. Although taxes are collected at various levels of production, all are ultimately paid by households—either in the form of higher prices for the things they buy or lower pay for the resources they own.

Government transfer payments to households may be thought of as *negative taxes*. These are the welfare payments, subsidies, and veterans' benefits we spoke of earlier. The difference between tax revenues collected and negative taxes paid is government's net income from taxes, or *net taxes*.

6. Wages and Salaries.   After taxes are paid, the remaining revenue from sales can be distributed to the resources that contributed to production. The largest class of resources used in production is labor, earning wages and salaries of $2,498 billion in 1986, or about 60 percent of GNP. Social Security contributions and personal income taxes are withheld from wages and salaries, and negative taxes (transfer payments) are paid to many households.

7. Rental Income.   Rental income is paid for land used in production. Rental income of persons was only $61 billion in 1986, amounting to about 1 percent of GNP. The percentage of business revenues paid for rent has declined fairly consistently over the past 50 years.

8. Interest Income.   Interest income is paid to the owners of financial capital that is used to purchase investments. In 1986, net interest was $295 billion, or about 7 percent of GNP. The interest share of income fluctuates with changes in interest rates and current investment spending.

9. Profit.   Profit income may be defined two ways. Accountants define *business profit* as revenue remaining after all production costs are paid. Individual entrepreneurs receive as business profit whatever remains after costs and business taxes. Corporate stockholders receive as dividends part of business profit after costs and corporate income taxes. The remaining business profit is held in the firm as a form of saving for investment and growth. Total profit in U.S. business firms amounted to $578 billion in 1986 and was 14 percent of GNP.

Economists define *profit* more precisely as a necessary payment to those who take the risks and provide the leadership for business enterprise. If business profit received in any single enterprise is insufficient to reward these individuals, they will turn their attention to other activities. This makes profit a most important use of business revenue.

10. Capital Consumption Allowance.   Like undistributed business profit, the final component of aggregate supply is not paid out as income but held in the firm as a part of business saving. *Capital consumption allowance* is a

FIGURE 14–1 Spending and Saving Flows

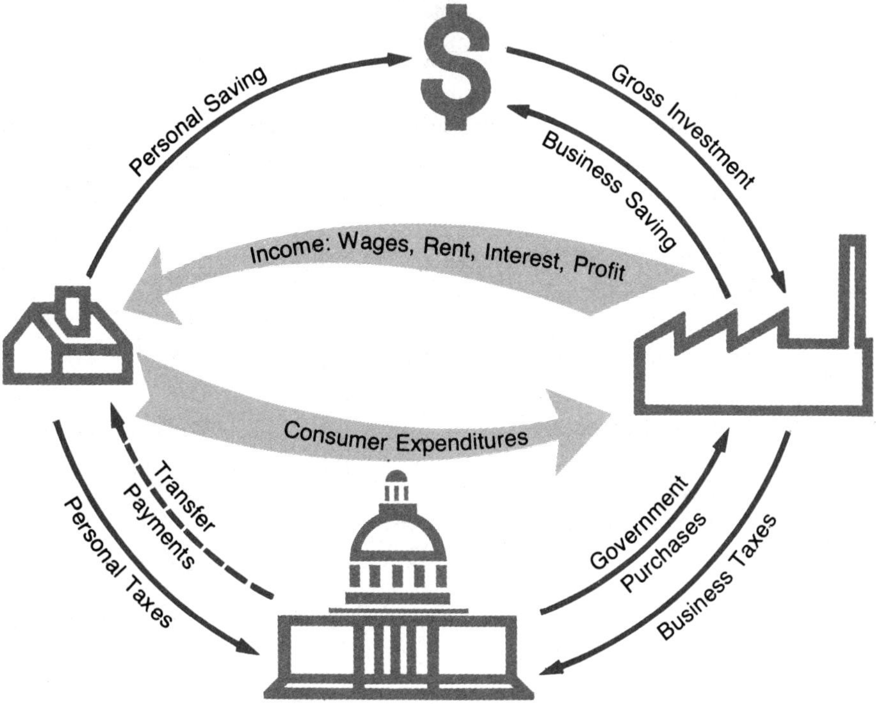

firm's regular contribution to a fund to replace depreciated capital equipment. Capital consumption allowance is considered a true cost of production and is not part of profit.

Spending and Saving Flows

Aggregate demand, measured on the left side of Table 14–1, is equal to aggregate supply or income, measured on the right:

$$C + I + G + F_n = T + w + r + i + \pi + \text{CCA}.$$

This is always true, because what is paid must be received by someone. The portion of income that is retained by households (after taxes) constitutes disposable income and is available for new consumer spending or for personal saving. The portion of income retained by business is business saving and is available for investment spending. The portion received by governments is available for government spending or for government saving in the form of budget surpluses. Amounts actually spent by these groups flow back into aggregate demand and constitute spending for GNP in the next period. Amounts saved drain out of spending and tend to reduce GNP.

Figure 14–1 illustrates flows of spending and income among households, business firms and governments. Follow the arrows that trace spending among the classes of income recipients.

The Keynesian Model

The Keynesian theory of income determination is based on all these flows of spending, which combine to yield income for the nation's households, businesses and governments. The theory is easily explained through the use of an economic model. The model illustrates the components of aggregate demand graphically and shows how spending affects the level of economic activity. Once we have fully described the Keynesian model of income, we will combine the Keynesian model with the theory of money. The result will be a more complete model of macroeconomic behavior: how spending affects and is affected by the supply of money, how both spending and the money supply influence economic activity, and finally, how policies to change spending and the money supply can work to change the level of economic activity.

The Consumption Function

Again we will begin with consumption (C), because consumption is the largest component of aggregate demand. Moreover, of the four kinds of spending, consumption is most closely associated with the level of economic activity. Not only does consumption depend strongly on the level of economic activity, but consumption strongly affects economic activity. Thus

$$C \rightarrow \text{Output} \rightarrow \text{Income} \rightarrow C.$$

Consumer spending is influenced by other factors, of course: the age level of the population, current attitudes toward spending versus saving, the stock of durable goods and wealth already owned by consumers, and the availability of credit. Still, the clearest and most easily measured determinant of consumer spending is income, which we have seen is equal to total production, or GNP. For convenience throughout this explanation we will use the letter Y to symbolize total production and income. Data on consumption and income for recent years are shown in Table 14–2.

Consumption data can be plotted on a graph relating consumption (C) to total production and income (Y), as shown in Figure 14–2a. As we predicted, the points reveal a rather stable relationship between consumption and income. The line on the graph slopes upward, because higher levels of

TABLE 14–2 Consumer Spending in the Long Run
(in billions of dollars)

Year	GNP = Y	C	*Average Consumption:* C/Y
1975	1,528.8	979.1	.64
1976	1,700.1	1,090.2	.64
1977	1,887.2	1,206.5	.64
1978	2,106.6	1,339.7	.64
1979	2,368.5	1,509.8	.64
1980	2,627.4	1,670.1	.64
1981	3,052.9	1,915.1	.63
1982	3,166.0	2,050.7	.65
1983	3,401.6	2,229.3	.66
1984	3,774.7	2,423.0	.64
1985	3,992.5	2,581.9	.65
1986	4,208.5	2,762.4	.66

FIGURE 14–2a The Long-Run Consumption Function, 1975–1985

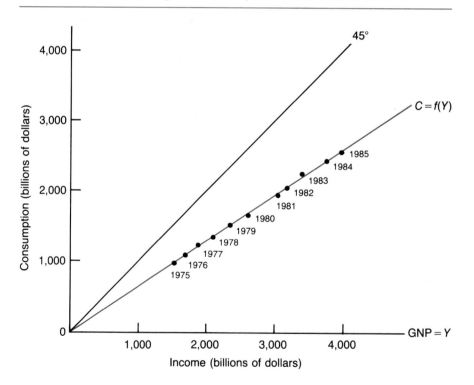

FIGURE 14–2b Saving Plus Taxes, 1975–1985

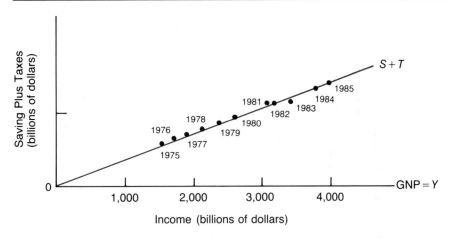

income are associated with higher levels of consumption. The relationship in Figure 14–2a can be stated formally: Consumption is a function of income: $C = f(Y)$.

The line in Figure 14–2a is called the long-run *consumption function*. It illustrates the tendency of consumption to rise with income and over time to remain a fairly constant fraction of income—in the United States about 65 percent. The slope of the line is less than 1, because not all income is spent for consumption. A 45° line from the origin has a slope equal to 1. The difference between a point on the consumption function and a point on the 45° line directly above is the amount of current income not spent for consumption. These quantities are plotted in Figure 14–2b and constitute saving plus net taxes at various income levels. At low income levels the sum of saving plus net taxes is low, and saving plus net taxes increases as income increases. Amounts saved and paid as taxes are available for use by business for capital investment and by government for government purchases.

Consumer Spending in the Short Run

The shape of the consumption function is different if data for shorter periods are used. Quarterly consumption and income data for 1984 and 1985 produce the series of points shown in Figure 14–3. The line on the graph is the short-run consumption function. Like the long-run consumption function, the short-run consumption function slopes upward to reveal a positive, or direct, relationship between consumption and income. The slope is somewhat flatter in the short run, however, suggesting a lagged response of consumption to income. Consumers appear to be somewhat slow to adjust their spending upward or downward with increases or decreases in income.

FIGURE 14–3   Short-Run Consumption Function, 1984–1985

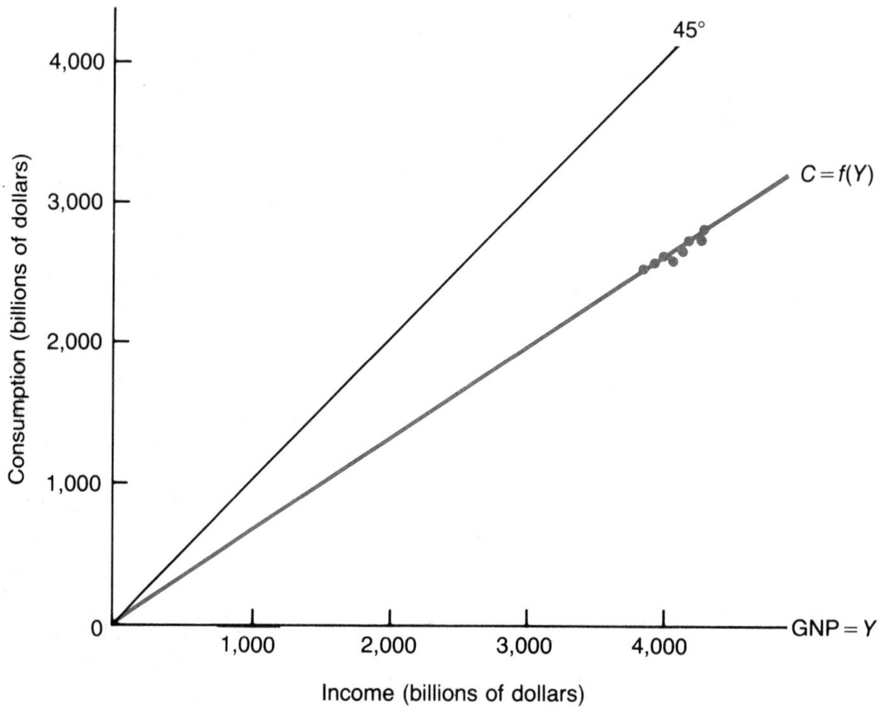

In the short run the marginal propensity to consume is $\Delta C/\Delta Y = .63$. The coefficient .63 also measures the slope of the consumption function.

The change in consumption relative to a change in income is called the marginal propensity to consume (MPC):

$$\text{MPC} = \Delta C/\Delta Y.$$

Because the marginal propensity to consume defines *changes* in the variable on the vertical axis, it is reflected in the *slope* of the line describing that variable.

The fact that the marginal propensity to consume is less than 1 means that the average *fraction* of income consumed might vary in the short run. When income is high, consumption is a smaller fraction of current income than when income is low. When income is very low, consumption may actually be greater than current income, as families spend from accumulated savings or borrow against expected future earnings.

The fraction of income consumed is called the average propensity to consume:

$$APC = C/Y.$$

Whereas the slope of the consumption function (and the MPC) is fairly constant, the APC differs at different income levels.

The relationship between consumption and income is easy to see if a 45° line from the origin is added to Figure 14–3. At low income levels, the consumption function lies above the 45° line, indicating consumption greater than income and, therefore, APC greater than 1. At high income levels, the consumption function lies below the 45° line, indicating consumption less than income and APC less than 1. Where the consumption function crosses the 45° line, consumption is equal to income, and APC is 1.

The Keynesian model uses the short-run consumption function, because it is the short run in which business cycles occur and in which policy is designed and put into effect for influencing economic activity. A hypothetical short-run consumption function has been drawn on Figure 14–4a as the first major component of aggregate demand. The equation for the hypothetical consumption function is:

$$C_s = 800 + .60(Y).$$

The constant 800 (billion) is a base level of consumption that would take place in the short run independent of changes in income. If income should drop to zero, in fact, consumer spending of 800 would require withdrawals from past savings or borrowing against future income. (Many other unpleasant things would happen in the economy if income were indeed to fall to zero. The base value here is intended only as a basis for locating the consumption function vertically on the graph.)

The coefficient .60 is the marginal propensity to consume: thus (MPC = .60) measures the change in consumer spending that results from a change in income. The MPC measures the slope of the consumption function. The value in parenthesis is current income.

The values 800 and .60 are the *parameters* of the equation. The parameters remain the same while the variables Y and C take on different values. In our equation, C is the *dependent variable* whose value depends on the *independent variable Y.*

Figure 14–4b is the graph of saving plus net taxes that is derived by subtracting consumer spending from income:

$$Y - C = S + T.$$

Note that saving plus net taxes is negative for low levels of income and increases as income increases, providing larger amounts for use by business and government.

Investment

The second major component of aggregate demand is business investment spending. Investment spending (I) is less responsive than consumption to short-run changes in income. This is because investment plans are made

FIGURE 14–4a   The Keynesian Model of Income Determination: Aggregate
Demand and Aggregate Supply

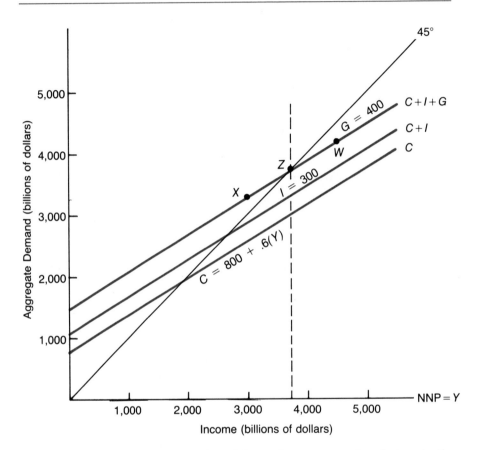

in advance of the current period and depend on many other factors in the economic environment: stock of capital already in place, changes in technology or expected changes, expected profitability of new investment, and credit conditions. For simplicity, we will assume that investment spending is a constant amount over the period shown in Figure 14–4a. We have added investment of $300 billion to Figure 14–4a by drawing a straight line parallel to the consumption function and labeling it (C + I).

Government Purchases

Like investment spending, government purchases (not including transfer payments) are based on factors other than current income. Thus, government purchases (G) are unresponsive to changes in income and fairly

FIGURE 14–4b Saving Plus Taxes and Investment Plus Government Spending

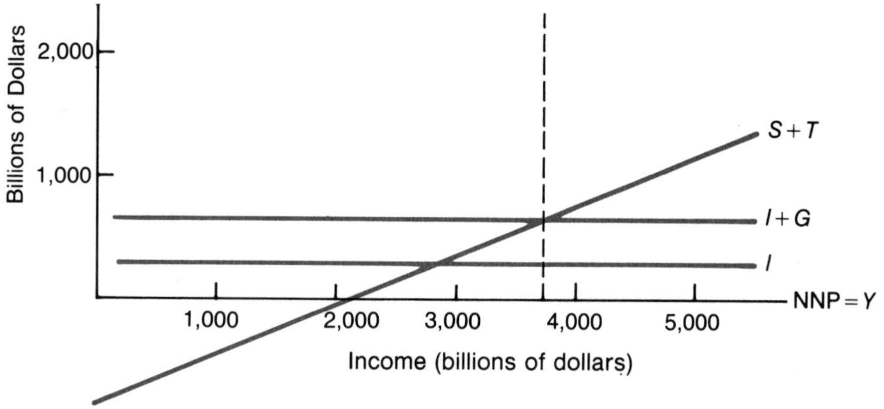

constant in the short run. We have added government purchases of $400 billion by drawing a straight line parallel to $(C + I)$ and by labeling it $(C + I + G)$.

Aggregate Demand

Because net foreign purchases require detailed explanation, we will omit them from our discussion at this point. This leaves:

$$C + I + G = AD.$$

The 45° line on Figure 14–4a shows the relationship between aggregate demand and income. At low levels of income, $(C + I + G)$ lies above the 45° line, indicating spending greater than current income. At high levels of income, $(C + I + G)$ lies below the 45° line, indicating spending less than current income. At income of $3,750 billion, where $(C + I + G)$ crosses the 45° line, total spending is precisely equal to income.

We have seen that points along the AD line measure total spending at various income levels, but the AD line provides other information as well. Remember that the difference between income and consumer spending is saving plus net taxes: personal and business saving (in the form of undistributed business profit and capital consumption allowance) plus net taxes paid to all governments. The saving plus net taxes function is shown in Figure 14–4b. Saving and net taxes may be used by business to finance investment or by governments to finance government purchases.

The sum of investment and government spending is also drawn on Figure 14—4b. At low levels of income, the excess of aggregate demand over income (Figure 14–4a) means that investment plus government spending is greater than saving plus net taxes (Figure 14–4b). Stated differently:

$$C + I + G > Y$$

means also:

$$I + G > S + T.$$

At high income levels, aggregate demand less than income (Figure 14–4a) means that investment plus government spending is less than saving plus net taxes (Figure 14–4b). Likewise:

$$C + I + G < Y$$

means

$$I + G < S + T.$$

At income of $3,750 billion, aggregate demand is equal to income (Figure 14–4a) and investment plus government spending is equal to saving plus net taxes (Figure 14–4b). Where

$$C + I + G = Y$$

then:

$$I + G = S + T.$$

Equilibrium

The 45° line helps us see the process by which aggregate demand determines income. Consider first the point X where $(C + I + G)$ lies above the 45° line. At point X, where Y equals $3,000 billion, total spending exceeds income, leading to higher than expected sales and stimulating increased production and employment. The result is a tendency for income to rise from $3,000 billion to $3,750 billion. The reverse is true at point W. At point W, where Y equals $4,500 billion, spending falls short of income, causing lower than expected sales and leading firms to cut back production and employment. Income tends to fall from $4,500 billion to $3,750 billion. Only at point Z is spending just equal to income, producing no tendency toward an increase or a decrease in economic activity. Income at Z is called the equilibrium level of income. It is the only income level that can be sustained with existing levels of consumer, business and government spending.

These results can be summarized algebraically:

1. $(C + I + G) >$ GNP means expansion.
2. $(C + I + G) <$ GNP means contraction.
3. $(C + I + G) =$ GNP means equilibrium.

Net Saving and Dissaving

The relationship between $(C + I + G)$ and GNP can be expressed another way. Refer to Figure 14–4b and compare saving plus net taxes with investment plus government spending. The difference between $(S + T)$ and $(I + G)$ may be named *net saving*: net saving is the portion of total saving plus net taxes that does not find its way into new spending. For incomes greater than $3,750 billion on Figure 14–4b, $(I + G)$ is less than $(S + T)$, so that net saving is positive. For incomes less than $3,750 billion, $(S + T)$ is less than $(I + G)$ and net saving is negative. In the first case, positive net saving pushes production and income to a lower level. In the second, negative net saving pushes income up. Only at point Z is investment plus government spending precisely equal to saving plus net taxes, with no net saving to push income up or down. Point Z is the point we have identified as the equilibrium level of income.

As before, these results can be summarized algebraically:

1. $(S + T) < (I + G)$ means expansion.
2. $(S + T) > (I + G)$ means contraction.
3. $(S + T) = (I + G)$ means equilibrium.

Planned and Unplanned Investment

We suggested earlier that business firms might accumulate unplanned inventory investment, as sales fall short of expectations. In this section, we will see that inventory accumulation (or depletion) is the way total production is made equal to aggregate demand. For this purpose, it is helpful to think of the 45° line as aggregate supply. Remember that aggregate supply is total production, measured in terms of resource costs. Because the sum of resource costs is income, the horizontal axis in Figure 14–4 measures aggregate supply as well as income: $AS = Y$. And the 45° line identifies positions of equality between aggregate demand on the vertical axis and aggregate supply on the horizontal axis.

First note points along $(C + I + G)$ above the 45° line. With aggregate demand greater than aggregate supply, sales must be made from inventories. When sales exceed expectations, firms find their inventories falling. In fact, as a result of negative net saving by consumers, businesses experience negative investment (or disinvestment). Now look at points along $(C + I + G)$ below the 45° line. With aggregate demand less than aggregate supply, firms accumulate inventory in excess of investment plans. As sales fall short of expectations, positive net saving by consumers calls for unplanned inventory investment by business firms. Only at equilibrium are sales consistent with business plans for inventory investment.

Unplanned inventory investment or disinvestment is the difference between the investment that actually occurs in business firms and their investment plans. Actual investment (I_a) is the sum of planned investment (I_p) and unplanned inventory changes:

$$I_a = I_p + \text{Unplanned Inventory Investment.}$$

When unplanned inventory investment is negative, actual investment is less than planned investment:

$$I_a < I_p.$$

Business firms increase production to build inventories to their desired level. When unplanned investment is positive, actual investment is greater than planned investment:

$$I_a > I_p.$$

Business firms reduce production to reduce inventories to the desired level. When unplanned investment is zero, actual investment will be equal to planned investment, so there is no tendency for businesses to change production plans.

The investment function in Figure 14–4b measures planned investment. To compute actual investment, it is necessary to add unplanned inventory investment (or disinvestment).

The existence of unplanned inventory investment means that actual investment plus government purchases will *always* be equal to saving plus net taxes:

$$I_a + G = S + T.$$

This is because the portion of total production not purchased by consumers, businesses or government must be purchased by someone. In fact, it is purchased by the firms that produced it—whether they planned to purchase it or not.

The equality between ($I_a + G$) and ($S + T$) can be stated another way:

$$I_a = S + T - G.$$

Actual investment is always equal to total saving: personal and business saving (S) plus government saving in the form of the budget surplus ($T - G$).

Differences between business plans for inventory investment and the investment that actually occurs cause firms to increase or reduce production. Actual investment depends on the saving decisions of individuals, businesses and governments. When business firms experience unplanned inventory investment (or disinvestment), they increase or decrease production and push the economy toward the equilibrium level of income.

Summary

The relationship between saving and investment is critical in Keynesian theory and policy. The following summary may help you understand the importance of the saving-investment relationship in the Keynesian model.

1. Business investment plans are made independently of the saving plans of consumers, business firms and governments. As a result, planned investment plus government spending is seldom precisely equal to saving plus net taxes:

$$I_p + G = S + T.$$

2. When planned investment and government spending exceed saving plus net taxes, the effect is to increase spending, production and income:

$$(I_p + G) > (S + T) \text{ means expansion.}$$

When planned investment plus government spending falls short of saving plus net taxes, the effect is to reduce spending, production and income:

$$(I_p + G) < (S + T) \text{ means contraction.}$$

If planned investment plus government spending should be precisely equal to saving plus net taxes, there is no tendency for production and income either to rise or fall. The economy is in equilibrium:

$$(I_p + G) = (S + T) \text{ means equilibrium.}$$

3. Actual investment will always equal saving, when saving is defined to include private saving plus the government surplus:

$$I_a = S + (T - G).$$

This is because of unplanned inventory investment or disinvestment. A low level of saving relative to planned investment leads to sales from inventory; inventory depletion means disinvestment, such that actual investment equals the low level of saving. Saving greater than planned investment leads to inventory accumulation, so that actual investment is equal to the higher level of saving: $I_a = I_p +$ unplanned inventory investment.

4. Unplanned changes in business inventories lead to changes in economic activity. Unplanned disinvestment causes business firms to increase production and income. Unplanned investment causes firms to cut production and income. In either case, the tendency is a movement toward the equilibrium level of income, at which planned investment is equal to saving, and investment plans are actually achieved.

Changes in Equilibrium Income: The Multiplier

The Keynesian model explains how individual spending plans combine to determine GNP. Business firms respond to individual spending plans by adjusting production, always tending toward a level of income we have called the *equilibrium* level. In reality, equilibrium may never be reached or maintained very long. This is because of frequent changes in spending and saving plans, which cause shifts in the lines representing the major components of aggregate demand. The most frequent shifts are associated with business investment spending.

Investment plans may vary widely from year to year, in response to new developments in the economic environment. The investment function in Figure 14–4b was drawn under the simplifying assumption that other factors in the economic environment do not change. At this point, we will relax this assumption and observe the effect on the Keynesian model of changes in investment spending.

One important determinant of planned investment spending is interest rates. Interest rates affect investment decisions for two reasons. When investment funds are to be borrowed, the cost of borrowing must be considered before making any new investment. A new investment must be expected to yield a higher rate of return than the cost of financing it. Interest rates are critical also to the firm that has internal funds for investment, however. Whether or not a firm plans to borrow, the interest it could earn on its own funds must be considered in any investment decision. Foregone earnings from using a firm's own funds are opportunity costs.

The relationship between the rate of return on investment and total investment spending is called the marginal efficiency of investment (MEI). (See Chapter 5 for further discussion of MEI.) Figure 4–5 shows the total quantity of investment associated with various rates of return. The MEI curve is drawn under the simplifying assumption that all other factors that influence investment remain constant. The line slopes downward, because firms normally make higher yielding investments before lower yielding investments. Figure 14–5 shows that investment spending of $300 billion yields a rate of return of at least 6 percent. If the current interest rate is no higher than 6 percent, we would expect total investment spending of $300 billion. This is the level of investment we used for drawing Figure 14–4a.

Now suppose the interest rate falls to 3 percent. The MEI schedule tells us that investment spending of $500 billion would yield a rate of return of at least 3 percent. We would expect the investment component of aggregate demand to shift upward to $500 billion, with a tendency toward a new equilibrium level of income. The new conditions are shown in Figure 14–6. Note that an increase in investment of $200 billion increases the equilibrium level of income (Y_e) by $500 billion.

The $500 billion increase in the equilibrium level of income is a result of what economists call the *multiplier*. The multiplier takes effect when recipients of new spending respend their new incomes. Respending adds to the incomes of others who, in turn, also respend and contribute to the incomes of still other income earners. At each stage of respending, the amount actually spent is smaller, but the total change in income is a multiple of the

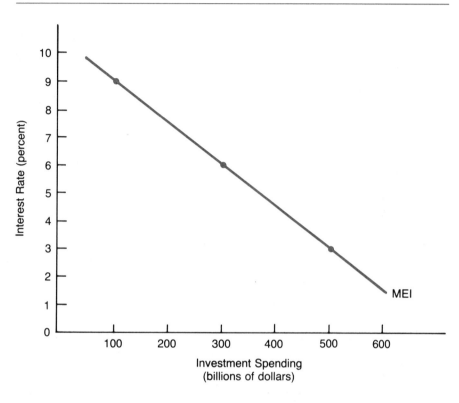

FIGURE 14–5   The Marginal Efficiency of Investment

initial change in spending. The size of the multiple depends on the rate at which consumers respend their incomes.

Remember that we described consumer spending in terms of the marginal propensity to consume:

$$MPC = \Delta C / \Delta Y.$$

A high MPC implies a high respending rate and a greater total change in income. A low MPC implies the reverse. If consumers respend at a rate equal to the MPC, the sum of all new spending is

    (MPC) $\times$ (initial change in spending)
+ (MPC) $\times$ (MPC) $\times$ (initial change in spending)
+ (MPC) $\times$ (MPC) $\times$ (MPC) $\times$ (initial change in spending)
+ . . . and so forth.

In terms of our example, the change in income that results from an initial change in investment is:

$$Y = (\Delta I) + (\Delta C / \Delta Y)(\Delta I) + (\Delta C / \Delta Y)^2 (\Delta I) + (\Delta C / \Delta Y)^3 (\Delta I)$$
$$+ \ . . . \text{ and so forth.}$$

FIGURE 14–6 A Change in Planned Investment

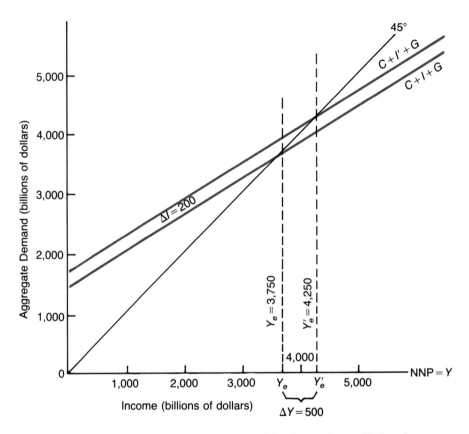

A change in planned investment yields a multiple change in equilibrium income:

$$\Delta Y = \Delta I \left(\frac{1}{1-\text{MPC}} \right).$$

Algebraically, this result is the sum of a geometric progression, for which the formula is the initial change times $1/(1-r)$, where r is the rate of respending. In terms of our example:

$$Y = \Delta I \left[\frac{1}{1 - (\Delta C/\Delta Y)} \right] = \Delta I \left[\frac{1}{1 - .60} \right] = 200(1/.40) = 500.$$

Thus, a $200 billion increase in investment causes the equilibrium level of income to increase by a multiple of $1/.40$, or 2.5, times the initial change in spending, or by $500 billion.

Alternatively, a $200 billion decrease in investment will cause a $500 billion decrease in the equilibrium level of income. A decrease in investment spending might be the result of an increase in the interest rate to 9 percent. The MEI curve in Figure 14–5 indicates this result, with investment of only $100 billion and a $500 billion drop in the equilibrium level of income. In fact, every point on the MEI curve implies a particular level of investment, a particular level of aggregate demand, and a corresponding equilibrium level of income.

The *IS* Curve

To include all possible quantities of investment and all possible equilibrium levels of income on the Keynesian model in Figure 14–4 would be confusing. Fortunately, it is possible to show the effect of different interest rates through another simple diagram.

Figure 14–7 shows the equilibrium level of income associated with any possible level of interest rates. Note first the equilibrium level with which we began: $3,750 billion with an interest rate of 6 percent and *I* of $300 billion. A change in the interest rate to 3 percent is associated with investment of $500 billion and equilibrium income of $4,250 billion. With *i* of 9 percent, investment is only $100 billion and income is $3,250 billion. All other interest rates may be expected to lead to particular levels of investment according to the MEI in Figure 14–5 and yield multiple income changes according to the MPC in Figure 14–4a. Connecting all these equilibrium points produces the *IS* curve in Figure 14–7.

The curve is called the *IS* curve because it identifies all positions of equality between investment and saving, where *I* is defined as planned investment plus government spending, and *S* is saving plus net taxes:

$$I_p + G = S + T.$$

Each point on the *IS* curve implies the level of planned investment that is equal to saving at the income level shown:

$$I_p + G = S + T.$$

Only points on the *IS* curve represent equilibrium positions; at any point off the curve planned investment is different from saving, and business firms make the necessary changes in production to bring actual investment into equality with planned investment.

Refer to Figure 14–7 and point A, which lies above and to the right of the *IS* curve. At point A interest rates are too high and income too high for equilibrium. We know this because at high interest rates planned investment is relatively low (by the MEI curve). At the high income level saving is

FIGURE 14-7 The *IS* Curve

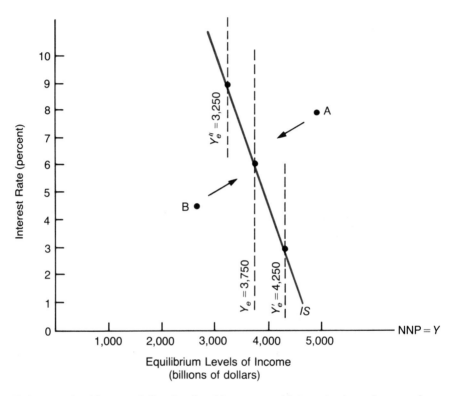

Points on the *IS* curve define levels of income and interest rates where saving is equal to investment.

relatively high (as shown by the difference between income and consumption at high income levels). Thus, planned investment plus government spending falls short of saving plus net taxes:

$$(I_p + G) < (S + T).$$

Inventories accumulate, leading business firms to cut production and incomes. Follow the arrow from point A to an equilibrium position on the *IS* curve where planned investment is equal to saving.

Movement from point A to the *IS* curve is helped by changes in interest rates. A low level of investment relative to saving puts downward pressure on interest rates, encouraging additional investment and bringing planned investment up to the level of saving.

Similar reasoning explains the process of movement to equilibrium from point B. At point B planned investment plus government spending exceeds saving plus net taxes:

$$(I_p + G) > (S + T)$$

leading to increases in income and rising interest rates. Adjustments continue until planned investment is equal to saving at a point on the *IS* curve. Thus, for every level of interest rates there is a corresponding equilibrium level of income.

The shape of the *IS* curve is a function of two circumstances: the responsiveness of business investment plans to interest rate changes and the responsiveness of consumer spending to changes in incomes. In the first instance, the MEI function relates investment plans to interest rates. A steep MEI implies little response to interest rate changes. If this is true for the economy, changes in interest rates will produce little change in the equilibrium level of income, and the *IS* curve will be rather steep as well. In the second instance, the MPC and the multiplier determine consumer respending rates. High values of the MPC and the multiplier translate into wide income changes whenever investment changes. Even small changes in investment produce substantial changes in equilibrium, making the *IS* curve rather flat. The steepness or flatness of the *IS* curve is important for predicting the effects of economic policy, as we will show in the next chapter.

Shifts in the *IS* Curve

The *IS* curve in Figure 14–7 was drawn under the assumption that many factors influencing spending remain constant. Only interest rate changes were included in the model. At this point, we may begin to relax this simplifying assumption and incorporate other factors in the model.

First, we might assume changes in the technical and economic conditions that affect business investment plans. Such changes would be shown as shifts in the MEI function (described in Chapter 5). Changes that improve business expectations of profit, for example, would be expected to shift the MEI function to the right. The rightward shift implies a higher level of investment for every level of interest rates shown. When higher levels of investment spending are included in aggregate demand, the result is higher equilibrium levels of income. This is shown in Figure 14–8 as a shift to the right of the *IS* curve to *IS'*. Stated differently, for every interest rate, a higher level of investment means that planned investment equals saving at a higher income level. Hence *IS* must lie farther to the right.

A change in the responsiveness of investment to interest rates also affects the *IS* curve. Substantial stocks of unused productive capacity, for example, discourage certain kinds of investment, regardless of the interest rate. The result is a steeper MEI function and a steeper *IS* curve. (See *IS"* in Figure 14–8.)

Changes in consumer spending also affect the *IS* curve. We have said that consumer spending is influenced by factors other than income. More

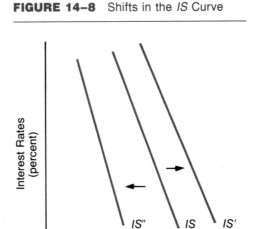

FIGURE 14–8   Shifts in the *IS* Curve

Equilibrium Levels of Income
(billions of dollars)

Changing technical or economic
circumstances shift the *IS* curve to the
right or left and may change its slope.

liberal credit policies, for example, and freer attitudes toward spending versus saving cause an upward shift in the consumption function. The result is increased aggregate demand, higher equilibrium income and a more rightward *IS* curve. These kinds of changes have affected consumer spending in the 1980s. Other changes such as expectations of rising prices might bring on increases in the MPC and the multiplier. Anticipating even higher incomes and prices in the future, families might tend to spend and respend their incomes faster. The result might be wider swings in equilibrium income and a flatter *IS* curve.

Finally, changes in government spending affect the *IS* curve. Increased government spending shifts the *IS* curve to the right, and increased taxes, to the left. In general, higher levels of spending—whether by business, government or consumers—shift *IS* to the right. Greater saving, whether business or personal, or in the form of larger government surpluses (or smaller deficits), shifts *IS* to the left. Changes in the slope of the *IS* curve are caused by changes in the responsiveness of investment to interest rates and consumers to income changes. Greater responsiveness means a flatter curve, and reduced responsiveness means a steeper curve.

We will find that the position and shape of the *IS* curve have a significant bearing on the choice of government economic policy and on its effectiveness. In the next chapter we will combine elements of the Keynesian model with the monetary theory of income determination. Then we will show how government decisions regarding spending and taxes affect the equilibrium level of income.

MONEY AND BANKING IN PRACTICE: KEYNES AND THE CONSERVATIVE REVOLUTION

During the Great Depression of the 1930s, students of economics were struggling to reconcile the theory they were learning from their professors with the events they were observing around them. Their professors were telling them that markets will always "clear": that there could be no unsold goods or services and no unemployed workers. Prices and wages would fluctuate to ensure it. Around them, on the other hand, students were seeing mortgage foreclosures, banks and business failures and desperation among vast numbers of unemployed.

It was hard to escape the conclusion that markets don't always clear and that surpluses in product and resource markets are evidence of an underemployment equilibrium.

One of the problems in the depression was that bank concerns about lending were reducing the money multiplier, and the Fed did not increase the money base by enough to offset the decrease. Instead of making new loans, many banks were using their excess reserves to acquire government securities, and interest rates had fallen so low

as to reduce the velocity of spending. Some economists speculated (facetiously) that even if money were to be dropped from airplanes, people were too worried about hard times to spend it. They even suggested that new money be printed with a date, after which it would be allowed to "expire." They hoped this would encourage people to spend their money quickly and bring on an increase in economic activity.

Paul Samuelson was a student of economics at the time and he later became the nation's foremost Keynesian economist. Samuelson noted a basic contradiction between what he called "mainstream economics and the commonsense views of amateurs." Many of the proposed remedies to the crisis seemed to make sense, according to Samuelson, but they ran counter to established theory. One commonsense idea talked about the multiplier and how new spending might so increase income as to pay back the initial spending. This seemed a remarkable idea at the time.

One of the chief concerns during the Great Depression was whether capitalism could actually survive. In fact, during the administration of President Franklin Roosevelt, many policymakers came to the conclusion that the poverty, unemployment and collapse of markets in agriculture, housing and health care would surely destroy the capitalist system—and soon. The only way to avoid total destruction was for government to intervene directly in markets to correct fundamental economic problems.

Keynes disagreed. He believed that capitalism was worth preserving and could be preserved with less radical means. Instead of direct government intervention in markets, Keynes proposed using the government budget to raise and stabilize production and employment. Thus, Keynesian recommendations were a *conservative* approach—to conserve capitalism without active government involvement in free markets.

Question for Discussion

1. How are Keynesian economic policy actions more conservative than other policy choices?

Glossary of Terms

aggregate demand. the sum of all spending of consumers, business, government and foreign buyers

aggregate supply. the sum of all incomes received from production

business profit. business revenues remaining after paying costs

capital consumption allowance. an amount set aside to reflect the cost of depreciating equipment

consumption. spending for consumer durable and nondurable goods and services

consumption function. an algebraic relationship between consumption and income

dependent variable. the variable in an equation whose behavior depends on the value of other variable(s)

equilibrium. a condition of income, employment, prices and interest rates toward which the economy tends to move

gross investment. total purchases of capital goods for the year

independent variable. the variable(s) in an equation whose value is determined outside the algebraic relationship

macroeconomics. the study of total output, income, and employment and the general price level

microeconomics. the study of output and prices in individual markets

microeconomics. the study of output and prices in individual markets

multiplier effect. the multiple increase in incomes that results from an exogenous increase in spending

negative taxes. payments received from government, including welfare payments, subsidies and veterans' benefits

net foreign investment. the difference between foreign purchases in the United States and sales to foreigners

net investment. total purchases of capital goods less depreciated capital for the year

net saving. the difference between saving plus net taxes and planned investment plus government spending

net taxes. the difference between taxes paid to government and transfer payments received from government

parameters. the values within an algebraic equation that remain the same when the values of variables change

transfer payments. payments by government to individuals or businesses; also called negative taxes

unplanned investment. accumulation or depletion of inventory beyond a firm's investment plans

---

Summary of Important Ideas

1. During the 1930s monetary theory and policy lost favor as a means of explaining and regulating economic activity. John M. Keynes developed a new theory based on individual decisions to spend, which together constitute aggregate demand.

2. The Keynesian model begins with consumer spending and shows that changes in consumption are a fairly constant fraction of changes in income. The difference between income and consumption is saving plus net taxes.

3. Investment spending responds slowly to income changes and may be regarded as a constant in the short run. The same is true of government purchases.

4. Equilibrium income occurs when planned investment plus government purchases equal saving plus net taxes. This is the same as saying that planned investment is equal to private and government saving. At any other level of income, aggregate demand is different from aggregate supply, and the difference pushes income toward a higher or lower level of income.

5. If aggregate demand differs from aggregate supply, the result is unplanned inventory investment or disinvestment. Thus, actual investment is always equal to total saving:

$$I_a = S + T - G.$$

Differences between actual investment and planned investment cause changes in production plans and bring on changes in income.

6. Changes in interest rates may lead to changes in investment plans. The marginal efficiency of investment (MEI) shows the relationship between interest rates and planned investment expenditures for any given state of economic and technological conditions. Changes in investment plans cause multiple changes in income according to the rate at which the community responds changes in income: the marginal propensity to consume (MPC).

7. Consumption, investment and government purchases can be combined in a single model showing interest rates and corresponding equilibrium levels of income. The *IS* curve defines equality between planned investment and saving:

$$I_p = S + T - G.$$

Its position depends on the constants of spending; its slope depends on the respending rate of consumers and the responsiveness of investment to interest rates. Changes in these parameters cause shifts in the *IS* curve.

Questions for Discussion and Research

1. Consult the current *Economic Report of the President* for recent data on gross national product (GNP), broken down into major spending and income components. What has been the behavior of each component over the past several years? What has been the behavior of net investment?

2. Explain the difference between the long-run and short-run consumption functions. What is the significance of each of the parameters of the consumption function:

$$C = a + b(Y)?$$

Distinguish between MPC and APC.

3. Explain the significance of positive and negative net saving. Illustrate the effect on national income. How is net saving related to unplanned investment? Explain the apparent contradiction between

$$I_a \text{ (always)} = S + T - G$$

and

$$I_p \text{ (not necessarily)} = S + T - G.$$

4. Use the hypothetical values for C and I given in the text to determine the effect on income if government expenditures (G) rise from 400 to 500. Verify that the change in income is consistent with the multiplier principle.

5. Assume that MPC is .6 and I is 500 minus 20(i). What is the change in income associated with a one-point change in the interest rate? Explain.

6. List as many circumstances as you can that would cause a rightward shift in the *IS* curve?

7. Illustrate the two factors that influence the slope of the *IS* curve. How do these factors differ from those that affect the position of the curve?

Additional Readings

Galbraith, J.K.   "Keynes, Roosevelt and the Complementary Revolutions." *Challenge* (January/February 1984): 4–8.

Juster, F. Thomas.   "Consumer Spending and the Outlook for 1987." *Economic Outlook USA* (Winter/Spring 1987): 5–7.

Lekachman, Robert.   *The Age of Keynes.* New York: McGraw-Hill, 1966.

Tobin, James.   *National Economic Policy.* New Haven, Conn.: Yale University Press, 1966.

Webb, Roy H.   "The National Income and Product Accounts." *Economic Review of Federal Reserve Bank of Richmond* (May/June 1986): 11–17.

C H A P T E R

15

LEARNING OBJECTIVES

- ■ To bring together the Keynesian model of income and the monetary model
- ■ To see how the product sector and the money sector react to changes in the economic environment
- ■ To project the consequences of monetary and fiscal policy
- ■ To learn the basis for disagreement regarding policies for influencing economic activity

Combining the Keynesian Theory with Monetary Theory

"After all, in a democracy like ours, effective policy in the end needs to rest on the base of an informed public—a public alert to the dangers and willing to accept the need for strong measures and for new policy initiatives to deal with them."

Paul A. Volcker

Anyone who doubts that economics is an evolving science should attend a seminar on economic policy. New ideas are constantly being offered, and old ones resurrected or discarded. Continuous debate is a substitute in economics for the laboratory experiments of the physical sciences.

The most vigorous debate in economics is the one regarding national income: specifically, the relative significance of the money supply and total spending as determinants of income, employment and prices. Economists who focus on the money supply are called Monetarists, and those who focus on spending are Keynesians.

Most modern economists are neither strict Monetarists nor Keynesians but believe that the level of economic activity depends both on the quantity of money and on total spending. This chapter will bring together the two theories of income determination and show how equilibrium is achieved in both theories simultaneously.

Equilibrium in the Keynesian Model

Equilibrium in the Keynesian model might be called *product-sector equilibrium*, because it emphasizes total spending for newly produced goods and services. In the Keynesian model many individual spending decisions combine to determine aggregate demand and, ultimately, production. Every level

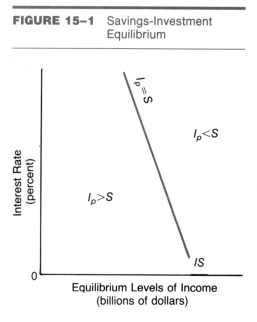

FIGURE 15-1   Savings-Investment Equilibrium

of production yields a corresponding level of income and employment. Equilibrium occurs when the saving plans of individuals, businesses and governments are equal to business investment plans:

$$I_p = S + T - G.$$

Because investment plans differ at different interest rates, various equilibrium levels are possible, each associated with a particular level of interest rates.

We have shown product-sector equilibrium levels as a series of points that form the *IS* curve. See Figure 15-1. Each point on the *IS* curve implies a level of income and interest rates at which the quantity of planned investment is equal to saving.

Only points on the *IS* curve represent equilibrium positions; at any point off the curve planned investment is not equal to saving, and income will either rise or fall. Points above and to the right of the *IS* curve indicate planned investment less than saving. This is because interest rates are too high (and thus planned investment too low) for equilibrium, and income too high (and thus saving too high) for equilibrium. Unplanned inventory investment would begin to accumulate, and firms would cut production. Similarly, points below and to the left of the *IS* curve indicate saving less than planned investment. Unplanned inventory disinvestment would lead firms to increase production. Thus, from either of these nonequilibrium positions, changes in production would take place to move the economy to a level of income on the curve.

Changes in planned investment and saving shift *IS* to a new series of equilibrium points. An increase in planned investment, for example, or a decrease in saving shifts *IS* to the right. Increased government spending or a reduction in taxes has the same effect. On the other hand, increases in saving of individuals, business firms or government and decreases in planned investment shift *IS* to the left.

Equilibrium in the Money Sector

The Keynesian Revolution focused attention on spending for goods and services and away from the supply of money. But the apparent neglect of the money sector was only temporary. Economists soon turned again to money matters and looked for ways to integrate monetary conditions into a more complete model that would include more of the factors that determine income.

The Demand for Money

Modern monetary economists believe that understanding the supply of money is not sufficient to explain income. It is necessary also to consider demand for money: people's desire to hold idle money balances as a part of their total portfolios of wealth.

A change in public holdings of idle money balances can offset changes in its supply. Changes in money holdings are reflected in changes in velocity (V), making the identity ($MV \equiv PQ$) less useful for deciding policy. Modern economists have changed the form of the money equation to one that emphasizes demand:

$$M = kPQ = kY.$$

The coefficient k is the fraction of income the public wants to hold in the form of money. Whereas V measures the spending rate of money, k reflects the holding rate.

We have seen that the chief reason for including idle money balances in a wealth portfolio is for making ordinary expenditures. Most families and business firms hold a portion of their income idle over the month as a fund for making everyday transactions. A family that sets aside two-fifths of monthly income at the beginning of the month and spends down to zero at the end of the month holds, on the average, one-fifth of its income idle. Its transactions demand for money is

$$L_t = l_t Y = .2Y.$$

Most families also hold a portion of income idle for use in emergencies. With precautionary holdings (l_pY) of .05Y, the *income-related demand for money* may be expressed

$$L_Y = l_tY + l_pY = lY = .25Y.$$

The coefficient ($l = .25$) measures the fraction of income held for transactions and precautionary purposes. It is an important part of the holding rate k.

Money held for transactions and precautionary purposes depends primarily on income. One-fourth of monthly income is a reasonable fraction of income for meeting normal expenditure needs. The fraction itself may vary, however, depending on current interest rates. Exceptionally high interest rates may encourage families to economize on their idle money balances, so that the fraction of money in a total portfolio declines. Funds would be transferred from non-interest-earning demand deposits to interest-earning deposits until they are needed for spending. Expected interest earnings must be sufficient to justify the time and trouble involved in transferring funds, however. There is probably some threshold of interest rates below which most families will not bother to economize on cash balances and above which funds are shifted about readily. Thus, the fraction l may be constant below some interest rate and decrease at higher rates.

In addition to the income-related demand for money, people hold idle money balances for what economists call speculative purposes. Remember that speculative holdings arise from the desire to purchase financial instruments at the most favorable terms. When terms are especially favorable, people use their idle money balances to purchase financial instruments, and speculative holdings drop to zero. When terms are relatively less favorable, people sell off their financial instruments and build up their idle money balances for making purchases later. Changes in speculative holdings cause wide swings in the holding rate and, alternatively, opposite swings in the spending rate.

To understand speculative holdings, suppose people decide that conditions for purchasing financial instruments are unfavorable; they reduce their purchases of corporate bonds and government securities and increase their holdings of idle money balances. The result is a reduced quantity of credit for business. Note that the higher value for k implies a lower level of V. Whatever the money supply, its turnover rate is lower and income is lower.

Now suppose conditions for purchasing financial instruments improve. People purchase more corporate bonds and government securities. Smaller idle money holdings have the effect of reducing k and increasing V. Whatever the money supply, its turnover rate is higher and income is higher.

Graphing the Demand for Money

The demand for money is shown graphically in Figures 15–2a to 15–2c. The market for idle money balances is a simple graph in which the

FIGURE 15–2a   Transactions and Precautionary Demand for Money

FIGURE 15–2b   Speculative Demand for Money

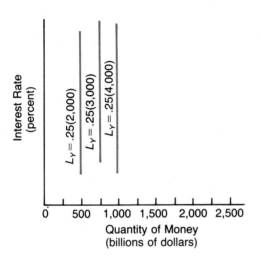

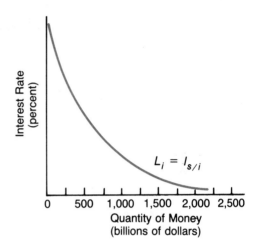

FIGURE 15–2c   Total Demand for Money

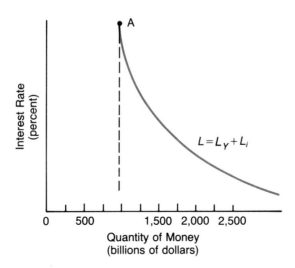

vertical axis measures the price of holding money (the interest rate) and the horizontal axis measures quantity. The demand for money appears as a typical demand curve. It is helpful to look at each of the components of money holdings separately.

Income-Related Demand for Money

Transactions and precautionary demand for money depend primarily on income. Therefore, the income-related demand for money must be drawn with respect to a particular level of income. With an l of .25, the income-related demand for money is a vertical line drawn at the quantity of money (L_Y) equal to .25Y. In Figure 15–2a the income-related demand has been drawn for incomes of $2,000 billion, $3,000 billion, and $4,000 billion. Similar lines could be drawn for every other income level, producing a dense array of vertical demand curves.

Interest-Related Demand for Money

Speculative money demand, or *interest-related demand*, depends on whether conditions for purchasing financial instruments are believed to be favorable or unfavorable. An important consideration is the level of interest rates. High interest rates make holding financial instruments attractive and reduce speculative holdings. When interest rates are relatively high, the prices of securities are low. Investors purchase securities to add to their wealth portfolios, expecting to experience a capital gain in the future when interest rates fall. Thus, high interest rates are associated with relatively low speculative demand for money. On the other hand, low interest rates mean high prices for securities and increased market risk: the risk that interest rates will rise and cause capital losses. Investors tend to increase their speculative money balances for buying securities later.

The Slope of the Money Demand Curve

The demand for speculative money balances is shown in Figure 15–2b. The curve slopes downward, in keeping with the public's attitudes toward holdings of idle money balances at various interest rates. Note that the curve flattens out at very low interest rates. Low interest rates imply low opportunity costs of holding money and low earning potential on securities. At very low interest rates the risk of loss may offset any expected gain, so that very little money is made available for purchasing financial instruments. Speculative demand increases to absorb the entire money supply.

The speculative demand for money may be expressed algebraically as:

$$L_i = l_s/i.$$

The term (l_s/i) is written as a ratio because of the inverse relationship between speculative money demand and interest rates.

Combining income-related demand at income of $3,000 billion with interest-related demand yields the money demand curve in Figure 15–2c. Like other demand curves, the demand for money curve slopes downward over most of its length. At high interest rates, speculative demand becomes very small, and money demand approaches $[L_Y = l_Y(Y)]$ only; thus the curve becomes almost vertical at high interest rates. At low interest rates speculative demand increases substantially, making the curve flatter and, at some level of interest rates, almost horizontal.

The demand curve in Figure 15–2c was drawn for income of $3,750 billion. Plotting all money demand equations for all possible incomes on a single graph would produce a dense array of curves, each with a vertical portion drawn at the quantity of money equal to $l(Y)$ for a particular level of Y.

k and the Demand for Money Curve

Every point on the demand for money curve implies a particular holding rate, k. To see why, begin with a point A high on the curve and move downward. Along the steep portion the demand for money is at a minimum: k reflects the public's desire to hold idle money for transactions and precautionary purposes only: $k = l$. All speculative balances have been used to purchase financial instruments, so that the nation's spending rate (V) is at a maximum. Along the downward-sloping portion of demand, k becomes larger as interest rates fall and money demand comes to include speculative holdings. Along the relatively flat portion, k becomes infinitely large as people sell off their financial instruments and hold the proceeds in speculative balances. With increased speculative balances the public's holdings of idle money absorb all the available money supply.

Variations in k complicate policy-making. If k remained constant at ($k = l = .25$), it would be possible to vary the money supply and achieve direct results in income by the equation: $M = kY$. A change in the money supply from $1,000 billion to $1,200 billion, for example, would change money income as follows:

Where:

$$M_1 = 1,000,$$
$$M_1 = kY_1 \text{ and}$$
$$1,000 = .25(Y_1)$$

then

$$Y_1 = 4,000.$$

Where

$$M_1 = 1,200,$$
$$M_2 = kY_2 \text{ and}$$
$$1,200 = .25(Y_1)$$

then

$$Y_2 = 4,800.$$

Variations in k make it necessary to consider changes in interest rates that affect the public's desire to hold speculative money balances, rather than interest-earning financial instruments. If the above increase in the money supply causes a drop in interest rates so that k increases to .30, there would be no change in income:
Where:

$$k = .30 \text{ and}$$
$$1{,}200 = .30(Y_3)$$

then

$$Y_3 = 4{,}000.$$

To complete our model of the market for money, we will look at supply and then determine the equilibrium price of money (the interest rate) and the actual quantity.

The Supply of Money

We have seen that the demand for money depends on the interest rate and the level of income. We know that the supply of money depends on decisions of the Federal Reserve, the U.S. Treasury, commercial banks and the public. An upper limit to supply is set by the reserve requirements and open market operations of the Federal Reserve. Reserves and cash in the hands of the public constitute the money base. When commercial banks expand lending to the maximum permitted by the money base, the money supply may be as much as:

$$M1 = B \left[\frac{1 + c}{r + e + c + r_t t} \right]$$

When reserves are used fully to support money creation, the supply of money curve is a vertical line at the quantity $M1$. (The derivation of the money multiplier was described in Chapter 8.)

Banks do not always lend the maximum amount, however. In fact, at lower interest rates their willingness to lend may fall short of the maximum by larger and larger amounts. (The value e in the denominator of the money multiplier increases.) Moreover, the public may withdraw more cash from the banks at lower interest rates, leaving less cash to satisfy bank reserve requirements. (The value c in the denominator of the money multiplier increases.) The result of these changes is a money supply that increases with interest rates and a money supply curve that slopes upward to the maximum permitted by the money base.

FIGURE 15–3a Supply of Money Curve

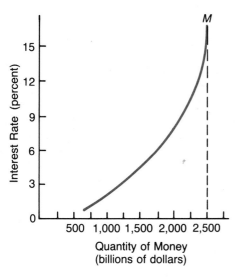

FIGURE 15–3b Money Supply and Equilibrium in the Money Sector

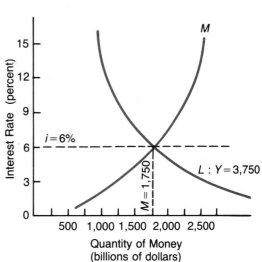

FIGURE 15–4 The Money Sector

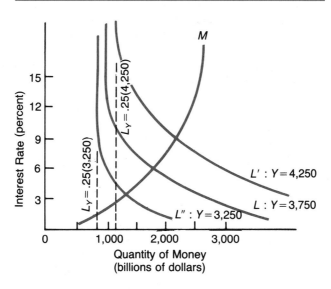

Various combinations of income and interest rates yield money-sector equilibrium.

Graphing the Supply of Money

The supply of money curve has been drawn in Figure 15–3a. It is a typical supply curve, sloping upward to indicate larger quantities supplied at higher interest rates. At i of 15 percent in this example, quantity reaches a maximum consistent with the given money base, and the money supply curve becomes vertical, with M at $2,500 billion.

Demand and supply are combined in Figure 15–3b. Equilibrium in the money sector occurs where demand and supply are equal: $L = M$. Equilibrium establishes three values: the actual quantity of money, its price (the interest rate) and the income level for which the demand curve was drawn. At equilibrium the existing supply of money is just enough to satisfy transactions and precautionary demand at the current level of income and to satisfy speculative demand at the current interest rate. The simultaneous decisions of commercial banks and individuals interact to push the money supply, income and the interest rate to levels consistent with these equilibrium conditions. Thus, with existing commercial bank reserves, equilibrium occurs when Y is 3,750 billion and i is 6 percent. The money supply is $1,750 billion.

Equilibrium in the Money Sector

Equilibrium in the money sector occurs when the demand for money is equal to the available money supply. The existing money supply must satisfy speculative, transactions and precautionary demand at various income levels and interest rates.

At high incomes, transactions and precautionary demand is relatively high, and less money is available for speculative balances. The relatively small amount available for speculative balances is consistent with a high interest rate. Figure 15–4 includes a second demand for money curve (L') drawn for income (Y) of 4,250. At the higher income level, transactions and precautionary demand absorbs a larger portion of the available money supply. Note that the vertical portion of the demand curve lies farther to the right, indicating larger income-related balances. Note also that the vertical portion of demand absorbs a larger quantity of the available money supply and that the equilibrium interest rate is higher, in keeping with the smaller speculative holdings. A third money demand curve (L'') reflects the opposite allocation of the money supply. L'' is drawn for income (Y) of 3,250. With lower incomes, income-related demand for money is low; with a larger amount remaining for speculative balances, the interest rate must also be low.

Any number of money demand curves could be drawn in Figure 15–4, each representing a different level of income and a different allocation of the existing money supply between transactions and precautionary demand, on the one hand, and speculative balances, on the other. For every level of income there is a corresponding equilibrium level of interest rates; high incomes are associated with high interest rates and low incomes with low rates.

The range of equilibrium incomes and interest rates can be shown graphically. For a given money supply, we have shown that equilibrium could occur with the following values:

$$L: \quad Y = 3,750 \text{ billion and } i = 6\%$$
$$L': \quad Y = 4,250 \text{ billion and } i = 9\%$$
$$L'': \quad Y = 3,250 \text{ billion and } i = 3\%.$$

These points are located in Figure 15–5 along with all other pairs of values taken from other money demand curves. Connecting all equilibrium points produces an income-interest rate curve appropriate to the given supply of money. Every point on the curve identifies a single equilibrium level of income and interest rates, and points off the curve are disequilibrium positions.

The *LM* Curve

The curve in Figure 15–5 is called the *LM curve* because it represents equality between money demand (*L*) with a given money supply (*M*). The *LM* curve slopes upward because with a fixed money supply higher income levels are associated with higher interest rates. At very high interest rates the *LM* curve becomes very steep. This is because speculative balances shrink to zero at very high interest rates, and all available money is allocated to transactions and precautionary balances. With all of the available money supply in income-related balances (*lY*), money is spent at the rate ($1/l = 1/k = V$). The result is the maximum income possible with the existing money supply. In our example, the maximum income possible with the given money supply is $10,000 billion.

The lower portion of the *LM* curve is generally believed to be rather flat. The explanation has to do with the behavior of speculative balances at low interest rates. As interest rates fall, a larger portion of the existing money supply is held in speculative balances. The reluctance to purchase financial instruments at very low interest rates finally places a lower limit on rates. Holders refuse to buy securities at all, believing that the interest rate must eventually rise, so that securities bought at low interest rates (high prices) would soon fall in value. At the minimum interest rate, income may vary over a wide range, depending on the allocation of money between transactions balances and speculative balances. But interest rates cannot fall below this level.

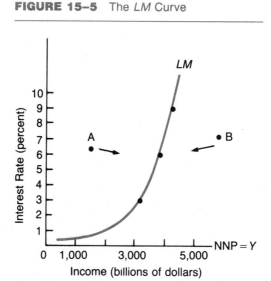

FIGURE 15-5   The *LM* Curve

Combinations of income and interest rates at
which the demand for money is equal to the
available money supply

Points along the *LM* curve represent equilibrium positions in the money
sector. At every point on the *LM* curve the public's demand for money is
equal to the available money supply. People are satisfied with the proportions of money and financial instruments in their portfolios, so there is no
change in income or interest rates. Points off the curve are disequilibrium
positions and cannot be maintained.

To see why, refer to point A to the left of the curve. At point A, interest
rates are too high and income too low for equilibrium. We know this because
high interest rates imply low speculative demand, and low incomes imply
low transactions demand. The result is a low level of money demand relative
to supply: $L < M$. With money demand less than supply, the public will
attempt to get rid of excess money balances. The excess supply in income-
related balances will be spent at the rate $1/l$, contributing to a rise in income.
Similarly, the excess speculative money balances will be used to purchase
securities, contributing to a drop in interest rates. The public will continue
to spend and purchase financial instruments until income and interest rates
reach levels consistent with the larger transactions and speculative balances.
Thus, the tendency is a movement toward a point on the *LM* curve.

Similar adjustments take place at point B. At point B, interest rates are
too low and income too high for equilibrium. Low interest rates imply large
speculative balances, and high incomes imply large transactions balances.

Thus, the demand for speculative and transactions balances exceeds supply: $L > M$. This time, the public attempts to build up money balances by reducing their spending and selling off their financial instruments. The result is a tendency for income to fall and interest rates to rise to levels consistent with the smaller transactions and speculative balances.

Only along the *LM* curve are actual money balances consistent with the public's demand for money. At any point on the curve, income and the interest rate call for transactions and speculative balances precisely equal to the available money supply. The public continues to spend and to purchase securities at the same rate, and there is no change in income or interest rates.

Shifts in the *LM* Curve

The *LM* curve was drawn under certain simplifying assumptions: that the public has rather stable preferences with respect to transactions and speculative money holdings, and that the money supply takes on a particular value based on bank reserves and bank responses to interest rates. A change in either of these circumstances causes a shift in the curve. In general, we may conclude that an increase in the public's demand for money shifts the *LM* curve to the left. This is because a larger demand for money relative to the existing supply reduces spending and reduces purchases of financial instruments, causing income to fall and interest rates to rise. Equilibrium points are located higher and farther to the left than before.

An increase in the money supply has the opposite effect. An increase in supply might come about through a Federal Reserve decision to increase reserves or through changes in public or commercial bank holdings of currency and excess reserves. When the supply of money comes to exceed demand at the current income and interest rate, people increase their spending and purchase more securities. The result is higher incomes for every level of interest rates. Equilibrium points are located farther to the right than before.

The *IS-LM* Synthesis

A *synthesis* brings together related ideas into a coherent whole. Combining two simple theories yields a more complex theory, but one that more correctly and completely describes the economic environment.

The Keynesian model of spending enabled us to express all product-sector equilibrium positions in a single curve (*IS*). The *IS* curve locates all

FIGURE 15–6   The *IS-LM* Synthesis

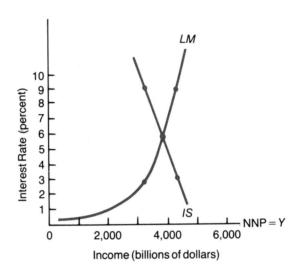

Only one combination of income and interest rates satisfies equilibrium conditions in both the product sector *(I = S)* and the money sector *(L = M).*

income levels and interest rates where planned investment is equal to saving. In the money sector, equilibrium occurs when money demand is equal to the available money supply (*LM*). The *LM* curve locates all income levels and interest rates where this condition is satisfied.

By combining product-sector equilibrium with money-sector equilibrium we can determine equilibrium in both sectors simultaneously. Typical *IS* and *LM* curves have been drawn together on Figure 15–6. Only one income level and one interest rate satisfy equilibrium conditions in both the product sector and the money sector. Any position other than Y at $3,750 billion and *i* at 6 percent sets in motion spending adjustments or adjustments in money balances that move the economy back to this point.

An illustration may be helpful. Refer to point A, a disequilibrium position in both sectors. At A, the interest rate is too high for equilibrium. In the product sector, planned investment falls short of saving, so that inventories build up and firms cut back production, causing income to fall. In the money sector, demand for money balances is less than the available money supply. Holders of excess money balances use them to purchase financial instruments, pushing the interest rate down.

Note that as the interest rate falls, planned investment tends to increase in response to the lower interest rate; the higher level of investment spending moderates the decrease in income. Adjustments in interest rates and incomes continue until equilibrium conditions are satisfied in both markets.

Now refer to point B. At point B, the interest rate is too low for equilibrium. In the product sector, planned investment exceeds saving, so that inventories are depleted, and production and income increase. In the money sector, demand for money balances exceeds the available money supply. People attempt to build up their money balances by reducing spending and by buying fewer financial instruments. The result is a rise in the interest rate that, in turn, moderates investment spending and moderates the increase in income. Adjustments continue in both the product sector and the money sector until all equilibrium conditions are satisfied.

The *IS-LM* model in Figure 15–6 is useful because it illustrates the process by which circumstances in one sector interact with those in another. The student should select other disequilibrium positions, say C and D, note the disequilibrium conditions in both sectors, and trace the series of adjustments through which the economy moves toward equilibrium.

Using the *IS-LM* Model

Understanding the *IS-LM* model enables us to trace the effects of changes in the product sector or money sector. When spending decisions change or Federal Reserve policies change, the curves shift or change their shape. In the product sector, individual decisions about consumer (C) or investment spending (I) and government decisions about spending (G) or taxes (T) affect the *IS* curve. In the money sector, personal or commercial bank decisions about holdings of money and financial instruments affect the *LM* curve. Federal Reserve decisions to change the money base also affect the *LM* curve.

Changes in these kinds of decisions take place all the time. Changes in the curves yield new equilibrium conditions in the product or money sector and set in motion the processes of adjustment we have talked about. The economy moves toward a new equilibrium income and a new interest rate.

Whether the new equilibrium level is efficient depends on the resulting employment of productive resources. If resources are fully employed in productive work, we would call the equilibrium income efficient. If there is significant unemployment or if the general price level is widely unstable, we would call the equilibrium income inefficient.

In the next chapter we will consider how decisions in the product sector or the money sector affect employment and the price level. Then we will describe how government policies can help produce an efficient equilibrium level.

MONEY AND BANKING IN PRACTICE: CONSTRUCTING AN ECONOMETRIC MODEL

Econometric forecasters use models similar to the one developed in this text to project future values of economic variables. They write algebraic equations describing the *IS* and *LM* curves, using values estimated from historical data. Then they solve the equations simultaneously to arrive at estimates of GNP and interest rates.

The IS Curve. To illustrate the process, remember we have defined the *IS* curve as comprising all levels of GNP and interest rates *(i)* at which aggregate demand is equal to aggregate supply: $AD = AS$. *AD* is a function of income *(Y)* equal to the sum of consumer, investment and government spending:

$$AD = f(Y) = C + I + G.$$

Consumer spending is defined more precisely as some base level of consumption C_o plus additional spending from additional income, as determined by the marginal propensity to consume:

$$C = C_o + MPC(Y).$$

Investment spending depends on many factors in the economic environment including interest rates and may be expressed as follows:

$$I = I_o - d(i),$$

where I_o is some base level of investment independent of interest rates and *d* measures the responsiveness of in-

vestment to interest rate changes. The sign for *d* is negative because a rise in interest rates, other things remaining the same, may be expected to cause a fall in investment expenditures.

Taxes may also be incorporated in the equation for the *IS* curve. Taxes affect consumer spending according to the marginal propensity to consume. Thus, taxes reduce consumer spending by $-MPC(T)$. The sign of the tax term is negative because taxes affect consumer spending in the opposite direction. Including taxes in the *IS* equation yields:

$$Y = [C_o + MPC(Y) - MPC(T)] + [I_o - d(i)] + G.$$

This is the equilibrium equation for GNP, which can be rearranged as:

$$Y = [C_o - MPC(T) + I_o - d(i) + G] [1/(1-MPC)].$$

This is also the equation for the *IS* curve, where income is written as the dependent variable. The first set of brackets contains the constants of consumption, investment, taxes and government spending, along with the quantity of investment that responds to interest rate changes. The second set of brackets contains the multiplier. Thus, a change in any of the constants of spending will change *Y* by the change in spending times the multiplier. Furthermore, a change in interest rates will change investment spending (in the opposite direction) and yield a multiple change in income.

Graphically, changes in the constants of spending or in interest rates are shown as shifts in the aggregate demand curve and multiple shifts in the *IS* curve. A change in policy that affects *G* and/or *T* causes a change in the equilibrium level of GNP and a shift in the *IS* curve. A change in the *MPC* changes the slope of the aggregate demand curve, the multiplier that affects income, and the slope of the *IS* curve. How will a change in the responsiveness of investment to interest rates be shown on the *IS* curve?

The LM Curve. The *LM* curve comprises all levels of GNP and *i* at which the supply of money is equal to the demand for money. The demand for money *(L)* is a function of income and interest rates and can be expressed algebraically as follows:

$$L = I_t(Y) + I_p(Y) + I_s/(i),$$

where I_t, I_p, and I_s describe transactions, precautionary, and speculative demand for money. The last term in the demand for money equation is a ratio because of the inverse relationship between the demand for speculative money balances and the interest rate.

The supply of money *(M)* depends on the money base and the money multiplier:

$$M1 = B [(1+c)/(r + e + c + r_t t)].$$

When the money base is used fully to support money creation, the supply of money curve would be a vertical line at the quantity *M1*. Banks are not likely always to lend the maximum amount,

however. In fact, at lower interest rates their willingness to lend may fall short by larger amounts. Moreover, the public may withdraw more currency from the banks at lower interest rates, leaving less cash to satisfy bank reserve requirements.

The result is a money supply curve that slopes upward to the maximum permitted by the money base. Up to this maximum the supply of money may be written algebraically as

$$M = M_o + m(i),$$

where M_o is some minimum quantity of money independent of current actions of banks. The coefficient *m* reflects the responsiveness of banks and the public to changes in interest rates. The sign of the coefficient *m* is positive, because higher interest rates encourage banks to activate more of their excess reserves for lending; also higher interest rates reduce public holdings of currency and allow more to flow into bank reserves.

Equilibrium in the money sector can be expressed algebraically as equality between the demand for money and the money supply: $L = M1$. Substituting the equations for demand and supply yields:

$$L = (I_t + I_p)(Y) + I_s/i$$
$$= M_o + m(i) = M1,$$

up to the maximum quantity of money determined by

$$M1 = B [(1 + c)/(r + e + c + r_t t)].$$

Solving the Equations. In this section we will propose hypothetical values for the variables in the *IS* and *LM* equations and solve them simultaneously for estimates of *Y* and *i*.

In the *IS* equation:

$C_o = 200$, $MPC = .75$, $I_o = 50$,
$d = 10$, $T = 100$, $G = 150$.

In the *LM* equation:

$(I_t + I_p) = .10$, $I_s = 7.5$, $M_o = 300$,
$m = 35$, $B = 65$,

and the money multiplier is 5.

Equilibrium in both sectors can be determined algebraically by substituting the hypothetical values and solving the equations for *IS* and *LM* simultaneously:

IS: $Y = [C_o - MPC(T) + I_o - d(i) + G]$
$[1/(1 - MPC)]$
$= [200 - .75(100) + 50$
$- 10(i) + 150] [4]$
$= 325(4) - 40(i)$
and $Y = 1300 - 40(i)$

LM: $(I_t + I_p)(Y) + I_s/i$
$= M_o + m(i) =$
$.10(Y) + 7.5/i = 300 + 35(i)$

and $Y = 3000 + 350(i) - 75/i$.

Setting *IS = LM* yields:

$1300 - 40(i) = 3000 + 350(i) - 75/i$,

or

$O = 1700 + 390(i) - 75/i$
$= 1700(i) + 390 (i^2) - 75$.

This is a quadratic equation, which can be solved through use of the quadratic formula or a pocket calculator. Solving the equation for *i* yields: $i = .0437$. Then substituting in either of the income equations yields:

IS: $Y = 1300 - 40(.0437) = 1298.25$
$= \$1298.25$ billion

LM: $Y = 3000 + 350(.0437) - 75/.0437$
$= 1298.25 = \$1298.25$ billion.

The money supply is determined by

$M = M_o + m(i) = 300 + 350(.0437)$
$= 315.29 = \$315.29$ billion.

This is less than the maximum permitted with the existing money base:
$65(5) = 325 = \$325$ billion.

Of course, econometric forecasters use much more complicated models than this, with many more equations defining specific components of consumption, investment and government spending. Still, the fundamental principle is the same.

Question for Discussion

1. Change one of the values in the equations and compute the changes in GNP and *i*. Can you explain the logic behind your results?

Glossary of Terms

income-related demand for money. transactions and precautionary demand for money

interest-related demand for money. speculative demand for money

IS curve. a curve showing all combinations of income and interest rates at which product-sector equilibrium occurs

LM curve. a curve showing all combinations of income and interest rates at which money-sector equilibrium occurs

money-sector equilibrium. a condition in which the demand for money is equal to the money supply; equilibrium implies a particular combination of income and interest rates

product-sector equilibrium. a condition in which total spending for goods and services is equal to total production; equilibrium implies equality between planned investment spending and net saving

synthesis. a combination that includes the Keynesian model of income determination and the monetary theory of income

---

Summary of Important Ideas

1. The *IS* curve defines positions of equilibrium in the product sector. A combination of an interest rate and income off the curve will set in motion changes in spending and production that move the economy back to the curve.

2. Equilibrium in the money sector depends on equality between money supply and demand: $M = L = kPQ$. The holding rate k is based on transactions, precautionary and speculative motives for holding idle money balances.

3. The given money supply is divided between transactions and precautionary balances, on the one hand, and speculative balances, on the other. A larger share for transactions and precautionary balances implies high income and a high interest rate. A larger share for speculative balances implies a low interest rate and low income.

4. Corresponding interest rates and income levels are shown on an *LM* curve that slopes upward from left to right. Its position depends on the given supply of money and its velocity; its slope depends on the responsiveness of speculative holdings and commercial bank lending to changes in interest rates. Changes in any of the constants or in the community's financial behavior are shown as shifts in the *LM* curve.

5. A sloping *LM* curve implies a changing value of k and a changing velocity of turnover (V), complicating the relationship between M and PQ.

6. When *IS* and *LM* are drawn together, it is possible to locate the equilibrium level of income and an interest rate that satisfy equilibrium conditions in both the product and the money sectors.

Questions for Discussion and Research

1. Use the *IS* model to illustrate the process of movement to product-sector equilibrium. Select a point off the curve and explain the disequilibrium conditions that push the economy toward equilibrium.

2. Outline the factors that constitute the demand for idle money, as reflected in the holding rate k. What are the effects of a change in k? How are changes in k shown by the shape and position of the *LM* curve? What is the maximum possible level of k?

3. List the factors that together determine the supply of money. Explain the basis for a maximum quantity of money at some level of the interest rate.

4. Use the *LM* model to illustrate the process of movement to money-sector equilibrium. Select a point off the curve and explain the disequilibrium conditions that push the economy toward equilibrium.

Additional Readings

Brunner, Karl. "Commentary on Monetary Economics: An Interview with Karl Brunner." *Federal Reserve Bank of St. Louis Review* 60 (November 1978): 8–12.

Friedman, Milton. "A Monetary and Fiscal Framework for Economic Stability." In *Essays in Positive Economics.* Chicago: University of Chicago Press, 1966.

Friedman, Milton. *A Theoretical Framework for Monetary Analysis.* New York: National Bureau of Economic Research, 1971.

Goldfeld, Stephen M. "The Demand for Money Revisited." *Brookings Papers on Economic Activity* 3: 577–646. Washington, D.C., 1973.

Radecki, Lawrence J., and Cecily C. Garver. "The Household Demand for Money: Estimates from Cross-sectional Data." *Federal Reserve Bank of New York Quarterly Review* (Spring 1987): 29–34.

Schultze, Charles L. *Other Times, Other Places.* Washington, D.C.: Brookings Institution, 1986, Chap. 3.

Teigen, Ronald L. "The Demand for and Supply of Money." In *Readings in Money, National Income, and Stabilization Policy*, 3rd ed., edited by W. L. Smith and R. L. Teigen. Homewood, Ill.: Richard D. Irwin, 1965.

Tobin, James. "The Interest-Elasticity of Transactions Demand for Cash." *Review of Economics and Statistics* 38 (August 1956): 241–247.

———. "Keynes' Policies in Theory and Practice." *Challenge* (November/December 1983): 5–11.

Wenninger, John, and Lawrence J. Radecki.   "Financial Transactions and the Demand for M1." *Federal Reserve Bank of New York Quarterly Review* (Summer 1986): 24–29.

Yosh, Mehra.   "Recent Financial Deregulation and the Interest Elasticity of M1 Demand." *Economic Review of Federal Reserve Bank of Richmond* (July/August 1986): 13–24.

C H A P T E R

16

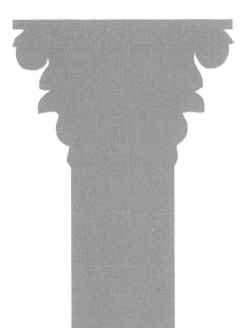

LEARNING OBJECTIVES

- To examine the composition of unemployment and its sources
- To understand the kinds of inflation and the relationship between inflation and unemployment
- To demonstrate the structure and recent behavior of the Phillips curve
- To understand the rational expectationists' explanation of inflationary unemployment
- To evaluate policies for correcting the problem of inflation

Unemployment and Inflation

"If you are a drowning man and you see a life raft with a hole in it, you will still jump, and this is a situation we are moving towards. Controls will not work, except very briefly. But when you are drowning, very briefly can look like a very good thing."

Otto Eckstein

If economics were like chemistry, we would not need the *IS-LM* model. Chemists have laboratories where they duplicate conditions in the environment and observe the effect of change. Without laboratories, economists have to use economic models.

The *IS-LM* model is particularly useful because it shows how individual decisions affect macroeconomic variables important to the nation as a whole: specifically, the level of employment and the general price level. It can be used to project the effect of changes in individual behavior, and it can show the expected result of policies designed to improve employment and the price level.

Why should we be concerned with these macroeconomic variables? As individuals we are naturally concerned with employment and prices, because they affect our jobs and purchasing power. Even more important, as citizens we are concerned about their consequences for *efficiency* in the way our nation uses resources, *equity* in the distribution of the benefits and costs of production, and the positive *externalities* that come with a prosperous economy. We are concerned about employment because resources are scarce; to fail to employ willing resources is grossly inefficient. We are concerned about prices because inflation changes the distribution of goods and services in ways that may be inequitable. We are concerned about both efficiency and equity because steady growth in production yields positive externalities in terms of better health, education, technical progress and improved standards of living.

In this chapter we will focus on employment and prices. We will use the *IS-LM* model to show how decisions in the private sector can push employment and prices to levels that may be inefficient and inequitable. Then we will discuss government policy that may or may not be effective in correcting the problem. Finally, we will suggest circumstances outside the model that may operate in the real environment to complicate policy-making.

Employment

Economists define the nation's labor force to include all persons over age 16 who work for pay or who are actively seeking work. The U.S. labor force has grown over time as a result of two causes. Population has grown faster than 1 percent a year over the past half century, and participation in the labor force has increased from 56 percent of the noninstitutionalized population in 1940 to 65 percent in 1986. The increase in participation is attributed primarily to females; 55 percent of adult women today are in the labor force versus only 28 percent in 1940. Among both males and females the participation rate of teenagers has increased by about 1 percent in the past 30 years. In contrast, the participation rate of adult men has declined, particularly middle-aged men who have chosen early retirement.

In 1986, the civilian labor force amounted to more than 120 million people. The size of the labor force is critical because it sets an upper limit to the productive capacity of the economy. With existing stocks of labor, land, capital equipment and entrepreneurial ability, a nation can produce a limited quantity of goods and services. Because our wants for goods and services are unlimited, it is important that we employ all available resources efficiently. In 1986, actual employment was only 110 million, for an unemployment rate of 7 percent. With more than 8 million willing workers unable to find jobs, the nation was failing to use its productive resources efficiently.

Even so, unemployment in 1986 was not as severe as that of 1982, when the economy was experiencing its worst recession since the Great Depression. (Unemployment reached 9.5 percent in 1982, and production for the year was down 2.5 percent.) Although 1984 brought recovery, unemployment was not expected to reach the low levels of the 1960s soon, if ever again. (Unemployment was only 3.5 percent in 1969.)

The problem of unemployment can be illustrated through the use of the *IS-LM* model. Figure 15–6 has been reproduced here as Figure 16–1. In Figure 16–1, income of $3,750 billion is associated with employment of 100 million workers of a total labor force of 125 million: an unemployment rate of 25/125, or 20 percent.

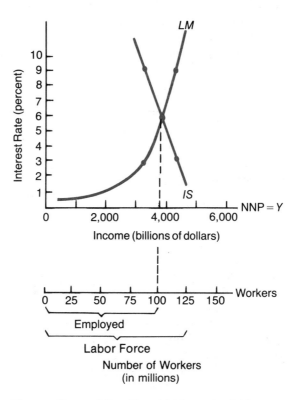

FIGURE 16–1 Total Output and Employment

The positions of the *IS* and *LM* curves yield an employment rate of 80 percent.

In Figure 16–1 the high level of unemployment is a result of the positions of the *IS* and *LM* curves. In the product sector, consumers are heavily in debt and worried about their job security; they have cut back purchases of durable goods and increased their saving to prepare for hard times ahead. Business firms have accumulated unplanned inventory and cut back new orders and production plans. They have evaluated proposals for new investments, in terms of the marginal efficiency of investment. Many investment proposals, whose rates of return have fallen below the cost of borrowing, have been put aside. With reduced spending from consumers and business firms, the *IS* curve has shifted far to the left.

In the money sector, the demand for money has increased relative to the existing money supply. Holders of transactions and precautionary balances have reduced their spending, so as to increase idle money balances to a larger fraction of income. Holders of speculative balances are worried about the risks of purchasing financial instruments; they have cashed in their securities to increase their idle money balances, in the hope that purchases of financial instruments will be more profitable in the future. The increased demand for idle money balances relative to the money supply has shifted the *LM* curve to the left, too. With both the *IS* and *LM* curves lying far to the left, the equilibrium level of production and income has fallen, and unemployment has increased.

Inflation

Unemployment has been a nagging problem of the 1980s. In the 1970s the more serious problem was inflation. Part of the reason for inflation was individual decisions regarding spending and the demand for idle money balances.

Increased Spending

Again the *IS-LM* model is useful. This time we would expect a high level of spending and a low demand curve for money to push the *IS* and *LM* curves far to the right.

One reason for the high level of spending in the 1970s was the age level of the population. A relatively low average age called for increased consumer spending for clothing, furniture, and health and recreation services. Increased consumer spending encouraged new business investment spending; housing construction in particular increased. Under these circumstances the *IS* curve shifted to the right.

Increased spending and higher incomes called for larger transactions and precautionary balances. When the money supply failed to grow fast enough to satisfy higher transactions and precautionary demand, the public reduced the fraction of income held in money balances (reduced k) and increased the rate of spending (increased V). The result was to shift the *LM* curve to the right, too. Still, the rightward shift in *LM* was not enough to avoid an increase in interest rates. As interest rates rose, people reduced the quantity of money held in speculative balances and used their funds to purchase financial instruments. Banks activated all their excess reserves to accommodate the increased demand for money.

Figure 16–2 illustrates the problem of inflation. In Figure 16–2 increased spending in the private sector has pushed *IS* to the right, so that equilibrium income is $4,700 billion. Production of $4,700 billion requires employment of 125 million workers, or 100 percent of the labor force. Zero unemployment is likely to cause prices to rise.

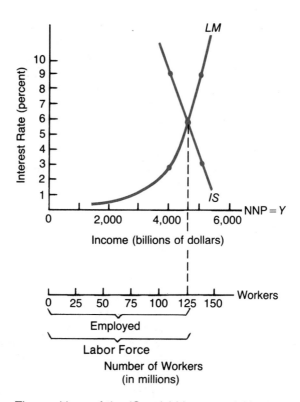

FIGURE 16–2   Total Output and Employment

The positions of the *IS* and *LM* curves yield an employment rate of 100 percent.

Employment, Productivity and Costs of Production

In general, high levels of employment are associated with rising prices. One reason is the effect of high employment on worker productivity. Worker productivity is defined as quantity of output per unit of work.

Over time, worker productivity in the United States has increased, in part because of improvements in other resources: more capital equipment and more advanced technology. Workers' skills have improved also, as have procedures for organizing and motivating workers. But advances in productivity have not come about regularly. Certain changes in worker productivity appear to be inversely related to the level of employment, rising when employment is falling and falling when the nation approaches full employment.

To understand this, consider the relationship between the number of workers in a factory and the quantity of fixed plant and equipment. When employment is low, each worker has more equipment to work with, and worker productivity is high. When the factory is fully employed, equipment is used more intensively, and worker productivity is less. (This result is associated with the principle of diminishing marginal productivity.) Moreover, as employment increases, there are fewer unemployed workers to choose among for expanding the work force; skill levels of additional workers are likely to be lower than those of currently employed workers. Lower worker productivity raises the cost of every unit of output produced.

There may be other cost increases at high levels of employment. Shortages of industrial commodities will allow suppliers to set higher prices. Managerial procedures may also become less efficient at very high levels of employment. When any of these production costs increases, the result is an increase in the price of the finished good or service.

Aggregate Demand and Aggregate Supply

The relationship between total output, employment and prices can be shown graphically, using the *IS-LM* model to determine equilibrium GNP and a model of product markets to determine the general price level. Look at Figure 16–3. At the top is the familiar *IS-LM* model. Below it is shown the relationship between the general price level and real output of goods and services up to the economy's maximum level of real production. The vertical axis measures the general price level around a price index of 1.00 for a particular base year. The horizontal axis measures real output of goods and services up to maximum total production at full employment. Thus, the horizontal axis extends from zero where employment and real output are zero, to production at full employment *Y*. At full employment, total production is the maximum quantity of real goods and services that could be produced with the nation's existing resources and technology.

The line labeled AS is aggregate supply. It shows the relationship between real production of goods and services and the general price level. Follow the AS curve along its horizontal portion to income and output of $3,750 billion. At income of $3,750 billion, employment is 80 percent. Employment of 80 percent involves no significant decrease in productivity and no cost pressures in labor or commodity markets. Thus, real production of goods and services can be carried on, with no tendency for the price index to rise above 1.00. But notice the behavior of prices at production and employment levels to the right of $3,750 billion. Beyond some level of production and employment further increases in total production mean rising employment and falling worker productivity. Competition for skilled work-

---

FIGURE 16-3 Total Output and the Price Index

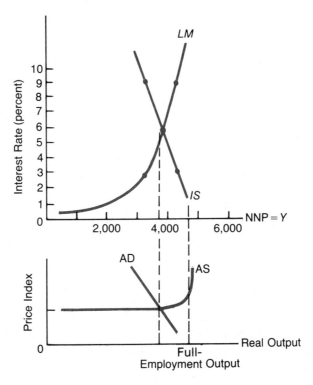

As real output approaches the full employment level
of output, the price index begins to rise.

ers and scarce materials causes some wages and materials prices to rise. All
these higher costs push prices up, so that additional production of real goods
and services is associated with a rising general price level. Finally, at the
economy's maximum real output of $4,700 billion (measured in constant
dollars) the potential price rise is infinite.

We have identified the AS curve in Figure 16-3 as aggregate supply.
Along its horizontal segment, production of real goods and services can
increase easily without a price increase. At some level of production, however, worker productivity begins to fall and shortages begin to develop.
Beyond this point, any further increase in production is accompanied by a
rise in the general price level. The aggregate supply curve begins to slope
upward. Maximum real production occurs at output of $4,700 billion, where
the aggregate supply curve becomes vertical. No further increases in production are possible—only increases in prices.

The actual level of prices is determined by the intersection of aggregate supply with aggregate demand, marked AD in Figure 16–3. Aggregate demand is derived from the *IS-LM* model. The aggregate demand curve reflects the spending decisions of individuals, business firms and governments in all the nation's product markets, at the current equilibrium level of income.

The aggregate demand curve shows the relationship between total purchases of real goods and services at the equilibrium level of income and the general price level. It slopes downward because of the effect of the price level on the real value of the money supply. A higher price level reduces the real value of M, so that fewer real goods and services can be purchased with the existing money supply. On the other hand, a lower price level increases the real value of M and increases the quantity of real goods and services associated with the equilibrium level of income.

The intersection of AS and AD marks equality between production and purchases of real goods and services. Thus the intersection determines the real quantity of output in the nation and the general price level. As long as AD intersects AS well short of the productive capacity of the economy, the price index remains 1.00. But as spending plans increase, the *IS* curve shifts to the right. At the new higher equilibrium income, more real goods and services will be bought at every price, and the aggregate demand curve will shift to the right as well. When aggregate demand comes to intersect aggregate supply along its rising segment, the price level will begin to rise.

Price fluctuations have been true of most business cycles in the past. Movements toward full production have generally brought on price increases; decreasing production with unemployment has generally brought decreasing prices or price stability. In both cases, the nation has suffered the inefficiency and inequity associated with abrupt changes in employment and prices and the negative externalities associated with uncertainty about the future.

We have described how shifts in AD can cause alternating periods of unemployment and inflation. Other factors have been at work to change AS. Advances in technology and investments in capital equipment have increased the nation's productive capacity. The result has been an increase in maximum real production over time, so that each year's aggregate supply curve remains horizontal over a wider range of real production than was true the year before. Our nation's increased productive capacity has enabled us to purchase larger quantities of many goods and services without price increases.

Regrettably, there is another possibility for the future. In future years new technology may not be applied so readily as in the past, and substantial new investment may not be undertaken. If productive capacity should fail to grow or even decline, the aggregate supply curve will turn upward at a lower level of real production, and price inflation will begin at a lower level of total spending. This possibility has become a major concern of the 1980s.

Demand-Pull and Cost-Push Inflation

Economists classify inflation according to its sources. Identifying the source of inflation is necessary before prescribing a cure. The inflation described above is classified as *demand-pull inflation* because it results from demand for real goods and services relative to productive capacity. If aggregate demand for goods and services grows faster than aggregate supply, there is upward pressure on prices. When markets become "tight," the price level rises.

Cost-push inflation is more often associated with the supply side of markets. On Figure 16–3 cost-push inflation would be shown as an upward shift of the entire AS curve, so that the horizontal segment lies somewhere above 1.00.

Cost-push inflation is sometimes the result of the use of market power to affect the prices and supplies of labor or materials. Labor unions insist on wage increases greater than increases in worker productivity; monopoly business firms set higher prices for industrial commodities; real or artificial scarcities raise the prices of vital materials or services. Higher prices in a few industries are built into production costs in many others. Finally, consumer goods prices rise, and workers insist on additional wage increases. Higher wages add another cost increase, so that cost-push inflation spreads widely throughout the economy.

Cost-push inflation may also result from conscious acts of government. In recent years, Congress has passed a host of laws designed to protect the environment and improve job health and safety. Agencies like the Environmental Protection Agency and the Occupational Safety and Health Administration have been established to set new standards and enforce them. Frequently, agency regulations require firms to install new equipment or new production processes to achieve long-range environmental and safety objectives. For many firms, such laws have meant higher production costs and higher prices for finished goods.

Environmental and safety regulations are generally defended on the grounds that they force business firms to include all the external costs of production in the prices of their output. The costs of polluted air and water, for example, would otherwise have to be borne by the community as a whole; and costs of industrial accidents would have to be borne by workers and their families. The goal of environmental and safety regulations is improved quality of life for citizens and workers. Still, such regulations increase costs of production, increase the general price level, and cause an upward shift in AS. It is important that environmental and safety regulations be cost effective; that is, that they achieve their goals at the lowest possible cost.

All these increases in costs of production can increase the general price level, whether or not aggregate demand is high.

The Phillips Curve

If prices tend to rise with employment, it follows that prices tend to fall with unemployment. We say there is normally an inverse relationship between prices and unemployment. A British economist, A. W. Phillips, was interested in the inverse relationship and collected data to illustrate their behavior over a century or so in Great Britain. As expected, he found a fairly consistent relationship: High unemployment was associated with low price inflation, and low unemployment with high inflation. The results of Phillips' investigation were presented on a graph called a *Phillips curve*, like the one in Figure 6–4.

A similar inverse relationship between prices and unemployment occurred in the United States over the years 1948 through 1969. During four business expansions, unemployment fell and the price level rose; during four recessions, unemployment increased and inflation fell.

Figure 16–5 is a graph of price and unemployment data in the United States for those years. The horizontal axis measures unemployment as a percent of the labor force, and the vertical axis measures price inflation. Each point represents unemployment and inflation for a particular year. The points are arranged around a downward sloping curve, with low inflation associated with high unemployment, and vice versa. During this period, the behavior of unemployment and inflation was consistent with Phillips' earlier study.

After 1969, the consistent behavior of prices and unemployment appeared to change. Increases in employment continued to be marked by increases in the general price level, but rising unemployment brought little decrease. Since 1969, the nation has experienced many years of high unemployment *and* high inflation. Points for these years have been added to Figure 16–5. These points lie farther and farther to the right of the curve, indicating higher levels of both variables.

Discomfort Index

The original Phillips curve illustrated the inverse relationship between price inflation and unemployment. High values for one variable were associated with low values for the other. If one value falls when the other rises, the sum of the two remains roughly constant. This was true of the 1960s but not true of the 1970s.

The late economist Arthur Okun suggested a way to measure the unemployment-inflation problem that he called the Discomfort Index. The Discomfort Index is the sum of inflation and unemployment for the year. A

FIGURE 16–4 A Phillips Curve

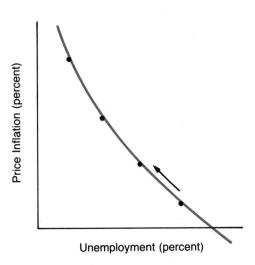

Lower levels of unemployment are
generally associated with higher price
inflation.

rising sum indicates worsening performance in both variables and a movement to the right off the Phillips curve. In fact, a series of years off the curve
like those of the 1970s may signal a shift of the entire curve. (Draw a line
through the points for the years 1974, 1979, 1977 and 1983 and the result
is an entirely new Phillips curve.) If policymakers are to deal with a new
Phillips curve, they must understand the reasons for the shift and design
policy to produce the most favorable results.

Changes in the Phillips Curve

What are we to make of the new inflation-unemployment relationship shown
in Figure 16–5? Is the Phillips curve dead? Or has it merely shifted to the
right? Must we become accustomed to higher levels of both variables? Or
can we find ways to move the curve back to its former position? Before
economists can answer such questions, they must first understand the reasons for the change. If the correct reasons can be identified, then correct
remedies may be decided on.

FIGURE 16–5   A Phillips Curve for the Years 1969 to 1985

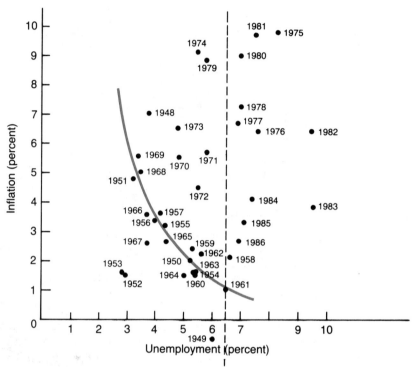

Points for the years since 1969 suggest the Phillips curve may have shifted to the right.

MONEY AND BANKING IN PRACTICE: LABOR SUPPLY AND PRICE INFLATION

The 1980s have been characterized by a gradual slowdown in the rate of price inflation, in part because of the severe recession early in the decade and increased foreign competition in markets for raw materials. From double-digit in- creases in consumer prices at the beginning of the decade, the Consumer Price Index rose only 1.1 percent in 1986. Falling price inflation has been as- sociated with an unemployment rate of around 7 percent.

In 1987, however, strains were appearing in labor markets that threatened a resumption of inflation. One reason was a change in consumer spending that called for different types of labor, some of which were in short supply. In particular, increasing consumer spending for services—including finance and insurance and medical and legal services—doubled the number of service workers in the nation in the space of only 15 years. Increasing demand for service workers came at a time when supply was not increasing as fast, so that labor costs began to rise.

In the past, many service industries benefited from employment of low-wage female workers, who constitute three-fifths of service workers in the above-named services compared with only one-third of manufacturing workers. Although the female labor force grew rapidly in the 1970s, growth slowed in the 1980s. In 1982 the unemployment rate of adult female workers fell below the male rate for the first time in 25 years.

It used to be that service industries could attract workers from declining manufacturing industries. But relatively low service wages make prospects poor for recruiting workers in the future. And finally, expanding service industries are not always located near areas of high unemployment.

Another factor in labor costs is the fact that labor productivity grows slowly (if at all) in service industries, adding to the cost pressures that arise from labor scarcity.

As a result of all these problems, service workers' wages have been increasing at an annual rate of almost 5 percent, compared with little more than 3 percent for manufacturing workers. Rising labor costs have pushed up the price of services by 5½ percent a year.

On the other side of this issue, inflation in the price of services may be overstated because of the difficulty of measuring improvements in service quality. Thus, the real output of services may be rising along with service prices.

Question for Discussion

1. How will conditions in this article affect the position and shape of the AS curve, drawn as a function of the general price level? How will they affect the Phillips curve?

The Effect of Changes in the Labor Force

One explanation for the shift in the Phillips curve has to do with the composition of the labor force. We have noted the increasing participation of the population in the labor force. Much of the increase has come through an influx of females and teenagers into labor markets. On the average, these workers differ from adult male workers in two ways. Their productivity is lower, and their job turnover is higher. Lower productivity may result from a generally lower commitment to a job. Because many of these workers have

TABLE 16–1   Unemployment Rates: 1986

	Percent
All Civilian Workers	7.0
Males	6.9
Aged 16–19 Years	19.0
Aged 20 Years and Over	6.1
Females	6.1
Aged 16–19 Years	17.6
Aged 20 Years and Over	6.2
Both Sexes	
Aged 16–19 years	18.3
White	6.0
Black and Other	13.1
Black	14.5
Experienced Workers	6.6
Married Men	4.4
Women Heads of Households	9.8

SOURCE: *Economic Report of the President*, January 1987.

not been the sole support of a family, they have not acquired the job skills appropriate to lifetime employment. Too, many females and teenagers have not been in the labor force long enough to gain job experience suitable for today's complex technology. Low productivity means that these workers will be the last hired, and that their output will cost more; hence higher unemployment will occur together with rising inflation.

High job turnover has the same effect. When women and teenage workers change jobs frequently because of family responsibilities or school schedules, employers must continually train new workers. Production costs are higher, adding to inflation even when there are large numbers of workers wanting jobs. In 1986, of the eight million people unemployed, almost half had never worked before or were returning to the labor force after an absence. Many of these were teenagers. Table 16–1 gives recent employment data. Note the relatively high unemployment rates of teenagers. What other groups experience relatively high rates of unemployment?

The Natural Rate of Unemployment

The growing number of high-unemployment groups in the labor force has led some economists to a new definition of unemployment. According to the new definition, there is some *natural rate of unemployment* below which unemployment cannot fall. Increased demand for workers will only drive up the wages of the more skilled workers, increasing production costs and prices without reducing unemployment very much. For these economists, full employment (zero unemployment) occurs at the level of employment that just excludes the natural rate.

In Figure 16–5 a vertical line has been drawn at a rate of 6.5 percent. This is the rate below which some economists believe unemployment cannot fall but at which inflation will increase.

The existence of a certain natural rate of unemployment does not necessarily cause serious economic hardship. High unemployment among females and teenagers may pose fewer problems than unemployment among males, who are more frequently the heads of households. (This is not to deny the serious problems faced by the growing numbers of female-headed households and those dependent, at least in part, on teenagers' wages.) Short periods of unemployment may be healthy for some young workers who want to change jobs, gain experience, upgrade job skills and improve opportunities for advancement.

Some economists recommend policies to increase the productivity and reduce the job turnover of workers, reduce the natural rate of unemployment, and shift the Phillips curve back to the left. Some suggested policies are job counseling and training programs and efforts to improve job satisfaction for low-skilled workers. A less politically acceptable proposal is to reduce the various types of income-support programs that prolong the job search for some workers, adding to the unemployment rate and keeping wages and prices high.

The Effect of Changes in Production Costs

The rightward shift of the Phillips curve has another explanation. It suggests that higher levels of inflation will continue to be associated with every level of unemployment.

We have discussed the effect of low worker productivity on production costs and prices, but we should not neglect the possibility of lower productivity of capital resources. In fact, many of the environmental and safety laws discussed earlier have reduced the productivity of capital equipment and reduced the profitability of capital investment. Some firms have hesitated to invest in new equipment that may be made obsolete by still more legislation in the future. As a result, advances in technology have slowed somewhat from the fast pace of the 1960s.

On the inflation side, there are other explanations for the generally higher inflation associated with every level of unemployment. Higher energy costs receive much of the blame. Energy costs are a part of the price of virtually every good or service. Higher food, housing and medical costs are also at fault. In every case, higher consumer prices are translated into cost-of-living wage increases for workers throughout all of industry. Table 16–2 shows price indexes for various years, beginning with the base year 1967. For each year compare the price indexes for particular goods and services with the Consumer Price Index as a whole. What category of good or service contributed most to price inflation over each period?

TABLE 16–2 Consumer Price Indexes for Selected Expenditure Classes

Year	Food and Beverages	Shelter	Fuel and Utilities	Trans-portation	Medical Care	All Items
1967	100.0	100.0	100.0	100.0	100.0	100.0
1968	103.6	104.8	101.3	103.2	106.1	104.2
1969	108.8	113.3	103.6	107.2	113.4	109.8
1970	114.7	123.6	107.6	112.7	120.6	116.3
1971	118.3	128.8	115.0	118.6	128.4	121.3
1972	123.2	134.5	120.1	119.9	132.5	125.3
1973	139.5	140.7	126.9	123.8	137.7	133.1
1974	158.7	154.4	150.2	137.7	150.5	147.7
1975	172.1	169.7	167.8	150.6	168.6	161.2
1976	177.4	179.0	182.7	165.5	184.7	170.5
1977	188.0	191.1	202.2	177.2	202.4	181.5
1978	206.3	210.4	216.0	185.5	219.4	195.4
1979	228.5	239.7	239.3	212.0	239.7	217.4
1980	248.0	281.7	278.6	249.7	265.9	246.8
1981	267.3	314.7	319.2	280.0	294.5	272.4
1982	278.2	337.0	350.8	291.5	328.7	289.1
1983	284.4	344.8	370.3	298.4	357.3	298.4
1984	295.1	361.7	387.3	311.7	379.5	311.1
1985	302.0	382.0	393.6	319.9	403.1	322.2
1986	311.8	402.9	384.7	307.5	433.5	328.4

In addition to price increases for food, energy, housing and medical care, other price increases may be caused by what economists call administered prices. Administered prices are prices not dictated by market conditions but by agreements among buyers and sellers. Administered prices are most likely when a few large groups decide among themselves to fix prices. This is true both in organized markets for labor and in markets for industrial commodities.

Vigorous enforcement of the antitrust laws can help prevent outright price fixing, but *similar* prices achieved without actual agreement among firms are difficult to prevent. In some industries, more competitive pricing may be encouraged by removing barriers to imports of competing commodities produced abroad. Perhaps a more difficult problem is that of *administered wages*: agreements between workers and employers for wage increases to offset the effects of inflation.

The Effect of Wage-Price Flexibility

We have described the inefficiencies, inequities and negative externalities associated with unemployment and price inflation. Economists look for

FIGURE 16–6a Equilibrium in *IS-LM* Model

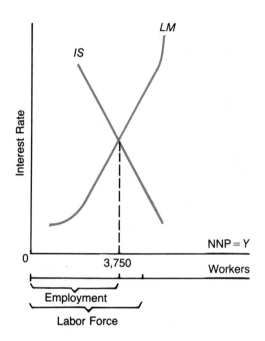

At the current equilibrium level, unemployment is 20 percent.

FIGURE 16–6b Automatic Change in *IS* and *LM*

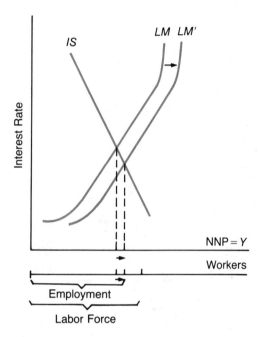

Falling wages and prices increase the real value of the money supply.

ways to correct such problems, ideally with a minimum of government intervention in our free market economy. Some economists look for automatic forces within free markets that would work to correct the problem of unemployment without any sort of government intervention at all. We have referred to their philosophy as a philosophy of laissez-faire, from the French phrase for "let alone."

The theory of laissez-faire depends on wage-price flexibility—in the downward direction as well as up. The effect of wage-price flexibility is illustrated on the *IS-LM* model in Figures 16–6a to 16–6d. Equilibrium with income of $3,750 billion and unemployment of 20 percent is shown in Figure 16–6a. According to laissez-faire economists, substantial unemployment will eventually cause wages to fall. With lower wages, costs of production will fall, and prices will fall as well.

Lower prices have two effects on the *IS-LM* model. The most obvious effect is to increase the real value of the money supply *M*. The real value

FIGURE 16–6c Automatic Change in *IS* and *LM*

FIGURE 16–6d Automatic Change in *IS* and *LM*

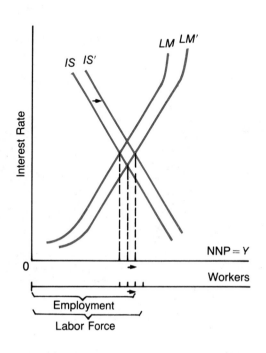

The higher value of savings causes an increase in consumer and investment spending.

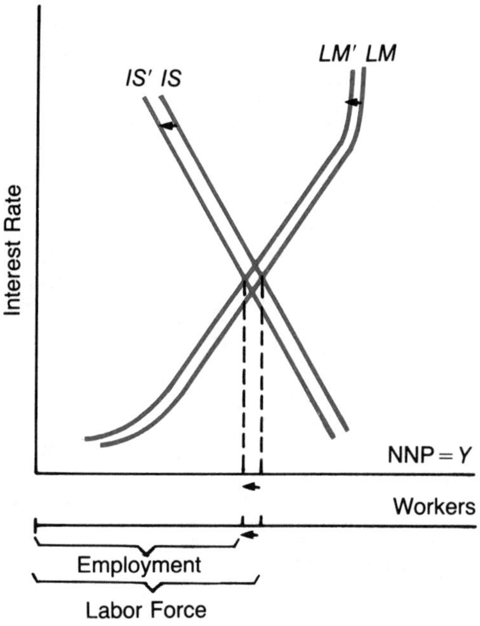

Rising wages and prices cause *LM* and *IS* to shift to the left.

of the money supply is its purchasing power in terms of current prices, M/P, where P is the current price index. When P falls, the real value of the money supply increases.

An increase in the real value of the money supply has the same effect as an actual increase in the money supply; that is, to shift the *LM* curve to the right. The reason is an increase in the real money supply relative to the demand for money balances: thus $M/P > kY$. When the real value of the money supply exceeds the demand for money, holders of the excess money use it to increase their spending or to purchase financial instruments. Incomes rise and interest rates fall, so that the *LM* curve shifts to the right. The rightward shift continues until there is no further tendency for wages and prices to fall. Income stabilizes at full employment.

These conditions are shown on Figure 16–6b.

Downward price flexibility may also affect the *IS* curve. Lower prices increase the real value of savings accumulated in years past. Consumers become wealthier as their dollar-denominated assets increase in real purchasing power. This is an example of Pigou's real-wealth effect, discussed in Chapter 13.

Increased consumer wealth enables families to increase their current spending, and the consumption function shifts upward. Higher spending rates may also occur in the business sector. Business firms experience lower production costs, which increase the expected profitability of new investment. An increase in the marginal efficiency of investment (MEI) means increased investment spending. Thus, the drop in wages and prices may also call for a rightward shift of the *IS* curve and a further increase in the equilibrium level of GNP.

This result is shown in Figure 16–6c.

Laissez-faire economists believe similar adjustments will take place to correct an equilibrium level that is too high. If the equilibrium level of income is too high, spending may be too high for price stability. As prices rise, the real value of the money supply falls: *M/P* falls and the *LM* curve shifts to the left. In this case, the Pigou effect reduces the value of accumulated savings, reducing consumer and business spending and causing the *IS* curve to shift to the left. The final result is an equilibrium level of income at which employment is just high enough to maintain price stability.

Both these latter conditions are shown on Figure 16–6d.

Some Criticisms

In practice, the conditions underlying laissez-faire theory may not exist. Downward wage-price flexibility does not work when wage and price contracts are established in advance to cover several years. Workers who have sufficient market power can resist a reduction in wage rates. Even if prices were to fall, consumers might not increase their spending if they believe prices might fall still further.

The main problem with laissez-faire theory is the long time required for automatic adjustments to have the desired effect. This is especially true in recession, when there is substantial unemployment.

When wages and prices are slow to fall, the economy may suffer severely before the curves finally shift to the right, stimulating increased spending and causing income and employment to rise. The social and political strains caused by unemployment or inflation may make laissez-faire policy unacceptable.

MONEY AND BANKING IN PRACTICE:
THE KEYNESIANS VERSUS THE CLASSICAL ECONOMISTS:
SUPPLY-SIDE ECONOMICS

We have emphasized that economics is an evolving science, in which new ideas are constantly being offered and old ones resurrected or discarded. We have compared the process of debate in economics with the laboratory experiments of the natural sciences.

The debate between the Classical economists and the Keynesians is the most vigorous in all of economics. It involves high levels of scholarship, as well as generous doses of political philosophy. To explain fully the positions of both groups would be impossible here, but some general observations can be made. One important distinction involves the emphasis of the Classical economists on the supply side of economics and the Keynesians on demand.

Classical economists tend to assume that the supply of goods and services is determined by *real factors* in the economic environment: the quantity of labor together with labor skills and motivation, the level of technology and available capital resources, and other resources along with cultural and organizational characteristics of the society as a whole. Real factors establish a production function that relates total output to employment. Then, full employment establishes a maximum level of total output for distribution among consumers, business firms and government. Per capita living standards depend on the ratio between total output at full employment and total population.

Figure 16–7a shows a production function. Levels of employment *(N)* are measured along the horizontal axis, and real production *(Y/P)* is measured on the vertical axis. As employment increases, total production increases at a decreasing rate. The reason is the principle of diminishing marginal product when additional variable resources are applied to a fixed stock of capital resources. Figure 16–7b is a graph of labor markets in which demand for labor is determined by the marginal product of labor *(MP_L)*, and supply reflects workers' willingness to supply labor at various *real wage* rates *(w/P)*. Equilibrium in labor markets determines the level of total employment at *N'* and total production at *Y/P'* in Figure 16–7a.

In the Classical view, *monetary factors* do not affect real production. Monetary factors only affect the general level of prices, wages and interest rates, leaving their *relative* values unchanged. An increase in money, for instance, leads to price and wage increases, but real wages (and living standards) remain constant. Employment does not change, and output continues at the level determined by the current production function.

Money, according to Classical economists, is only a "veil" obscuring

FIGURE 16–7a A Production Function

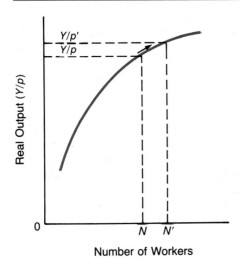

Number of Workers

FIGURE 16–7b The Market for Labor

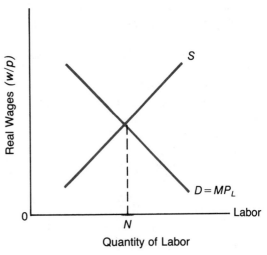

Quantity of Labor

FIGURE 16–7c An Increase in the Supply of Labor

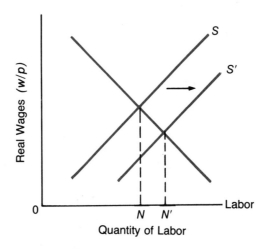

Quantity of Labor

real variables; therefore, an active monetary policy would only disturb monetary variables.

Look again at Figure 16–7b. An increase in prices has no effect on workers' marginal product and the real wage;

neither does a price increase affect the supply of labor, because workers will understand the effect of price increases on real wages and insist on proportional increases in money wages. Thus, changes in the money supply have no actual effect on employment and real production.

Keynesian economists focus on aggregate demand for goods and services, reasoning that employment and real production might be affected by the total level of consumer, business and government spending. In this view, price and wage flexibility do not occur so smoothly that real wages do not change. Workers will be slow to insist on proportional changes in money wages; then, lower real wages will push the supply of labor curve in Figure 16–7b downward as in Figure 16–7c, and employment will increase to the equilibrium shown at N'. Higher employment moves the economy along the production function (Figure 16–7a) to a higher level of total output at Y/P'. A decrease in aggregate demand has the opposite effect; prices fall faster than wages, increasing real wages and reducing total employment. Keynesian economists favor *demand management* policies to maintain a level of total spending consistent with the nation's employment goals.

These two points of view represent contrasting positions on the aggregate supply curve shown on Figure 16–3. The Classical equilibrium is shown by the vertical segment of aggregate supply where the nation experiences full employment and full production. Along this segment, changes in the supply of money do not affect the total quantities of goods and services but cause wide

fluctuations in the price level. The Keynesian equilibrium is shown along the horizontal and upward-sloping segments of aggregate supply, where changes in the money supply affect employment and production without wide fluctuations in the price level.

For roughly a half century, Keynesian economics dominated policy decisions. There were some successes and some failures. Demand management worked well to increase employment and production, but the cost was periods of excessive price inflation. Over the past decade, fears of inflation have further complicated economic policy; cost-of-living adjustments have been included in many labor contracts to keep real wages from falling in inflation, so that the labor supply curve has not shifted downward. Employment has grown more slowly than the labor force, worsening the problem of unemployment at the same time that prices have been rising. Rising costs of production have pushed the aggregate supply curve upward.

Lately, economic policymakers have become so discouraged with Keynesian economics that they have turned again to the supply side and to the policy proposals of the Classical economists. The success of Classical policy depends on wage-price flexibility, competition in resource and product markets, and policies to affect the real variables in the economic environment. Thus, *supply-side economists* recommend policies to moderate the bargaining power of unions and the price-fixing power of business firms. Most important, supply-side economists favor programs to increase the productive capacity of the nation's economy: improvements in labor skills, removal of unnecessary regulations governing resource use, and tax incentives to increase and modernize capital equipment. Programs like these require the enthusiastic cooperation of labor, business management and government, as well as support from the nation's financial sector. Our living standards, our international competitive position and perhaps our way of life depend on their success.

Questions for Discussion

1. What other policies would help invigorate the supply side of our nation's economy?

2. Cite current examples of programs that aim at improving the productivity capacity of U.S. industries.

Glossary of Terms

administered prices. prices that result from market power rather than from the free operation of supply and demand

cost-push inflation. price inflation that results from increases in the costs of producing output

demand management. policies that seek to affect the equilibrium level of income through manipulation of total spending

demand-pull inflation. price inflation that results from spending beyond the productive capacity of the economy

natural rate of unemployment. a level of unemployment that includes the least productive and least stable portions of the labor force

Phillips curve. a line graph showing the historical relationship between unemployment and price inflation

real wages. wages corrected for inflation; the real purchasing power of wages

supply-side economics. emphasis on the real factors that determine a nation's productive capacity; a distrust of policies that emphasize consumption relative to investment

Summary of Important Ideas

1. Independent decisions of spenders, savers, banks, government and the Federal Reserve may produce unacceptable levels of unemployment or inflation. Too little spending aggravates unemployment, because de-

mand for goods and services is low. Too little saving aggravates inflation, because productivity falls when demand for goods and services pushes against productive capacity.

2. The tendency toward price inflation is shown by an aggregate supply curve that slopes upward as the economy approaches full employment.

3. Technological advances have the effect of increasing the level of output at which price increases begin. The exercise of market power has the effect of shifting upward the entire aggregate supply curve. Environmental and safety regulations have the same result.

4. The historical relationship between unemployment and inflation is shown on a Phillips curve. Movements in one variable have generally been accompanied by opposite movement in the other.

5. The inverse relationship between unemployment and inflation has broken down in recent years, complicating the job of economic policy-making for bringing about more acceptable levels of both variables. Changes in the current relationship are attributed to: the changing composition of the labor force with lower average productivity, environmental regulations that reduce the productivity of capital, higher energy costs of production, and administered pricing in concentrated industries. Each case would require specific policy actions to correct.

6. In recent years some disillusionment with Keynesian demand-side theories of income determination has led to greater emphasis on supply-side theories. Supply-side economists recommend policies to affect the real factors that contribute to increased productive capacity.

Questions for Discussion and Research

1. Explain the derivation of the aggregate demand and aggregate supply curves. What factors determine their shapes? How can the curves be used to show demand-pull and cost-push inflation? How are demand-pull and cost-push inflation shown on the Phillips curve?

2. What current economic conditions tend to increase the natural rate of unemployment? Cite specific examples.

3. Explain why wage and price increases may be (a) ineffective and (b) inefficient as protection against inflation.

4. Distinguish between demand-side theories and supply-side theories for explaining economic behavior. How do their fundamental assumptions differ and what types of policies would they support?

Additional Readings

Berman, Peter I. "The Basic Cause of Inflation, I." *Across the Board* 14 (November 1977): 23–27.

Berman, Peter I. "The Basic Cause of Inflation, II." *Across the Board* 15 (May 1978): 67–70.

Bosworth, Barry P. "Conflicts in Economic Policy." *Economic Outlook U.S.A.* 7 (Spring 1980): 27–29.

Chandler, Lester V., and Stephen M. Goldfeld. *The Economics of Money and Banking.* 7th ed. New York: Harper and Row, 1977, Chap. 16.

McCulloch, J. Huston. *Money and Inflation: A Monetarist Approach.* New York: Academic Press, 1975, Chap. 6.

McNees, Stephen K. "The Phillips Curve: Forward or Backward Looking?" *New England Economic Review*, Federal Reserve Bank of Boston (July/August 1979): 46–54.

Marshal, Ray. "The Inflation Battle: Winning Labor's Support." *Challenge* 21 (January/February 1979): 18–25.

Okun, Arthur M. "The Invisible Handshake and the Inflation Process." *Challenge* 22 (January/February 1980): 5–12.

Osterman, Paul. "Youth, Work, and Unemployment." *Challenge* 21 (May/June 1978): 65–69.

Rappoport, Peter. "Inflation in the Service Sector." *Federal Reserve Bank of New York Quarterly Review* (Winter 1987): 35–45.

Spechler, Martin C. "Big Inflations Need Potent Cures." *Challenge* (November/December 1986): 26–32.

Stein, Herbert. "Price-Fixing as Seen by a Price-Fixer." *Across the Board* 15 (December 1978): 32–43.

Tatom, John A. "Does the Stage of the Business Cycle Affect the Inflation Rate?" *Federal Reserve Bank of St. Louis Review* 60 (September 1978): 7–15.

Trebing, Michael E. "The Economic Consequences of Wage-Price Guidelines." *Federal Reserve Bank of St. Louis Review* 60 (December 1978): 2–7.

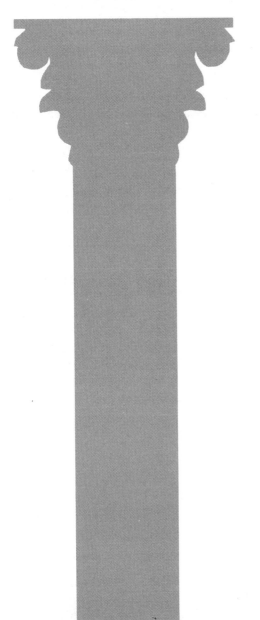

C H A P T E R

17

LEARNING OBJECTIVES

■ To understand the division of
responsibility among various levels
of government
■ To examine the source and
historical behavior of government
deficits and surpluses
■ To see how government budgets
affect the money supply
■ To consider the significance of
government debt
■ To look at the procedure for
determining the government budget
and its predicted course over the
coming decade

The Effects of Government on the *IS-LM* Model

"If each of us was consistently 'neither borrower nor lender,' as Polonius advised, no one would ever need to violate the revered wisdom of Mr. Micawber. But if the prudent among us insist on running and lending surpluses, some of the rest of us are willy-nilly going to borrow to finance budget deficits."

James Tobin

This chapter describes the activities performed by government and the ways those activities affect the equilibrium level of employment and the general price level.

Activities performed by government call for an allocation of resources away from private purposes and toward purposes of the society at large. A shift in government's responsibility reflects a shift in the priorities of voters: a shift from private to public or a shift from state and local governments to the federal government. Whenever such a shift occurs, it is important to make sure that the change in government responsibilities is an efficient change and that it does not cause inequities or negative externalities that offset the gain in efficiency. Thus, a policy that increases employment is intended to make production more efficient. But if it causes inflation, it may distort the distribution of goods and services in ways we consider inequitable. Rampant inflation may break apart established patterns of production and lead to other negative externalities like fraud and crime.

Citizens must evaluate the projected consequences of government policies and judge whether the gains in efficiency are worth the costs.

The Historical Role of Government

In the beginning, governments were supposed to do for citizens the things citizens could not do for themselves: first, to protect life and property and to enforce contracts so that buying and selling could be carried on peacefully;

then, to provide a standard money so as to encourage production for exchange; eventually, to operate certain social services collectively—namely education, health and safe water systems—so as to ensure maximum levels of well-being for the community.

Although certainly significant, these functions did not require big government in the sense we know it today. In recent years, we have asked government to take on broader responsibilities for managing the nation's economy: providing jobs and income supplements to the unemployed and transferring income and wealth through tax policies. Whereas many community services can be provided by state and local governments, broad macroeconomic responsibilities like these require actions of the federal government.

In this chapter we are concerned with the economic functions of government at the state, local and federal levels. We will look first at the tax and spending powers of governments and then at the impact of taxes and government spending on income and employment. We will consider the implications of government borrowing for the money supply and, finally, projections of government's influence over the coming years.

Economic Responsibilities of State and Local Governments

Maintaining the proper balance between state and local responsibilities and federal responsibilities has always been an important objective of our political system. From the beginning, Americans have feared excessive government and resisted efforts to change the power balance in favor of more centralized control. In general, we prefer to deal with social needs at the lowest level at which they can be handled efficiently. We encourage citizens to express their preferences for services locally and to accept the responsibility themselves for financing them.

This means that most civilian services are provided by state and local governments: education, sanitation, police and fire protection, health, and highway maintenance. Our increasingly urban and affluent population has been demanding more and better services of this type to improve the quality of life. Moreover, lately our population has included more young people and more elderly, increasing the need for comprehensive education and health services provided by state and local governments.

In recent years, citizens have begun to complain about the high state and local taxes needed to finance such services. Voter resistance to new taxes has forced cuts in services in some areas and a reduction in quality in others. Lacking local support, some social services may ultimately become the sole responsibility of the federal government, constituting a major gain in its power over local affairs. Whether the change will bring more efficiency, equity and positive externalities is a subject for political debate.

Economic Responsibilities of the Federal Government

The great increase in the responsibilities of the federal government began in 1946, when the United States was emerging from almost two decades of political and economic turmoil. During the 1930s, the Great Depression had held production far below capacity and deprived millions of workers of jobs and income for their families. Then World War II depleted much of our nation's capital resources and distorted production toward military purposes. When peace came, Congress strongly felt its obligation to use its powers to establish a more efficient level of production and employment.

The Employment Act of 1946 gave this responsibility the force of law. In effect, the law required Congress to use its tax and spending powers to regulate total spending in such a way as to enhance economic stability. The use of government tax and spending to stabilize economic activity is called *fiscal policy*. (We will have more to say about fiscal policy later.) Consistent with its new responsibility, Congress called on the executive branch to carry out the budget decisions of Congress. Each year, the President must report to Congress on the state of the economy and on progress toward solution of the nation's economic problems in the *Economic Report of the President*.

By 1978, new problems seemed to call for amendments to the Employment Act. The Full Employment and Balanced Growth Act (Humphrey–Hawkins Act) passed that year requires the President to set specific goals for such variables as employment, production and prices, and to establish government spending and revenue targets to achieve the goals. The President meets regularly with the Federal Reserve Board and the Joint Economic Committee of Congress to coordinate government policies toward these goals.

The Impact of Government Budgets

In order to carry out their various responsibilities, governments must collect taxes and make payments. The impact on income, employment and prices depends on the size of tax revenues (*T*) and government purchases (*G*).

Government Outlays

Government outlays comprise what government pays out: payments for purchases of goods and services as well as transfer payments that supplement the incomes of particular groups.

Government *purchases* include both what government employees produce (from education to flu shots) and what governments purchase from private firms (from jet planes to copying machines). In 1986, the total of government production and government purchases amounted to about 20 percent of GNP. *Transfer payments* include payments to the elderly, the unemployed, the sick, and the disabled. The growth in Social Security and new programs like Medicaid and food stamps have increased transfer payments to about half of the total government budget. Total government outlays, including transfer payments, were about 33 percent of GNP in 1986. (For computing GNP, government expenditures constitute the value G. Transfer payments appear as negative taxes for computing taxes, T. Thus, tax revenues collected minus transfer payments paid equals net taxes, T.)

Wars in the 1940s, 1950s and 1960s and costly social programs of the 1960s increased federal outlays relative to state and local outlays. During the 1970s, state and local spending increased faster than federal outlays, in part because of the baby boom, which increased education needs, and because of the move of the population toward urban areas, which increased demand for city services.

Tax Revenues

Tax revenues collected at various levels of government depend on the *base* to which the tax is applied. The base for the greatest federal tax revenues is income. In 1986 federal personal income tax payments were $356 billion and corporate income taxes were $83 billion. Contributions to Social Security were $324 billion, and other federal taxes brought in $52 billion. Income taxes are *progressive*; that is, the tax rate increases with the size of the base income. Social Security taxes are *regressive*; because there is a maximum base for Social Security taxes ($43,800 in 1986), the fraction of income paid in tax diminishes at higher incomes.

The base for the greatest state and local tax revenues is retail sales, with property a close second. Retail sales taxes brought in $126 billion in 1986 and property taxes $104 billion. Personal and corporate taxes brought in $89 billion, and other fees were $172 billion. About one-fifth of state and local revenues is grants-in-aid from the federal government: $106 billion in 1986.

The base for federal taxes has been rising over the years, raising federal tax revenues relative to revenues of state and local governments. In contrast, the property tax base has been shrinking in some cities as a result of the movement of industry from the city and because much of city land has been taken out of the tax base for building highways, rapid transit systems, and civic centers. Retail sales tax revenues tend to fluctuate with changes in consumer spending during business cycles. Federal grants-in-aid have been shrinking, too, down from the mid-1970s when the federal government was

TABLE 17-1 Federal Government Receipts and Expenditures, 1986

	Billions of Dollars	Percentage of Total
RECEIPTS		
Personal Tax and Nontax Receipts	396.5	41
Corporate Profits Tax Accruals	130.2	13
Indirect Business Tax and Nontax		
Accruals	56.6	6
Contributions for Social Insurance	384.8	40
Total	968.1	100
EXPENDITURES		
Purchases of Goods and Services:		
National Defense	301.0	28
Other Purchases	93.8	9
Transfer Payments	427.3	39
Grants-in-Aid to State and Local		
Governments	100.0	9
Net Interest Paid	140.5	13
Subsidies less Current Surplus of		
Government Enterprises	26.1	2
Total	1,088.6	100
Government Deficit	120.5	

more generous. Table 17–1 shows receipts and expenditures of governments in 1986.

Deficits and Surpluses

The macroeconomic effect of government budgets depends on the difference between total government expenditures (G) and net taxes collected at all levels of government (T). A high level of expenditures relative to net taxes produces a *deficit* in the government sector:

$$G - T = \text{Deficit.}$$

A high level of net taxes relative to expenditures produces a *surplus*:

$$T - G = \text{Surplus.}$$

Since 1969, the federal budget has consistently been in deficit and state and local budgets in surplus. Total government surpluses and deficits during the 1970s and 1980s are shown in Table 17–2.

If the combined government budget is in surplus, government exerts a contractionary effect on economic activity. Government has been contractionary in years of economic peaks: 1973 and 1979. If the combined budget

TABLE 17–2   Federal and State and Local Government Receipts and Expenditures, 1970–1986 (billions of dollars)

Year	Federal Government			State and Local Government			
	Receipts	Expenditures	Deficits/Surpluses*	Receipts	Expenditures	Deficits/Surpluses*	Total
1970	195.4	207.8	− 12.4	135.8	134.0	+ 1.8	− 10.6
1971	202.7	224.8	− 22.0	153.6	151.0	+ 2.6	− 19.5
1972	232.2	240.0	− 16.8	179.3	165.8	+13.5	− 3.4
1973	263.7	269.3	− 5.6	196.4	182.9	+13.5	+ 7.9
1974	293.9	305.5	− 11.6	213.1	205.9	+ 7.2	− 4.3
1975	294.9	364.2	− 69.4	239.6	235.2	+ 4.5	− 64.9
1976	340.1	393.7	− 53.5	270.1	254.9	+15.2	− 38.4
1977	384.1	430.1	− 46.0	300.1	273.2	+26.9	− 19.1
1978	441.1	470.7	− 29.3	330.3	301.3	+28.9	− .4
1979	505.0	521.2	− 16.1	355.3	327.7	+27.6	+ 11.5
1980	553.8	615.1	− 61.3	390.0	363.2	+26.8	− 34.5
1981	639.5	703.3	− 63.8	425.6	391.4	+34.1	− 29.7
1982	635.3	781.2	−145.9	449.4	414.3	+35.1	−110.8
1983	659.9	835.9	−176.0	487.7	440.2	+47.5	−128.6
1984	726.5	896.5	−170.0	540.8	472.4	+68.5	−101.5
1985	786.8	984.9	−198.0	577.5	515.8	+61.7	−136.3
1986	826.2	1,030.2	−204.0	618.8	557.9	+60.8	−143.1

*Deficits (−) and surpluses (+).

is in deficit, the effect is expansionary, most strongly so in recession years like 1975 and 1983.

Saving-Investment Equilibrium

If combined federal, state and local budgets are in surplus ($T > G$), the government sector is said to be a net saver. If budgets are in deficit ($T < G$), the government is a net dissaver. Government saving or dissaving combines with personal and business saving to yield total saving for the nation's economy:

$$S + T - G.$$

If the expression ($S + T - G$) is positive, the economy as a whole is experiencing net saving; if negative, net dissaving.

All these circumstances can be shown on the *IS* curve. Remember that points on the *IS* curve show positions of equality between planned investment and total saving:

$$I_p = S + T - G.$$

This relationship may be stated another way:

$$I_p - S = T - G.$$

The expression on the left measures the excess of planned investment over saving in the private sector, a value we will call net dissaving. The expression on the right measures the excess of tax revenues over government spending in the government sector, a value we will call net saving. Thus, we can say that points on the *IS* curve show positions of equality between net dissaving in the private sector and net saving in the government sector. In practice, this means that the excess of planned investment over private saving ($I_p - S > 0$) is financed by a surplus in the government budget ($T - G > 0$). Government uses its excess tax revenues to pay off government debt, and the funds are loaned instead to private investors.

If both sides of the saving-investment equation are negative, the left side measures net saving in the private sector: $I_p - S < 0$ means net saving. The right side measures net dissaving in the government sector: $T - G < 0$ means net dissaving. Points on the *IS* curve show positions of equality between net saving in the private sector and net dissaving in the government sector. In this case, the excess of private saving over investment is loaned to government for spending in excess of tax revenues. These conditions are summarized in Table 17–3.

TABLE 17–3   Equilibrium Conditions in Product Markets

Private Sector	*Government Sector*
1. $I_p - S > 0$	$T - G > 0$
Net private dissaving: a deficit in private budgets	Net government saving: a surplus in government budgets
2. $I_p - S < 0$	$T - G < 0$
Net private saving: a surplus in private budgets	Net government dissaving: a deficit in government budgets
3. $I_p - S = 0$	$T - G = 0$
Zero net private saving: balanced budget	Zero net government saving: balanced budget

---

Satisfying either of the conditions in the table yields equilibrium in the product sector and defines the *IS* curve. Because planned investment differs at different interest rates, the *IS* curve shows all possible equilibrium positions. Changes in decisions in the private or government sector change the variables in the saving-investment equation and shift the *IS* curve to new equilibrium positions. For example, an increase in net saving in either the private or the government sector shifts the *IS* curve to the left. An increase in net saving can take place either through a decrease in I_p, an increase in S, and increase in T, or a decrease in G. On the other hand, an increase in dissaving shifts the *IS* curve to the right; this can happen through an increase in I_p relative to S, or an increase in G relative to T.

Shifts in the *IS* curve affect income and production, employment, and prices. When decisions in the private sector cause unemployment or price inflation, the federal government may use fiscal policy to offset these decisions.

Fiscal Policy

Governments influence the *IS* curve by their tax and spending decisions. Changes in taxes and spending affect consumption, business investment and government expenditures and create disequilibrium in the product sector. The result is to shift the *IS* curve to the right or left. Decisions that yield a net increase in aggregate demand shift the *IS* curve to the right; a net decrease, to the left.

Fiscal policy is characterized as *contractionary fiscal policy* or *expansionary fiscal policy*. Contractionary fiscal policy involves lower levels of government spending (*G*) and/or higher taxes (*T*). The result is a larger surplus (or smaller deficit) in the government budget. An increase in government saving affects the *IS* curve in the same way as would an increase in private saving. Remember that an increase in saving makes saving equal to planned investment at a lower level of income, so that the *IS* curve shifts to the left. In the same way, a decrease in government spending or an increase in taxes reduces aggregate demand, causes a lower equilibrium level of income at every interest rate, and shifts the *IS* curve to the left.

Expansionary fiscal policy involves greater government spending and/or lower taxes; the result is a larger deficit (or smaller surplus) in the budget. A larger government deficit (*G* > *T*) affects the *IS* curve in the same way as would an increase in private spending. Remember that an increase in private spending requires a decrease in private saving. A decrease in saving makes saving equal to planned investment at higher levels of income, so that the *IS* curve shifts to the right. In the same way, an increase in government spending or a decrease in taxes increases aggregate demand, increases the equilibrium level of income at every interest rate, and shifts the *IS* curve to the right.

Effect on Income and Interest Rates

The effect of contractionary fiscal policy is shown in Figure 17–1a. The effect of increasing the government surplus (or reducing the deficit) is a leftward shift of *IS* and a lower equilibrium level of income and lower interest rates. The effect of expansionary fiscal policy is shown in Figure 17–1b. The effect of increasing the government deficit (or reducing the surplus) is a

FIGURE 17–1a Contractionary Fiscal
                  Policy

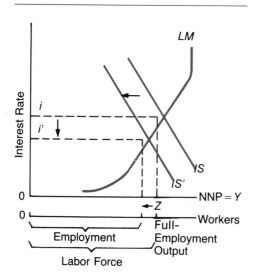

FIGURE 17–1b Expansionary Fiscal
                  Policy

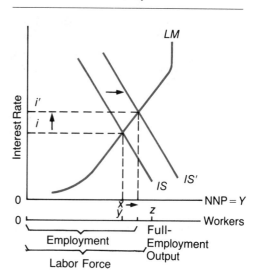

rightward shift of *IS* and a higher equilibrium level of income and interest rates.

The magnitude of the shift in *IS* depends on the amount of the change in government spending or taxes and the multiplier associated with the change. The multiple effect of increased government purchases (*G*) is based on the public's rate of respending income, causing the *IS* curve to shift:

$$\text{Shift in } IS = \Delta G \left[\frac{1}{1 - MPC} \right]$$

The multiple effect of a change in taxes (*T*) is less than that of government expenditures, because not all of a tax change is reflected in spending. With a given marginal propensity to consume, the public will react to a tax change with a spending change of only *MPC* times the amount of the tax change. This makes the multiple effect of a tax change only:

$$\text{Shift in } IS = - MPC \, \Delta T \left[\frac{1}{1 - MPC} \right]$$

The sign of the change is negative because an increase in taxes, like an increase in private saving, causes the *IS* curve to shift to the left. A decrease in taxes, like a decrease in private saving, causes the *IS* curve to shift to the right.

Expansionary Fiscal Policy

Fiscal policy involves the use of the federal budget to influence the level of production and employment. To increase employment, government might reduce the level of government saving at the equilibrium positions shown in Figure 17–1b. Employment is shown on the scale beneath the *IS-LM* model as numbers of workers required to produce particular levels of output. Thus, equilibrium at *x* is associated with employment of *y* workers. The unemployment rate at equilibrium depends on the size of the total work force, as indicated by the full employment level of output, *z*.

Let us suppose that the labor force is, in fact, *z* and that unemployment is shown by the distance *yz*. Unemployment of *yz* may be regarded as an inefficient level of resource use, calling for expansionary fiscal policy. In this case, government may reduce its own saving by reducing *T* and/or increasing *G*. The result is

$$I_p - S > T - G$$

at every level of interest rates and a shift to the right of the entire *IS* curve.

A reduction in taxes may be expected to shift the *IS* curve by:

$$- MPC \; \Delta T \; [1/(1-MPC)],$$

and an increase in government spending by:

$$\Delta G \; [1/(1-MPC)].$$

The shift in the *IS* curve produces a new equilibrium level of GNP, with employment closer to the full-employment level. Notice that the change in GNP is not the full amount of the shift in the *IS* curve, however. The reason for the difference is what economists call *crowding out*.

Crowding Out

Crowding out occurs when the expansionary effects of increased government spending are offset by contractionary changes in private spending. It occurs because government spending greater than tax revenues must be financed by borrowing. To the extent that the money supply is fixed, greater government borrowing competes with private borrowers for funds, and the result is upward pressure on interest rates. When business firms are unable to borrow at rates that allow investment projects to be profitable, private investment spending falls. Thus, additional government spending is partly offset by a reduction in private investment spending.

Critics of fiscal policy worry about crowding out. They say that expansionary fiscal policy has little effect on output but affects primarily the composition of output: in particular, the portion of output purchased by government relative to the portion purchased for use in the private sector. If expansionary fiscal policy is to be fully effective in increasing output and employment, the money supply must be increased to avoid a scarcity of credit for investment. This makes the money supply particularly important when deciding to use expansionary fiscal policy.

We will have more to say about the supply of money later. But first let us consider the consequences for the money supply of government decisions regarding taxes or borrowing to finance government spending.

Government Budgets and the Money Supply

Governments finance their expenditures in two ways: collecting taxes and/ or borrowing. The effect on the money supply depends on which of the two methods is chosen. This is important because unless the money supply changes along with government spending (or taxes), changes in private spending may offset changes in government spending. Expansionary or contractionary fiscal policy may not affect production and employment at all.

Financing Expenditures Through Taxes

Consider first the effect on the money supply when government expenditures are financed by taxes, so that the government budget is balanced. Tax payments are normally made by check, reducing taxpayers' deposit accounts and reducing commercial bank reserves. Government deposits increase by the amount of taxes collected. But because government deposits are not counted in the money supply, the money supply falls. If all tax revenues are then spent for government purchases or paid as transfer payments, the money returns to private accounts and the money supply increases. Thus, when government budgets are balanced, there may be no change in the money supply.

Financing a Deficit Through Borrowing from the Public

Now consider what happens when government outlays are greater than federal tax revenues, so that the Treasury must borrow. Remember that spending greater than taxes is called expansionary fiscal policy. Normally, the objective of expansionary fiscal policy is to increase total spending and bring on an increase in production and employment. Whether expansionary fiscal policy is effective, however, depends on how the deficit is financed. If government borrows from individuals or business firms, the effect on the money supply is the same as taxes. Buyers of government bonds write checks to the government; their deposits and commercial bank reserves decline; the money supply falls. When government pays out the funds, the money supply increases by an equal amount. Thus, like balanced budgets, borrowing from the public may involve no change in the money supply.

Note that in both cases—tax collections and borrowing from the public—government outlays take the place of what might have been private expenditures. Families might have spent for consumption what they paid in taxes; savers might have bought corporate securities rather than government securities. Thus, expansionary fiscal policy has produced no change in total spending and, very likely, no effect on output and employment.

Coordinating Government Borrowing with the Federal Reserve

The federal government may want to spend more without causing the private sector to spend less. In this way, it can achieve the maximum effect from expansionary fiscal policy. The way to do this is by coordinating government borrowing with actions of the Federal Reserve.

Although the Treasury does not normally borrow directly from the Federal Reserve, it may sell new securities *to the public* while the Federal Reserve is buying existing securities *from the public*. While private buyers of government securities are paying by writing checks and *reducing* the money supply, the Federal Reserve would be issuing checks for its purchases and *increasing* the money supply. In this case, Treasury borrowing does not reduce the money supply. Then, when the Treasury spends its borrowed funds, commercial bank deposits and reserves and the money supply all increase. If Federal Reserve bond purchases precisely offset Treasury sales, government outlays can take place without a corresponding drop in private spending.

Disposing of a Surplus

We have considered the money supply consequences when government is conducting expansionary fiscal policy. The reverse adjustments are required when government is conducting contractionary fiscal policy and running a surplus. In this case the federal government is collecting more in taxes than it is paying out, and it must decide how to dispose of the surplus. Again, the effect on the money supply depends on how the surplus is used. Unless the surplus causes a reduction in the money supply, the decrease in government spending may be partly offset by an increase in private spending. (The reason is that lower government spending and higher taxes produce a larger surplus—or smaller deficit—which reduces borrowing and causes interest rates to fall. At lower interest rates investment spending may be expected to increase.) The contractionary fiscal policy may have no effect on production and employment.

Normally, when the Treasury spends less than tax revenues, it uses its excess funds to redeem existing debt. As their bonds mature, bondholders receive checks from the Treasury and deposit them in their commercial bank accounts. Reserves increase, and the money supply increases to offset the amount not spent by the Treasury. Without a decrease in the money supply, however, private spending could increase by the amount that government spending has fallen.

The result is different if surplus tax revenues are used to redeem securities held by the Federal Reserve Banks. Checks received by the Federal Reserve do not appear in commercial bank reserves and do not add to the money supply. This time, the government surplus causes a reduction in the money supply, because neither Treasury expenditures nor debt repayment checks find their way into private hands. What is not spent by the Treasury is not available to be spent by the private sector either. In this case, surplus tax revenues impose a sacrifice on private individuals and business firms that is not offset by additional government outlays. And the contractionary fiscal policy has its maximum effect on production and employment.

Monetary Policy

Decisions to change the nation's money supply are called *monetary policy*. Monetary policy involves Federal Reserve operations affecting commercial bank lending. Operations to reduce the money supply are called contractionary monetary policy. *Contractionary monetary policy* is achieved through open market sales of securities, increases in commercial bank reserve requirements, and/or higher discount rates on commercial bank borrowing.

The effect of contractionary monetary policy is to reduce the money supply (M) and to shift the LM curve to the left. This is because a smaller supply of money is equal to money demand at a lower income level. A reduced money supply is less than transactions and precautionary demand at the existing income level. Spending will be cut and income will fall until income reaches a level consistent with the smaller money supply.

Policies to increase the money supply are called expansionary monetary policy. *Expansionary monetary policy* is achieved through open market purchases and reductions in reserve requirements and discount rates. The increase in reserves allows banks to increase their lending, and the money supply grows. An increase in the money supply (M) causes a rightward shift in the LM curve. This is because the larger supply of money is greater than transactions and precautionary demand at the existing income level. Larger money balances allow individuals and business firms to increase their spending until their larger transactions and precautionary balances are consistent with a new, higher income level.

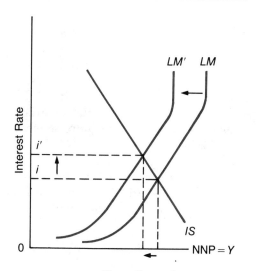

FIGURE 17–2a   Contractionary Monetary Policy

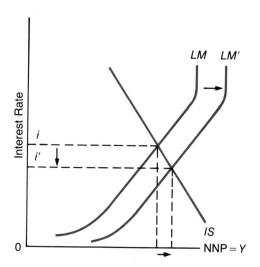

FIGURE 17–2b   Expansionary Monetary Policy

The effect of contractionary monetary policy is shown in Figure 17–2a by a leftward shift of *LM* to *LM'*. A reduction in the money base reduces banks' ability to create money. At the old equilibrium level of GNP the demand for idle money balances exceeds supply. People cut back their spending to a level consistent with smaller holdings of transactions and precautionary balances, and income falls.

The effect of expansionary monetary policy is shown in Figure 17–2b by a rightward shift in *LM* to *LM"*. An increase in the money base allows banks to create additional money so that supply exceeds transactions and precautionary demand at the existing level of income and the interest rate. The public increases its spending to amounts consistent with larger transactions and precautionary balances, and income increases.

Look at the vertical segment of the *LM* curve to understand the magnitude of the shift in *LM*. Remember that the vertical portion of *LM* is drawn at the maximum income level where the entire money supply is being spent at the rate $1/l$. The public is holding no speculative balances, and commercial banks are holding no excess reserves. In this case a change in the available money supply shifts the vertical segment of the *LM* curve by $\Delta M(1/l)$.

The shift of *LM* is not as easy to see along the sloping segment of the curve. Along the sloping segment speculative balances and excess commercial bank reserves absorb some of the change in *M*, so that not all the change is reflected in spending and income. Along the horizontal segment of *LM*, the new curve lies along the old, as all changes in the money supply are absorbed into idle money balances.

Interest Rate Effects of Monetary Policy

Now look back to see the effect of monetary policy on interest rates. In Figure 17–2a contractionary monetary policy causes a leftward shift of the *LM* curve. Move up the *IS* curve to locate the new higher equilibrium level of interest rates. The decrease in the money supply requires changes in people's asset portfolios. With smaller speculative balances, people sell off their securities, so that interest rates rise. In Figure 17–2b expansionary monetary policy causes a rightward shift in the *LM* curve. Move down the *IS* curve to locate the new lower equilibrium level of interest rates. The increase in the money supply means larger speculative balances and allows people to add securities to their portfolios, with the result that the interest rate falls.

In both these cases, people adjust their portfolios to hold financial instruments and speculative money balances consistent with new interest rates.

Changes in interest rates affect behavior in product markets, as shown on the *IS* curve. With contractionary monetary policy, interest rates tend to rise, and business investment spending tends to fall, according to the marginal efficiency of investment (MEI). Lower investment spending has a multiple effect on income, according to the marginal propensity to consume (MPC). (Can you explain the opposite adjustments that are associated with expansionary monetary policy?)

In both these cases, the resulting equilibrium levels of income and interest rates depend on the positions and slopes of the two curves. The positions of the curves reflect the magnitude of the change in spending and the money supply, and the slopes reflect the response of spenders and lenders to these changes.

Summary

We might summarize the interest rate effects of fiscal and monetary policy as follows:

1. In the case of fiscal policy, interest rates are expected to move in the same direction as income. Contractionary fiscal policy ($G < T$) has the effect of reducing interest rates as well as income. This is because lower government spending or higher taxes mean less government borrowing and downward pressure on interest rates. Too, government surpluses might be used to pay back government debt, leaving more funds available for private borrowers at lower interest rates. On the other hand, expansionary fiscal policy ($G > T$) tends to increase both income and interest rates, because government deficits must be financed by borrowing.

2. The interest rate effects of monetary policy are different: Income and interest rates are expected to move in opposite directions. Con-

tractionary monetary policy reduces the supply of credit and tends to push interest rates up. At the same time, the lower level of transactions balances reduces income. In contrast, expansionary monetary policy puts downward pressure on interest rates at the same time it is pushing income up.

Fiscalists and Monetarists

We have distinguished between Monetarists and Keynesians with respect to differences in their theories of income determination. Now we will see that differences in theories of income determination imply differences in the kinds of policies Monetarists and Keynesians recommend for affecting income.

In general, Keynesian economists are classified as *fiscalists*. Because they attach greater importance to spending decisions as determinants of income, they tend to look to government spending policies as the best way to affect economic activity. Because Monetarists believe that the quantity of money is the fundamental basis for spending decisions, they look to monetary policy as the best way to affect economic activity.

Most modern economists are neither strict fiscalists nor strict Monetarists but recommend both types of policies, as well as some others, for influencing economic activity. Under most conditions this latter group is probably correct, but there are circumstances in which even a vigorous use of a particular policy tool will not affect income at all. If policy is to affect economic activity, the other policy must be used.

To illustrate, consider simultaneous and roughly equal use of both expansionary fiscal and monetary policies, as illustrated in Figure 17–3. In the figure, government deficits (or smaller surpluses) shift *IS* to the right by the amount of the multiplier:

$$\text{Shift in } IS = \Delta G \left[\frac{1}{1 - MPC} \right]$$

or

$$\text{Shift in } IS = -MPC\ \Delta T \left[\frac{1}{1 - MPC} \right]$$

The higher level of total spending requires a larger money supply, if interest rates are to remain stable. Therefore, the Federal Reserve acts to increase commercial bank reserves, and the vertical segment of the *LM* curve shifts to the right:

$$\text{Shift in } LM = \Delta M \left[\frac{1}{l} \right]$$

FIGURE 17–3 Simultaneous Use of Expansionary Monetary and Fiscal Policy

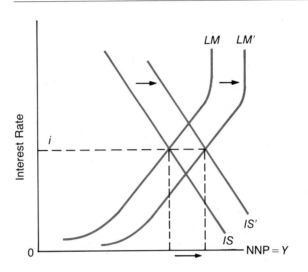

Note that simultaneous use of both policies can avoid an increase in interest rates. The increase in spending (shown on *IS*) is carried out through the use of new money (shown on *LM*), and there is no tendency for interest rates to rise. Contractionary policies used together are expected to produce similar results. Income falls, but there is no reduction in interest rates. In both examples, coordinated use of fiscal and monetary policy might be expected to change income without interest rate changes to disrupt financial markets.

When *IS* Is Steep and *LM* Is Flat

Now consider a situation where monetary policy would have no effect on income, and the entire change in income must come from fiscal policy. The conditions when this is true are reflected in the slopes of the *IS* and *LM* curves in Figures 17–4a and 17–4b. In particular, the *IS* curve is relatively steep and the *LM* curve relatively flat. Steepness of the *IS* curve means two things:

1. Business investment spending is not very responsive to changes in interest rates; MEI is steep.
2. The marginal propensity to consume is low, and the multiple effect of new spending is small: MPC is relatively low and $1/(1-MPC)$ is small. With a steep *IS* curve, changes in the money supply have virtually no effect on spending and income but cause wide fluctuations in interest rates.

FIGURE 17–4a Expansionary Monetary Policy

FIGURE 17–4b Expansionary Fiscal Policy

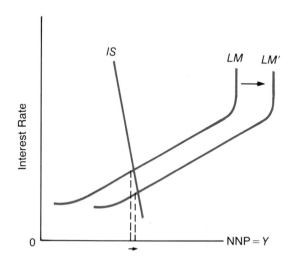

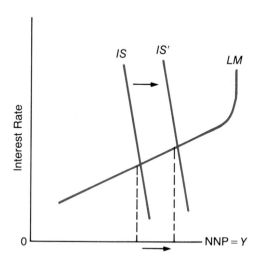

Flatness of the *LM* curve reflects two conditions as well:

3. Holders of speculative money balances are strongly responsive to changes in interest rates.
4. Commercial banks also respond readily to interest rate changes, varying their holdings of excess reserves substantially with interest rates.

Look first at Figure 17–4a, where the *IS* curve is relatively steep. Suppose expansionary monetary policy is used to increase income, and note its effects. The larger quantity of money has the effect of reducing interest rates but according to (1) above, business investment does not increase very much, and according to (2), consumers respend a small fraction of changes in income, so that income rises only slightly. Meanwhile, according to (3), the fall in interest rates causes much of the new money to be added to speculative balances and, according to (4), causes commercial banks to increase their holdings of excess reserves.

With a steep *IS* curve and flat *LM* curve, as illustrated in Figure 17–4a, it appears that expansionary monetary policy has little effect on income. The effect on interest rates may also be slight, because money held in speculative balances or in commercial bank excess reserves is not available for purchasing financial instruments and cannot put downward pressure on interest rates.

These conditions may prevail at the depths of a recession. Business pessimism about the potential for profitable investment is reflected in a steep

IS curve. (Can you explain why?) Public holdings of idle money balances are reflected in a flat *LM* curve. (Can you explain why?) Both conditions reduce the effectiveness of monetary policy. Exceptionally low interest rates do not encourage people to purchase financial instruments or banks to make loans. Keynesians describe this condition as a *liquidity trap*, an extreme desire for liquidity that paralyzes money and product markets. Under these conditions, a greater emphasis on fiscal policy may be called for.

Now look at Figure 17–4b and note the effect of expansionary fiscal policy under these same conditions. Because greater government spending or reduced taxes do not depend on business expectations of profit or people's willingness to purchase financial instruments, they can be carried on in amounts appropriate to the public's respending rate for accomplishing the desired increase in income. *IS* shifts to the right:

$$\text{Shift in } IS = \Delta G \left[\frac{1}{1 - MPC} \right] \text{ or } -MPC \, \Delta T \left[\frac{1}{1 - MPC} \right]$$

When the public is holding substantial speculative balances, the government can finance its deficit easily, because increases in interest rates coax idle dollars from speculative balances. Too, increases in interest rates encourage banks to activate more of their excess reserves. With a steep *IS* curve and flat *LM* curve, fiscal policy alone appears sufficient for increasing income without seriously disrupting financial markets.

When *IS* Is Flat and *LM* Is Steep

Under other conditions, monetary policy may be more effective. Look at Figures 17–5a and 17–5b where the *IS* curve is relatively flat and the *LM* curve relatively steep. The flatter *IS* curve suggests (1) greater business responsiveness to interest rate changes (a flatter MEI) and (2) a higher respending rate among consumers (higher MPC). The steeper *LM* curve suggests (3) relatively smaller holdings of speculative balances and (4) fuller use of excess reserves by commercial banks. In part, these conditions are a result of higher interest rates in years of expanding economic activity.

With a flat *IS* curve and steep *LM* curve, expansionary monetary policy has its greatest effect on income and little effect on interest rates. This is because, according to (1) above, only a small reduction in interest rates calls forth a substantial increase in investment spending and, according to (2), consumers respend a relatively large fraction of increases in income. Moreover, according to (3), little of the new money goes into speculative balances or (4) into excess reserves of commercial banks.

In contrast, expansionary fiscal policy, shown in Figure 17–5b, produces little income change, working primarily to increase interest rates. This is because the increased government deficits must be financed by borrowing,

FIGURE 17–5a   Expansionary Monetary Policy

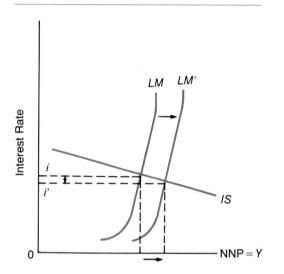

FIGURE 17–5b   Expansionary Fiscal Policy

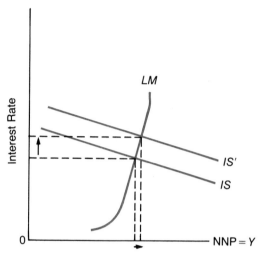

putting upward pressure on interest rates. The results are a substantial drop in investment spending and a negative multiplier effect on income from the drop in investment.

When the *IS* curve is flat and the *LM* curve steep, expansionary fiscal policy puts upward pressure on interest rates without improving income and employment very much. The reason is that the nation's money supply is already being used fully to finance spending. Much of the increase in government spending (relative to tax revenues) requires an offsetting drop in other types of spending. When necessary government spending crowds out private spending, the appropriate policy might be to provide additional money. As we demonstrated in Figure 17–3, coordinated use of fiscal and monetary policy would ease pressures in financial markets and help achieve employment objectives.

The Phillips Curve Again

The goal of economic policy—and the central theme of this text—is to achieve the maximum level of employment possible with price stability. Full employment and price stability will ensure efficiency in resource allocation, allow for improved equity in distribution, and yield positive externalities from a prosperous economy.

FIGURE 17–6a A Phillips Curve

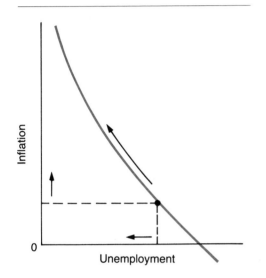

FIGURE 17–6b Expansionary Monetary and Fiscal Policy

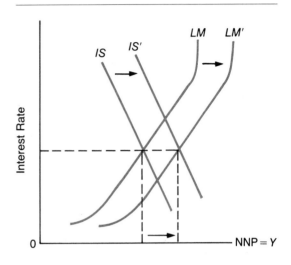

In Chapter 16 we showed that it may be impossible to achieve both full employment and price stability. In fact, we showed on the Phillips curve that the two goals may be contradictory. Full employment is often accompanied by price inflation, and price stability may be impossible unless there is some amount of unemployment.

Look at the Phillips curve in Figure 17–6a. Positions low on the curve reflect high unemployment and low price inflation. Many economists would recommend expansionary fiscal and monetary policies to increase income and employment. Expansionary fiscal policy would take the form of increased government spending and/or lower tax rates. The *IS* curve shifts to the right by a multiple of the changes, as shown in Figure 17–6b. Expansionary monetary policy would take the form of open market purchases and reductions in the discount rate and reserve requirements. As commercial banks receive excess reserves, the money supply increases and the *LM* curve shifts to the right. If expansionary policies are precisely coordinated, there may be no change in interest rates to disrupt financial markets.

The expected result of expansionary fiscal and monetary policies is a movement up the Phillips curve, with lower unemployment and an increase in price inflation. The student should select a point high on the Phillips curve and suggest the kinds of policy that would move the economy down the curve to a more acceptable level of both variables.

Now consider a point to the right of the Phillips curve, a point representing exceptionally high unemployment as well as inflation. In fact, points to the right of the Phillips curve represent the chief problem of policymakers in recent years.

You might say that points to the right of the Phillips curve present policymakers with a dilemma: Should expansionary policies be used to reduce the unacceptably high level of unemployment—even though expansionary policies may cause inflation to go through the roof? Or should contractionary policies be used to reduce the unacceptably high level of inflation—even though contractionary policies will cause severe distress to larger numbers of unemployed workers?

The Theory of Rational Expectations

A group of modern economists has a theory to explain points to the right of the Phillips curve and a prescription for dealing with policymakers' dilemma. The Theory of Rational Expectations blames high levels of unemployment together with inflation on workers' insistence on protection against inflation.

Rational expectations means that workers base their wage demands on all the information they have regarding price trends. When their information suggests that prices are going to rise, workers insist on higher wages to offset the expected price rise. The result is to cause prices to rise—as expected.

According to the Theory of Rational Expectations, the traditional Phillips curve describes employment and price behavior only for short periods when workers are unaware of the effect of inflation on their real wages. Real wages measure the purchasing power of money wages after correcting for the effects of inflation. When prices rise faster than money wages, real wages fall.

Money Illusion

Consider again a point low on the Phillips curve in Figure 17–6a, with high unemployment and low inflation. Suppose expansionary fiscal and monetary policies are used to move the economy up the curve; employment increases and there is some increase in prices. Unfortunately, the gain in employment may be only temporary; permanent gains in employment are possible only if workers suffer from money illusion. Money illusion is the belief that more money received as wages necessarily means more purchasing power; it ignores the effect of higher prices on the buying power of wages.

If workers do, in fact, have money illusion, the traditional Phillips curve will correctly show the results of expansionary policies. More likely, however, as the higher inflation takes hold, workers will come to understand that their real wages have fallen. Some workers will refuse to work for the

FIGURE 17-7 The Loss of Money Illusion

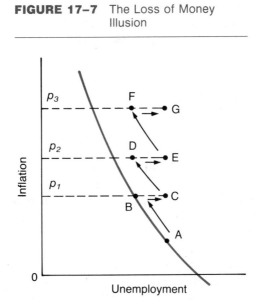

current money wage, and unemployment will begin to rise. Figure 17–7 shows the temporary effect of expansionary policies and the eventual increase in unemployment when workers lose their money illusion. When this happens, the inflation rate (p_1) becomes the basis for new wage demands. Moreover, because wage increases are eventually built into price increases, p_1 becomes the lower limit below which price inflation cannot fall.

Price Expectations

If the expansionary policies are repeated, inflation will rise still further. Again the gain in employment is only temporary. In fact, as workers come to expect increases in prices, they may insist on wage increases before prices actually increase. Successive levels of inflation (p_2 and p_3) become the lower limits for new wage demands. The long-range result is accelerating inflation accompanied by continued high employment.

Note that under these conditions expansionary fiscal and monetary policies will not increase employment. To make matters worse, contractionary policies will work only to increase unemployment while inflation remains high. According to the Theory of Rational Expectations, only a prolonged period of high unemployment will finally convince workers that inflation is over, so that wage demands fall.

Because money illusion is only temporary, the traditional Phillips curve can exist only in the short run. When workers insist on wage increases to offset expected inflation, the curve becomes vertical at some rate of unemployment—perhaps the natural rate we discussed in Chapter 16. Price inflation ratchets upward with each attempt to reduce unemployment. Expansionary policies worsen inflation without improving employment.

The Policy

If the Theory of Rational Expectations is correct, an appropriate policy would be to change workers' expectations about price trends. One way to do that is to undertake fiscal and monetary policies opposite to those workers have come to expect. Specifically, because workers expect that rising unemployment will call for expansionary fiscal and monetary policies, the rational expectationists recommend no such policy at all. In fact, the rational expectationists might recommend contractionary fiscal and monetary policies to bring inflation down. As workers come to expect a decreasing price trend, they will find their real wages growing along with their money wages and will drop their insistence on inflationary wage increases.

Other economists would deal with the shifted Phillips curve differently. They worry about the prolonged period of high unemployment that might be necessary to change workers' expectations and bring down wage demands. Instead they recommend some sort of wage-price controls.

Wage-Price Controls

The United States used controls during World War II to hold down wartime inflation. Because price controls created shortages, rationing was necessary in many product markets, and a sense of patriotism kept workers on the job at controlled wages. After controls were lifted, there was a significant bulge in prices, and since then we have tried to avoid outright controls. (Controls reappeared briefly during the Korean War in the 1950s.)

In the early 1960s, the nation was experiencing a recession with high unemployment and low inflation. The Kennedy-Johnson Administration attempted to use expansionary policies while holding wage and price increases within guidelines. Under the guidelines, wages were allowed to increase only in line with productivity growth, averaging 3.2 percent a year. If wages rose only by the amount of productivity growth, wage costs would remain stable, and finished goods prices would not rise. Industries that experienced less than average productivity gains could set higher prices; but these were to be offset by lower prices in industries with greater than average productivity gains.

The guidelines were moderately successful in holding down prices in markets subject to control. The problems occurred in markets not subject to control. Prices could not be controlled in sectors producing raw commodities; to do so would have discouraged production and worsened shortages. For this reason, agricultural products were exempt from controls. Rising prices for food and other agricultural products eventually led to demands for wage increases in manufacturing. In addition, crude oil production was increasingly outside the jurisdiction of U.S. price controllers, and health services experienced quality gains accompanied by sharply rising prices. The result of price increases in these sectors was renewed inflation, worsened by expenditures associated with the Vietnam War later in the 1960s.

President Nixon's economic goals in 1972 were the same as those of Presidents Kennedy and Johnson in the 1960s: expansionary policies to reduce unemployment while preventing an increase in inflation. Wages and prices were first frozen and then increases were subject to limits: 5½ percent for wages and cost "pass-throughs" for prices. Controls were removed in 1973, which turned out to be a particularly bad year for prices. Worldwide crop failures increased demand for U.S. grain, driving up the prices of grain and livestock products. Then, Arab oil producing nations sharply increased their prices for petroleum, raising the prices of gasoline, chemical fertilizers, synthetic fibers, electricity and a host of other petroleum-related products. Consumer prices jumped by 22 percent between June 1973 and December 1974.

The Need for Limits

The poor performance of wage-price controls has reduced their popularity. Still, policymakers recognize the need to place limits on wage increases and anticipatory price increases. The explanation is simple. Workers should not be compensated for every increase in living costs. Higher costs for particular goods reflect shortages and should encourage conservation. Consumers should cut down on their consumption of a scarce good or reduce consumption of some other good in its place. If everyone continues to consume as if there were no shortage, shortages worsen and prices increase further. The burden of conservation falls on those least able to achieve increases in income: the elderly, savers and persons on relatively fixed incomes.

The Full-Employment Budget

Concern with full employment has led to a new method for measuring the federal budget and assessing its impact on the economy. Economists look not at the existing budget—its surplus or deficit—but at what the budget would be if the economy were operating at full employment. If the economy is actually operating at less than full employment, tax revenues are likely to be lower than they would be at full employment. Moreover, government outlays will include more income-support payments than would be the case at a higher level of employment. The result is likely to be a deficit in the actual budget. On the other hand, if the economy were to be at full employment, government outlays would be lower and tax revenues higher (given the existing structure of progressive income tax rates). With no change in patterns of taxes and spending, the *full-employment budget* might be in balance or even surplus.

The concept of the full-employment budget permits economists to judge the impact of the budget on economic activity: contractionary, stimulative or neutral. A full-employment *surplus* indicates a contractionary effect; the existing tax structure and spending programs may be holding down private spending and may prevent a move to full employment. A full-employment *deficit* indicates stimulus; the high level of government spending relative to tax rates may be increasing total spending and pushing the economy beyond its productive capacity. Perhaps the ideal would be a neutral effect: rough balance at full employment (or a small surplus).

To accomplish balance in the full employment budget is not an easy job. It requires accurate projections of such variables as labor force productivity, taxable income at full employment, and government outlays at full employment. Then tax rates must be set to collect just enough revenue to offset government outlays if all workers were actually employed. The actual budget would be in deficit, but the stimulus would be just enough to move income up to the full employment level and not beyond. As the economy approaches full employment, the budget would move toward balance.

There is a corollary to this, of course. It is that increases in productive capacity will continue to push the full employment goal higher. The full employment budget concept would require frequent reductions in tax rates and frequent deficits in the actual budget. The goal of balance at full employment may be an elusive one.

MONEY AND BANKING IN PRACTICE: DEALING WITH GOVERNMENT DEFICITS

In the mid-1980s, the chief concern among participants in U.S. financial markets was continuing federal budget deficits. Private econometric forecasters were projecting deficits as high as $165 billion to $180 billion for the foreseeable future. Official forecasters tended to be somewhat more optimistic; the latter is indicated in Table 17–4.

By 1987, concern about federal deficits was moving Congress toward a showdown with President Reagan. The Gramm-Rudman-Hollings Law, passed in 1985, required across-the-board spending cuts every year to achieve a balanced federal budget by 1991. Some spending programs were exempted from cuts: specifically, social welfare programs, including Social Security, Medicaid and food stamps. But other programs were to face automatic spending cuts of between 6 percent and 8 percent. Applying automatic cuts to all programs would result in the sharpest cuts for defense, which the President wanted to increase by 3 percent above inflation. The Gramm-Rudman-Hollings Law could be set aside, of course, but that would cast doubt on the President's resolve to reduce the federal deficit.

Congress was willing to compromise on a solution to the deficit problem. It agreed to accept the President's proposed increases in defense spending in return for a tax increase, but the President was adamant in his refusal to allow a tax increase.

To make matters worse, sluggish economic growth in the mid-1980s and rising interest rates were worsening prospects for budget balance. Both the OMB and CBO forecasts were based on the assumption that tax revenues would increase with economic growth. But economic growth was slowing, and productivity growth was disappointing as well. With more slowly rising incomes, tax payments were expected to rise more slowly, too. The Tax Reform Act of 1986 helped increase revenues in the current tax year, but it was expected to worsen future revenues. This is because the increase in capital gains taxes encouraged holders of capital gains to liquidate them in 1986 and pay the lower tax in that year.

TABLE 17–4 Official Deficit Projections
(billions of dollars as of January 1987)

Fiscal Year	Office of Management and Budget (OMB)	Congressional Budget Office (CBO)
Actual:	220.7	220.7
1986		
Estimate:		
1987	175	174
1988	150	169
1989	147	162
1990	125	134
1991	101	109
1992	78	85

Another problem was a tendency for government expenditures to increase. The new federal employees retirement system was expected to add $3 billion a year to expenditures, and Social Security cost-of-living adjustments were scheduled to increase as well. Interest charges on government borrowing were beginning to rise, and the Treasury was expected to rescue the savings and loan industry and the Farm Credit System with massive infusions of capital.

There were other potential problems in the late 1980s, such as an expected spurt in health care costs and the possibility of a military crisis or a new recession.

Question for Discussion

1. The conflict between the President and Congress on the budget issue demonstrates the danger of running a federal deficit in periods of recovery from recession. Explain the process by which a deficit in the recovery stage can worsen as the economy expands and contributes to further economic instability.

The National Debt

Government dissaving ($T < G$) creates government debt. Net dissaving in a recession year may be followed by net saving in a more prosperous year, with surplus tax revenues used to pay off the previous year's borrowing. The result would be increases in debt during recessions and decreases during periods of prosperity, with no long-term change in total government debt. Spending for wars and national defense has made it unlikely that deficits and surpluses will ever come into precise balance. During World War II, the federal debt grew from $43 billion to $259 billion. The Vietnam conflict in the 1960s and severe recessions in the 1970s pushed the debt close to $1 trillion by 1981. In the 20 years since 1966 the federal budget has been in surplus only one year ($8.5 billion in 1969), and accumulated deficits have been more than $1.5 trillion.

Most of the Treasury's debt is held by private individuals, commercial banks, mutual savings banks, insurance companies, and other financial and nonfinancial corporations. State and local governments frequently use their own surpluses to purchase U.S. government securities and held almost one-tenth of the debt in 1986. Federal Reserve Banks held $200 billion in 1986, and various agencies of the federal government held another $325 billion.

The largest single group of holders of government securities is now foreign investors, with 15 percent of the total in 1987. This is a substantial increase over 1970, due in part to increased purchases by foreign central banks. (Central bank holdings are a result of actions to stabilize the value of the dollar, a subject of Chapter 12.) Much of foreign individuals' holdings of debt is short-term and could cause troubles for the Treasury if foreigners should decide to liquidate their securities at once.

Interest payments on the *national debt* are classified in the federal budget as transfer payments, because they do not represent purchases of real goods or services. The growing size of the debt itself and the increase in interest rates has made interest payments a substantial part of Federal outlays: 15 percent in 1987, third in size after defense and income security payments. Thus, debt borrowed in earlier years continues to exert its impact on the economy through taxes collected to pay interest to bondholders.

A Balanced-Budget Law?

Many citizens favor legislation to require balance in the federal budget. Such a requirement would place a limit on spending and on the size and power of the federal government. It would make government more responsive to the will of the people, because without the ability to borrow Congress would need taxpayer approval for new spending programs.

Opponents of a balanced-budget law argue that the goal of a balanced budget is less important than the goals of efficiency in the use of productive resources and equity in the distribution of output. They point out that government debt, like personal and corporate debt, can be used to increase productivity and income over the long run. Greater productivity means higher incomes and higher tax payments, so that deficits may become *automatically self-liquidating*.

The Growth of Entitlement Programs

Still, the size of the debt and its recent growth require careful attention. The prolonged series of federal deficits in the 1970s and 1980s may be the result of a changed pattern of revenues and outlays. In fact, there has been a major shift in budget outlays from expenditures for goods and services to transfers of purchasing power from one group to another: transfers of tax revenues from income earners to dependent persons and transfers of federal tax revenues to states whose borrowing and taxing powers are limited. In general, transfers like these do not have as large a multiple effect on income as do government purchases; hence debt incurred for these purposes is less likely to be self-liquidating. Moreover, transfer payments may be less expansionary for moving the economy out of recession than government purchases of goods and services.

Transfer payments financed by incurring debt seem to be more and more a result of voters' insistence on larger *entitlement programs*. Entitlement programs are payments to particular groups and include price-support payments to farmers, aids to private education, veterans' benefits and so forth.

At the same time they are demanding increased programs of these kinds, voters resist tax increases to pay for them; so they must be financed by borrowing. When the growth of entitlement programs pushes aggregate demand beyond the productive capacity of the economy, the result is price inflation. The loss in real purchasing power has the effect of a tax increase, even though a tax increase was never approved by the voters.

The Gramm-Rudman-Hollings Law

In 1986 Congress passed a new law intended to slow the growth in federal debt. The Gramm-Rudman-Hollings Law requires that Congress gradually reduce federal deficits until by 1991 the federal budget is in balance. Unless the deficit is reduced each year by a specified amount, the law gave officials of the executive branch the responsibility to cut most spending programs by a specified percentage. This last requirement was declared unconstitutional by the courts, and Congress has looked for other ways to ensure compliance with the deficit requirements in the law.

Glossary of Terms

automatically self-liquidating.   a condition in which the use of borrowed funds yields incomes and tax revenues sufficient to pay off the debt

crowding out.   the condition in which the expansionary effects of increased government spending are offset by contractionary changes in private spending

deficit.   an excess of government expenditures over tax revenues

entitlement programs.   government outlays to particular groups

fiscalists.   economists who recommend government tax and spending policies to influence economic activity

fiscal policy.   the use of government tax and spending policy to influence the level of economic activity

full-employment budget.   a budget that measures what tax revenues and government expenditures would be at full employment

liquidity trap.   a condition in which interest rates are too low to compensate for the risks of lending, so that additions to the money supply are held in idle speculative balances

monetary policy.   manipulation of the money supply to affect income and employment

money illusion.   a failure to recognize the effect of inflation on real wages

national debt.   the accumulated net debt of the federal government

progressive taxes.   taxes for which the rate paid rises with an increase in the tax base

rational expectations.   the theory that thoughtful people's expectations regarding economic policy lead to the kinds of behavior that offset the effects of policy

regressive taxes.   taxes for which the rate paid falls with an increase in the tax base

surplus.   an excess of government tax revenues over expenditures

tax base.   the economic variable on which taxes are levied

Summary of Important Ideas

1.   In recent decades citizens have come to demand that government use its budget to influence economic activity. Government outlays include expenditures and transfer payments (or negative taxes).

2.   Federal tax revenues are based on income that rises with prosperity and economic growth; state and local tax revenues are based on property, retail sales and income. Some federal tax revenues are paid to state and local governments as grants-in-aid. The net government deficit or surplus depends on outlays and tax revenues at all levels of government.

3.   Product sector equilibrium occurs when planned investment in the private sector is equal to total saving:

$$I_p = S + T - G.$$

Stated differently, net dissaving (saving) in the private sector ($I_p - S$) is offset by net saving (dissaving) in the public sector ($T - G$). Changes in saving plans are shown as shifts in equilibrium positions at all interest rates.

4.   Government outlays can be financed by taxes or by borrowing. Taxing or borrowing from private savers an amount equal to outlays requires no change in the money supply.

5.   When the Federal Reserve increases its lending to finance government outlays, the money supply increases. When Treasury borrowing is repaid to the Federal Reserve, the money supply decreases. Increasing the money supply through Federal Reserve lending helps to avoid crowding out: the reduction of private borrowing for investment purposes.

6.   Government borrowing creates debt, which is owned by individuals and business firms in the United States and abroad. A growing debt requires rising allocations for interest charges.

7.   To the extent that borrowed funds are used to increase productivity and tax collections, the debt may be self-liquidating. However, much of today's borrowings go to finance entitlement programs and are probably not self-liquidating.

8. An appropriate focus for evaluating the current budget is the full employment deficit or surplus. Balance (or a small surplus) at full employment helps ensure that the budget's effect will neither be inflationary nor contribute to unemployment.

Questions for Discussion and Research

1. What are the philosophical bases for assigning certain functions to federal or state and local governments? How has the allocation of functions changed over time?

2. Consult the *Economic Report of the President* for data on federal and state and local government spending. Trace the relative shares of total spending over recent decades. Comment on the results.

3. What circumstances determine the tax base at various levels of government? What characteristics of a tax base constitute an advantage or disadvantage for the level of government involved?

4. Explain the relationship between deficits and surpluses in the public sector and the private sector. How is this relationship significant for the problem of crowding out?

5. Under what circumstances is government debt self-liquidating?

6. Debate the question of legislation requiring a balanced federal budget.

7. Explain the relationship between the actual budget and the full employment budget. What is the expected trend in the full employment budget and the implication for policymakers?

Additional Readings

Break, George F. *Intergovernment Fiscal Relations in the United States.* Washington: Brookings, 1967.

Brimmer, Andrew F. "The Political Economy of Limitations on Federal Spending." *Challenge* 23 (March/April 1980): 6–11.

Carlson, Keith M. "Estimates of the High-Employment Budget and Changes in Potential Output." *Federal Reserve Bank of St. Louis Review* 59 (August 1977): 16–22.

Friedman, Benjamin M. "Crowding Out or Crowding In?" *Brookings Papers on Economic Activity* no. 3, 594–694. Washington, D.C., 1978.

Jianakoplos, Nancy Ammon. "The Growing Link Between the Federal Government and State and Local Government Financing." *Federal Reserve Bank of St. Louis Review* 59 (May 1977): 13–20.

Maxwell, James A. *Financing State and Local Governments.* Rev. ed. Washington: Brookings, 1971.

Nathan, Richard P., and Fred C. Doolittle. "The Budget Cuts: The Day After." *Challenge* (January/February 1984): 29–36.

Smith, Delos R. "Tax for the Memories: Interview With Former IRS Commissioner Roscoe L. Egger, Jr." *Across the Board* (June 1987): 46–51.

Stevens, Neil A. "Government Debt Financing—Its Effects in View of Tax Discounting." *Federal Reserve Bank of St. Louis Review* 61 (July 1979): 11–19.

CHAPTER

18

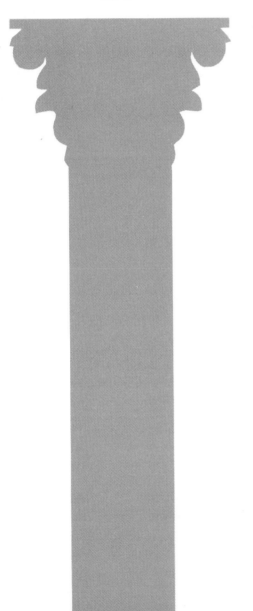

Recent Economic Policies
and Their Consequences

"Economists of every persuasion have much to be humble about."

Arthur Okun

How well have we used our monetary and fiscal powers to produce a high employment–low inflation level of income? How well have the nation's policymakers used their understanding of economics to achieve efficiency, equity and positive externalities from the way we use resources? This chapter will describe how the theories explained in this text have been applied to achieve our nation's fundamental economic goals.

You will not be surprised to learn that there are gaps between theory and fact. Economic models cannot include all the many different factors that affect spending and saving, and they cannot anticipate all the changes in these factors. Policymakers cannot always act quickly enough to prevent periods of rising unemployment or worsening inflation. Occasional failures to achieve our goals may be the price we pay for a free market economy—where, after all, the decisions of individuals count for more than the decisions of a central authority.

We will begin this chapter with a description of how monetary policy really works. Then we will consider problems and policies of the recent past, along with their consequences for output, employment and prices.

Monetary Policy: Goals, Targets and Instruments

The Federal Reserve likes to describe its role as "to take away the punch bowl when the party is going good." With a job like that, the Federal Reserve is bound to make enemies—both when it performs its responsibilities as required by law and when it performs them at the wrong time to do much good.

We have described the Federal Reserve's job as to regulate the money supply to achieve the highest possible levels of income and employment with price stability. These are the ultimate *goals* of all national economic policy, and they would ensure maximum possible levels of living with the nation's existing resources and technology. In order to achieve these goals, the Board of Governors must decide on intermediate *targets* for day-to-day policy action. Targets are specific money and credit variables whose behavior may be influenced by Federal Reserve policies. The Federal Reserve carries out its policy decisions through the various *instruments* we described in Chapter 11: reserve requirements, the discount rate and open market operations.

Money Supply and Credit Market Targets

Whatever the ultimate goal of policy, the immediate concern must be how to instruct the Account Manager in carrying out day-to-day market operations. The Account Manager must have a fairly clear target, first for deciding open market purchases and sales, and second for evaluating their effectiveness. The target may be a single variable or a weighted average of several variables. If more than one variable is used as a target, their behavior must be consistent; that is, they must move in relation to each other in fairly predictable ways. Otherwise, policy decisions would be confused.

In general, targets may be divided into two groups: aggregate money supply measures and interest rates. *Money supply aggregates* include values of M1, M2, M3, bank credit (commercial bank loans and investments), the money base (reserves plus currency in the hands of the public), and reserves. A money target has the advantage that the money supply is explicitly related to spending and total production. It has the disadvantage that reliable information is not always immediately available. When banks report their data to the Federal Reserve, the data may need to be *seasonally adjusted* and may be incomplete. Without current information on money aggregates, it is difficult to make quick decisions and to evaluate their effects.

Interest rates fall in the second group of targets, often referred to as money market or credit market targets. *Credit market targets* include the federal funds rate on interbank borrowing and the U.S. Treasury bill rate. Interest rate data are always readily available, making this a more convenient decision-making target. Still, there is not complete agreement on the most appropriate interest rate target to use.

Targets as Indicators

To be an effective target, a variable must have certain characteristics:

1. It must be economically meaningful; that is, it must have a clear relationship to the Federal Reserve's ultimate goals with respect to income and employment.

2. It must clearly reflect the force of Federal Reserve policy. When this characteristic is true, a target can also be useful as an *indicator*. An indicator signals to investors the direction of Federal Reserve policy.

Suppose, for example, that weekly reports of the Federal Reserve show abnormally fast growth in *M*1. Investors may interpret this information as a sign of expansionary monetary policy, with the objective of increasing income and employment. Their reaction would depend on whether they believe expansionary policy is desirable for stimulating economic activity or dangerously inflationary and subject to change. In the first case, they might increase their own investment plans and help meet Federal Reserve goals; in the second, they might reduce their own spending plans and help bring on a recession.

Movements in interest rates might produce similar reactions. An increase in the federal funds rate signals a scarcity of reserves and tight money; a decrease signals easy money for encouraging economic expansion. Investors who approve of the current direction of policy would behave optimistically, with increased investment spending and increased purchases of stocks and bonds. If many investors believe current policy must soon be reversed, however, investment would fall, and purchases of stocks and bonds might be replaced by purchases of nonproductive assets like gold.

Using a target as an indicator has another disadvantage. Occasionally a change in the target variable may be simply a temporary change in Federal Reserve tactics to deal with a short-run change in bank reserves. (In Chapter 10 we characterized such actions as defensive policy—in contrast with dynamic policy, which aims at a fundamental change in economic activity.) Or the value of the target variable may change independently of any Federal Reserve action at all. Interest rates are especially subject to abrupt movement in response to shifts in credit demand, and they may send out misleading signals. To avoid falsely signaling a major policy change to investors, the Board of Governors may sometimes postpone actions to affect the target until conditions have become seriously out of line with the goals of economic policy.

Outside Influences on the Target

Although influencing a money or credit market target is the immediate aim of Federal Reserve policy, target variables cannot be controlled directly. The only significant money supply variable directly controlled by the Federal Reserve is open market operations. Federal Reserve purchases and sales of U.S. government securities are expected, in turn, to influence the target: commercial bank reserves, the money supply and/or interest rates.

Other factors operate to influence the target, too, making the Federal Reserve's job more difficult. Commercial bank reserves, for example, depend not only on open market operations but also on commercial bank decisions to borrow reserves, Treasury movements of its deposit accounts, and public holdings of cash. M1 and bank credit depend on borrowed and excess reserves, Treasury deposits, and investors' decisions as to the structure of asset portfolios. In order to hit a money supply target, the Account Manager must correctly predict the behavior of all these uncontrollable variables and the possible feedbacks between open market operations and any of the outside variables.

Interest rate targets are also affected by a range of uncontrollable supply and demand conditions in all the markets for borrowed funds. It would be impossible to predict changes in all these conditions.

When outside factors are predicted incorrectly, targets will be missed. Misses result also from incorrectly specifying the relationship between the controlled variable or policy instrument, on the one hand, and the money supply or credit market target, on the other. Using open market operations, the Account Manager must determine the correct level of purchases or sales to produce the reserves for yielding the targeted growth of, say, M1 and the targeted value of, say, the federal funds rate. The Account Manager must decide if a miss is only a temporary result of a short-run change in outside factors or a more fundamental error in specifying the underlying relationships that guide policy. This is not an easy job.

Choosing a Target

We may summarize Federal Reserve operations as relating to goals, targets and instruments. Goals are broad, long-range objectives with respect to income, employment and prices; targets are intermediate objectives believed to be consistent with economic goals; and instruments are the day-to-day processes by which the Federal Reserve seeks to achieve its targets.

We have divided Federal Reserve targets into two categories: money supply and interest rate variables. An example of the first is a target growth of between 5 percent and 6 percent in M1; an example of the second is a federal funds rate of 8 percent.

The Federal Reserve might reasonably expect to hit a 5 percent to 6 percent money growth target *or* an 8 percent federal funds target but cannot normally expect to hit *both* targets at once. The reason is that a certain rate of growth in M1 may turn out to be less (or greater) than money demand, in which case market interest rates would begin to rise (or fall). On the other hand, a decision to keep interest rates at a certain level might require frequent changes in money growth so that the supply of money is always equal to demand at precisely the target rate of interest.

Because two targets cannot normally be achieved with a single set of policies, the Board of Governors has to choose between them. While establishing a target range for both variables, policymakers must give greater priority to one or the other. Suppose, for example, that money growth is within its target range, but the federal funds rate is pushing above its range. Should money growth be speeded up to relieve interest rate pressure? Or should interest rates be allowed to rise above the target so as to ration the targeted supply of money and to slow down expansion?

Whether the money supply or interest rates should have priority may depend on the structure of the economy and especially the behavior of particular groups in the economy. Before choosing the primary target, it is necessary to identify the source of instability that is pushing one of the targets outside its range. Two possibilities might be considered:

1. Is the instability due to changes in the public's demand for money balances? Changes in the fraction of income the public wants to hold as money can shift the money demand curve. Unless the money supply changes, too, the *LM* curve will shift, causing interest rates to change. Interest rate changes disrupt financial markets and may also change the equilibrium level of income and employment.

     If a change in the public's demand for money is indeed the source of instability, the correct policy would be to adjust money growth more frequently. Changes in the money supply would offset changes in money demand and hold interest rates steady. Keynesians tend to support this position.

2. Is the instability due to changes in spending plans and accompanying changes in the public's demand for credit? Changes in consumer, business or government spending plans shift the *IS* curve and cause interest rates to rise or fall. If changes in credit demand are the source of instability, the correct policy would be to hold money growth constant at a rate appropriate to the potential growth of real output. Interest rates would be allowed to fluctuate, so as to curtail spending if it threatens to grow too fast or to stimulate spending if there are unemployed resources available for use.

Monetarists tend to accept the second explanation of instability. In general, they recommend a fixed rate of money growth, and they look to financial markets to allocate credit according to changes in interest rates. However, Keynesians are also attuned to shifts in spending plans; therefore, it is not entirely correct to say that explanation (2) is Monetarist and explanation (1) is Keynesian.

In one important sense, Keynesians would object to a fixed money supply target, with changes in interest rates to regulate spending. Research into the relationship between interest rates and spending has not produced a clear relationship. High interest rates have not always worked to discourage high levels of consumption, investment and government spending. This is particularly true when inflation is pushing up the buying plans of households and business firms, as was the case in 1980. During inflation, interest rates might have to reach astronomical levels before spending is actually reduced. In the meantime, financial markets may suffer severely. In this case, Keynesians might recommend expansionary monetary policy and strongly contractionary fiscal policy, along with other policies directed precisely at the sectors of the economy where spending is growing too fast.

Keynesians would respond similarly under the opposite situation—when spending is low and interest rates are tending to fall below the target range. In this case, even very low interest rates may not encourage additional spending. Keynesians might recommend contractionary monetary policy and expansionary fiscal policy to stimulate economic activity.

Credit-Market Targets in the 1950s and 1960s

During the 1950s and early 1960s, Federal Reserve policymakers gave greater priority to credit market targets, holding interest rates within a target range. This policy was more in keeping with the Keynesian explanation of the sources of instability: explanation (1) above, which blames monetary instability on changes in the public's demand for money. Open market operations were used to adjust the supply of money to satisfy changing money demand so that interest rates would not fluctuate widely. The result was irregular money growth over the period.

Use of a stable credit market target had some disadvantages. Like prices of goods and services, free market interest rates rise and fall with supply and demand in credit markets. Higher interest rates reflect a scarcity of credit. The expected result of high interest rates is to discourage the use of scarce financial capital and allocate it toward its most productive uses. Lower interest rates encourage borrowing and stimulate spending. To prevent fluctuations in interest rates involves a sacrifice of these important functions. It may also aggravate business cycles, because a possible result of stable interest rates is to encourage excessive borrowing during inflation and to discourage needed borrowing for investment in recession.

A policy that worsens a tendency toward business cycles is said to be *pro-cyclical*. Irregular money growth to accommodate shifts in the demand for money during the 1950s and 1960s may have contributed to irregular growth in output and employment. A change in this policy took place in 1966 when the Federal Open Market Committee inserted a proviso clause in its instructions to the Account Manager. The revised instructions required the Account Manager to change interest rate targets as needed whenever irregular money growth appeared to be aggravating the business cycle.

MONEY AND BANKING IN PRACTICE: DOES MONETARY POLICY REALLY WORK?

Before deregulation of financial institutions, monetary policy worked primarily through restricting the quantity of money. Open market sales reduced bank reserves, limiting the level of bank lending and forcing a slowdown in economic activity. Interest rate ceilings prevented both banks and savings and loan associations from competing vigorously for new deposits. As a result, people continued to hold a fairly constant fraction of their incomes in idle deposits and to spend their incomes at a relatively stable rate.

With deregulation, the opportunity to pay interest on deposits reduced the dependence of financial institutions on reserves provided through the Fed's open market operations. By offering to pay interest rates on new deposit liabilities, they could acquire reserves to support new lending—but lending at higher interest rates. Thus, with deregulation higher interest rates have become the means by which monetary policy forces a slowdown in economic activity.

One important difference between the effects of policy before and after deregulation involves particular sectors of the domestic economy. Before deregulation, restrictions on the quantity of money primarily affected housing and small business—sectors that depend most strongly on financial institutions to satisfy their need for financial capital.

Today, interest rate restrictions may have their greatest effect on sectors that are particularly sensitive to interest rates—consumer durable goods, producers' durable equipment and residential construction. Changes in spending in these sectors spread broadly to other sectors of the economy and may be expected to affect economic activity according to Federal Reserve objectives.

Another difference between the effects of monetary policy before and after deregulation involves the relationship between the U.S. economy and the international economy. Changes in interest rates in the United States affect the attractiveness of deposits held in U.S. financial institutions. Changes in foreign holdings of dollar-denominated deposits affect the dollar's exchange rate. Therefore, rising U.S. interest rates tend to be associated with a rising dollar exchange rate, and vice versa. The effects of both reinforce each other. Rising interest rates are likely to reduce spending in interest-sensitive sectors of the U.S. economy, but at the same time a rising dollar exchange rate permits an increase in spending in international markets and further reduces spending in the domestic economy.

Researchers at the Federal Reserve Bank of New York have measured the responsiveness of various kinds of spending to interest rate changes and produced these results:

1. In the housing sector a 10 percent change in interest rates leads to an 8 percent change in expenditures (in the opposite direction).
2. In housing and producers' and consumers' durables taken together, a 10 percent change in interest rates leads to a 3.2 percent change in expenditures (in the opposite direction).
3. The interest-rate sensitivity of spending for producers' and consumers' durables has increased in the 1970s and 1980s over its value in the 1960s.

These results seem to confirm the notion that deregulation and rising interest rates have not weakened the effectiveness of monetary policy for influencing economic activity in the United States.

The exchange rate effects on international spending were also significant over a period long enough for trading relationships to respond:

1. A 10 percent change in the exchange value of the dollar leads to a 7 to 8 percent change in imports (in the same direction, because a rising dollar makes imports cheaper).
2. A 10 percent change in the exchange value of the dollar leads to a 4 percent change in exports (in the opposite direction, because a rising dollar makes exports more expensive).

Again, the results seem to confirm a strong link between contractionary monetary policy and decreasing domestic spending, on the one hand, and expansionary monetary policy and increasing domestic spending, on the other. Can you describe the interest and exchange rate changes that yield these results?

The researchers concluded that the combined effect of interest rate and exchange rate changes can be substantial. In fact, a 10 percent increase in both leads to a drop in spending for residential construction and consumers' and producers' durables of almost 6 percent. This represents nearly 1⅓ percent of GNP, a significant change in economic activity, which is likely to yield a further multiplier effect as well.

Although these results suggest a significant link between monetary policy and the nation's economic activity, the researchers caution that continuing changes in the financial sector and the increasing openness of the U.S. economy may have resulted in weakening the link between Federal Reserve policy instruments and financial variables.

(From M.A. Akhtar and Ethan S. Harris, "Monetary Policy Influences on the Economy—An Empirical Analysis," *Federal Reserve Bank of New York Quarterly Review*, Winter 1987, 19–34.)

Question for Discussion

1. How does the openness of the U.S. economy affect the link between open market operations, for example, and interest rates?

An Attempt at Monetarism in the 1970s

In 1970 Arthur Burns became Chairman of the Board of Governors of the Federal Reserve System. Burns had been a professor of economics whose student, Milton Friedman, is regarded as the leader of the nation's Monetarists. Burns favored the Monetarists' approach to economic policy: a stable money growth target in line with growth of the nation's productive capacity. In this view, interest rates should be allowed to fluctuate so as to keep spending and income within a noninflationary, high employment range. As you will see, events of the 1970s made this policy unattractive, with the result that money growth varied widely and may have worsened a tendency toward business cycles.

When Burns took over as Federal Reserve Chairman, the economy was moving into recession. GNP growth had slowed from a high growth path through most of the 1960s. Unemployment was rising, and prices were increasing about 5 percent annually. Long-term interest rates clustered around 7 percent, and the annual growth of *M*1 was only 2.5 percent. Moderately expansionary monetary and fiscal policies were begun, with the goal of increasing GNP growth. Regrettably, the Vietnam War heated up, requiring greater government spending and aggravating inflation. Unemployment worsened as well, and GNP failed to grow as expected. President Nixon and Congress urged still faster money growth to stimulate private spending and hold down the interest cost of Treasury borrowing to finance the war.

Contrary to the advice of its monetarist critics, the Federal Reserve turned more expansionary. Still, growth in total production remained below the desired GNP growth path. Stronger medicine appeared to be needed, and in August 1971 President Nixon proclaimed a 90-day freeze on prices, to be followed by wage-price controls. Fiscal and monetary policy became strongly expansionary in 1972, in anticipation (it was said) of the coming Presidential election. Production increased significantly in 1973 but inflation increased, too, when wage-price controls were relaxed.

Federal Reserve policymakers faced a difficult dilemma during the period of wage-price controls. The problem arose because short-term interest earnings are an important source of income to many investors. Reducing money growth to slow inflation might raise the interest incomes of these individuals and institutions, a result that seemed inappropriate when other wages and prices were being controlled. There was some discussion in Congress of imposing additional controls on interest rates, a decision that would have interfered with the use of monetary policy to curb inflation. Some critics complained that in order to avoid interest rate controls, the Federal Reserve allowed the money supply to grow much too fast and held rates down. The result was more fuel for inflation, which ultimately destroyed the controls system entirely.

The OPEC Recession of 1974–1975

Late in 1973 the Organization of Petroleum Exporting Countries (OPEC) raised crude oil prices and declared an embargo on oil exports to the United States. Unemployment and inflation increased sharply, and total output fell by 1.4 percent in 1974. Money growth slowed by about a percentage point, and interest rates climbed to historic highs. High interest rates placed many large banks in difficulty, because high rates were necessary to attract short-term deposits but many banks had made long-term loans at lower rates. The Franklin National Bank appealed to the Federal Reserve for help and received substantial loans; nevertheless, the bank failed in October 1974. Mounting inflation finally brought on strongly contractionary fiscal and monetary policies, and the economy moved into recession.

March 1975 was marked by two events: the trough of the worst post–World War II recession (to date) and passage of Congressional Resolution 133, which removed some of the Federal Reserve's isolation from political pressures. Resolution 133 instructed the Federal Reserve to act to reduce long-term interest rates, to announce its targets for money growth, and to report regularly to Congress to outline and defend its policy objectives.

Increasing Velocity Fuels the Expansion

The recession of 1975 differed importantly from its recent predecessors. It left the economy with an extremely high rate of inflation. Price increases of the immediate past had become firmly embedded in industry cost structures and would take a long time to abate. As recovery began, real growth increased but unemployment remained high. The wide swings in interest rates moderated, and financial markets grew calmer. The demand for credit increased only moderately during the recovery.

The Federal Reserve attempted to set money growth high enough to permit real growth in production but low enough to squeeze out inflationary pressures. Slower money growth was partly offset by increased velocity, typical of recovery from recession. New developments in financial intermediaries also contributed to an increase in velocity, particularly the development of new kinds of checkable deposits.

Throughout 1976, 1977 and 1978 labor productivity grew slowly (less than 6 percent over three years) while hourly wages rose almost 30 percent. Rising wage rates pushed up production costs and worsened inflation. Policymakers struggled to discover the correct policy for absorbing the growing labor force into productive jobs while at the same time gradually reducing inflation. It was feared that too sharp a reduction in money growth might plunge the nation again into recession. These fears grew stronger in 1978.

Slowing Growth and Accelerating Inflation

In 1978 the nation began its fourth year of expansion. Four years of continuous expansion exceeded all post–World War II records except for the phenomenal expansion of the 1960s and, in fact, growth was beginning to slow. Consumer spending was high as a fraction of total spending—a result of beat-the-price-rise psychology, particularly in markets for durable goods. But slow growth in real income and rising consumer debt were beginning to cut into consumer spending. Business investment spending was increasing only moderately, with slower profit growth and higher borrowing costs beginning to take hold. Planned inventory investment was cautious.

Government had generally turned less expansionary in 1978, with a reduction in the federal deficit and only moderate spending by state and local governments. Federal expenditures declined in real terms, while higher Social Security taxes and higher income tax brackets for many taxpayers increased federal revenues. Exports of goods and services increased in 1978, however, partly in response to the decline in the value of the dollar and partly because economies abroad were finally recovering from the 1975 recession.

Moderate increases in aggregate demand continued to shift the *IS* curve to the right, but by smaller amounts throughout 1978. GNP grew by almost 4 percent in real terms, and unemployment fell by a full percentage point (to 6 percent) in spite of the addition of 3 million workers to the labor force. Inflation was accelerating: from 6.8 percent in 1977 to 8.1 percent in 1978. One reason was the sharp decrease in the value of the dollar; a cheaper dollar made imported goods and commodities more expensive and raised production costs in many industries. (We will have more to say about the dollar in international trade in Chapter 19.)

Policy for the "Turning Point"

G. William Miller became Chairman of the Board of Governors in mid-1978, just in time to preside over turbulent monetary conditions and to suffer harsh criticism for his conduct of monetary policy. For most of the year, Miller appeared to be following the policy of his predecessor: allowing money growth to increase along with the increase in credit demand so as to hold interest rates constant. As inflation accelerated, however, policy finally turned contractionary. The discount rate was raised in steps to 9.5 percent, until then the highest rate ever. Reserve requirements on large certificates of deposit were increased as well. Open market sales reduced Federal Reserve holdings of securities by $5 billion during the first half of 1979, and commercial bank reserves fell by $1.4 billion. Money growth slowed from 4.1 percent in the closing months of 1978 to −2.1 percent in early 1979.

Then abruptly monetary policy turned expansionary. Critics complained that expansionary policy was continuing to fuel inflation and adding to the distortions that would have to be corrected in the next recession. Miller reasoned that expansionary policy would be effective only after a lag of about a year and that increasing money growth would soften the coming recession and ease the recovery afterward.

Lags in the Effectiveness of Monetary Policy

Chairman Miller's decision to increase money growth late in the expansion stage of a business cycle illustrates a fundamental problem of policymakers. The problem involves the timing of monetary policy relative to its expected effects. Like any government policy, monetary policy is subject to lags. There are four lags between the time when policy is needed and when it finally becomes effective:

1. The first lag may be called the *identification lag*. It is the time required to acknowledge that a problem exists and that it can be remedied by policy action.
2. The second lag may be called the *decision lag*. It is the time required for evaluating alternatives, deciding on a plan of action, and putting the plan into place.
3. The third lag may be called the *money sector lag*. It is the time required before Federal Reserve policy actually affects bank reserves and, ultimately, the money supply. Some time must elapse before banks understand that policy changes are more than simply defensive tactics but intended as dynamic changes in Federal Reserve targets. Then time is needed to alter banks' credit policies safely and with a minimum of problems for borrowers.
4. The fourth lag may be called the *product sector lag*. It is the time required before changes in the availability of credit produce real changes in economic activity. If the goal of policy is to influence output, employment and prices, completing this final step is especially critical.

The timing of the four lags is important because, between the time a problem is first noticed and the effects of policy felt, the problem may have disappeared. A policy intended for fighting unemployment may become effective when the economy is experiencing full employment with inflation. Of course, the reverse is also true.

Many economists believe that policy operates with a lag that is distributed over a period of 6 to 18 months. Less than half the effect of a change in policy is felt within 6 months, so that by the time one policy change is taking hold, an offsetting change may be working—at least partly—to cancel it out. This means that a brief change in the money growth target will have little or no effect on production and employment.

The time lag for the effectiveness of monetary policy is important in the debate over whether money growth should ever be varied for stabilization purposes. In general, monetarists say "no," but for different reasons. On the one hand, Milton Friedman has estimated a lag of 15 months between changes in bank reserves and changes in GNP. If Friedman's estimate is correct, then policy changes are risky without reliable predictions of economic activity 15 months in the future. This is why Friedman prefers a constant rate of money growth in line with potential growth of output.

Other economists recommend steady money growth, too, but for different reasons. Arthur Laffer reports that policy changes have an immediate and permanent effect on GNP. This makes tampering with the money supply particularly dangerous, because mistakes are hard to correct. More recent evidence supports a position between these extremes, with a lag of from 6 to 18 months between the time a change in policy takes place and the time its effects are fully reflected in real production.

Getting Serious about Monetarism

Events of the fall of 1979 illustrated another problem: the difficulty of separating monetary policy from politics. As part of a major change in his cabinet, President Carter appointed William Miller Secretary of the Treasury and Paul A. Volcker Chairman of the Federal Reserve Board. Volcker had served previously as President of the Federal Reserve Bank of New York and had a reputation as a "tight money man." In general, U.S. investors and finance ministers abroad applauded his appointment, believing that a turn toward slow and steady money growth would curb U.S. inflation and help maintain the dollar's value internationally.

When Paul Volcker took office, real GNP was increasing at a 2.5 percent annual rate. Retail sales and consumer installment debt were growing sharply, spurred by beat-the-price-rise psychology. Volcker was afraid that spending was growing too fast and that there would soon be a severe drop in spending, with a reduction in production and employment. To make matters worse, high energy prices were combining with rising wages and other costs to push inflation to a 9 percent annual rate.

On October 6, 1979, Volcker put into place a package of contractionary monetary policies, including a shift from a credit market target to a money supply target—bank reserves. The development of new money forms had made transactions and precautionary demand for money increasingly hard to predict, so that short-term interest rates were fluctuating widely. Banks and other financial intermediaries had come to believe they could depend on additional reserves to satisfy borrowers whatever the interest rate. Volcker intended to change that impression.

The new policy also included a one percentage point increase in the discount rate to 12 percent, higher reserve requirements on certain liabilities, and moral suasion to banks to lend only for productive purposes—farming and small business—and to avoid speculative loans. The federal funds rate leaped 3.5 percentage points to 13.8 percent. Other short- and long-term rates rose sharply, and stock and bond prices collapsed. Money growth, which had averaged more than 10 percent during the summer of 1979, slowed to 2.2 percent in the fall.

The contractionary monetary policy had been strongly recommended by economists for some time. Many doubted its success in reducing inflation, however. They were afraid that political pressure would force Volcker to become expansionary again before prices could be brought down. Business firms would respond to tight money by cutting output and employment rather than prices. Expecting an eventual return to easy money with continuing inflation, they would continue to raise prices. Meanwhile, rising unemployment would raise calls for expansionary policies, and the Federal Reserve would eventually give in.

Volcker continued to repeat his commitment to monetary restraint through the early months of 1980. In February the discount rate was raised again, and banks raised their prime lending rate. Many small business firms were charged as much as 25 percent on bank borrowings, and some were forced out of business entirely. Volcker insisted that lower interest rates would come about only through a reduction in inflation. And a reduction in inflation would require slower money and credit growth over a substantial period of time. All this is necessary, he said, if public expectations of inflation are to be changed and if spending is to slow to a more sustainable level of real economic growth.

Selective Credit Controls

In March 1980 the Board of Governors took even stronger contractionary actions: a special 15 percent deposit requirement on new consumer loans from all lending institutions, a 15 percent deposit requirement on new purchases of money market fund shares, an increase in reserve requirements on certain liabilities, a 3 percent surcharge above the 13 percent discount rate for certain bank borrowings, and new interest rate ceilings on securities issued by bank holding companies. (The Board acted in response to President Carter's executive order issued under authority of the Credit Control Act of 1969.) Some critics complained that the new credit policies were "too little and too late," that a severe recession had already begun.

The "Double-Dip" Recession

The recession of 1980 was short but severe. Consumer spending and real GNP dropped at an annual rate of 8 percent, and unemployment rose almost two percentage points to 7.8 percent. Auto sales and homebuilding suffered most. With recession, credit controls were removed and interest rates fell, so that consumer spending quickly rebounded. By the end of the year interest rates had moved back up above previous highs, and inflation, which had never slowed significantly, began to pick up again.

According to the rational expectationists, decisions about wages and prices were still responding to expectations of continued inflation. Along with the Monetarists, they urged continued monetary restraint to reduce consumer borrowing for installment purchases and home mortgages. Treasury borrowing was also rising as the recession cut into tax revenues, and state and local governments issued new tax-exempt bonds they had postponed during the recession.

The Federal Reserve responded to the increase in spending by raising the discount rate a full percentage point, and the economy moved back into recession in 1981.

The recession of 1981 and 1982 was part of a worldwide slump, the severest since the Great Depression. In the United States, unemployment rose to 10.7 percent. Housing and auto production continued to suffer from high interest rates, and other firms cut inventories rather than cut prices. U.S. export sales fell, too. Tight monetary policy placed severe strains on heavy borrowers: major manufacturing and service firms, financial intermediaries, and even foreign governments, whose commercial bank borrowings had doubled while their own export sales were falling. Concerned about a major default on Mexico's borrowing, the Federal Reserve abandoned its tight money policy late in 1982.

The Expansion: 1983 to 1987

The change to easy money brought a strong expansion, with 10 percent real growth over the next two years. Remarkably, inflation dropped below 4 percent, and unemployment dropped 2 percentage points. Consumer spending and business investment spending rose; but exports continued to fall while imports rose sharply. Relatively high real interest rates and expectations of increased borrowing by the U.S. Treasury brought foreign holdings of dollars back into the United States and helped hold nominal interest rates down.

Falling nominal interest rates and declining oil prices stimulated the stock market, increasing consumer wealth and fueling additional consumer spending. Unemployment fell from 10.7 percent to 8.2 percent but, surprisingly, inflation did not accelerate. Lower inflation was attributed to two things: (1) the highly valued dollar, which kept import prices down, and (2) deregulation in industry, which brought competitive price cuts.

The expansion begun in 1983 continued four years into 1987, and inflation remained low. Unemployment dropped further to 6 percent, and real GNP increased at an average annual rate of 2.5 percent. In the fall of 1987, however, a sharp drop in stock prices seemed to signal a slowdown in consumer and investment spending, with the possibility of a new recession.

Some Continuing Problems

The chief problem facing monetary policymakers in the mid-1980s is massive government deficits, a result of tax laws of 1981 that sharply reduced tax rates while government defense spending was increasing. Annual deficits have increased to between 5 percent and 5.5 percent of GNP and are absorbing a larger and larger part of total saving in the nation. The full employment deficit is expected to be as high as 5 percent of GNP at least until 1990. Unless money growth is speeded up to accommodate Treasury borrowing, high real interest rates will crowd out private investment spending, and economic growth will slow. High interest rates will also keep the dollar's value high and destroy the ability of U.S. firms to compete with lower cost producers abroad. To increase money growth, on the other hand, will increase the risk of renewed inflation.

Another problem is the increasing confusion over money targets. The development of new money forms has made it more difficult to set targets and to measure the relationship between target variables and spending. To deal with the confusion, the Federal Reserve has decided to be more flexible in setting targets and to focus less on target variables and more on long-term goals of production, employment and prices.

Another dangerous imbalance in the world economy is the differential growth rates among nations, which hold down U.S. exports and damage export firms. Trade imbalances create massive deficits in international accounts. The inflow of financial capital from other nations helps keep nominal interest rates from rising, but the long-term threat of heavy loan repayments hovers over financial markets.

The inflow of financial capital has the advantage in the United States of dampening inflation and spurring improvements in productivity. It places a burden on the less developed countries (LDCs), however, whose debt repayment problems are worsening and threatening the solvency of U.S. commercial banks.

Interest Rates and Economic Activity

Wide fluctuations in economic activity during the 1970s and 1980s have created some confusion regarding interest rates. In general, the behavior of interest rates depends on the interaction between money supply and money demand. As economic activity picks up, money demand may move ahead of supply and cause interest rates to rise. The first interest rate to feel the effect of changes in money demand is generally the federal funds rate. Other short-term rates follow, and finally long-term rates adjust so that the yield curve resumes its usual slope.

The expected rise in interest rates is consistent with historical experience. As the economy recovers from recession, investment demand increases and consumers increase their purchases of durable goods. If government budgets remain expansionary in the early stages of recovery, government purchases add to the shift in aggregate demand, pushing the *IS* curve farther to the right. Money growth will ordinarily accommodate the higher spending, at least until employment moves into an inflationary range. When money growth finally slows, rightward shifts in *LM* will no longer be adequate to prevent a sharp rise in interest rates. Sharply higher borrowing costs will depress investment spending, consumption of durable goods, and Treasury borrowing to finance a deficit. With recession, lower levels of these components of aggregate demand act further to contract income until the economy reaches a noninflationary level of employment.

Interest rate behavior should be evaluated relative to the price level. As the economy approaches full employment, certain prices and wages may begin to rise. Increases in the general price level reduce the real value of interest earnings. Economists distinguish between *nominal* and *real interest rates*. The nominal rate is the actual percentage paid, and the real rate is corrected for inflation. Thus:

$$\text{Nominal Rate} - \text{Rate of Inflation} = \text{Real Rate.}$$

When inflation exceeds the nominal rate, the real rate is negative.

As expansion slowed throughout 1979, the real rate was indeed negative. Double-digit inflation exceeded most interest earnings. With the prime rate for corporate borrowing 12.25 percent in the fall of 1979 and inflation at 13.7 percent, critics reasoned that monetary policy was too easy. Real interest rates of −1.45 percent (12.25–13.70) indicated strongly expansionary monetary policy. Nominal interest rates had to rise to 15 percent or 16 percent to exert significant contraction.

When nominal interest rates finally moved above the rate of inflation, real interest rates became positive; many current investment projects could not pay their high borrowing costs and had to be abandoned. Many holders of financial instruments experienced capital losses. The result was a serious recession, with liquidations, foreclosures and bankruptcies, and with a significant drop in business and consumer confidence throughout the remainder of the year. The lost output and economic distress in recession were substantial. Furthermore, high borrowing costs contributed to inflation, particularly in building construction, adding to shortages and increasing housing costs.

Over the long run, the results of contractionary policy might be different. Slower money growth would remove some of the basis for price inflation; reduced economic activity would have the same effect. As inflation slows, the nominal rate of interest falls, too, so that savers can receive the same real return for a lower nominal return. Thus, high interest rates in the short run may contribute to lower rates in the long run.

MONEY AND BANKING IN PRACTICE: GIBSON'S PARADOX

Reducing the supply of money should cause interest rates to rise. Right? And increasing the supply should cause interest rates to fall. At least that's what a shifting money supply curve might lead us to expect. But in 1980 Paul Volcker appeared to promise the reverse. To bring interest rates down, he said, would require a reduction in money growth.

Volcker was referring to a paradox observed around the turn of the century by an Englishman named Gibson. Gibson wondered if it was true that increasing the money supply would cause prices to rise and interest rates to fall. So he looked at prices and interest rates

over the previous century. He expected to see the kind of inverse behavior illustrated at the left in Figure 18–1, but instead he saw parallel behavior like that at the right. Apparently, increases in the money supply brought on *both* price increases and increases in interest rates.

Gibson explained the perverse behavior of interest rates in terms of the public's expectations of future prices. Experience of price inflation in one period can lead to increased *inflationary expectations*, so that nominal interest rates rise. Even if money growth brings on a temporary decrease in interest rates, lenders will eventually realize that their real returns have fallen, and refuse to lend at the lower nominal rates. Volcker hoped that reducing money growth might also reduce expectations of inflation and help bring down the high nominal rates of interest that prevailed in 1980.

FIGURE 18–1   Hypothetical Time Series Illustrating Gibson's Paradox

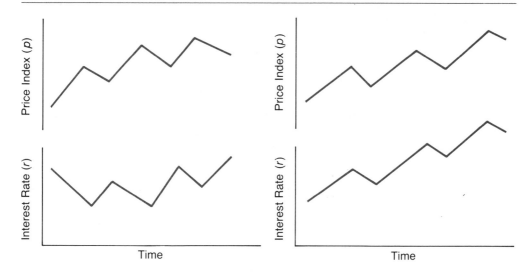

Question for Discussion

1. Explain Gibson's paradox in terms of the *LM* curve.

The New Financial Climate

Today's financial climate is influenced strongly by the effects of deregulation in financial markets. Deregulation has allowed more kinds of financial intermediaries to accept more kinds of deposits and make more kinds of loans. For some financial intermediaries, the result has been a mismatch between accounts on the two sides of the balance sheet. Recessions have created more problems. Declining earnings in agriculture, energy, and in the less developed countries (LDCs) have reduced the creditworthiness of borrowers and increased the risks of lending.

To deal with the increased risks, financial intermediaries have created new financial instruments to transfer risk: interest rate and foreign exchange options and futures contracts are the most obvious. High real interest rates and increased sources of borrowed funds (including direct borrowing by many firms) have reduced the level of liquidity in many business firms and financial intermediaries. Many have adopted liquidity enhancing instruments, like cash management programs, money market funds and new kinds of negotiable deposits.

The higher level of competition in financial markets keeps interest rate spreads narrow. A spread is the difference between what a financial intermediary earns on its assets and what it pays on its liabilities. Rapid telecommunications equipment has increased the speed and increased the risks of financial markets. The increased use of arbitrage has increased the emphasis on short-term financial performance and magnified the risks. For many financial intermediaries, the most profitable strategy is to run payments imbalances during the day and settle accounts at night. This practice increases the risk of settlement failure. Credit risks are not monitored as well as they should be. With all these problems, some members of Congress are beginning to push for new forms of regulation, particularly in the market for government securities.

MONEY AND BANKING IN PRACTICE: TWO PROPOSALS FOR REFORM

Fundamental disagreements over the proper role of money continue to divide U.S. economists. The strongest critic of recent monetary policy is Milton Friedman.

According to Friedman, discretionary policies of the Federal Reserve have not stabilized economic activity but instead have worsened tendencies toward instability. The Fed has shifted its focus frequently from target to target and has allowed too much variability in money growth. The Fed's frequent changes in the procedures for hitting the target have been the source of erratic changes in economic activity. They have contributed to instability of prices and employment but have failed to affect real production.

According to Friedman, the Fed's unbroken record of failure calls for reform, and he has two proposals. One proposal would change the rules under which the Fed operates but leave the basic institution unchanged. The other would fundamentally change the institution itself.

Friedman's first proposal would call for a single target for monetary policy, basic *M*1 money, and a money rule mandating an annual 3 to 5 percent increase. To ensure hitting the target level of *M*1, Friedman would apply the same percentage reserve requirement to all deposit components of the target. Then he would link the discount rate to a market rate and set it high enough to be regarded as a "penalty" borrowing rate. Finally, he would eliminate Federal Reserve actions classified as "defensive" operations. Thus, the Fed would be limited to long-range, "dynamic" operations designed to promote long-range economic goals.

To carry out this proposal would require, first, the calculation of the total level of bank reserves needed to hit the target over, say, six months; second, announcement of the schedule of open market purchases over that period; and, finally, the resolve to stick to the schedule, regardless of short-range fluctuations in financial variables.

Friedman's second proposal would be more radical than this. It would eliminate Federal Reserve control of the money supply and would allow the supply of money to be determined entirely by free markets.

Under Friedman's second proposal, the Federal Reserve would become a department of the Treasury, with power only to maintain the current money base. The Fed's regulatory and supervisory functions would be allocated to the other agencies that now participate in bank supervision. All new money would be issued by private financial institutions, in the form of new liability accounts: like checking accounts, lines of credit, travelers checks, and other bank drafts. The terms of the issue would be determined by the institutions that issue the liabilities and the people who hold them.

To carry out Friedman's second proposal, the rate of money growth would have to be brought down from an annual rate of 7 percent in 1986 to zero in about five years. Then the money base would be frozen, and the Fed would supply new money only when it was necessary to replace worn-out currency.

Friedman does not worry that money growth would be erratic under his second proposal. As the economy grows, he says, the nation's financial intermediaries and innovations would grow, too, so that the money multiplier would increase. This would allow the existing money base to support a larger and larger money supply, consistent with the growing needs of the economy. If this did not happen, prices would decline. However, falling prices would not be a problem; understanding the downward tendency of prices, people would adjust their contracts to allow for the gradual increase in the value of money.

According to Friedman, some of these results are already occurring. Economic growth between 1870 and 1970 was accompanied by a rise in the ratio of the money supply to the money base by an average of about 1 percent a year.

Moreover, since World War II the growth of financial intermediaries and financial instruments has allowed velocity to increase about 3 percent a year.

These developments seem to indicate that private financial institutions have the means and the incentives to supply the nation's money—without interference by the Federal Reserve.

Questions for Discussion

1. What do you think about Friedman's two proposals? What are the advantages and disadvantages of each?

2. What are the theoretical underpinnings of Friedman's radical proposal regarding the Fed?

Glossary of Terms

credit market targets.   interest rates

Gibson's Paradox.   a condition in which increasing money growth aggravates expectations of inflation and causes interest rates to rise

goals.   ultimate objectives in terms of output, employment and prices

identification lag.   one of four time lags between the implementation and the effects of monetary policy; others are decision, money sector and product sector lags

indicator.   a variable whose behavior suggests the direction of current policy

instruments.   monetary policy tools by which Federal Reserve targets are to be achieved

money aggregates.   total reserves or money according to $M1$, $M2$, or $M3$ definitions

nominal interest rate.   the interest rate actually paid on loans

pro-cyclical.   a policy that worsens a tendency toward overexpansion or collapse

real interest rate.   the nominal interest rate corrected for the effects of inflation

targets.   immediate objectives of the Federal Reserve's monetary policy

Summary of Important Ideas

1. To meet its goal of full employment with price stability, the Federal Reserve selects intermediate targets for guiding and evaluating current policy. Targets include broad monetary aggregates or credit market variables.

2. The behavior of target variables may serve as an indicator of the Federal Reserve's goals to financial analysts and investors. Target variables are influenced by other factors, however: commercial bank borrowing and lending, the location of Treasury deposits, public holdings of cash and time deposits, and private demand for credit. Moreover, the relationship between Federal Reserve policy instruments and target variables is not well defined.

3. Because hitting both a monetary aggregate target and a credit market target is difficult, the Federal Reserve must give priority to one or the other. If the source of instability is shifts in the demand for money, a credit market target is believed appropriate. If the source is shifts in the demand for credit, a money supply target is appropriate.

4. Monetarists tend to favor steady money growth with interest rate variability to allocate credit and regulate spending. Keynesians fear that high interest rates will not restrain spending in inflation, nor low rates encourage spending in recession.

5. During the 1950s and 1960s the use of a stable credit market target was believed to have been pro-cyclical: validating excesses in private spending. Stated objectives to hold money growth constant in the 1970s were generally unfulfilled. Vietnam War expenditures, OPEC price increases and a wage-price control program complicated policy-making.

6. In 1975 Congress began to exert more influence on Federal Reserve policy-making.

7. During the late 1970s productivity growth slowed, consumer and investment spending slowed, but inflation remained high. Contractionary monetary policy was finally applied, and the nation moved into recession as the decade ended.

8. Because of the time lag between policy actions and their effects, policy is frequently contrary to current economic conditions. Moreover, other factors in the private and public sector influence the timing and results of policy.

9. During the 1980s, the Federal Reserve has generally acted to restrain money growth to hold down price inflation, at a time when strongly expansionary fiscal policy has caused major increases in spending.

Questions for Discussion and Research

1. Distinguish clearly between goals, targets and instruments. Why is each important? How is each determined?

2. What considerations make targets poor indicators? How might the use of indicators be useful or damaging to investors?

3. Describe the two classes of Federal Reserve targets and explain why it may be necessary to choose between them. What circumstances should govern selection? Discuss the difficulties involved in the selection and the debate that surrounds it.

4. Define *pro-cyclical* and illustrate the pro-cyclical effects of certain kinds of policy. How is this question related to efficiency in credit allocation? What circumstances during the early 1970s led to the move to a money-supply target in 1975?

5. What product-sector and money-sector events of the late 1970s increased the complexities of economic policy-making? What specific changes in financial markets affected the definitions of money targets?

6. Discuss the question of the proper timing for monetary policy actions. How is timing significant for achieving intended results? How are the philosophies of monetary economists significant to their policy recommendations?

7. Explain the different rates of change of the various money measures. Demonstrate how changing variables of the money equations act to affect money growth.

8. Explain changes in nominal interest rates over the business cycle and the likely changes in real rates. What policy conclusions might be drawn?

9. The difference between total commercial bank holdings of excess reserves and borrowed reserves is "net free" reserves (or if the difference is negative, "net borrowed" reserves). What credit conditions would you expect to influence the behavior of "net free" reserves? Why are "net free" reserves not an appropriate indicator of Federal Reserve objectives?

10. During April 1980 the nation's money supply by the *M*1 measure fell at an annual rate of 18 percent. Meanwhile, the money base rose 5 percent and interest rates fell by 5 to 9 percentage points. Point out the apparent contradictions in this report and explain the monetary circumstances that helped bring them about.

Additional Readings

Andersen, Leonall. "Money Market Conditions as a Guide for Monetary Management." In *Targets and Indicators of Monetary Policy*, edited by Karl Brunner. San Francisco: Chandler Publishing Company, 1969.

Andersen, Leonall. "Selection of a Monetary Aggregate for Economic Stabilization." *Federal Reserve Bank of St. Louis Review* 57 (October 1975): 9–15.

Berkman, Neil G. "A Rational View of Rational Expectations." *New England Economic Review*. Federal Reserve Bank of Boston (January/February 1980): 18–29.

Berkman, Neil G. "Some Comments on the New Monetary Aggregates." *New England Economic Review*. Federal Reserve Bank of Boston (March/April 1980): 45–63.

Blinder, Alan S. "The Policy Mix: Lessons from the Recent Past." *Economic Outlook USA* (Fall 1986): 3–8.

Burger, Albert E. "The Relationship between Monetary Base and Money: How Close?" *Federal Reserve Bank of St. Louis Review* 57 (October 1975): 3.

Burns, Arthur F. "Burns' Parting Thoughts." *Across the Board* 15 (May 1978): 78–80.

Danziger, Sheldon, Robert Haveman, Donald Nichols, and Barbara Wolfe. "Reviewing Reagan's Economic Policy." *Challenge* (January/February 1984): 42–50.

Davis, Richard G. "The Monetary Base as an Intermediate Target for Monetary Policy." *Federal Reserve Bank of New York Quarterly Review* 4 (Winter 1979/1980): 1–10.

Heller, Walter W. "Open Letter to G. William Miller." *Challenge* 21 (March/April 1978): 18–19.

Hetzel, Robert L. "Monetary Policy in the Early 1980s," *Economic Review of the Federal Reserve Bank of Richmond* (March/April 1986): 20–31.

Keyserling, Leon. "Will It Be Progress or Poverty?" *Challenge* (May/June 1987): 30–36.

Kopcke, Richard W. "Financial Assets, Interest Rates, and Money Growth." *New England Economic Review* (March/April 1987): 17–30.

Lang, Richard W. "The FOMC in 1979: Introducing Reserve Targeting." *Review of the Federal Reserve Bank of St. Louis* 62 (March 1980): 2–17.

McCallum, Bennett T. "The Significance of Rational Expectations Theory." *Challenge* 22 (January/February 1980): 37–43.

Poole, William. "Interpreting the Fed's Monetary Targets." *Brookings Papers on Economic Activity* 1:247–259. Washington, D.C., 1976.

Poole, William. "Burnsian Monetary Policy: Eight Years of Progress?" *Journal of Finance* 34 (May 1979): 473–504.

Poole, William. "Ignoring the Funds Rate." *The American Banker* (July 23, 1979): 4.

Poole, William. "The Monetary Deceleration: What Does It Mean and Why Is It Happening?" *Brookings Papers on Economic Activity* 1: 231–240. Washington, D.C., 1979.

Tobin, James. "Monetary Semantics." In *Targets and Indicators of Monetary Policy*, edited by Karl Brunner. San Francisco: Chandler Publishing Company, 1969.

Wallich, Henry C. "Wallich's Approach to Fighting Inflation." *Across the Board* 26 (December 1979): 69–74.

CHAPTER

19

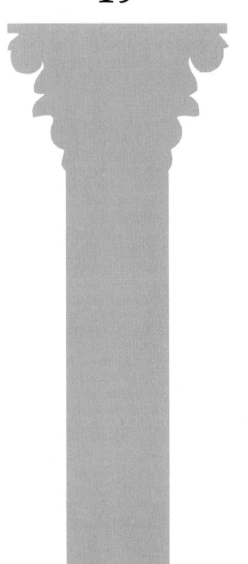

LEARNING OBJECTIVES

- To show how international transactions affect national income, employment and prices
- To distinguish between internal and external balance
- To learn about practices and policies for achieving balance in both the domestic and international sectors
- To explore international agreements for achieving balance, along with their disadvantages

Achieving Internal and External Balance

"Inasmuch as a deficit in foreign payments means drawing on real resources of other countries, and inasmuch as unemployment is sometimes due to an insistence on higher wages than the market can provide, an ethical judgment that more employment should be secured even if it involves prolonged deficits says in effect that it is more ethical to call for a sacrifice of others than to tolerate a sacrifice oneself."

Fritz Machlup

It is government's responsibility to design and carry out policies that promote maximum levels of well-being for its citizens. Fulfilling this responsibility is difficult because the goal of maximum well-being may conflict with other important goals. Moreover, policies to improve citizens' well-being may produce side effects that conflict with other policy objectives. In this chapter we will confront two types of policy objectives that frequently come into conflict. We will show how policy actions taken to improve one type of problem often worsen problems of another type. And we will mention the criteria that determine a government's decision to favor one objective over the other.

We will characterize these two sorts of problems as problems of internal balance and problems of external balance. Internal balance means an efficient equilibrium level of domestic output and employment, with the improved equity and positive externalities that accompany stable prices. External balance means Balance of Payments equilibrium with a nation's trading partners. External balance implies efficiency in the global use of resources and equity in the distribution of global production.

Defining Internal Balance

A nation's income, employment and prices depend on aggregate demand and aggregate supply. We have seen that aggregate demand is the sum of all spending for goods and services produced for the market. Spending provides incentives to business firms to hire resources up to the productive capacity of the economy. Beyond the point of full employment, further spending worsens the scarcity of resources and threatens price inflation. Throughout this process, the supply of money and the financial institutions that manage it help provide the spending power necessary for carrying out private and public decisions in the market.

In Chapters 15 through 17 we used the *IS-LM* model to illustrate the result of spending decisions and decisions regarding the supply of and demand for money. We characterized the equilibrium level of income and employment as efficient or inefficient, depending on the level of employment and price inflation. Then we showed how the coordinated use of fiscal and monetary policy can help move equilibrium to a more efficient level of employment with stable prices.

The *IS* Curve: Product-Sector Equilibrium

To include international transactions in our analysis requires some small changes. First, we must expand the Keynesian model of income determination to include foreign spending. Specifically, we must include U.S. sales to foreigners minus U.S. purchases of goods and services produced abroad:

$$\text{Net Foreign Investment} = \text{U.S. Exports} - \text{U.S. Imports}$$
$$= X_f - M_f = F_n.$$

Net foreign investment (F_n) combines with domestic consumption (C), investment spending (I), and government purchases (G) to yield aggregate demand and to determine the position of the *IS* curve. Including (F_n) changes the equilibrium positions on the *IS* curve to

$$Y = C + I + G + F_n$$

at various interest rates. Including F_n in product-sector equilibrium is illustrated in Figures 19–1a and 19–1b.

Let us look at F_n in more detail. International spending is determined by many factors in the world economy: resource supplies and their productivity, changes in productivity trends among nations, the technology of transportation and communication, and incomes. Incomes provide the ability to participate in international markets just as they do in domestic markets. In effect, incomes measure contributions to global production and define the maximum amounts that can be withdrawn from global production. Thus, U.S. imports depend on U.S. incomes, and U.S. exports depend on incomes abroad.

Note that the expression

$$F_n = X_f - M_f$$

measures the merchandise trade balance in Part 1 of the Balance of Payments statement. The net value of merchandise trade is added to (or subtracted

FIGURE 19–1a   An Open Economy: The
Keynesian Model

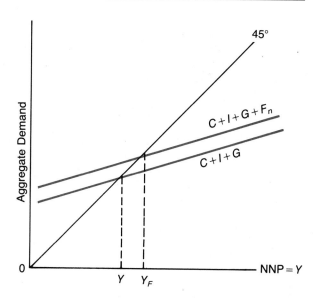

FIGURE 19–1b   International Trade and
Product-Sector
Equilibrium

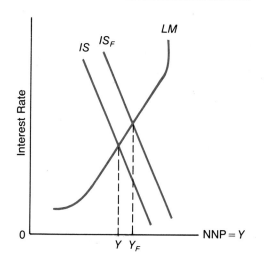

FIGURE 19–1c   International Money
Flows and Money-
Sector Equilibrium

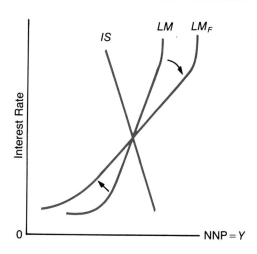

from) domestic spending to define the *IS* curve. Remember that the *IS* curve defines all combinations of income and interest rates at which saving is equal to planned investment. Increases in exports (X_f) shift the *IS* curve to the right, and decreases shift the curve to the left. Because imports reduce domestic purchases, increases in imports (M_f) shift the *IS* curve to the left, and decreases shift it to the right.

The *LM* Curve: Money-Sector Equilibrium

The second change in the Keynesian model is to adapt money-sector equilibrium to include the effects of international transactions on the money supply. We have defined the *LM* curve as comprising all equilibrium positions between the demand for and the supply of money. Money demand (*L*) depends on income and interest rates that determine transactions and speculative balances. The quantity of money demanded is higher with higher incomes and lower with higher interest rates. The nation's money supply (*M*) depends on the open market policies of the Federal Reserve and on decisions of banks, the Treasury, and the public with respect to holdings of demand deposits. Higher interest rates tend to increase the money supply, as banks and individuals attempt to maximize interest income from their asset portfolios.

Including international transactions means that some of the nation's money flows in and out in response to trade or investment opportunities the world over. In effect, the money supply in the United States becomes subject to the changing effects of international trade and investment. When more money flows out through trade than in, the domestic money supply falls. The Federal Reserve may have to create additional bank reserves just to maintain the domestic money supply at a level sufficient for spending at full employment. Then foreign holdings of money become a potentially disruptive addition to the domestic money supply.

When the Federal Reserve creates additional money to offset a money outflow, we say it has sterilized the effects of trade. *Sterilization* also takes place when the Federal Reserve reduces the money supply to offset an inflow of money from increased exports. Unless the Federal Reserve acts continuously to sterilize international money flows, the effect may be unwanted changes in the money supply and unwanted shifts of the *LM* curve.

Apart from spending for trade, short-term investments are another source of international money flows. Short-term investment flows depend strongly on interest rates. Differences in rates among nations encourage "hot money" to move in and out quickly, to take advantage of higher expected interest earnings. When U.S. interest rates are relatively high, we would expect inflows of short-term deposits, which will increase the lending capacity of U.S. banks. When U.S. interest rates are relatively low, we would expect deposit outflows and a lower value of *M*.

The result of all this is to make the money supply more variable, so that the *LM* curve is flatter. The effect of international money flows on money-sector equilibrium is illustrated in Figure 19–1c.

The Effect on Fiscal and Monetary Policy

In practice, a flatter *LM* curve means that fiscal policy produces relatively greater changes in income and smaller changes in interest rates. The reason is that a money shortage or money glut is partially offset by international deposit flows. An increase in money demand, for example, does not push interest rates up as far, because money held abroad flows into the United States to earn the higher yields. On the other hand, a drop in domestic spending plans encourages U.S. investors to shift funds abroad where money demand is greater. We might say that international money flows reduce the crowding out that might otherwise result from expansionary fiscal policy.

A flatter *LM* curve also influences the effectiveness of monetary policy. The reasons are simple. An attempt to increase the money supply and reduce interest rates can be thwarted by money outflows. Interest rates cannot fall as far or income rise as much as in a closed economy. Contractionary monetary policy suffers from the same problem. If the Federal Reserve Bank reduces reserves so that interest rates rise, money held abroad can flow freely back to the United States.

Policymakers may even hesitate to use monetary policy vigorously because of its implications for international money flows. To understand this point, suppose expansionary policy is needed to combat unemployment, but holders of dollars abroad fear that expansionary fiscal policy will bring on inflation. Any action by the Federal Reserve to increase commercial bank reserves would cause foreign holders to dump dollars on foreign exchange markets. Speculators would go short, and investment funds would flow out. On the other hand, contractionary policies might bring on expectations of reduced inflation, with higher values for the dollar. But in this case U.S. export industries are harmed by the higher international prices for their products.

Summary

We may summarize the international aspects of internal balance as follows:

1. Net foreign investment ($X_f - M_f$) is an increasingly important component of aggregate demand.
2. Shifts in *C, I* or *G* have less effect on domestic output and employment when citizens can spend (or reduce their spending) for goods and services produced abroad.

3. The money supply is influenced by international spending flows and by the responsiveness of short-term investment to interest rates.

4. Fiscal policy produces wider swings in income and smaller changes in interest rates when international money flows accommodate government spending needs.

5. International money flows reduce the effectiveness of domestic monetary policy by narrowing the resulting changes in incomes and interest rates.

6. Finally, because international flows of spending and lending respond to a myriad of causes outside our model, they are difficult to predict and plan for. This makes policy-making much less precise. Unforeseen developments may turn routine policy moves into major mistakes, with many frustrations for government and for the financial sector as well.

Defining External Balance

We have outlined some of the complexities international transactions add to our model of domestic equilibrium. Now we will examine the problem of external balance. External balance involves equilibrium in Balance of Payments accounts. Equilibrium does not mean balance; we have seen that international accounts must always balance. Equilibrium or disequilibrium depends on the size and direction of compensatory transactions (Part 3 of the Balance of Payments statement). A repeated need to borrow or repeated lending indicates a fundamental disequilibrium and the absence of external balance.

External balance means that a nation is withdrawing from global production goods and services equal in value to those it contributes. In this sense, external balance ensures equity in the distribution of global output and minimizes the potential for international conflict. It helps promote free trade and the positive externalities that follow from international specialization.

Lack of external balance may have several causes. The terms of trade may turn against a nation, so that every unit of exports buys fewer imports than before; needed imports may continue to be purchased on credit, with the result that accounts continue out of balance. Price inflation, not offset by equal and opposite changes in currency exchange rates, may change the attractiveness of imported and exported goods, shifting accounts out of balance. Growth of incomes may be irregular among trading nations, changing the patterns of consumer purchases. We dealt with all these causes in Chapter 12. Here we will deal with the third cause in greater detail.

FIGURE 19–2a Balance of Trade

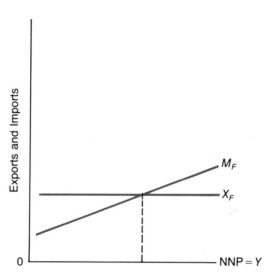

Exports are shown as a constant relative to
domestic incomes.

FIGURE 19–2b Effect of Shift to Lower
Domestic Income

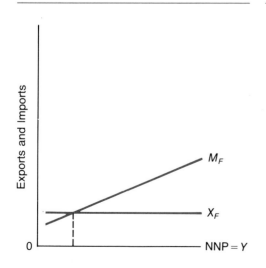

FIGURE 19–2c Effect of Shift to Higher
Domestic Income

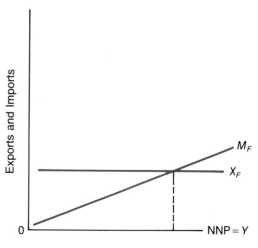

A nation's exports depend on incomes abroad, and imports depend on domestic income. Figures 19–2a to 19–2c illustrate the effect of income changes on the trade balance. Imports (M_f) are shown as an increasing function of domestic income according to the marginal propensity to import (MPI). The MPI is defined as the change in imports associated with a change in domestic incomes:

$$\text{MPI} = \Delta M_f / \Delta Y.$$

Higher domestic incomes encourage increased spending for imported autos and equipment, clothing and ornaments, travel and recreational services. Exports (X_f) depend on incomes in many other nations, some of whose incomes may be rising and some falling. Therefore, exports are shown in Figures 19–2a to 19–2c as a constant relative to domestic incomes. The level of exports may shift from year to year with changes in incomes abroad. Or income changes in some of a nation's trading partners may be offset at least in part by opposite changes in others, leaving X_f roughly stable.

To determine the balance of trade, compare the value of exports with imports. Note that low levels of income are associated with balance of trade surpluses; domestic incomes are so low that imports are also low. On the other hand, high levels of income are associated with balance of trade deficits, as high-income consumers spend heavily for goods and services produced abroad. Only one level of income yields balance of trade equilibrium. The effects of levels of income on the balance of trade can be expressed algebraically:

$$X_f - M_f > 0 = \text{Surplus}$$
$$X_f - M_f < 0 = \text{Deficit}$$
$$X_f - M_f = 0 \ = \text{Trade Equilibrium}$$

The positions of X_f and M_f are drawn *ceteris paribus*; that is, with other factors held constant. Circumstances outside the model are assumed to be unchanging so that we may observe the relationship between X_f and M_f only. On this basis, we may conclude that low national income tends to be associated with balance of trade surpluses and high income with deficits. Changing any of the conditions held constant (ceteris paribus) shifts the position of X_f and M_f and changes the location of balance of trade equilibrium. Thus, an unfavorable change in terms of trade reduces the trade value of exports relative to imports; the result is a downward shift in X_f, an upward shift in M_f, and deficits over a wider range of incomes. This situation, shown graphically in Figure 19–2b, is illustrative of recent events in many less developed countries, whose necessary imports of Arab oil now cost more in terms of their own exports of raw commodities.

Whatever the cause of changes in terms of trade—uneven gains in productivity, changes in global consumer demand, or faulty exchange rates—shifts in X_f and M_f can bring extended deficits or surpluses in international accounts. Domestic price inflation, uncorrected by exchange rate movements, can have the same effect. The United States experienced increasing inflation during the late 1970s, but the dollar's exchange value did not fall enough to reflect its reduced purchasing power. With their overvalued dollars, U.S. citizens spent lavishly for lower priced imports, while foreigners were unable to pay the high prices of U.S. exports. Exports (X_f) shifted down and imports (M_f) shifted up, producing a series of deficits.

Figure 19–2b illustrates both these circumstances, but it implies that elsewhere in the world other countries are experiencing the opposite shifts in exports (X_f) and imports (M_f). Those are the countries where favorable changes in terms of trade or lower price inflation, not corrected by changes in exchange rates, yield balance of trade surpluses over a wider range of incomes. Germany, Japan and some oil-producing states fit this category.

Combining Internal and External Balance

If government is to fulfill its responsibility to ensure high levels of employment and price stability on the one hand and Balance of Payments equilibrium on the other, it must have effective instruments for carrying out policy. In terms of internal balance, it must have appropriate fiscal and monetary policy tools; for external balance it must have the means of influencing international trade and finance.

Fiscal and Monetary Policy

To illustrate the process, we have combined the familiar *IS-LM* model of internal equilibrium in Figure 19–1a with Figure 19–2a, representing external equilibrium. In Figure 19–3, the equilibrium level of income is Y^*. Employment is 80 percent, a noninflationary level of employment. Income of Y^* is associated with exports of Y^*a and imports of Y^*b. The relatively low level of income yields a balance of trade surplus of ab.

The hypothetical economy shown in Figure 19–3 is achieving neither internal nor external balance. Unemployment of 20 percent suggests inefficient use of the nation's productive resources, with inadequate living standards for its people. A balance of trade surplus suggests that the nation is withdrawing less from global output in the form of imports than it contributes in exports. Again, domestic standards of living are lower than need be.

Expansionary fiscal and monetary policy can be used together to shift the *IS* and *LM* curves to the right, as shown in Figure 19–4, increasing income to full employment at, say, 95 percent of the labor force. At the same time, higher incomes will encourage greater spending for imports and eliminate

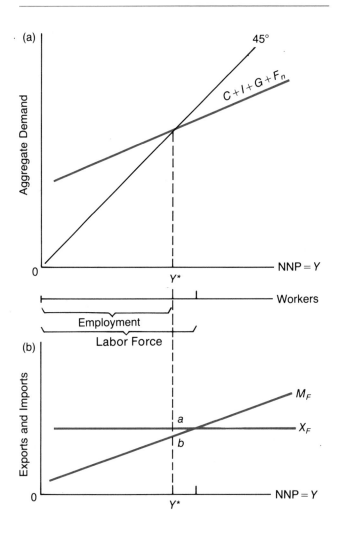

FIGURE 19-3   Internal and External Imbalance

the balance of trade surplus. Note that achieving internal balance is consistent with the goal of external balance. A single set of policies can accomplish both objectives.

The same result is true of the opposite situation shown in Figure 19-5. In Figure 19-5 the equilibrium level of income exceeds the noninflationary level of employment at 95 percent. With exports (X_f) and imports (M_f) as shown in the figure, the balance of trade is in deficit. In these circumstances, achieving internal balance would require contractionary fiscal and monetary policies, accomplishing external balance at the same time.

FIGURE 19–4 Expansionary Fiscal and Monetary Policy to Achieve Internal and External Balance

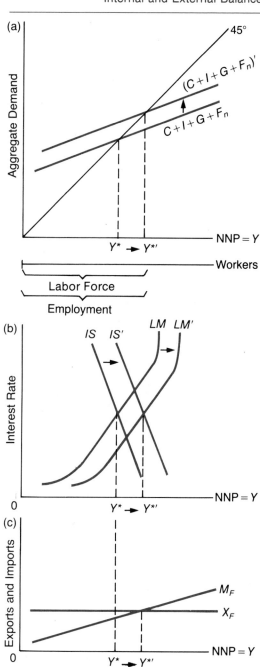

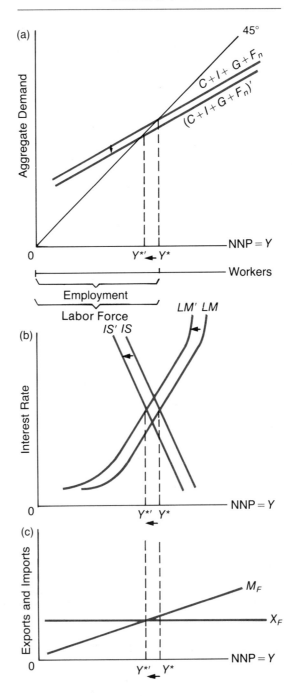

FIGURE 19–5 Contractionary Monetary and Fiscal Policy to Achieve Internal and External Balance

The Effect on Short-Term Investment Flows

In Figures 19–4 and 19–5 monetary policy designed to achieve internal balance may promote external balance as well. In the surplus nation, expansionary monetary policy will tend to push interest rates down. Lower interest yields will discourage short-term investment, stimulating an outflow of currency to eliminate a Balance of Payments surplus. In the deficit nation, contractionary monetary policy will push interest rates up and encourage an inflow of short-term investment. In both cases, interest rate changes would help achieve external balance.

The result of contractionary monetary policy in the deficit nation may be higher borrowing costs, reduced capital construction and fewer jobs. During the 1950s the United States attempted to avoid these results while using contractionary monetary policy to reduce the deficit. The procedure was nicknamed Operation Twist because it involved twisting the yield curve. Instead of its usual upward slope, the yield curve was twisted to slope downward; that is, short-term rates were pushed up and long-term rates were pushed down. Higher short-term rates, it was reasoned, would encourage short-term currency inflows and reduce the deficit in the capital account. Lower long-term rates would encourage domestic borrowing for capital construction. The "twist" was expected to be accomplished by Federal Reserve purchases of long-term securities, driving their prices up and interest yields down. Meanwhile, sales of short-term securities were expected to push their prices down and cause interest yields to rise.

Conflicts Between Internal and External Balance

Figures 19–4 and 19–5 illustrate conditions where one set of policies can accomplish both internal and external balance. In the real world, imbalances are rarely so easily corrected. Figures 19–6 and 19–7 illustrate the more likely possibilities.

In Figure 19–6 the equilibrium levels of income and employment are too low, but the balance of trade is in deficit. Expansionary monetary and fiscal policies to increase employment would worsen conditions for external balance. Contractionary policies to reduce the balance of trade deficit would increase domestic unemployment.

Figure 19–7 illustrates the opposite dilemma. Income is too high for domestic wage and price stability, but contractionary monetary and fiscal policies would increase the balance of trade surplus. In both types of circumstances, government must choose between the objectives of internal and external balances and decide on the fiscal and monetary policies that will achieve the desired objective. Pursuing one objective means sacrificing the other.

FIGURE 19–6 Both Internal and External Imbalance

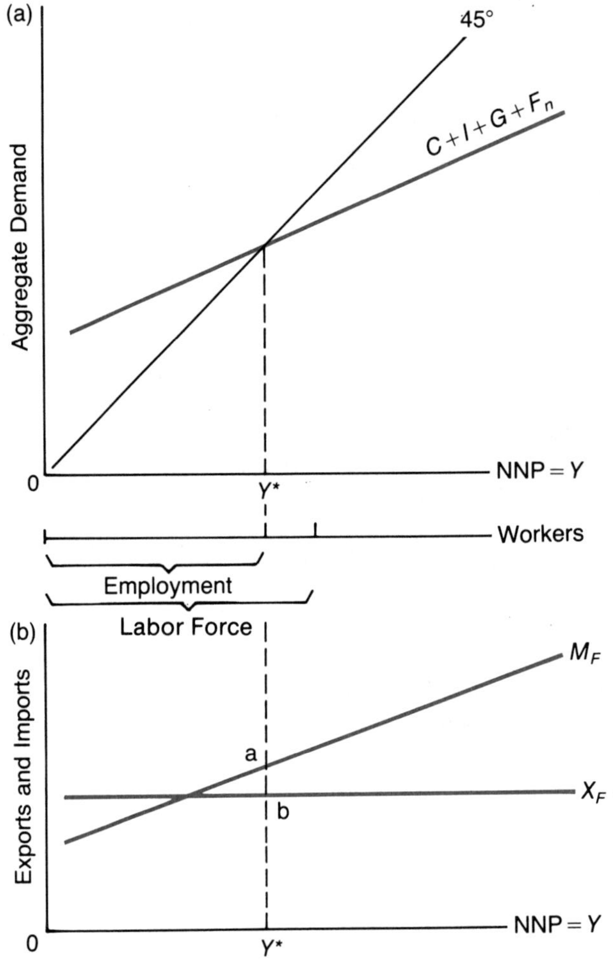

Recent Experiences

The circumstances illustrated in Figures 19–6 and 19–7 do not clearly reflect conditions in any single nation. The model is a simplified view of reality, excluding many of the factors that affect real world variables. Still, we may suggest that Figure 19–6 more nearly describes recent conditions in Great Britain, and Figure 19–7, those in Germany.

During the 1970s Great Britain experienced years of expansionary policies, with inflation as high as 25 percent. Until the development of North Sea oil, British trade balances were generally in deficit, with millions of

FIGURE 19–7   Both Internal and External Imbalance

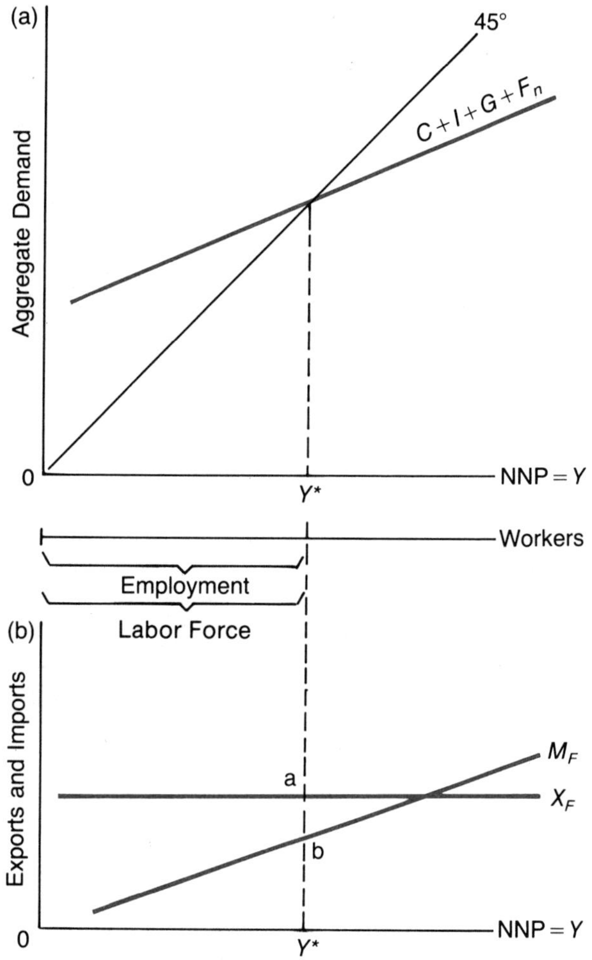

British pounds flowing out to foreign exchange markets around the world. The decrease in the pound's exchange rate made imports more costly and worsened British inflation, giving another unfavorable jolt to the trade balance and perpetuating the decline of the pound's value. In 1979, the British elected a conservative government that promised contractionary fiscal and monetary policies to achieve external balance and stabilize the pound. Voters appeared willing to suffer an increase in unemployment to get inflation under control and regain Britain's competitive position in world trade.

The German government made the opposite choice. As shown in Figure 19–7, to achieve external balance would require expansionary fiscal and monetary policies and risk inflation. Historical experience has aggravated German fears of inflation, so that policymakers have chosen to maintain internal balance and endure continuing surpluses in the balance of trade. The German government was helped in this decision by the fact that many domestic workers were "guest workers" from other European nations. Contractionary policies forced these workers out of jobs and out of the country without increasing employment among German workers.

In both these cases, governments were forced to sacrifice internal or external balance. At least temporarily, their citizens have been willing to forego the advantages of either full employment with price stability or Balance of Payments equilibrium.

Offsetting Fiscal and Monetary Policies

Under some circumstances, offsetting fiscal and monetary policies may be used together to achieve both internal and external balance. Success depends on changes in interest rates and flows of short-term investments.

To illustrate, suppose a nation is experiencing unemployment and a trade deficit as shown in Figure 19–8. Expansionary fiscal policy can be used to shift the *IS* curve to the right and increase output and employment. While expansionary fiscal policy tends to worsen a balance of trade deficit, simultaneous use of contractionary monetary policy might raise interest rates enough to encourage an inflow of investment spending. The Balance of Payments deficit would shrink. On the other hand, suppose the nation is experiencing inflation and a balance of trade surplus, as in Figure 19–9. In this case, contractionary fiscal policy to reduce inflation might be used together with expansionary monetary policy to reduce interest rates. Short-term investments would flow out and reduce the Balance of Payments surplus.

MONEY AND BANKING IN PRACTICE: EXPORTING MONETARY POLICY

Early in the 1980s, the Federal Reserve determined to stop inflation in the United States by slowing money growth. Even as economic activity continued sluggish into 1981, Chairman Paul Volcker showed no willingness to ease mone-

FIGURE 19–8   Offsetting Fiscal and Monetary Policies to Achieve Internal and External Balance

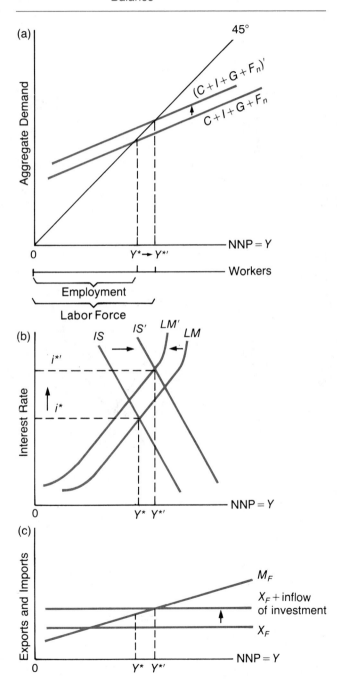

FIGURE 19–9   Offsetting Fiscal and Monetary Policies to Achieve Internal and External Balance

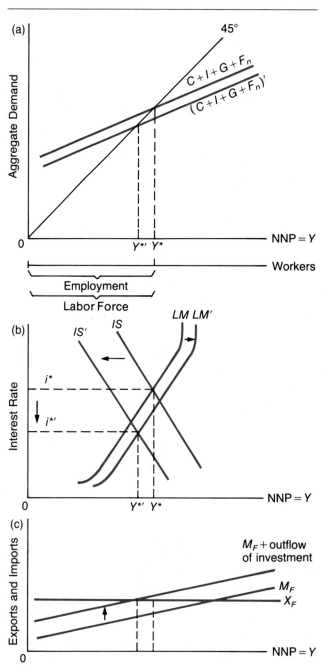

tary policy and help push interest rates down. How did this decision affect economic activity in other nations?

The immediate effect of contractionary monetary policy in the United States was to reduce expectations of inflation so that dollar-denominated assets became more valuable. Investors came to expect an increase in net return—the sum of the expected increase in the dollar's value and the relatively high U.S. interest rates.

Tight money and high interest rates in the United States reduced the monetary policy choices available to policymakers in other countries. In Germany, monetary policy was contractionary all along, consistent with German fears of inflation. In France and Great Britain,

unemployment and recession were calling for expansionary policy to stimulate recovery. But more rapid monetary growth would have reduced interest rates and aggravated inflationary expectations, so that outflows of short-term investment would have increased. Moreover, increasing supplies of their currencies in foreign exchange markets would have reduced exchange rates, so that necessary imports would have cost even more.

While leaders of all major industrial nations suffer politically from slow money growth, most seem to accept contractionary policy as a "necessary evil" for bringing down worldwide inflation and paving the way for more sustainable growth over the long run.

Question for Discussion

1. Interpret the circumstances above in terms of internal and external balance. Why are fluctuating exchange rates not always sufficient for bringing about external balance?

MONEY AND BANKING IN PRACTICE: AGAIN A COLONY?

The United States was once a colonial possession of European nations. Investors in Britain, France, Germany and Spain used their savings to purchase shares in the developing productive capacity of North America. In return for their investments, they received income from U.S. railroads, manufacturing plants and farms.

As incomes grew in the United States, savings grew also, and U.S. savers were able to buy back U.S. prop-

erties and purchase additional properties in Asia, Africa and Latin America. Income from these properties became an important part of the U.S. Balance of Payments.

More changes may be occurring in international savings-investment flows today.

Expansionary fiscal policy in the United States has produced government deficits amounting to two-thirds of current U.S. saving. Competition for financial capital has threatened to drive up U.S. interest rates and crowd out private investment spending. Without sufficient new investment, U.S. productivity growth could slow. Lower incomes, lower employment and lower standards of living could be the result.

Fortunately, foreign investors have again welcomed the opportunity to purchase shares in U.S. industry. Foreign investors have brought new technolo-

gies and new management techniques, and they have provided jobs for U.S. workers. On the other hand, the increasing participation of foreigners in U.S. industry suggests some problems for the long run. In the long run, more of the profits from U.S. industry must be paid to owners abroad. Less will remain for reinvestment, and more decisions regarding future investments will be made abroad.

Questions for Discussion

1. It seems almost as if the United States is returning to its former status as a colony of foreign investors. Our ancestors did not enjoy colonial status. Might we be any different?

2. Cite the pros and cons of foreign investment in the United States.
3. What are the efficiency, equity and externality bases for increased foreign investment?

Policies to Restrict Trade

In the previous sections, we discussed the problem of achieving internal and external balance and the domestic fiscal and monetary policies used toward these objectives. We showed how the two objectives may be incompatible, so that the nation's policymakers must choose between them. Frequently, the choice favors internal balance, because a nation's voters are more immediately concerned with domestic employment and prices than they are with Balance of Payments equilibrium.

Over time, however, a nation cannot afford to ignore a fundamental disequilibrium in its international accounts. Thus, specific policies and institutions must be designed to help resolve international trade and investment disequilibrium. Some of these policies and institutions involve restrictions on trade.

When a nation restricts trade, it sacrifices the benefits of international specialization. In order to maintain full employment it must protect domestic producers from foreign competition. Then domestic consumers suffer higher prices and reduced selections of goods. Moreover, the global economy suffers a loss of efficiency and reduced incentives for technical innovation.

Consider a nation that is experiencing a balance of trade deficit, with decreasing exports (X_f) and an increase in imports (M_f). We showed these conditions on Figure 19–6. A decrease in exports relative to imports reduces the net foreign investment component of aggregate demand:

$$F_n = X_f - M_f.$$

In fact, for a nation with a trade deficit, the value of net foreign investment is negative. A decrease in net foreign investment (F_n) shifts the *IS* curve to the left by a multiple and reduces the equilibrium level of income and employment. Expansionary fiscal and monetary policy could restore internal balance, but the balance of trade deficit would grow even larger.

To minimize the effects of fiscal and monetary policy on the balance of trade, nations have attempted to restrict trade through tariffs, quotas, subsidies and even foreign exchange controls.

Tariffs

One of the oldest and most enduring political issues in the United States has been the issue of tariffs. Tariffs were a topic for debate at the time our government was formed; they were a source of conflict between the North and South in the years leading up to the Civil War; and they continue to divide workers and consumers in the United States today.

A tariff is a tax on imported goods. It raises the price of foreign made goods and encourages consumption of domestic substitutes.

In the beginning, the purpose of tariffs was to raise the price of goods manufactured abroad so as to protect *infant industries* from foreign competition. It was expected that the nation's young industries would eventually mature and become efficient enough to compete on their own. Then the infant-industry tariff could be removed. Frequently, the time for removal was slow in coming. In fact, the trend of U.S. tariffs was generally upward until 1930 when Congress passed our highest tariff ever. The Hawley-Smoot tariff added about 60 percent to the average price of imported goods.

In the 1920s and 1930s tariffs were high around the world. This time, the reason was to save domestic jobs. Worsening unemployment in many nations increased the pressure for protection to keep F_n positive and keep income and employment high. To protect domestic jobs by restricting imports has the effect of exporting unemployment. This is because one nation's fewer imports are another's fewer exports. Other nations retaliated by imposing tariffs of their own to restrict their imports and export their own unemployment elsewhere. The result was a cumulative series of trade restrictions in many nations, with a drop in aggregate demand for all. The collapse of world trade contributed to a collapse of income and employment throughout Western nations.

President Franklin Roosevelt began a program of Reciprocal Trade Negotiations in 1935. Agreements were made with individual nations to reduce tariffs together by comparable amounts. After World War II, negotiations continued with groups of nations who agreed to the membership rules of the General Agreement on Tariffs and Trade, or GATT. Members of GATT continue to meet regularly for tariff negotiations in which tariff reductions are put into effect for all members at the same time. Furthermore, any single reduction for a favored nation is extended to other nations on a *most favored nation* basis. Recent tariff reductions have helped to revive world trade, but there are still problems. U.S. workers continue to want job protection from imports.

Other supporters of tariffs ignore the issue of efficiency and comparative advantage and stress the nation's *strategic industries*. Because certain industries are necessary for defense and for sustaining our population during war, they say, these industries should be protected from competition. Difficulties with this argument are, first, to determine the industries that are in fact strategic and, second, to decide if there are better ways than tariffs to protect such industries. Economists generally favor subsidies to permit truly strategic industries to survive. And they question whether allocating the nation's scarce resources to inefficient industries is really in our "strategic" interest after all.

Quotas

The goal of tariffs is to reduce imports, to maintain a high positive value of F_n and to achieve external balance. Quotas have the same objective, but they are more restrictive in their effects than tariffs. Quotas are numerical limits on imports of certain goods; thus they protect domestic producers from substantial foreign competition. The result is greater domestic production of the good, whether or not domestic production is efficient, with higher prices for consumers than would be true with free trade.

Quotas are illegal to member nations of GATT. But the United States has negotiated *orderly market agreements*, or voluntary agreements to limit sales to the United States. Voluntary quotas now in effect limit imports of Japanese automobiles and television sets, Japanese and European specialty steel, textile products and some agricultural products, including meat and milk.

In the 1950s and 1960s the United States enforced quotas on imports of petroleum products. The intent was to protect high-cost U.S. producers from cheap foreign oil. The oil quota may have backfired in a particularly damaging way. Unable to earn sufficient foreign exchange from their limited sales in the United States, foreign producers raised their prices above U.S. prices, and the rest is history.

Export Subsidies and Countervailing Duties

Whereas GATT forbids new tariffs, recent negotiations now allow a nation to impose *countervailing duties* when another nation pays export subsidies to domestic producers. Export subsidies promote foreign sales by reducing the selling price of the export item. They are a means of raising F_n, shifting the *IS* curve to the right, and achieving a balance of trade advantage. Export subsidies are paid by most European countries by refunding the domestic value-added tax (or VAT) when a manufactured good leaves the country. The VAT is a percentage of the good's value, making it easily refundable. (Because most U.S. taxes are income taxes and not a clearly defined percentage, it would be difficult to refund taxes on U.S. exports.) This gives European exporters an advantage in U.S. markets and in other markets around the world.

When a foreign government pays an export subsidy, the United States is allowed to collect a tariff equal to the subsidy. When imported steel prices fall below a certain *trigger price*, for example, U.S. tariff commissioners assume that a subsidy is being paid and impose a tariff. If other import prices fall below what is believed to be their true production costs, a nation is said to be *dumping* surplus goods in the U.S. market. Charges of dumping are brought before the U.S. Tariff Commission and, if proved, may result in the imposition of a tariff. In all these cases, the tariff is called a countervailing duty because it is meant to offset an unfair trade tactic of another nation.

The United States provides advantages to U.S. exporters in a way that some producers abroad regard as a subsidy. The Export-Import Bank makes low interest loans to foreign buyers of U.S. exports. In fact, however, the funds are generally paid directly to the U.S. exporter. Low interest loans enable U.S. producers to underprice producers abroad, gaining an advantage similar to that of a subsidy.

Nontariff Barriers

Possibly the most difficult trade restriction to deal with is nontariff barriers. Nontariff barriers are product standards that tend to exclude foreign manufacturers from the market. Standards that exclude illegal or harmful materials are certainly justified, but some standards are actually disguised attempts to protect local producers.

Florida tomato farmers, for example, attempted to impose size standards on imported tomatoes, a regulation that would have excluded vine-ripened Mexican tomatoes from a U.S. market. Safety and pollution equipment standards have excluded some foreign-built autos. Standards on grades of leather have excluded some shoe imports.

It is difficult to separate standards that have the legitimate aim of protecting the health of U.S. consumers from those that aim at protecting U.S. producers from competition. Whenever nontariff barriers are enforced, the result is to exclude imports, raise domestic prices and reduce quantities available to consumers.

MONEY AND BANKING IN PRACTICE: AN OIL IMPORT TARIFF

As 1987 began, the United States was suffering from both internal and external imbalance. Expansionary fiscal and monetary policy had stimulated a strong recovery from recession, but unemployment remained stubbornly at 7 percent, and the government deficit was running close to $200 billion a year. At the same time, a low level of exports relative to imports was yielding annual Balance of Payments deficits of around $200 billion.

Policymakers desperately sought solutions for the twin deficits. One action was to impose a tariff on oil imports. Supporters of the oil import tariff claimed that it would reduce imports and at the same time collect revenue for the U.S. Treasury.

On the other hand, opponents argued that the disadvantages of a tariff would offset these advantages. For example, they said that reduced oil imports will reduce real output in the United States and raise prices. Lower output will mean higher unemployment and larger transfer payments for the federal government; higher prices will mean higher incomes and higher tax revenues. When these effects are added to the effects of the oil import tariff, the net effect on the government's budget may not be very great. Moreover, the cost in terms of lost output may make the tariff an inefficient solution to the federal deficit.

The oil import tariff may not improve the Balance of Payments deficit either. Higher prices for oil will raise costs of production for all U.S. manufacturers and worsen any disadvantages they suffer relative to foreign competitors. There might be another long-run disadvantage. By encouraging consumption of limited domestic supplies, an oil import tariff may increase the nation's dependence on foreign suppliers.

Probably the best argument against an oil import tariff is the efficiency argument. Interference with the free flow of trade creates distortions that reduce the efficiency of resource allocation and disturb the equity of distribution. Loss of efficiency and equity create negative externalities that call for additional interferences.

Questions for Discussion

1. Can you think of other arguments against the oil import tariff? Hint: What is likely to be the reaction of oil exporting nations?

2. How does this article demonstrate the dilemma policymakers face when the nation is suffering both internal and external imbalance?

Exchange Controls

The most restrictive trade policy of all is when government takes over all trade and restricts imports to only those goods and services that serve the purpose of government. It does this by exchange control: requiring exporters to turn over all foreign exchange earnings to government and paying out foreign exchange only for government-approved imports. Correcting disequilibrium through exchange control was discussed in Chapter 12.

Embargoes and Boycotts

Certain U.S. trade restrictions may serve foreign policy objectives. Examples are embargoes and boycotts that restrict trade with Cuba, Vietnam, Cambodia, North Korea, Zimbabwe and Uganda. In general, prohibitions on trade aim at protecting national security by limiting the spread of nuclear explosives and other military technology. Other objectives are to reflect U.S. principles on human rights and to discourage other nations from harboring political terrorists. Export financing is limited to countries where the above principles are honored. Moreover, since the Trade Act of 1974, Export-Import Bank loans have been denied Communist nations that restrict the rights of citizens to emigrate.

Policies to Promote Trade

When economists criticize trade restrictions, it is generally on the basis of economic efficiency. Economists want to promote specialization according to comparative advantage, so as to use the world's resources efficiently. Instead of restricting imports, economists recommend policies to promote exports.

Grants and Loans

Frequently the U.S. government promotes exports through grants to poor and developing countries. U.S. farmers and food processors benefit, as do manufacturers of military and industrial equipment. U.S. incomes and employment increase, and the U.S. balance of trade improves. Other less pleasant results include higher food costs for U.S. consumers and higher wage costs in U.S. industries. The Export-Import Bank mentioned earlier is another source of loans for promoting exports.

To the extent that grants and loans stimulate domestic production of goods for which the nation has comparative advantage, they make production more efficient. Grants and loans enable developing nations to use U.S. equipment and farm commodities to develop their own industrial potential. Then they can become full participants in trade on an equal basis with other nations. Some countries regard grants and loans as a form of dumping, however. They see cheap U.S. exports as a strategy to drive competing industries out of the market.

Research and Development

Another way to promote exports is through research and development of technology-intensive products. By a common definition of technology intensive, about half of U.S. imports and about three-fourths of U.S. exports are technology-intensive items. Our technology-intensive imports are primarily consumer goods like autos, television sets and other consumer electronics. Technology-intensive exports are primarily capital goods such as aircraft, computers and satellite communication equipment. Foreign producers are beginning to develop technologies for producing these goods, but U.S. production remains generally superior. Foreign firms are often too small to enjoy the economies of scale necessary to compete with U.S. firms.

If U.S. manufacturers are to continue to export technology-intensive goods, U.S. products must be attractive to foreign buyers. This may require marketing research and product engineering especially for export. It also requires basic and applied research for developing new technologies and new products. As other nations adopt U.S. technology, we must be prepared to move on to still more advanced types of production.

As a percentage of U.S. GNP, expenditures for research and development have fallen in recent years. Government-sponsored research has declined because of high budget deficits and efforts to balance the federal budget. Industrial research has declined because of high risks, low profits, and fears of new environmental and safety regulations. Private business firms have been slow to develop products for foreign markets, preferring instead to increase their shares of a relatively protected domestic market. All of this poses particular problems for technology-intensive exports.

Tax Advantages

In the 1960s Congress approved certain tax advantages designed to promote U.S. exports. Firms were allowed to establish Domestic International Sales Corporations (DISCs) abroad for marketing their products. One-half of profits earned on foreign sales were exempt from U.S. corporate income taxes until they were actually returned to this country. This encouraged firms to invest profits abroad for substantial gain. When profits are eventually returned to the United States, the amount of tax due is reduced by the amount of taxes paid the foreign government.

Although such tax advantages are intended to help solve U.S. balance of trade problems by stimulating exports, a side effect was to encourage greater investment abroad. Foreign investment earns income for its owners and is a valuable source of credits in the Balance of Payments, as we have seen. Still, the result of substantial foreign investment may be fewer jobs in the United States. This has been a source of controversy and a basis for attempts to change these tax advantages. A tax advantage may also be looked upon by foreign governments as an export subsidy, illegal under the rules of GATT.

MONEY AND BANKING IN PRACTICE: INTERNATIONAL FINANCIAL INTERMEDIARIES

The collapse of trade in the Great Depression of the 1930s and frequent payments problems in the years since then have led Western nations toward greater cooperation in trade and international finance. An important first step toward international cooperation was the Bretton Woods Conference of 1945, which established postwar currency values. Another achievement of the Bretton Woods conference was the establishment of an international financial institution for dealing with Balance of Payments problems, the International Monetary Fund (IMF).

The IMF has 138 members with the goal of easing flows of international payments. Members are assigned shares in the fund according to their own GNP and their participation in world trade. They contribute gold and foreign and domestic currencies in the amount of their shares. Then any nation can borrow back a portion of its share for settling a payments deficit. Loans are expected to be short term, and borrowers must agree to use fiscal and monetary policy to help correct chronic payments problems.

In the 1970s world demand for liquidity rose faster than IMF holdings of gold and foreign exchange. To deal with the shortage of liquidity, the IMF created a new form of money to be used only in international settlement transactions by central banks. The new money was called Special Drawing Rights (SDRs) and was essentially "unlimited rights to borrow." SDRs were issued to member nations in proportion to their IMF shares. Actual decisions to use SDRs are made by a nation's Treasury when the Treasury deposits its SDRs in its central bank. Depositing SDRs provides the funds for Treasury purchases of foreign exchange for settling international accounts.

The value of an SDR is determined by weighting 25 currencies together in a "basket." In 1987 the value was about $1.21. SDRs are sometimes called paper gold because they substitute for what in years past might have been new gold production.

Occasionally a member nation may need to borrow large amounts over several years. Mexico, Argentina, the Philippines and Great Britain have been granted continuing loans from the IMF. But as a condition of the loans, their governments were required to impose sharply contractionary fiscal and monetary policies. The goal was to reduce domestic incomes and prices and bring international trade accounts into balance: that is, to sacrifice internal balance for external balance. This process is especially difficult for nations that are already poor and has not been completely successful.

More frequently, long-term credit is extended through the International Bank for Reconstruction and Development, or World Bank. The World Bank makes loans for development projects, both large and small: power plants, steel mills and transportation networks, on the one hand, and farm irrigation systems, rural roads and vocational training on the other. About $6 billion is loaned every year.

The World Bank acquires funds for lending by selling stock to IMF nations and selling bonds to private investors. Its loans must be guaranteed by the governments of borrowing nations. Moreover, loans must be repaid in "hard" currencies, currencies that are convertible to other currencies at stable rates. International Development Association (IDA) loans are repayable in "soft" currencies over a longer period of time and at a smaller interest rate. Funds for lending come entirely from IMF countries.

Questions for Discussion

1. Explain why contractionary monetary and fiscal policies may be required of a nation receiving a long-term IMF loan. What are the difficulties associated with such policies?

2. What are the advantages and disadvantages of "hard" currency and "soft" currency loans?

Glossary of Terms

countervailing duties. tariffs imposed to offset subsidies granted to foreign producers by their governments

dumping. selling goods in a foreign market at prices below their domestic costs of production

embargoes and **boycotts.** refusals to trade with a nation for political reasons

infant industries. newly established industries whose costs of production may exceed those of established industries in other countries

marginal propensity to import. the fraction of a change in income that will be used to increase or to decrease foreign purchases

most favored nation arrangements. agreements to extend favorable trade advantages to all parties to the agreement

orderly market agreements. voluntary agreements to limit sales of particular goods or commodities in a country

quotas. legal limits on the import of particular goods or commodities

sterilization. action by the Federal Reserve to offset international flows of money with changes in the domestic money supply

strategic industries. domestic industries whose output may be necessary for national defense

subsidy. a payment made to domestic industries that makes their products cheaper to foreign buyers

trigger price. a price at which government would enter the market for a good or service to influence its price

Summary of Important Ideas

1. Policies to promote full employment and price stability may conflict with Balance of Payments equilibrium.

2. Including net foreign investment in the *IS-LM* model causes the *IS* curve to shift by $(F_n = X_f - M_f)$ times the multiplier. International capital flows change the slope and position of the *LM* curve and may require offsetting actions by the Federal Reserve. Shifts in the *IS* and *LM* curves make the results of fiscal and monetary policy difficult to predict.

3. Because the balance of trade depends on income, policy to change income affects the Balance of Payments. Unemployment and a balance of trade surplus can be corrected by expansionary policies. Price infla-

tion and a balance of trade deficit can be corrected by contractionary policies. In both cases, interest rate effects of monetary policy encourage short-term investment flows that help achieve external balance.

4. "Operation Twist" attempted to affect short- and long-term interest rates differently, so as to encourage short-term investment inflows while also encouraging long-term capital construction.

5. Unemployment and a balance of trade deficit cannot be corrected by a single set of policies. (The same is true of inflation and a balance of trade surplus.) In these cases expansionary (contractionary) fiscal policy can be combined with contractionary (expansionary) monetary policy. It is expected that the appropriate fiscal policy will help achieve internal balance while the interest effects of the opposite monetary policy will contribute to external balance.

6. Tariffs may protect infant industries, preserve local jobs, maintain high domestic wage scales, and serve a nation's (short-run) strategic interests. But they also raise domestic prices, reduce selection of goods and services, and promote inefficiency in the allocation of resources.

7. Quotas are more damaging than tariffs, because supply cannot expand to satisfy rising demand. Although quotas are illegal under international agreements, the United States has concluded orderly market agreements with some of our trading partners. The resulting higher prices may push up many other domestic prices.

8. Some nations promote exports by awarding subsidies to export industries. Subsidies may result in accusations of dumping, which may be met by countervailing duties. If foreign subsidies succeed in driving domestic producers out of business, prices may be raised to the level of monopoly.

9. Nontariff barriers exclude foreign goods for reasons of health and safety or to protect local suppliers. Quality standards reduce trade, raise prices and limit selection.

10. Some governments control the use of foreign exchange so that it can be allocated for purposes consistent with national goals. Governments may prohibit trade altogether for the sake of national security or international political considerations.

11. Policies to promote trade may contribute to payments equilibrium. Grants and loans aid export industries but may be regarded as subsidies. Research and development expenditures may contribute to the growth of technology-intensive exports. Tax advantages also promote exports but may also promote investments abroad.

Questions for Discussion and Research

1. Describe the effect on internal output and employment of increased domestic demand for foreign automobiles. Consider the consequences in the product sector and the monetary sector. Clearly state your assumptions with respect to domestic spending habits, commercial bank lending practices, and Federal Reserve policy targets.

2. Under what circumstances will expansionary fiscal policy not cause a worsening of a nation's balance of trade? Distinguish between short- and long-term effects.

3. In what sense are international capital flows "accommodating" to domestic fiscal policy?

4. Precisely how did the Federal Reserve and the Treasury attempt to "twist" the yield curve? What assumptions about investors' behavior are necessary if the strategy is to be successful?

5. What considerations determine a government's decision to favor internal or external balance in its policies?

6. Explain why internal imbalance often leads to the imposition of tariffs. How can tariffs export unemployment?

7. Evaluate the various arguments for tariffs. How is GATT working to reduce tariffs?

8. Illustrate graphically the effect of dumping on domestic output, employment and prices. What are the long-range effects?

9. How might changes in U.S. tax laws enhance our nation's position in international trade?

10. Consult recent news stories for information on current quality standards on imports. To what extent do you think these nontariff barriers are disguised attempts to exclude competition?

Additional Readings

Balogh, Thomas. "Monetarism and the Threat of a World Financial Crisis." *Challenge* 20 (May/June 1977): 40–47.

Bundy, William P., ed. *The World Economic Crisis.* New York: W. W. Norton, 1975.

Corrigan, E. Gerald. "Coping with Globally Integrated Financial Markets." *Federal Reserve Bank of New York Quarterly Review* (Winter 1987): 1–5.

de Vries, Rimmer, and Derek Hargreaves. "The Dollar's Decline and Trade: Mission Accomplished?" *Challenge* (January/February 1987): 37–46.

Hartland-Thunberg, Penelope. "Tales of a Onetime Tariff Commissioner." *Challenge* 20 (July/August 1977): 6–12.

Kindleberger, Charles P. *The World in Depression, 1929–1939.* Berkeley: University of California Press, 1973.

Krauss, Melvyn B. "Stagnation and the 'New Protectionism.' " *Challenge* 20 (January/February 1978): 40–49.

Leontieff, Wassily. "Observations on Some Worldwide Economic Issues of the Coming Years." *Challenge* 21 (March/April 1978): 22–30.

Luttrell, Clifton. "Imports and Jobs—The Observed and the Unobserved." *Federal Reserve Bank of St. Louis Review* 60 (June 1978): 2–10.

McCracken, Paul, et al. *Toward Full Employment and Price Stability.* Paris: Organization for Economic Cooperation and Development, 1977.

Tarshis, Lorie. "Disarming the Debt Bomb." *Challenge* (May/June 1987): 18–23.

Wood, Geoffrey E., and Nancy Ammon Jianakoplos. "Coordinated International Economic Expansion: Are Convoys or Locomotives the Answer?" *Federal Reserve Bank of St. Louis Review* 60 (July 1978): 11–19.

Wood, Geoffrey E., and Douglas R. Mudd. "Do Foreigners Control the U.S. Money Supply?" *Federal Reserve Bank of St. Louis Review* 59 (December 1977): 8–11.

End-of-Book Glossary

(Numbers in parentheses indicate chapters for more detailed discussion of topics.)

absolute advantage.   the ability to produce a good or service more cheaply than it can be produced elsewhere (7)

Accelerationists.   economists who blame increasing inflation on attempts of labor and business to protect against expected inflation (16)

Accord of 1951.   an agreement between the Federal Reserve and the U.S. Treasury that the Federal Reserve would no longer "support the government bond market" (11)

administered pricing.   pricing that results from market power rather than from the free operation of supply and demand (16)

advances.   loans from the Federal Reserve to commercial banks on the basis of suitable collateral (10)

aggregate demand.   the sum of all spending of consumers, business, government, and foreign buyers (14)

aggregate supply.   the sum of all incomes received from production (14)

amortize.   to pay off a portion of the amount borrowed with each regular interest payment (3)

announcement effect.   the reactions in the financial community that frequently follow the announcement of a change in Federal Reserve policy (11)

arbitrage.   the simultaneous purchase and sale of two currencies with the aim of making a profit (7)

assay.   to evaluate a precious metal in terms of its purity and weight (1)

asset management. acquiring additional reserves by selling some of a bank's assets (3)

assets. real and financial properties owned (3)

automatically self-liquidating. a condition in which the use of borrowed funds yields incomes and tax revenues sufficient to pay off the debt (17)

autonomous transactions. international transactions initiated by private individuals or business firms (12)

balance sheet. a financial statement listing bank assets, liabilities and capital accounts (3)

bank credit. the total of bank loans and investments (8)

bank credit multiplier. a ratio that determines the effect on bank credit of new reserves or excess reserves (8)

bankers acceptances. agreements to pay debts incurred in international trade (4)

Banking School. economists who believed banks should create additional credit money in line with growth of production of goods and services (9)

barter. the exchange of goods for other goods without the use of money (1)

bill of exchange. a promise to pay, issued by an importer, used to pay the exporter (1)

bills. securities with maturity of less than one year (3)

bimetallic money system. a money system that uses two precious metals (1)

bonds. securities with maturities of one or more years (3)

branch banks. banks that operate more than one closely linked banking institution (3)

business profit. business revenues remaining after paying costs (14)

call loans. loans that are due when "called" by the lender (3)

capital accounts. accounts listing the value of stockholder shares plus accumulated profits (3)

capital consumption allowance. an amount set aside to reflect the cost of depreciating equipment (14)

capital deepening. producing enough new capital to increase the amount available for each worker (5)

capital gains tax. a tax on the gain from resale of an asset (5)

capital markets. markets for lending funds for more than a year (4)

capital widening. producing enough new capital resources to supply a growing labor force with a constant quantity of capital (5)

cartel. an organization of producers for controlling the supply of an export good (7)

cash balance theory of money. the theory that the public's decisions to hold idle money balances determine the relationship between money and income (13)

cash management. the practice of minimizing idle cash balances so as to increase yield on financial assets (8)

CDs. savings certificates issued for certain time deposits (3)

commercial paper. unsecured short-term debt instruments of corporations (4)

commodity agreement. an agreement to export specific quantities of a good (7)

commodity money. money that is valuable in itself, apart from its value as money (1)

common and preferred stock. shares of ownership issued by corporations (4)

comparative advantage. the ability to produce a good or service more cheaply in terms of its opportunity costs (7)

compensatory transactions. official transactions made to settle outstanding claims from autonomous transactions (12)

compounding. applying interest on interest earned on a long-term asset (5)

consumption. spending for consumer durable and nondurable goods and services (14)

consumption function. an algebraic relationship between consumption and income (14)

conventional mortgage. a home loan made by a savings and loan association to a home buyer without the intervention of a government agency (6)

corporate bonds. long-term debt·instruments issued by corporations (4)

cost-effective. a condition in which programs accomplish their objectives at minimum costs (16)

cost-push inflation. price inflation that results from increases in the costs of producing output (16)

countervailing duties. tariffs imposed to offset subsidies granted to foreign producers by their governments (19)

coupon rate. interest to be paid regularly on the face value of a long-term debt instrument (4)

credit market targets. interest rates (18)

credit money. money that has no value apart from its value as money; fiat money (1)

credit transactions. international transactions that result in an inflow of payments to the United States (12)

crowding out. the condition in which the expansionary effects of increased government spending are offset by contractionary changes in private spending (17)

Currency School. economists who believed banks should be simply depositories of the public's money (13)

cyclical asymmetry. the fact that Federal Reserve policy is more effective during one phase of the business cycle than the other (11)

debase.   to reduce the value of money through chipping, overissue, etc. (1)

debit transactions.   international transactions that result in an outflow of payments from the United States (12)

debt instrument.   agreement stating the amount borrowed and the terms for repayment (4)

default risk.   the risk that a borrower will not pay interest and principal as agreed in the debt instrument (4)

defensive operations.   Federal Reserve policy actions designed to correct short-run changes in the supply of money (10)

deficit.   an excess of government expenditures over tax revenues (17)

deflation.   general decreases in prices that reflect changes in the value of money (1)

demand deposits.   commercial bank deposits that may be withdrawn on demand (8)

demand management.   policies that seek to affect economic equilibrium through manipulation of total spending (16)

demand-pull inflation.   price inflation that results from spending beyond the productive capacity of the economy (16)

dependent variable.   the variable in an equation whose behavior depends on the value of other variable(s) (14)

deposit multiplier.   a ratio that determines the effect on bank deposits of new reserves or excess reserves (8)

derivative deposit.   a deposit created by bank lending (8)

devaluation.   reducing the value of one nation's currency in terms of other currencies (7)

diminishing marginal product.   a principle that describes the decline in additional output as larger amounts of variable resources are added to fixed resources (7)

discount.   a reduction in the selling price of a debt instrument that reflects the interest paid the lender (4)

discounting.   reducing the value of a future revenue according to the interest rate and the distance in the future it is to be received (5)

discounts.   sales of commercial bank loans and investments at discount to the Federal Reserve Bank (10)

discretion.   the use of judgment to determine the appropriate changes in the money supply (9)

diseconomies of scale.   the rising unit costs that result from producing a larger volume of output (7)

disequilibrium.   a condition in which a nation experiences repeated deficits or surpluses in international payments (12)

disintermediation.   withdrawing funds from a financial intermediary to use for direct purchase of securities (6)

diversification. selection of a variety of securities whose behavior is likely to differ with cycles in economic activity (5)

dual banking system. a system in which banks are chartered both by states and by a national authority (3)

dumping. selling goods in a foreign market at prices below domestic costs of production (19)

dynamic operations. Federal Reserve policies designed to produce long-run changes in the money supply and in economic activity (10)

economies of scale. the lower unit costs that result from producing a larger volume of output (7)

efficiency. a condition in which productive resources are allocated in a way to achieve the greatest production with the smallest expenditure (6)

efficient frontier. the curve showing the portfolios with the highest return relative to risk (5)

elastic currency. a money supply that expands and contracts along with the needs of the economy (9)

embargoes and boycotts. refusals to trade with a nation for political reasons (19)

entitlement programs. government outlays to particular groups (17)

equilibrium. a condition of income, employment, prices and interest rates toward which the economy tends to move (14)

equity. fairness in the distribution of benefits and costs of production (6)

ERISA. The Employee Retirement Income Security Act, passed by Congress in 1976 to mandate standards of retirement plans (6)

Eurodollars. dollars or dollar deposits owned by foreigners (3)

excess reserves. reserve accounts in excess of the required fraction (8)

exchange rate. the price of one nation's currency in terms of another's for use in trade (2)

expected return. the weighted average of past returns on an asset (5)

external economies. improvements in productivity that result from a general expansion of industry (7)

externalities. benefits and costs that occur outside the primary activity of exchange in markets (6)

face value. the amount marked on the face of a debt instrument to be paid at maturity (4)

federal funds rate. the interest rate paid on borrowings among banks (3)

financial capital. savings that are made available for borrowers to use in constructing new capital resources (4)

financial intermediaries. institutions that stand between savers and borrowers (3)

fiscal policy. the use of government taxing and spending policies to influence the level of economic activity (17)

float. the difference between checks not yet deducted from reserve accounts and checks being held for 48 hours before being added to reserve accounts (10)

floating exchange rates. exchange rates that fluctuate according to supply and demand (7)

fixed resource. a resource whose quantity is fixed in the short run (7)

foreign exchange. currency issued by a foreign government (7)

forward transactions. contracts to purchase or to deliver foreign exchange at some specified date in the future (12)

4 percent rule. a rule that the money supply should grow at a steady rate equal to average annual increases in productive capacity (9)

fractional reserve banking. an arrangement by which banks hold only a fraction of depositors' funds in reserve; fractional reserve banking enables banks to lend from holdings in excess of this fraction (3)

full employment budget. a budget that measures what tax revenues and government expenditures would be at full employment (17)

futures contracts. contracts promising to deliver a certain asset on a certain day at a certain price (2)

general obligation bonds. bonds issued by governments, interest and principal to be paid from the government's general revenue (4)

Gibson's paradox. a condition in which increasing money growth aggravates expectations of inflation and causes interest rates to rise (18)

goals. ultimate objectives in terms of output, employment and prices (18)

gold standard. a money system in which paper currency is evaluated according to a specific weight of gold; the Treasury buys and sells gold at the stated price (2)

gross investment. total purchases of capital goods for the year (14)

hedgers. market participants whose purchases and sales reflect their own needs for funds or for interest-earning assets (4)

holding companies. firms that own stock in other companies and manage them for a profit (3)

"hot money". short-term investment capital that moves freely from nation to nation in response to differences in interest rate (12)

identification lag. one of four time lags between the implementation and the effects of monetary policy; others are decision, money sector and product sector lags (18)

independent variable. the variable(s) in an equation whose value is determined outside the algebraic relationship (14)

indexed funds. investment funds that own a portfolio of assets corresponding to those used in a particular market index (6)

indicator. a variable whose behavior suggests the current direction of policy (18)

indifference curves. curves representing individual preferences with respect to risk and return (5)

infant industries. newly established industries whose costs of production may exceed those of established industries in other countries (19)

inflation. general increases in prices that reflect changes in the value of money (1)

instruments. monetary policy tools by which Federal Reserve targets are to be achieved (18)

Interdistrict Settlement Fund. a fund of central bank assets used for transferring payments among Federal Reserve districts (10)

interventionist currency. a currency used to purchase other currencies for the purpose of influencing their relative values (12)

"J"-effect. the immediate effect of currency devaluation, when a given volume of imports calls for a greater expenditure of domestic currency and worsens a payments outflow (12)

L. M3 plus nonbank public holdings of government securities, commercial paper and bankers' acceptances; net of money market fund holdings of these assets (1)

laissez-faire. the belief that economic activity is most efficient when government interferes least (2)

liabilities. amounts owed to lenders (3)

liability management. acquiring additional reserves by attracting new bank liabilities (3)

liquidity. the ease of converting an asset to purchasing power without significant loss of value (1)

liquidity preference. the preference for holding liquid assets rather than illiquid assets (4)

liquidity trap. the condition in which interest rates are too low to compensate for the risks of lending, so that additions to the money supply are held in idle speculative balances (17)

lock-in effect. the tendency to hold securities whose value has fallen, so as to avoid a capital loss (11)

M1. currency and checkable deposits in the hands of the public (1)

M2. M1 plus savings and small time deposits, repurchase agreements and money market deposit accounts (1)

M3. M2 plus large deposits, U.S.-owned Eurodollars and institutional money market mutual funds (1)

margin requirements. minimum down payment requirements for purchases of securities, when the security is to serve as collateral for the loan (11)

marginal efficiency of investment. rates of return on investment projects arranged in descending order to form a firm's demand curve for financial capital (5)

marginal propensity to import. the fraction of a change in income that will be used to increase or to decrease foreign purchases (19)

market ratio. the ratio between the values of two precious metals when sold in the market (1)

market risk. the risk that the resale value of a security will fall as a result of a rise in current interest rates (4)

medium of exchange. the use of money for making purchases (1)

microeconomics. the study of output and prices in individual markets (14)

mint ratio. the ratio between the values of two precious metals when sold to the mint (1)

Monetarists. economists who place the greatest importance on the supply of money for determining economic activity and guiding economic policy (9)

monetary policy. manipulation of the money supply to affect equilibrium for the economy (17)

money aggregates. total reserves or money according to M1, M2 or M3 (18)

money base. the total of bank reserves and cash held by the public (8)

money illusion. a failure to recognize the effect of inflation on real wages (16)

money market certificate. a short-term savings instrument issued by savings and loan associations in denominations of $10,000 and earning interest tied to the Treasury bill rate (6)

money markets. markets for lending funds for less than a year (4)

money multiplier. a ratio that determines the effect on the money supply of new reserves or excess reserves (8)

mortgage. long-term lending, usually for the purpose of buying a home or commercial property (4)

most favored nation agreements. agreements to extend favorable trade arrangements equally to all parties to the agreement (19)

multinational corporation. a corporation that conducts operations in more than one nation (12)

multiple exchange rates. a schedule of exchange rates based on the expected use of the foreign exchange (12)

multiplier effect. the multiple increase in incomes that results from an exogenous increase in spending (14)

national debt. the accumulated net debt of the federal government (17)

natural rate of unemployment. a level of unemployment that includes the least productive and least stable portions of the labor force (16)

net foreign investment. the difference between foreign purchases in the United States and sales to foreigners (14)

net investment. total purchases of capital goods less depreciated capital for the year

net present value. the difference between an asset's present value and its current cost; net present value may be either positive or negative (5)

net saving. the difference between saving plus net taxes and planned investment plus government spending (14)

net taxes. the difference between taxes paid to governments and transfer payments received from government (14)

nominal interest rate. the interest rate actually paid on loans (18)

nominal money supply. the money supply measured in terms of current dollars (9)

notes. securities with maturity of one or more years (3)

NOW accounts. savings accounts in mutuals and savings and loans on which checks can be written (6)

opportunity cost. a sacrifice experienced as a result of choosing one alternative over another (13)

opportunity set. an arrangement of points representing the risk and expected return on available investments (5)

orderly market agreements. voluntary agreements to limit sales of particular goods or commodities in a country (19)

overvalued currency. a currency whose exchange value exceeds its domestic purchasing power (12)

par. the face value of money or securities (1)

parameters. the values within an algebraic equation that remain the same when the values of variables change (14)

pensions. funds in which worker and employer contributions accumulate for investment (6)

Phillips curve. a line graph showing the historical relationship between unemployment and price inflation (16)

portfolio. a collection of real and financial assets owned by an individual or institution (1)

precautionary motive. holding money for taking care of emergencies (13)

present value. the value of a future stream of revenues, discounted according to the interest rate and the distance in the future revenues are to be received (5)

price ceiling. a maximum price maintained by government sales of a commodity from stockpiles (2)

price floor. a minimum price maintained by government purchases of a commodity for adding to stockpiles (2)

primary deposit. a deposit of new funds from outside the banking system (8)

primary markets. financial markets where the initial borrowing and lending is done (4)

prime rate. the interest rate charged a bank's most creditworthy corporate customers (3)

pro-cyclical. an economic policy that worsens a tendency toward inflation or recession (18)

progressive taxes. taxes for which the rate paid rises with an increase in the tax base (17)

purchasing power parity. a condition in which exchange rates reflect the real domestic purchasing power of different currencies (7)

quantity theory of money. the theory that prices change proportionally to changes in the supply of money (13)

quotas. legal restrictions on the import of particular goods or commodities (19)

rate of return. the discount rate that makes the present value of an asset equal to the initial outlay (5)

real bills doctrine. a principle that loans should be made only for productive activity (9)

real interest rate. the interest rate corrected for the effects of inflation (18)

real money supply. the money supply measured in terms of dollars of constant purchasing power (9)

real wages. wages corrected for inflation; the real purchasing power of wages (16)

real-wealth effect. the changes in the value of money holdings that result from price changes (13)

regressive taxes. taxes for which the rate paid falls with an increase in the tax base (17)

REIT. Real Estate Investment Trust, a subsidiary of a bank-holding company organized for lending for commercial construction (9)

representative commodity money. certificates that stand for a certain quantity of commodity money (1)

repurchase agreement. the purchase of a government security with the condition that the seller will buy it back after a certain time; also called a *repo* (11)

required reserves. accounts that represent a fraction of total deposits, required by state- and federal-chartering institutions (8)

reserve accounts. a portion of a bank's deposits, generally held on deposit in another bank (3)

reserve currency. a currency held as a financial asset (12)

revaluation. increasing the value of one nation's currency in terms of other currencies (12)

revenue bonds. bonds issued by governments to build a particular project, the revenue from which will be used to pay interest and principal (4)

reverse repos. the sale of securities under an agreement to repurchase (11)

risk. the average of squared deviations of past returns from expected return on an asset (5)

saving and investment. refraining from consumption and using resources to produce capital goods (5)

SDRs. Special Drawing Rights issued by the International Monetary Fund for the purpose of increasing world liquidity (19)

second mortgage. a mortgage whose collateral is the homeowner's equity (6)

secondary markets. financial markets for trading previously issued debt instruments (4)

seigniorage. the difference between the face value of money and the cost of producing it (1)

self-liquidating. the characteristic of a loan through which productive activity earns the funds for paying the lender (9)

self-regulating. the characteristic of a loan through which the supply of credit money parallels the growth of production (9)

share drafts. check-like devices for making payments from shares held in credit unions (6)

solvency. a condition in which assets are greater than liabilities (3)

specie. coins made of precious metals, usually gold or silver (1)

specie-flow principle. the principle that describes how flows of gold lead to proportional changes in income and prices (2)

speculative motive. holding money because current lending conditions are less favorable than expected future conditions (13)

speculators. market participants who purchase and sell financial assets with the aim of profiting from differences in their prices (4)

standard of deferred payment. the use of money for paying in the future for goods and services obtained in the present (1)

standard deviation. a statistic that measures the risk of an investment (5)

strategic industries. domestic industries whose output may be necessary for national defense (19)

standard of value. the use of money to compare the values of different goods or services (1)

store of value. the use of money to hold a claim for goods and services to be purchased in the future (1)

subsidy. a payment made to domestic industries that makes their products cheaper to foreign buyers (19)

supply-side economics. emphasis on the real factors that determine a nation's productive capacity; a distrust of policies that emphasize consumption relative to investment (18)

surplus. an excess of government tax revenues over expenditures (17)

synthesis. a combination that includes the Keynesian model of income determination and monetary theory (15)

targets. immediate objectives of monetary policy (18)

tariff. a tax on imported goods and services (7)

tax base. the economic variable on which taxes are levied (17)

terms of trade. the quantity of goods imported per unit of goods exported (7)

transactions currency. a currency used for exchanging goods and services (12)

transactions motive. holding money for the purpose of making everyday transactions (13)

transfer payments. payments by government to individuals or businesses; also called negative taxes (14)

undervalued currency. a currency whose exchange value is less than its domestic purchasing power (12)

unit banks. banks that operate only one banking institution (3)

unplanned investment. accumulation or depletion of inventory beyond a firm's investment plans (14)

variable resource. a resource, various quantities of which can be added to available fixed resources (7)

velocity. the rate at which the existing supply of money is spent during the year (13)

yield. the return on an asset including interest earned and increase in resale value (6)

yield curve. a graph showing the term structure of interest rates (4)

Index